REAL-LIFE APPLICATIONS OF THE INTERNET OF THINGS

Challenges, Applications, and Advances

REAL-LIFE APPLICATIONS OF THE INTERNET OF THINGS

Challenges, Applications, and Advances

Edited by
Monika Mangla, PhD
Ashok Kumar, PhD
Vaishali Mehta, PhD
Megha Bhushan, PhD
Sachi Nandan Mohanty, PhD

APPLE ACADEMIC PRESS

First edition published 2022

Apple Academic Press Inc.
1265 Goldenrod Circle, NE,
Palm Bay, FL 32905 USA

4164 Lakeshore Road, Burlington,
ON, L7L 1A4 Canada

CRC Press
6000 Broken Sound Parkway NW,
Suite 300, Boca Raton, FL 33487-2742 USA

2 Park Square, Milton Park,
Abingdon, Oxon, OX14 4RN UK

© 2022 Apple Academic Press, Inc.

Apple Academic Press exclusively co-publishes with CRC Press, an imprint of Taylor & Francis Group, LLC

Library and Archives Canada Cataloguing in Publication

Title: Real-life applications of the Internet of things : challenges, applications, and advances / edited by Monika Mangla, PhD, Ashok Kumar, PhD, Vaishali Mehta, PhD, Megha Bhushan, PhD, Sachi Nandan Mohanty, PhD.

Names: Mangla, Monika, editor. | Kumar, Ashok (Assistant professor), editor. | Mehta, Vaishali, editor. | Bhushan, Megha, editor. | Mohanty, Sachi Nandan, editor.

Description: First edition. | Includes bibliographical references and index.

Identifiers: Canadiana (print) 20220140936 | Canadiana (ebook) 20220140995 | ISBN 9781774638477 (hardcover) | ISBN 9781774638484 (softcover) | ISBN 9781003277460 (ebook)

Subjects: LCSH: Internet of things. | LCSH: Internet of things—Industrial applications. | LCSH: Blockchains (Databases) | LCSH: Cloud computing.

Classification: LCC TK5105.8857 .R43 2022 | DDC 004.67/8—dc23

Library of Congress Cataloging-in-Publication Data

....

CIP data on file with US Library of Congress

....

ISBN: 978-1-77463-847-7 (hbk)
ISBN: 978-1-77463-848-4 (pbk)
ISBN: 978-1-00327-746-0 (ebk)

About the Editors

Monika Mangla, PhD
Associate Professor, Department of Information Technology,
Dwarkadas J. Sanghvi College of Engineering, Mumbai, India

Monika Mangla, PhD, is working in the Department of Information Technology at Dwarkadas J. Sanghvi College of Engineering, Mumbai, India. She has two patents to her credit as well as over 20 years of teaching experience at undergraduate and postgraduate levels, and she has guided many student projects. Her interest areas include IoT, cloud computing, network security, algorithms and optimization, location modelling, and machine learning. She has published several research papers and book chapters (SCI and Scopus-indexed) with reputed publishers. She has also been associated with several SCI-indexed journals such as the Turkish Journal of Electrical Engineering & Computer Sciences (TUBITAK), Industrial Management & Data Systems, etc., as a reviewer. She is a life member of the Computer Society of India and the Institution of Electronics and Telecommunication Engineers. Dr. Mangla received her PhD from Thapar Institute of Engineering & Technology, Patiala, Punjab, India.

Ashok Kumar, PhD
Assistant Professor, Chitkara University Research and
Innovation Network (CURIN) Department, Punjab, India

Ashok Kumar, PhD, is currently an Assistant Professor in Chitkara University Research and Innovation Network (CURIN) Department, Punjab, India. He has over 15 years of teaching and research experience. He has filed three patents and has published a number of publications in international journals and conferences of repute. His current areas of research interest include cloud computing, Internet of Things, and mist computing. Further, he is supervising four PhD scholars and two ME students. His teaching interests includes Python, Haskell, Java, C/C++, advanced data structures, and data mining. He has been a guest editor of the *International Journal of Cloud Computing* (Inderscience). Dr. Kumar holds a PhD in Computer Science and Engineering from Thapar University, Punjab, India.

Vaishali Mehta, PhD
Professor, Department of Information Technology,
Panipat Institute of Engineering and Technology, Panipat, Haryana, India

Vaishali Mehta, PhD, is an Professor in the Department of Information Technology at Panipat Institute of Engineering and Technology, Panipat, Haryana, India. She has done her PhD in facility location problems from Thapar University. She has two patents published to her credit. She has 17 years of teaching experience at the undergraduate and postgraduate levels. Her research interests include approximation algorithms, location modeling, IoT, cloud computing, and machine learning. She has published research articles in quality journals (SCI and Scopus indexed), national and international conferences, and books of reputed publishers. She has reviewed research papers of reputed journals and conferences.

Megha Bhushan, PhD
Assistant Professor, School of Computing, DIT University, Dehradun, India

Megha Bhushan, PhD, is an Assistant Professor in the School of Computing, DIT University, Dehradun, India. She has received her PhD degree in Computer Science and Engineering from Thapar University, Punjab, India. She has four years of research experience as a junior research fellow and senior research fellow under the University Grants Commission (UGC), New Delhi, Government of India. She was awarded a fellowship by UGC, Government of India, in 2014. In 2017, she was a recipient of the Grace Hopper Celebration India (GHCI) fellowship. She has filed four patents and published many research articles in international journals and conferences of repute. Her research interest includes software quality, software reuse, ontologies, artificial intelligence (AI), and expert systems. She is also a reviewer and editorial board member of many international journals.

Sachi Nandan Mohanty, PhD
Department of Computer Science & Engineering, Vardhaman College of Engineering (Autonomous), Hyderabad, India

Sachi Nandan Mohanty, PhD is working in the Department of Computer Science & Engineering at Vardhaman College of Engineering, Hyderabad, India. Professor Mohanty's research areas include data mining, big data analysis, cognitive science, fuzzy decision making, brain-computer interface, and computational intelligence. He has received three best paper awards during his PhD studies and has since published 20 papers in SCI journals. As a Fellow of the Indian Society Technical Education, The Institute of Engineering and Technology, and the Computer Society of India, and as a member of the Institute of Engineers and IEEE Computer Society, he is actively involved in the activities of the professional bodies/societies. He has received several awards, including Best Researcher Award from Biju Pattnaik University of Technology in 2019, Best Thesis Award (first prize) from the Computer Society of India in 2015, and Outstanding Faculty in Engineering Award from Dept. of Higher Education, Govt. of Odisha in 2020. He has also received international travel funds from SERB, Dept of Science and Technology, Govt. of India, for chairing a session at international conference USA, 2020. Dr. Mohanty is currently acting as reviewer of many journals, including *Robotics and Autonomous Systems, Computational and Structural Biotechnology, Artificial Intelligence Review,* and *Spatial Information Research.* He has also published four edited books and three authored books.

He did his postdoctoral from IIT Kanpur in the year 2019 and earned a PhD from IIT Kharagpur in the year 2015, with an MHRD scholarship from the Government of India.

Contents

Contributors

Alpana Agarwal
Thapar Institute of Engineering and Technology, Patiala, Punjab–147001, India

Ravinder Agarwal
Thapar Institute of Engineering and Technology, Patiala, Punjab–147001, India

Altaf Ahmad
Faculty of Science and Technology, ICFAI Foundation for Higher Education, Hyderabad–501203, Telangana, India

Rakhi Akhare
Assistant Professor, Computer Department, LTCoE, University of Mumbai, Maharashtra, India

Smita Sanjay Ambarkar
Assistant Professor, Computer Department, LTCoE, University of Mumbai, Maharashtra, India, E-mail: smita.ambarkar27@gmail.com

Rajiv Bansal
JMIT Radaur, Haryana, India, E-mail: rajivbansal@jmit.ac.in

Vinayak Ashok Bharadi
Department of Information Technology, Finolex Academy of Management and Technology, Ratnagiri, Maharashtra, India, E-mails: vinayak.bharadi@famt.ac.in; vinayak.bharadi@outlook.com

Tarandeep Kaur Bhatia
School of Information Technology, Deakin University, Geelong, VIC–3220, Australia, Chitkara University Institute of Engineering and Technology, Punjab, India, E-mails: tkbhatia@deakin.edu.au; tarandeep.bhatia@chitkara.edu.in

Shantanu Bhattacharya
Faculty of Science and Technology, ICFAI Foundation for Higher Education, Hyderabad–501203, Telangana, India

Chaitrali Chaudhari
Lokmanya Tilak College of Engineering, Koperkhairane, Navi Mumbai, Maharashtra, India, E-mail: chaitralichaudhari13@gmail.com

Sangita Chaudhari
Department of Computer Engineering, Ramrao Adik Institute of Technology, Nerul, Maharashtra, India

Rajesh Chauhan
Assistant Professor, School of Mass Communication, Chitkara University, Punjab

Satish Devane
Datta Meghe College of Engineering, Airoli–400708, Navi Mumbai, Maharashtra, India, E-mail: srdevane@yahoo.com

Rashmi Dhumal
Department of Computer Engineering, Ramrao Adik Institute of Technology, Nerul, Maharashtra, India

Sushopti Gawade
Pillai College of Engineering, Panvel, Mumbai, Maharashtra, India, E-mail: sgawade@mes.ac.in

Neha Goyal
NIT Kurukshetra, Haryana, India, E-mail: Neha.goyal2309@gmail.com

Anuj Kumar Gupta
Chandigarh Group of Colleges, Landran, Mohali, Punjab, India

Rohit Gupta
Thapar Institute of Engineering and Technology, Patiala, Punjab–147001, India

Gitanjali Kalia
Associate Professor, School of Mass Communication, Chitkara University, Punjab, India

Sakshi Kapoor
Chitkara University Institute of Engineering and Technology, Punjab, India,
E-mail: sakusakshi100@gmail.com

Gaganpreet Kaur
Department of Computer Science and Engineering, Chandīgarh University, Punjab, India,
E-mail: ghuliani04@gmail.com

Rajbir Kaur
Department of Electronics and Communication Engineering, Punjabi University, Patiala, India,
E-mail: rajbir277@yahoo.co.in

Dishant Khosla
Chandigarh Group of Colleges, Landran, Mohali, Punjab, India

Meenu Khurana
Chitkara University Institute of Engineering and Technology, Punjab, India,
E-mail: meenu.khurana@chitkara.edu.in

Umesh Kulkarni
Vidyalankar Institute of Technology Wadala, Mumbai, Maharashtra, India,
E-mail: umesh.kulkarni@vit.edu.in

J. Sai Praveen Kumar
Thapar Institute of Engineering and Technology, Patiala, Punjab–147001, India

Shubham Kumar
Faculty of Science and Technology, ICFAI Foundation for Higher Education, Hyderabad–501203,
Telangana, India

Tabassum Maktum
Department of Computer Engineering, Ramrao Adik Institute of Technology, Nerul, Maharashtra, India

Monika Mangla
Associate Professor, Department of Information Technology, Dwarkadas J. Sanghvi College of
Engineering, Mumbai

Anjanna Matta
Faculty of Science and Technology, ICFAI Foundation for Higher Education, Hyderabad–501203,
Telangana, India, E-mail: anjireddyiith@ifheindia.org

Sachi Nandan Mohanty
Vardhaman College of Engineering (Autonomous), Hyderabad, India

Surya Narayan Panda
Chitkara University Institute of Engineering and Technology, Punjab, India,
E-mail: snpanda@chitkara.edu.in

Amrutanshu Panigrahi
Research Scholar, Department of CSE, SOA University, Bhubaneswar, Odisha, India,
E-mail: amrutansup89@gmail.com

Ramkumar Ketti Ramachandran
Chitkara University Institute of Engineering and Technology, Punjab, India,
E-mail: k.ramkumar@chitkara.edu.in

Ridhima Rani
Chitkara University Institute of Engineering and Technology, Punjab, India, E-mail: rdahiya7@gmail.com

Bibhuprasad Sahu
Assistant Professor, Department of CSE, Gandhi Institute for Technology, Bhubaneswar, Odisha, India

Piyush Samant
Chandigarh University, Punjab–140413, India, E-mail: piyushsamantpth@gmail.com

Amandeep Sharma
Associate Professor, Department of Electronics and Communication Engineering, Chandigarh University,
Gharuan, Punjab–140413, India

Bikramjit Sharma
Thapar Institute of Engineering and Technology, Patiala, Punjab, India

Manvinder Sharma
Chandigarh Group of Colleges, Landran, Mohali, Punjab, India, E-mail: manvinder.sharma@gmail.com

P. S. Sheeba
Department of Computer Science & Engineering (IoT & Cyber Security including Blockchain
Technology), Lokmanya Tilak College of Engineering, Navi Mumbai, Maharashtra, India,
E-mail: sheebaps@gmail.com

Narendra Shekokar
Professor, Computer Department, DJSCE, University of Mumbai, Maharashtra, India

Pramod Shitole
Adarsh Institute of Technology and Research Center, Vita, Maharashtra, India,
E-mail: mail2pramodshitole@rediffmail.com

Harjinder Singh
Punjabi University, Patiala, Punjab, India

Prabhdeep Singh
Department of Computer Science and Engineering, Punjabi University, Patiala, Punjab, India,
E-mail: ssingh.prabhdeep@gmail.com

Rajat Tiwari
Department of Electronics and Communication Engineering, Chandigarh University, Punjab–140413,
India, E-mail: er.rajattiwari@gmail.com

Bhanu Priyanka Valluri
Research Scholar, Department of Electronics and Communication Engineering, Chandigarh University,
Gharuan, Punjab–140413, India, E-mail: bhanu.priyanka1904@gmail.com

Abbreviations

4G	fourth generation
ACHE	acetylcholinesterase
ACL	access control list
ACL	agent communication language
ADEPT	autonomous decentralized peer-to-peer telemetry
AI	artificial intelligence
AMQP	advanced message queuing protocol
ANNs	artificial neural networks
AoA	angle of arrival
API	application programming interface
BCoT	blockchain of things
BDA	big data analytics
BLE	Bluetooth
BP	blood pressure
C&C	command and control
CIS	cloud information service
CNN	convolutional neural network
CoAP	constrained application protocol
CPE	customer premises equipment
CRLB	Cramér-Rao lower bound
CTV	connected TV
DBN	deep belief networks
DDoS	disturbed denial of service
DES	discrete event simulations
DGA	domain generation algorithm
DICOM	digital imaging and communications in medicine
DLT	distributed ledger technology
DNS	domain name system
DOD	direction-of-departure
DoS	denial of service
dPBFT	developed delegated PBFT
DPI	deep packet inspection
DPOS	delegated proof of stake
DSD	data distribution service

DSNs	deep stacking networks
ECC	elliptic curve cryptography
ECG	electrocardiogram
ED	entity disambiguation
EDI	electronic data interchange
FAO	Food and Agriculture Organization
FCN	fully convolution network
FinTech	financial technology
GA	genetic algorithms
GBs	gigabits
GEO	geostationary satellite
G-IoT	green IoT
GPS	global positioning system
GPU	graphics processing units
GSM	global service for mobile
GUI	graphical user interface
HDFS	Hadoop distributed file system
HEO	highly elliptical orbit
HIPS	host-based intrusion prevention systems
HIS	hospital information system
HPC	high performance computing
IaaS	infrastructure as a service
IAM	identity and access management
ICT	information and communication technologies
IDS	intruder detection system
IIoT	industrial internet of things
IoE	internet of energy
IoMT	internet of medical things
IoT	internet of things
IoV	internet of vehicles
IPM	integrated pest management
ITU	international telecommunication units
K	potassium
KIF	knowledge interchange format
KQML	knowledge query and manipulation language
LDR	light dependent resistor
LED	light-emitting diode
LEO	low earth orbit
LI	laboratory interface
LIFS	localization information fusion system

LoS	line-of-sight
LPWA	low-power wireless access
LPWAN	low power wide area network
LSCSH	lattice-based secure cryptosystem
LSTM	long short-term memory
M2M	machine to machine
M2P	includes machine to people
MAC	message authentication code
MEMS	micro-electro-mechanical systems
ML	machine learning
MPA	microstrip patch antenna
MPI	message passing interface
MQTT	message queue telemetry transport
MTC	machine-type correspondence
MTL	multi-task learning
N	nitrogen
NDVI	normalized difference vegetation index
NE	named entity
NER	named entity recognition
NFC	near field communication
NLP	natural language processing
NPK	nitrogen-phosphorus potassium
NRC	National Research Council
OMA-DM	open mobile alliance device management
OTT	over-the-top
P	phosphorus
P2P	peer-to-peer
P2P	people-to-people
PaaS	platform as a service
PACS	picture archiving and communication system
PBFT	practical byzantine fault tolerance
PI	path lab interface
PIR	passive infrared
PN	personal network
PoET	proof of elapsed time
PoS	proof of stake
PoT	proof of trust
PoW	proof of work
QoS	quality of service
RDF	resource description framework

RFID	radio frequency identification
RFM	reference fingerprinting map
RI	radiology interface
RIS	radiology information system
RMS	remote monitoring system
RNNs	recurrent neural networks
RPi	raspberry Pi
RSS	received signal strength
RSSI	received signal strength indicator
SaaS	software as a service
SAR	synthetic aperture radar
SD	secure digital
SIM	subscriber identification module
SIoT	satellite IoT
SIT	secure IoT
SLAs	service level agreements
SMS	short message service
SSWE	sentiment-specific word embeddings
SVM	support vector machine
T&D	transmission and dissemination
TDOA	time difference of arrival
ToA	time of arrival
ToF	time of flight
UAVs	unmanned aerial vehicles
UGT	uses and gratification theory
UNFCCC	UN Framework Convention on Climate Change
USB	universal serial bus
UUID	universally unique identifier
V2G	vehicle-to-grid
VLC	visible light communication
VRI	variable rate irrigation
WAN	wide area network
WAP	wireless access point
WFC	weighted fingerprint construction
WHO	World Health Organization
WSN	wireless sensor network
WTFM	weighted text feature model
XMPP	extensible messaging and presence protocol

Acknowledgments

First of all, we express our gratitude to the Almighty, who blessed us with the zeal and enthusiasm to complete this book successfully.

We are extremely thankful to Prof. Jitender Chhabra, Head of Department, NIT, Kurukshetra, Prof. Deepak Garg, Head of Department, Bennett University, Prof. Nonita Sharma, NIT, Jalandhar, for their continuous guidance and support throughout the life cycle of this book.

We would like to acknowledge the assistance and contribution of all the people engaged in this project. We especially thank our authors for contributing their valuable work, without which it was impossible to complete this book. We express our special and most sincere thanks to the reviewers involved in the review process who contributed their time and expertise to improve the eminence, consistency, and arrangement of the chapters in the book. We also take the opportunity to express our thanks to personnel from the publishing house for giving it a final shape and presenting this book in this manner.

This book would not have been possible without the heartiest support of our family. Our deepest regards to our parents for their blessings and affection even during the tough period. Last but not least, we thank GOD for giving us the strength and wisdom to carry out this work successfully.

—*Editors*

Preface

The internet of things (IoT) paradigm is on its way to making objects such as web cameras, wireless sensors, consumer electronic devices, mobile phones, home appliances, clinical support systems, etc., communicate with each other. Thus, it creates a networking environment comprising various objects. It has opened avenues to establish interaction among human and non-living things. Additionally, it enables to development of smart cities, infrastructures, and services so as to improve the lifestyle of mankind alongside the utilization of resources.

IoT is an emerging paradigm for new generation computing. The data that is produced by IoT devices, commonly known as smart devices or sensors, are integrated and analyzed efficiently with the help of IoT technology. The IoT is a new revolution of the networking world and is gaining the attraction of researchers and scientists due to its rapid advancements in technologies and smart devices. Analysts have predicted that there will be a total of 50 billion IoT devices/things by the year 2050.

This book covers many of the powerful features and applications of IoT, such as weather forecasting, agriculture, medical science, surveillance system, and many more. This book is a collection of chapters on diverse issues on the Internet of Things, written for educational programs at universities and institutes and also for experts from industry and for scientists and researchers.

The book structure consists of three divisions, with a total of 20 chapters. Part I covers the issues and challenges arising from the Internet of Things (IoT) and their characteristics. Taxonomy of security issues of IoT systems is presented comprising of various IoT levels of security in different domains. Part II introduces various application areas of IoT, including agriculture, healthcare, and finance. A depth study of various applications of IoT is provided so that readers can enhance their knowledge about smart devices and equipment and their use in agriculture, finance, medical industry, home automation systems, logistics, retail, etc. Part III introduces the readers to advanced topics on IoT, including the integration of IoT with blockchain, cloud, and big data. It is expected that diligent readers of this book can improve their knowledge and skills in order to develop their own IoT applications. We assume that readers of this book possess some basic knowledge about

IoT technology, the general idea of programming, awareness about wired/ wireless technologies, and the concept of embedded systems. Our focus is on providing the reader a complete knowledge about different IoT domains for developing robust IoT applications.

We trust that the book will let readers find innovative ideas that are helpful for their educational research. Also, they can find an opportunity to setup some innovative business or develop their own smart application.

Organization of the Book

- ➤ **Chapter 1:** This chapter presents a detailed tutorial in the context of the IoT along with its description, merits, demerits, and challenges. This chapter elaborates on the main challenges faced by the field of IoT, such as unpredictable behavior, robustness, concurrency, coordination, and many more.
- ➤ **Chapter 2:** This chapter proposes an identification model that uses a random forest algorithm. This chapter also discusses the various botnet detection approaches in existence.
- ➤ **Chapter 3:** This chapter explores various challenges present in IDS over IoT. The authors also analyzed various types of available IDS Intrusion detection system techniques over IoT technology.
- ➤ **Chapter 4:** This chapter explains about empowering innovations of IoT, including distributed computing and various stages for information investigation.
- ➤ **Chapter 5:** This chapter explores IoT along with the emerging technologies and its implementation in the agriculture sector to achieve a greater result than traditional farming. SMART farming techniques along with the usage of various sensors, devices, and technologies are also elaborated section-wise.
- ➤ **Chapter 6:** This chapter discusses the capability of IoT in agribusiness, different periods of IoT in horticulture, and the challenges involved.
- ➤ **Chapter 7:** In this chapter, the authors present a weed monitoring system in crop production using various techniques, including manual surveys, sensors on land vehicles, or remote sensing. An optic mechanical system has been developed and installed with the reliability needed to operate the weed sensor under the outside area.
- ➤ **Chapter 8:** In this chapter, inset fed Microstrip Patch Antenna (MPA) is designed and analyzed for 7 GHz frequency for satellite communication which can be used to be mounted on IoT/OiE-based smart agriculture devices.
- ➤ **Chapter 9:** This chapter proposes a health monitoring system for cancer care using cloud-based IoT with wireless sensor network (WSN) to enhance the healthcare solution. The cloud services are used to achieve

transmission of data accurately, a good decision-making environment to enhance the cancer treatment facility.

➢ **Chapter 10:** The authors in this chapter propose a WSNs based system that collects data from different sensors deployed at various identified nodes in the field and communicates it through a wireless protocol. A solution has been provided for farmers which require less time and reduce the use of pesticides.

➢ **Chapter 11:** A lot of technological advancements were observed in financial sectors in the last decade. This chapter reviews various risks involved owing to the rapid increase in digitalization and mobilization of financial sectors.

➢ **Chapter 12:** In this chapter, a review on cloud computing as well as IoT with an attention on the need of the convergence of both innovations and security and privacy issues is presented.

➢ **Chapter 13:** This chapter proposes an effective summarization of surveillance videos by combining the advent of deep learning to IoT. Deep CNN is used for the selection of significant video features and LSTM is used for generation of video summary.

➢ **Chapter 14:** This chapter gives the complete insight of state of the art for blockchain and IoT. The chapter addresses research challenges, issues, and the concept of convergence of blockchain and IoT into BCoT. It also discusses the architecture, deployment, benefits, and challenges of BCoT.

➢ **Chapter 15:** This chapter presents the role of blockchain in IoT with respect to fault-tolerance, adaptability, security, and cost, etc.; additionally, it also discusses the associated challenges and issues.

➢ **Chapter 16:** In this chapter, the authors' emphasis is on the OTT platforms and their current market scenario. The authors also focus on understanding the theoretical perspective from the consumer viewpoint through cognitive dissonance theory.

➢ **Chapter 17:** The healthcare sector is always growing while technologies are updating and emerging. In this chapter, fog assisted IoT-based framework for the healthcare sector of a smart city is proposed that utilizes the concept of artificial intelligence by integrating with fog computing.

➢ **Chapter 18:** The authors in this chapter propose a novel activity recognition framework by the fusion of sensor technology with machine learning techniques. The framework is developed under real-time embedded implementation constraints and can be implemented in real-time sensor networks for accurate recognition of malicious wood logging activities.

➤ **Chapter 19:** The authors of this chapter propose a learning model system that takes IoT data from sensor devices, geographical locations, Twitter feeds, and SAR images. The authors propose a decision-making system for anomaly detection to minimize the risks.

➤ **Chapter 20:** This chapter focuses on the usage of Bluetooth Low Energy (BLE) devices beacons for indoor localization. Authors in this paper aim to present state-of-the-art for various developments in indoor localization.

PART I
Issues and Challenges in IoT

CHAPTER 1

Detailed Review on Security Challenges Associated with the Internet of Things

TARANDEEP KAUR BHATIA[1,2] and RAMKUMAR KETTI RAMACHANDRAN[2]

¹School of Information Technology, Deakin University, Geelong, VIC–3220, Australia, E-mails: tkbhatia@deakin.edu.au; tarandeep.bhatia@chitkara.edu.in

²Chitkara University Institute of Engineering and Technology, Punjab, India, E-mail: k.ramkumar@chitkara.edu.in (R. K. Ramachandran)

ABSTRACT

Internet of things (IoT) is the trending technology in this 21st century that aims at the interconnection of all the things in our surroundings via the internet. This chapter presents a detailed tutorial in the context of the IoT along with its description, merits, demerits, and challenges. This chapter elaborates on the main challenges faced by the field of IoT, such as unpredictable behavior, robustness, concurrency, co-ordination, and many more. However, in today's world, one of the major challenges that IoT has to deal with is the extremely dangerous security attacks that even can destroy the entire network. So, maintaining a balance between security and privacy is a challenging task for the IoT field. Therefore, this chapter explores and reviews good journal articles that discuss the security problems in the domain of IoT also elaborate on the technology used, as well as a solution to overcome the discussed problems. Based on the knowledge gathered from all the reviewed articles, this chapter discussed the research gaps for the current going on research in the domain of IoT security that need to be addressed in the upcoming future. IoT application provides a lot of benefits to the user, but in the case, if the IoT could not be able to secure the user information as well as data from hackers, outbreaks, and vulnerabilities, then IoT would not be considered as a secure domain. Furthermore, a critical analysis has been presented graphically for the evolution of the cybersecurity market in the domain of IoT. By reading this chapter, the readers will have a complete picture of the IoT domain as well as know the necessity for managing and controlling the security challenges faced by the field of IoT. Moreover, this chapter also allows the readers to understand and choose the research issues to carry out for their future research.

1.1   INTRODUCTION

The IoT (internet of things) is the novel technology in the present period that aims at the inter-connection of every single entity in a real-world scenario [1]. With the help of this technique, we can trail anything from a distant position using Internet set-up. Also, the IoT states the association of gadgets to the internet. Cars, kitchen machines as well as pulse rate all would be associated through IoT [2]. Furthermore, as the IoT progresses in a subsequent couple of ages, further new devices will connect that rundown. IoT is considered as a structure of interrelated substances ready to collect and skill data using embedded sensors. In order to deliver the entire systems intended for a service or product, IoT acts as advanced computerization as well as analytics systems that feats big data, networking, sensing, and artificial intelligence (AI) technology. These systems allow more notable straightforwardness, control, and performance when applied to any industry or framework [3]. The IoT is a framework of interconnected computing gadgets, motorized as well as digital machinery, articles, faunas, or humans that are equipped with the unique identifier as well as the capability of transferring information over a setup without requiring a human to PC or else human to human associations [4].

The word "thing," in the IoT things might be a human being with a heart screen implant, an animal with a bio-chip transponder, a car that has functioned in sensors to aware the car owner when tire weight is low or some other natural or man-made thing that can be allocated an IP address as well as outfitted with the capability to transfer above an internet. IoT has developed from the conjunction of wire-less skills, micro-electro-mechanical systems (MEMS), small-scale administrations as well as the web. Kevin Ashton, prime supporter as well as official chief of the Auto-ID focus at MIT, first whispered the IoT in an introduction he made in front of Procter and gamble in 1999 [5]. As per the novel research by Gartner, The IoT, which ignores PCs, tablets, and cell phones, will produce incremental income of more than $300 billion in amenities by 2020. The services involve equipment, embedded software, communications facilities as well as information amenities related to the things [6], [7]. Gartner predicted that 2.9 billion associated things will be in practice in the user area in the year 2015 and will spread over 13 billion in the year 2020. The motorized field will display the maximum progress rate at 96% in the year 2015.

Cryptography refers to the approaches and techniques which are developed and implemented for secured communication for specific channels [8, 9]. It is traditionally associated with the encryption approaches to secure the overall transmission. Security ideas can be executed simply by applying tools of cryptography for example message authentication outlines or encryption. Table 1.1 displays the evaluation of cryptography hash approaches applied in the network environment. Table 1.1 depicts different security-related algorithms with their description of various parameters. Also, Figure 1.1 shows the graphical illustration of traditional cryptography hash approaches using several parameters.

1.1.1 IoT: MERITS

The benefits of IoT navigate over each zone of lifespan as well as business. Here is a rundown of certain merits that IoT brings to the notice [7]:

1. **Enhanced Client Engagement:** In the current analysis, there occurs numerous flaws in the accuracy so involvement of the client becomes quite essential.
2. **Innovation Optimization:** The similar innovations that enhance client knowledge also improves gadget utilization, and help in more intense changes to advancement [8].
3. **A Decrease in Waste:** Current analysis provides us shallow understanding, but IoT provides real-world information provoking a more effective organization of assets.
4. **Improved Data Gathering:** Modern gathering of data encounters from its limitations and its design for passive use.

1.1.2 IoT: DEMERITS

Despite the way that IoT provides numerous benefits, it also offers a substantial number of challenges [9]. Here is a summary of a couple of its noteworthy issues:

1. **Security:** IoT presents an environment of frequently related devices communicating over the networks.
2. **Privacy:** IoT gives extensive individual data in extreme detail without the customer's active involvement.
3. **Complexity:** IoT systems are quite complicated regarding design as well as deployment.
4. **Flexibility:** Many are stressed over the flexibility of an IoT structure to facilitate quickly with another [10].
5. **Compliance:** IoT, like some other innovation in the area of business, must consent to guidelines.

TABLE 1.1   Evaluation of Cryptography Hash Approaches in Network Environment

Algorithm	Rounds	Word Size	Internal State Size	Block Size	Output Size (bits)
GOST	32	32	256	256	256
HAVAL	5	32	256	1,024	128
MD2	18	32	384	128	128
MD4	3	32	128	512	128
MD5	64	32	128	512	128
PANAMA	32	32	8,736	256	256
RIPEMD	48	32	128	512	128
RIPEMD-128/256	64	32	128/256	512	128/256
RIPEMD-160	80	32	160	512	160
RIPEMD-320	80	32	320	512	320
SHA-0	80	32	160	512	160
SHA-1	80	40	160	512	160
SHA-256	64	56	256	512	256
SHA-3	24	64	1,600	3,200	512
SHA3-224	24	64	1,600	1,152	224
SHA3-256	24	64	1,600	1,088	256
SHA3-384	24	64	1,600	832	384
SHA3-512	24	64	1,600	576	512
Tiger2	24	64	192	512	128
WHIRLPOOL	10	8	512	512	512
BLAKE2b	12	64	1,024	512	512
BLAKE2s	10	32	512	256	256

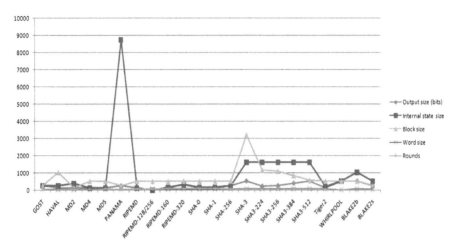

FIGURE 1.1   Graphical evaluation of traditional cryptography hash approaches.

1.2   CHALLENGES OF IoT

There are several challenges that IoT faces beyond costs and the ubiquity of devices such as [5]:

1. **Device Similarity:** IoT gadgets are genuinely uniform. They use a similar association innovation as well as modules [6]. In this, if one framework or gadget experiences powerlessness or suffers from a susceptibility then many more have a similar issue.
2. **Long Device Life and Expired Support:** One of the advantages of IoT gadgets is lifespan, although, that long life furthermore implies that they may outlast their gadget sustenance that is possible to some extent only.
3. **No Upgrade Support:** Many IoT gadgets acts in the same way as other portable and little gadgets do, which is not intended to permit redesigns or any alterations.
4. **Poor or No Transparency:** Many IoT gadgets neglects to furnish straightforwardness concerning their usefulness. Clients cannot watch or access their procedures and are left to accept how gadgets act. They have no influence over undesirable capacities or information accumulation; moreover, when a producer modernizes the device, it may bring more unwanted functions.
5. **No Alerts:** Another objective of IoT stays to give its unimaginable usefulness without being prominent. This presents the issue of client

mindfulness. Clients do not screen the gadgets or know when something turns out badly. Security breaches can persist over long periods without recognition.

6. **Mobility Induced Sensor Network Design:** The IoT gadgets think that it would be hard to interface with each other as well as any other components of IoT organizes in the existence of movability.

7. **Robustness:** The topology of the system in the case of IoT will be exceptionally unverifiable as well as may changes frequently [7]. In such cases keeping up of a long-lived and dynamic framework is dangerous. In this manner, there are challenges in gadget discoverability, control use, and communication protocols.

8. **Co-Ordination:** The real-time coordination among all the mobile device senses as well as actuation platforms is a crucial research challenge that needs to be addressed if IoT is to become fruitful.

9. **Concurrency:** For instance, a web associated auto traveling through more traffic could show variable portability patterns and travel times between its source and goal, managing communication and input/output tasks among various autos, every one of them is varying with their portability patterns and this would be additionally challenging.

10. **Optimal Data Capture and Processing:** A key issue in the IoT framework with more information is created and transmitted on the system. Since the greater part of the information is pointless for the client, methods for ideally filtering the information before storage, and this will rise as a critical research zone.

11. **Location-Based Data Representation and Storage:** Optimal representation, as well as storage of IoT information, is a vital subject, given the information volumes that may be put away from future examination and for review reason.

12. **Serve Implementation via Actuation:** Users need to roll out improvements in the IoT system through the actuation process.

13. **Integration with Opportunistic Computing:** The key research challenge is to decide the most ideal ways to deal with encourage decentralized resourceful directions among human clients and the IoT system [8].

1.3   BACKGROUND OF THE STUDY

IoT is highly susceptible as well as vulnerable to the assaults in assorted layers. There are many issues related to the field of IoT that have been revealed in

Figure 1.2. IoT integrates the low powered devices which communicate with the real-world objects in limited resources and thereby the need to associate the secured cryptography arises. In this research-based study, the need to integrate lightweight cryptography and secure authentication is required. A number of approaches that are devised and implemented here are in a need to integrate the high-performance approaches including quantum cryptography and effectual paradigms that can elevate the overall performance with the secured authorization and authentication in multiple channels.

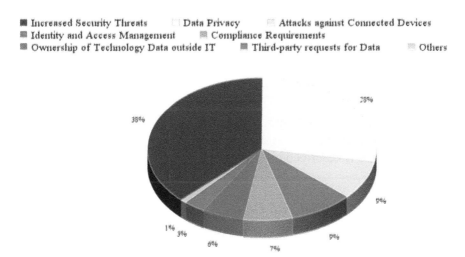

FIGURE 1.2   Top governance issues with the internet of things.

Following are the key assaults in the network environment of IoT:

1. **Sniffing:** In this type of attack, the secretly sniffing or intercepting the channel is done. The forceful evaluation of network channels is done in this type of assault to breach the security in a wireless network.
2. **Base Attack:** In this type of assault, the virtual work is created to intercept the network by hidden layers.
3. **Blackhole Attack:** In this attack, the hacker changes the data packets and the fake channel is used for the distribution of signals. The malicious nodes create a false route to send the fake data to damage the network.
4. **Convoluted Attack:** In this attack, the Convolutional path or complex path is allocated to the network for the damaging purpose. It is used

to exploit the network nodes with the fetching of data packets without permissions.

5. **Hastening Attack:** It energizes the resources so that a higher degree of energy can be consumed in an unethical way. The rushing attacks can damage the network environment to a huge extent with the luring factors by the non-genuine nodes in the environment.

6. **Choke Down Attack:** In this attack, the network channel, as well as bandwidth, are choked down with the evaluation and forcing the bandwidth to deplete a huge level. Using this way, the network bandwidth is consumed and heavily loaded to damage as well as stop the overall communication by the genuine or authenticated users in the network.

1.4   LITERATURE REVIEW

In this section, 23 reputed journal papers are considered, and an extract of each paper is mentioned below as well as the complete summary of all the reviewed papers is described in Table 1.2.

1.4.1   EXCERPTS FROM THE EXISTING WORK AND REVIEW OF LITERATURE

The approach of a certificate-less public key is presented whereby the industrial internet of things (IIoT) can be secured [10]. In this approach, the random public key is introduced rather than the public key of the user. The proposed SCF-MCLPEKS approach is found effective and executed in less time as compared to the approach by Peng et al.'s.

The work presents the lattice-based secure cryptosystem (LSCSH) for the implementation of higher security in the smart cities-based environment [11]. The proposed approach makes use of a lightweight key exchange mechanism with the secured authentication module having multiple layers so that the security can be enriched. The Access Right Verification Mechanism is used so that the permissions can be set for the nodes in the communication scenario.

The author of this chapter proposed the CP-ABE scheme to protect the user attributes values in contradiction of AA-based on the 1-out-of-n Oblivious transfer method [12]. Attributes Bloom Filter adopted to defend the attributes types of access strategy in the cipher-text. The outcome consequences proved that the planned model is much improved in terms of efficiency as well as security.

TABLE 1.2 Summary of Review

Year	Paper Title	Objective	Technology/ Technique	Problem	Solution	Advantages	Limitations
2018 [10]	Certificateless searchable public-key encryption scheme for industrial internet of things.	To elevate the security with dynamic encryption	SCF-MCLPEKS approach	Security, integrity, authentication, and authorization	Time	Execution time reduce	Cost factor
2018 [11]	LSCSH: Lattice-based secure cryptosystem for smart healthcare in smart cities environment	Lattice oriented cryptosystem development specifically for the smart cities and medical records	Lattice-based secure cryptosystem (LSCSH)	Security, integrity, authentication, and authorization	Security	Higher degree of security	Higher cost factor
2018 [12]	Efficient and robust attribute-based encryption supporting access policy hiding in internet of things.	Fault-tolerant and robust approach for security and integrity in the IoT	CP-ABE scheme	Security, integrity, authentication, and authorization	Security, efficiency, performance	Time and cost	Complexity may be compromised
2017 [13]	Privacy-preserving and lightweight key agreement protocol for V2G in the social internet of things.	Grid-based implementation of cryptography approach	Lightweight key agreement protocol	Security, integrity, authentication, and authorization	Communication complexity, functionality, and computational cost	Higher degree of security and reduce complexity	Time factor
2017 [14]	Secure data access control with cipher-text update and computation outsourcing in fog computing for internet of things.	Security aware IoT environment development with fog computing-based implementation for higher level of security	Secure data access control outline by using fog computing on CP-ABE as well as ABS is proposed	Security, integrity, authentication, and authorization	Encryption and decryption computational overhead	Overall computational overhead	May not be generic for multiple networks

TABLE 1.2 *(Continued)*

Year	Paper Title	Objective	Technology/ Technique	Problem	Solution	Advantages	Limitations
2017 [15]	Secure signature-based authenticated key establishment scheme for future IoT applications.	Secured key and signature associated authentication approach	Signature-based authenticated key establishment arrangement	Security, integrity, authentication, and authorization	Throughput as well as end-to-end delay	Throughput as well as end-to-end delay	Higher level of cost factor
2017 [16]	Lightweight three-factor authentication and key agreement protocol for internet-integrated wireless sensor networks.	Development of multi-level and multi-factor authentication approach for security in advanced wireless networks of IoT	Proposed lightweight and secure user authentication protocol based on Robin cryptosystem	Security, integrity, authentication, and authorization	Efficiency	Higher efficiency	Complexity factor
2017 [17]	Lightweight cybersecurity schemes using elliptic curve cryptography in publish-subscribe fog computing.	Association of ECC based approach for cryptography in IoT security	Fog computing based publish-subscribe lightweight protocol using elliptic curve cryptography (ECC)	Security, integrity, authentication, and authorization	Overall security	Higher degree of security	Cumulative performance on assorted networks
2017 [18]	Elliptic curve cryptography with efficiently computable endomorphisms and its hardware implementations for the internet of things.	Integration of ECC (elliptic curve cryptography) that is a prominent approach for security and its performance in IoT	Offer trade-off and optimization between resources and performance	Security, integrity, authentication, and authorization	Security and performance	Higher degree of security and performance	Greater value of complexity

TABLE 1.2 *(Continued)*

Year	Paper Title	Objective	Technology/ Technique	Problem	Solution	Advantages	Limitations
2017 [19]	Sit: A lightweight encryption algorithm for secure internet of things.	Analysis and implementation of Secured algorithm with lightweight resources in IoT	Secure IoT (SIT) a lightweight encryption algorithm	Security, integrity, authentication, and authorization	Correlation and entropy, histogram comparison	Correlation and entropy, histogram comparison and correlation comparison	Overall performance may be compromised
2016 [20]	An efficient user authentication and key agreement scheme for heterogeneous wireless sensor network tailored for the internet of things environment.	Implementation of security-based approach that can be integrated with assorted networks of IoT with heterogeneous properties	Improved the key agreement and user authentication for heterogeneous WSN	Security, integrity, authentication, and authorization	Storage, computational	Storage, computational, and communication cost	Cost factor and complexity can be optimized further using high performance approaches
2016 [21]	S3K: scalable security with symmetric keys— DTLS key establishment for the internet of things.	Development of a framework with implementation using symmetric key-based approach	Symmetric key (S3K) for security in the IoT	Security, integrity, authentication, and authorization	Time as well as energy overhead	Time as well as energy overhead, memory-overhead	Complexity factor
2016 [22]	SecIoT: a security framework for the internet of things.	Development of an outline for effective safety in IoT	Prototype security framework with a transparent security feature.	Security, integrity, authentication, and authorization	Study results of access control model	Study results of access control model and study results of risk indicator	Complexity factor

TABLE 1.2 *(Continued)*

Year	Paper Title	Objective	Technology/ Technique	Problem	Solution	Advantages	Limitations
2016 [23]	FairAccess: a new blockchain-based access control framework for the internet of things.	Development of blockchain integrated approach for secured authentication and cumulative security in internet of things	Proposed a novel outline for access control in IoT using blockchain technology	Security, integrity, authentication, and authorization	Performance and security	Better performance and increased security	Complexity factor
2016 [24]	DCapBAC: embedding authorization logic into smart things through ECC optimizations	Usage of the embedded framework for authorization and secured authentication in IoT	This model proposed IP based technology for the IoT based scenario	Security, integrity, authentication, and authorization	AVISPA and authentication	Trade-off between security and performance is better	Cost factor and complexity can be optimized further using high performance approaches
2016 [25]	A lightweight message authentication scheme for smart grid communications in power sector.	Smart grid-based framework for energy optimization and security in power segment	Hybrid Diffie-Hellman based authentication scheme	Security, integrity, authentication, and authorization	Computational cost	Communication overhead and computational cost	Cost factor and complexity can be optimized further using high performance approaches
2015 [26]	OSCAR: Object security architecture for the internet of things.	Development of a new approach for security and secured framework	Address and overcome the issue of the E2E safety approach in the IoT	Security, integrity, authentication, and authorization	Computational overhead and scalability	Computational overhead and scalability	The generic performance on assorted topologies required

TABLE 1.2 *(Continued)*

Year	Paper Title	Objective	Technology/Technique	Problem	Solution	Advantages	Limitations
2015 [27]	Optimized ECC implementation for secure communication between heterogeneous IoT devices, sensors.	Integration of ECC based cryptography approach for security and authorization with the key management	Elliptical curve cryptography algorithm	Security, integrity, authentication, and authorization	Usage of network	Network usage	Cumulative performance on assorted networks
2015 [28]	Triathlon of lightweight block ciphers for the internet of things.	Lightweight approach for security with minimum resource consumption	Framework in the embedded platform	Security, integrity, authentication, and authorization	Evaluate the memory parameters, resources	Evaluate the RAM, footprints, and binary code size.	Cost factor and complexity can be optimized further using high performance approaches
2015 [29]	SEA: a secure and efficient authentication and authorization architecture for IoT-based healthcare using smart gateways.	Smart healthcare integrated approach for overall performance in IoT	This proposed model adopted better key-management schemes between sensor nodes as well as a smart gateway	Security, integrity, authentication, and authorization	Transmission overhead and communication overhead	Better performance with Transmission overhead and communication overhead parameters	Cumulative performance on assorted networks
2015 [30]	Talos: Encrypted query processing for the internet of things.	Data encryption-based model for increasing the privacy of the network	Encryption and key management approach	Security, integrity, authentication, and authorization	Time and energy	Reduced time and energy	Cumulative performance on assorted networks

TABLE 1.2 *(Continued)*

Year	Paper Title	Objective	Technology/Technique	Problem	Solution	Advantages	Limitations
2015 [31]	IoT-OAS: An OAuth-based authorization service architecture for secure services in IoT scenarios.	Usage of open authentication for security and effectual services in cloud and IoT based environment	An innovative architecture for providing HTTP as well as CoAP service workers with an authorization sheet.	Security, integrity, authentication, and authorization	Energy consumption	Energy consumption and memory footprints	The generic performance on assorted topologies required
2014 [32]	Lightweight collaborative key establishment scheme for the internet of things.	An effectual approach integrating the collaborative key in IoT	Lightweight collaborative key exchange scheme	Security, integrity, authentication, and authorization	Overall energy consumption	Overall energy consumption reduced	Cost factor and complexity can be optimized further using high performance approaches

This chapter addresses the security as well as privacy problems in the V2G (vehicle-to-grid) network of the internet of thing and also proposed a lightweight key agreement protocol for making networks more secure and enhance the privacy [13]. The effectiveness of the proposed model is represented by comparison with the ECC based protocol.

In this, a secured data access control outline intended for IoT in the Fog-Computing on CP-ABE as well ABS is proposed [14]. The efficiency of the planned outline that is represented by the time taken by the proposed scheme for encryption, decryption as well as signing for the user is small and constrained. The simulation results proved that the planned outline is secure in contradiction to the attacks.

The Author of this chapter proposed a secure signature-based Genuine key establishment outline for an IoT which becomes more secure and reliable [15]. The planned structure of security is tested by using Burrows Adadi Needham logic, informal safety as well as formal safety verification by means of broadly accepted automated authentication of internet safety protocol and NS2 simulator.

The work presents a lightweight and secure user authentication protocol based on Robin cryptosystem with the characteristics of the computational asymmetry [16]. The proposed model support dynamic security features. The simulation results proved that the proposed model is suitable for providing security and higher efficiency in a more balanced way.

This chapter proposed a secure, fog computing-based publish-subscribe lightweight protocol using elliptic curve cryptography (ECC) for the IoT network [17]. Basically, ECC provides shorter key length, reduce message size, and lower the resources usage. This scheme provides better scalability and less overhead such as storage and communication.

This chapter offers trade-off and optimization between resources and performance because they both are important in the IoT network [18]. In this chapter, a twisted Edward curve with an efficient endomorphism is also used. The author also described how endomorphism exploited to speedup dual scalar multiplication. 100-bit security level trade-off offers between security and performance.

Author proposed secure IoT (SIT) a lightweight encryption algorithm [19]. This is a 64-bit cipher and always required a 64-bit key to perform a task and encrypt data. The simulation outcomes proved that the planned outline offers substantial safety only in five encryption rounds.

Author projected a new outline for improving the key agreement and user authentication for heterogeneous WSN [20]. This proposed model tackles and eliminates all security attacks. The security results proved that this model provides higher security.

The work presents Symmetric Key (S3K) for security in the IoT [21]. S3K is a lightweight as well as possible to use in the resource-constrained gadgets also at a similar time, it is scalable to numerous IoT gadgets.

The author of this chapter proposed a prototype security outline with a clear security feature [22]. The core aim of this chapter is to address the security matter as well as provide a real framework.

The author of this chapter proposed a novel framework for access control in the IoT using block-chain technology [23]. This new outline leverages and consistently provide block-chain based cryptography such as bit-coin to offer stronger as well as a transparent access control tool.

This work is dependent on a capability-based access control outline [24]. This model uses IP based technology for the IoT based scenario. The trade-off between security and performance is better.

A new approach named hybrid Diffie-Hellman based verification arrangement using AES as well as RSA for the session key creation is proposed in this chapter [25]. This communication overhead of this scheme is 23% that is much low than the existing schemes.

The author projected a new technique to overcome the problem of E2E security in IoT [26]. The application and security concepts are discussed in this chapter as well as Cooja simulator is used for simulating the work.

This chapter proposed the elliptical curve cryptography algorithm for dealing with the security issues in the IoT network [27]. Basically, ECC optimization is available for secure communication.

This chapter presents the framework for benchmarking of the lightweight block cipher on a multitude of embedded platforms [28]. This platform evaluates the RAM, footprints, and binary code size.

This model architecture was developed with a focus to make a network more secure than the existing systems [29]. This proposed model adopted better key-management schemes among sensor nodes as well as a smart gateway. The outcome proved that the communication overhead is reduced by 26%.

This chapter projected a data encryption-based technique for increasing the privacy of the network and reducing the encryption time [30]. The main emphasis of this chapter was to develop a more secure and higher privacy-based network scheme.

The author of this chapter planned an innovative architecture for providing HTTP and CoAP service workers with an authorization sheet [31]. The proposed approach is able to handle multiple smart objects with limited computational power.

This chapter represents a light-weight collaborative key exchange outline for increasing the security of the IoT network [32]. The proposed approach is better in terms of energy consumption as through this approach, the energy is saved by 80% as compared to existing strategies.

1.5 OVERVIEW OF CURRENT STATE OF THE FIELD AS WELL AS THEORETICAL UNDERPINNINGS OF THE RESEARCH

Today's era is encompassed by numerous devices and gadgets that are interlinked through technologies offering high performance. This technological communication is handled under the umbrella of the IoT. IoT based communication is being used at a rapid pace in the fields of defense, highway patrolling, smart cities, smart toll collections, satellite televisions, business communications, smart offices, traffic systems of interrelated webcams for the social security [33–35]. IoT is also linked with the terms like Pervasive Computing, Ubiquitous Computing (UbiComp), or Ambient Computing to provide virtual connections among devices for making decisions as well as remote monitoring. Because of the linking of enormous devices and objects through a virtual environment, severe challenge related to security and privacy arises. But with the advent of IoT, the risks to security and privacy are demolishing to a great extent.

There are numerous attacks that can harm the IoT environment at various layers [36, 37]. The hackers can damage as well as control the IoT system by distributing malicious packets and signals with the aim of practically destroying the structure [38, 39]. These attacks are in the list of the highest priority as they can affect the overall functionality of the system:

1. **DoS Attack:** In *the DoS attack*, the availability of the network is blocked by the attacker node or malicious packet by arresting the communication channel or bandwidth. In this case, genuine users will not be able to access the network facilities. This attack is treated as the main attack that occurs on the network layer of IoT based situation [40]. These kinds of attacks become much more dangerous when it turns out to be a Distributed Denial-of-Service (DDoS) attack. In this attack, the malicious node or hacker accomplish the attack through numerous as well as diverse locations.

2. **Sybil Attack:** In the *Sybil attack,* the network layer is greatly affected. This attack helps in manipulating the identity of the source. The malicious node fabricates the original source node to pretend

like it and then manipulates the identity of the source node. In a Sybil attack, with the help of replication, the attacker node creates dissimilar nodes and compels other nodes either to move quickly or leave the network path [41]. With the help of Resource testing, which is based on the assumption that vehicles have limited resources, these attacks can be detected. Moreover, Public-key cryptography may be used to diminish Sybil attacks through the means of public keys for authentication of vehicles.

3. **Application-Level Attack:** The *application-level attack* in the IoT environment, there is interference which results in the retransmission of messages to destination thus making it insecure. For instance, high traffic lanes can be relayed as Congestion Free Lane on the internet of vehicles (IoV), thus resulting in disasters. The main concerns in IoT based network environments are security and privacy which requires secure communication without any intrusion. To enforce a high level of security, IPv6 is implemented with dynamic hybrid cryptography for generating and authenticating key. The IPv6 based approach can be implemented with fully secured algorithms [42]. With the application of IoT in various scenarios, it becomes essential to handle the IoT security aspects by the secured routing of packets to ensure secure transmission without any interruption. IoT has an IPv6 Based Protocol named, RPL, which is combined with IPv6 over Low Power WPAN and works with DODAG (Destination-Oriented Directed Acyclic Graph) that supports unidirectional also with bi-directional communication. RPL permits each node to decide whether the packets are to be sent to the root or the child nodes.

1.5.1   *IDENTIFICATION OF GAPS IN RESEARCH*

- There is a need to integrate and associate the high-performance approaches of security in IoT including quantum cryptography;
- Quantum cryptography integrates Heisenberg's uncertainty principle and the no-cloning theorem which are effective and can give better results in the security as well as integrity;
- Quantum key distribution is required to be connected because of its current minimum usage and giving the better-predicted results;
- Lightweight cryptography is currently used that can be improved with the use of soft computing and meta-heuristic approaches.

1.6 CRITICAL ANALYSIS

An IoT involves the growing occurrence of objects as well as elements that are referred to in this setting as things-provided along with the capacity to naturally exchange data over the system [43]. A great portion of the development in IoT communication invents from computing gadgets as well as implanted sensor frameworks utilized in modern machine-to-machine (M2M) communication, a vehicle-to-vehicle communication, home, and building robotization, and also wearable computing gadgets.

Most of the time, IoT items are sold with previously used and improper working frameworks. Apart from this, customers either do not feel the need to change the default passwords or set new passwords. To improve security, IoT gadgets that directly open on the internet should be portioned into their system and should have constraints for accessing the network [44]. The statistic that demonstrates the IoT security spending worldwide from 2014 to 2022 (in million U.S. dollars) have been shown in Figure 1.3.

Following are the key points from the study which can be worked out for security and challenges with IoT:

- IoT API security;
- IoT tokens generation;
- IoT PKI;
- IoT encryption;
- IoT authentication.

Frameworks and libraries for implementation of IoT [45, 46]:

- *OpenIoT* (URL: http://www.openiot.eu/);
- *Zetta* (URL: http://www.zettajs.org/);
- *DSA* [Distributed Services Architecture] (URL: http://www.iot-dsa.org/);
- *Node-RED* (URL: http://nodered.org/);
- *IoTivity* (URL: https://www.iotivity.org/);
- *Cooja* (URL: http://www.contiki-os.org).

1.7 CONCLUSION

IoT applications are becoming vital in day-to-day routine for instance, smart home, smart parking, healthcare, smart grid, and many more. As we all know, IoT application provides a lot of benefits to the user, but in this case, if the IoT will not be able to secure the user information and data from hackers,

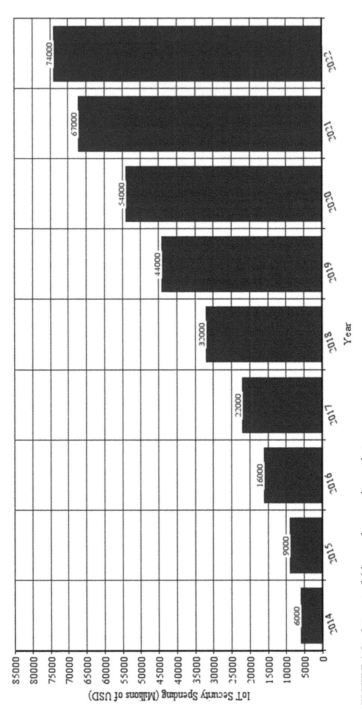

FIGURE 1.3 Internet of things cybersecurity market.

IoT will not have the future. Light-weight encryption is an area of traditional cryptographic algorithms that are relevant for resource-constrained gadgets in IoT. Using such integration, the overall escalation can be done in the IoT-based environment. This chapter covers the complete description of the security challenges linked with the IoT. Also, this chapter discusses the problems as well as the solutions faced by the domain IoT. Researchers will get a precise and clear idea for the problems that need to be addressed in the future to deal with the challenges of IoT after reading this chapter.

KEYWORDS

- **cryptography**
- **distributed denial-of-service**
- **internet of things**
- **networking attacks**
- **privacy**
- **security**

REFERENCES

1. Gubbi, J., Buyya, R., Marusic, S., & Palaniswami, M., (2013). Internet of things (IoT): A vision, architectural elements, and future directions. *Future Generation Computer Systems, 29*(7), 1645–1660.
2. Kelly, S. D. T., Suryadevara, N. K., & Mukhopadhyay, S. C., (2013). Towards the implementation of IoT for environmental condition monitoring in homes. *IEEE Sensors Journal, 13*(10), 3846–3853.
3. Lee, I., & Lee, K., (2015). The internet of things (IoT): Applications, investments, and challenges for enterprises. *Business Horizons, 58*(4), 431–440.
4. Guo, B., Zhang, D., Wang, Z., Yu, Z., & Zhou, X., (2013). Opportunistic IoT: Exploring the harmonious interaction between human and the internet of things. *Journal of Network and Computer Applications, 36*(6), 1531–1539.
5. Farooq, M. U., Waseem, M., Mazhar, S., Khairi, A., & Kamal, T., (2015). A review on internet of things (IoT). *International Journal of Computer Applications, 113*(1), 1–7.
6. Mirocha, U., (2015). *The Internet of Things at the Crossroads: Smart Home and Smart City Implementation Models*. Working Paper Delab Uw, No. XX (2/2015 Smart Economy & Innovation, Warshaw.
7. Mishra, A., Nadkarni, K., & Patcha, A., (2004). Intrusion detection in wireless ad hoc networks. *IEEE Wireless Communications, 11*(1), 48–60.

8. Kumari, S., Karuppiah, M., Das, A. K., Li, X., Wu, F., & Kumar, N., (2018). A secure authentication scheme based on elliptic curve cryptography for IoT and cloud servers. *The Journal of Supercomputing, 74*(12), 6428–6453.

9. Diffie, W., & Hellman, M., (1976). New directions in cryptography. *IEEE Transactions on Information Theory, 22*(6), 644–654.

10. Ma, M., He, D., Kumar, N., Choo, K. K. R., & Chen, J., (2017). Certificateless searchable public-key encryption scheme for industrial internet of things. *IEEE Transactions on Industrial Informatics, 14*(2), 759–767.

11. Chaudhary, R., Jindal, A., Aujla, G. S., Kumar, N., Das, A. K., & Saxena, N., (2018). LSCSH: Lattice-based secure cryptosystem for smart healthcare in smart cities environment. *IEEE Communications Magazine, 56*(4), 24–32.

12. Han, Q., Zhang, Y., & Li, H., (2018). Efficient and robust attribute-based encryption supporting access policy hiding in internet of things. *Future Generation Computer Systems, 83*, 269–277.

13. Shen, J., Zhou, T., Wei, F., Sun, X., & Xiang, Y., (2017). Privacy-preserving and lightweight key agreement protocol for V2G in the social Internet of Things. *IEEE Internet of Things Journal, 5*(4), 2526–2536.

14. Huang, Q., Yang, Y., & Wang, L., (2017). Secure data access control with ciphertext update and computation outsourcing in fog computing for internet of things. *IEEE Access, 5*, 12941–12950.

15. Challa, S., Wazid, M., Das, A. K., Kumar, N., Reddy, A. G., Yoon, E. J., & Yoo, K. Y., (2017). Secure signature-based authenticated key establishment scheme for future IoT applications. *IEEE Access, 5*, 3028–3043.

16. Jiang, Q., Zeadally, S., Ma, J., & He, D., (2017). Lightweight three-factor authentication and key agreement protocol for internet-integrated wireless sensor networks. *IEEE Access, 5*, 3376–3392.

17. Diro, A. A., Chilamkurti, N., & Kumar, N., (2017). Lightweight cybersecurity schemes using elliptic curve cryptography in publish-subscribe fog computing. *Mobile Networks and Applications, 22*(5), 848–858.

18. Liu, Z., Großschädl, J., Hu, Z., Järvinen, K., Wang, H., & Verbauwhede, I., (2016). Elliptic curve cryptography with efficiently computable endomorphisms and its hardware implementations for the internet of things. *IEEE Transactions on Computers, 66*(5), 773–785.

19. Usman, M., Ahmed, I., Aslam, M. I., Khan, S., & Shah, U. A., (2017*). SIT: A Lightweight Encryption Algorithm for Secure Internet of Things.* arXiv preprint arXiv:1704.08688.

20. Farash, M. S., Turkanović, M., Kumari, S., & Hölbl, M., (2016). An efficient user authentication and key agreement scheme for heterogeneous wireless sensor network tailored for the internet of things environment. *Ad. Hoc. Networks, 36*, 152–176.

21. Raza, S., Seitz, L., Sitenkov, D., & Selander, G., (2016). S3K: Scalable security with symmetric keys—DTLS key establishment for the internet of things. *IEEE Transactions on Automation Science and Engineering, 13*(3), 1270–1280.

22. Huang, X., Craig, P., Lin, H., & Yan, Z., (2016). SecIoT: A security framework for the Internet of Things. *Security and Communication Networks, 9*(16), 3083–3094.

23. Ouaddah, A., Abou, E. A., & Ait, O. A., (2016). FairAccess: A new Blockchain-based access control framework for the internet of things. *Security and Communication Networks, 9*(18), 5943–5964.

24. Hernández-Ramos, J. L., Jara, A. J., Marín, L., & Skarmeta, G. A. F., (2016). DCapBAC: Embedding authorization logic into smart things through ECC optimizations. *International Journal of Computer Mathematics, 93*(2), 345–366.

25. Mahmood, K., Chaudhry, S. A., Naqvi, H., Shon, T., & Ahmad, H. F., (2016). A lightweight message authentication scheme for Smart Grid communications in power sector. *Computers & Electrical Engineering, 52*, 114–124.

26. Vučinić, M., Tourancheau, B., Rousseau, F., Duda, A., Damon, L., & Guizzetti, R., (2015). OSCAR: Object security architecture for the internet of things. *Ad. Hoc. Networks, 32*, 3–16.

27. Marin, L., Pawlowski, M. P., & Jara, A., (2015). Optimized ECC implementation for secure communication between heterogeneous IoT devices. *Sensors, 15*(9), 21478–21499.

28. Dinu, D., Le Corre, Y., Khovratovich, D., Perrin, L., Großschädl, J., & Biryukov, A., (2019). Triathlon of lightweight block ciphers for the internet of things. *Journal of Cryptographic Engineering, 9*(3), 283–302.

29. Rahimi, M. S., Nguyen, G. T., Rahmani, A. M., Nigussie, E., Virtanen, S., Isoaho, J., & Tenhunen, H., (2015). SEA: A secure and efficient authentication and authorization architecture for IoT-based healthcare using smart gateways. In: *Procedia Computer Science* (Vol. 52, pp. 452–459). Elsevier.

30. Shafagh, H., Hithnawi, A., Droescher, A., Duquennoy, S., & Hu, W., (2015). Talos: Encrypted query processing for the internet of things. In: *Proceedings of the 13th ACM Conference on Embedded Networked Sensor Systems* (pp. 197–210).

31. Cirani, S., Picone, M., Gonizzi, P., Veltri, L., & Ferrari, G., (2014). IoT-OAS: An OAuth-based authorization service architecture for secure services in IoT scenarios. *IEEE Sensors Journal, 15*(2), 1224–1234.

32. Saied, Y. B., Olivereau, A., Zeghlache, D., & Laurent, M., (2014). Lightweight collaborative key establishment scheme for the internet of things. *Computer Networks, 64*, 273–295.

33. Farahat, I. S., Tolba, A. S., Elhoseny, M., & Eladrosy, W., (2019). Data security and challenges in smart cities. In: *Security in Smart Cities: Models, Applications, and Challenges* (pp. 117–142). Springer, Cham.

34. Sawhney, H., (1996). Information superhighway: Metaphors as midwives. *Media, Culture & Society, 18*(2), 291–314.

35. Herrera, J. C., Work, D. B., Herring, R., Ban, X. J., Jacobson, Q., & Bayen, A. M., (2010). Evaluation of traffic data obtained via GPS-enabled mobile phones: The mobile century field experiment. *Transportation Research Part C: Emerging Technologies, 18*(4), 568–583.

36. Nastase, L., (2017). Security in the internet of things: A survey on application layer protocols. In: *2017 21st International Conference on Control Systems and Computer Science (CSCS)* (pp. 659–666). IEEE.

37. Burhan, M., Rehman, R. A., Khan, B., & Kim, B. S., (2018). IoT elements, layered architectures and security issues: A comprehensive survey. *Sensors, 18*(9), 2796.

38. Jan, M. A., Nanda, P., He, X., Tan, Z., & Liu, R. P., (2014). A robust authentication scheme for observing resources in the internet of things environment. In: *2014 IEEE 13th International Conference on Trust, Security and Privacy in Computing and Communications* (pp. 205–211). IEEE.

39. Khan, M. A., & Salah, K., (2018). IoT security: Review, blockchain solutions, and open challenges. *Future Generation Computer Systems, 82*, 395–411.

40. Anirudh, M., Thileeban, S. A., & Nallathambi, D. J., (2017). Use of honeypots for mitigating DoS attacks targeted on IoT networks. In: *2017 International Conference on Computer, Communication and Signal Processing (ICCCSP)* (pp. 1–4). IEEE.
41. Evangelista, D., Mezghani, F., Nogueira, M., & Santos, A., (2016). Evaluation of Sybil attack detection approaches in the internet of things content dissemination. In: *2016 Wireless Days (WD)* (pp. 1–6). IEEE.
42. Razzaq, M. A., Gill, S. H., Qureshi, M. A., & Ullah, S., (2017). Security issues in the internet of things (IoT): A comprehensive study. *International Journal of Advanced Computer Science and Applications, 8*(6), 383.
43. Bonomi, F., Milito, R., Natarajan, P., & Zhu, J., (2014). Fog computing: A platform for internet of things and analytics. In: *Big Data and Internet of Things: A Roadmap for Smart Environments* (pp. 169–186). Springer, Cham.
44. Al-Fuqaha, A., Guizani, M., Mohammadi, M., Aledhari, M., & Ayyash, M., (2015). Internet of things: A survey on enabling technologies, protocols, and applications. *IEEE Communications Surveys & Tutorials, 17*(4), 2347–2376.
45. Mazhelis, O., & Tyrväinen, P., (2014). A framework for evaluating internet-of-things platforms: Application provider viewpoint. In: *2014 IEEE World Forum on Internet of Things (WF-IoT)* (pp. 147–152). IEEE.
46. Ammar, M., Russello, G., & Crispo, B., (2018). Internet of things: A survey on the security of IoT frameworks. *Journal of Information Security and Applications, 38*, 8–27.

CHAPTER 2

Advanced Attack Detection and Prevention Systems by Using Botnet

ANJANNA MATTA, ALTAF AHMAD, SHANTANU BHATTACHARYA, and SHUBHAM KUMAR

Faculty of Science and Technology, ICFAI Foundation for Higher Education, Hyderabad–501203, Telangana, India, E-mail: anjireddyiith@ifheindia.org (A. Matta)

ABSTRACT

A botnet is a string of connected computers organized together to perform a task; good technologies for bad intentions are the best example. The criminal organizations behind the implementation of this new online threat are well planned. Turning our focus now to the defense side in computer security, it needs to continuously find innovative ways of countering the threats, and one way to deploy honeypots on top of standard security mechanisms. It can design a novel feature extraction module and adopt an extended decision fusion algorithm, to achieve three-level fusions of data, feature and decision which enables the detection. Honeypots never try to replace traditional security mechanisms, but add another layer of security Botnets generally involve computers from several countries, and making tracking more difficult. Co-operation between law enforcement agencies and communication services providers has started, but there is a need for more resources and more structure.

2.1 INTRODUCTION

An increasing number of articles in the media discuss the developing criminal activity involving botnets. According to current generation, botnets have become one of the major attacks in the internet because of their illegal profitable financial gain. The composition of the words "robot" and "network" is botnet. The term is generally used with a damaging or malicious connotation [1]. A botnet is a string of connected computers organized together to perform a task, good technologies for bad intentions is the best example. Their purpose is to establish communications channel from the herders to the bots; all things are managed by a criminal or an organized crime syndicate [2]. The criminal organizations behind the implementation of this new online threat are well planned. They used to employ software developers, they buy and sell infrastructure for their criminal activities and they hire people for money laundering to hide their identification. They have the technical resources to continuously improve their attacks; these conditions make online frauds more successful than offline ones. Lack of user security combined with the common habit of using old and unpatched operating system increase the success of criminal exploitation (Figure 2.1).

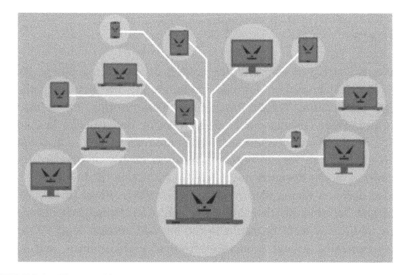

FIGURE 2.1   The set of honeypots.
Source: https://www.kaspersky.com/blog/botnet/1742/.

Once upon a time a set of computers has been compromised, they can be involved in many kinds of online criminal activity, including identity theft, unsolicited commercial e-mails, scams, and massive attacks [3]. According to the report, more than 6 million infected computers worldwide are connected to a botnet, with China, Germany, Spain, the USA, and France the top five countries for the numbers of infected computers.

Turning our focus now to the defense side in computer security, it needs to continuously find innovative ways of countering the threats, and one way to deploy honeypots on top of standard security mechanisms [4]. A 'honeypot' is a "trap" network that appears to have important information and a fake network for hackers to somewhat easily gain access to. As a honeypot is basically used for malware collection, database, spam, and client. The main purpose of honeypots is to gather information about the attacker and the attack methods. As more number of peoples uses honeypots in monitoring to avoid honeypot traps, botnets will sooner try to find out. Botnets. Honeypots never try to replace traditional security mechanisms, but add another layer of security Botnets generally involve computers from several countries, and making tracking more difficult. Close co-operations between ISPs and private companies are essential.

To counter this threat, a significant effort is necessary from public and private stakeholders in the information society. The legal basis for prosecution of cybercrime needs to be improved, especially in relation to cross-border scenarios [5]. Co-operation between law enforcement agencies and communication services providers has started, but there is a need for more resources and more structure. Users' awareness programs should be adjusted to this changing threat. To improve the security of operating system and application software, continuous investment should be required.

In this chapter, when constructing and maintaining the botnet how botmasters attempt to remove honeypot traps. Honeypot can be setup inside, outside or in the DMZ of a firewall design or even in all of the locations, although they are most often deployed inside of a firewall for control. In a sense, they are variants of standard intruder detection system (IDS) but with more of a focus on information gathering and deception [6]. With the widespread use of deception technology, honeypot detection methods also need improvement, which means researchers need to modify their honeypots more realistic to cheat potential attackers instead of easily distinguished. Based on the analysis of the existing honeypot detection technology, the chapter proposed a new automatic identification model based on random forest algorithm with three features group: network-layer features, application-layer feature and other system layer features [7]. If they fail to perform due to diligence by securing their honeypots from damage, the other machines will be considered negligent.

For botnet detection the importance of information fusion, most of the existing work does not focus on this field. This chapter highlighted, to some extent, the existing botnet detection schemes can discover bots, but they do not make the full use of multifarious information related to botnet activities and the botnet infiltration are not able to handle the entire situation [8]. In recent years multi-sensors information fusion has been rapidly developed and applied in network security. The complicated information from hetero-geneity and multi-source is efficient by the view of integrating. Based on information fusion techniques you propose a botnet detection architecture [9]. You design a novel feature extraction module and adopt an extended decision fusion algorithm, to achieve three-level fusions of data, feature, and decision which enables the detection.

For detection of the bot botmasters use DNS by monitoring whether the IP value changed or same [10]. Botmasters matches the value of IP and detect whether the network is infected by malicious bot or not. DNS is a protocol within the TCP protocol that uses a set of standards for how computers exchange data on the internet and on many private networks [11]. A massive database that links domain names to their respective IP addresses, instead a connection is made through domain name server. Woefully, besides being used for obvious benign purposes, domain is widely famous for malicious use.

In this chapter, you present peer-to-peer (P2P) networks that have in common that all network nodes are both clients and servers: at the same time, any node can provide and retrieve information [12]. P2P networks are extremely robust against node failures, i.e., high resilience. To monitor and eliminate, a P2P botnet is much harder for the security community.

2.2   HISTORY AND ORIGIN OF BOTNET

After examining the process of botnets, and what steps they are used for it. It would be delightful to include a few words about their history and where they develop from [13]. As most tools on the World Wide Web, bots did not start as a malicious tool that were used by hackers to cause desolation and ruination, but as a tool that was allowed to monitor activity on IRC channels and perform actions for the channel operators while he was pre-occupied with other activities. The earliest IRC bot, would play a game of "Hunt the Wampus" with IRC users [14].

Although all of the original IRC bots that were constructed were conceived to assist the users in enjoying their IRC experience or in managing IRC connections and performing mindless operations for the IRC operators [15]. On all sides this time, is when dissimilar IRC servers offered OS shell accounts, which permit the users to run commands on IRC hosts [16]. After 1999 various release of dissimilar bots develop, that would employ different methods to steal personal information and spread to different department [17].

The major evolution occurred in rapid 2002 when the SDbot develop, which was write down in C++, and the author sent the source code to the internet for everybody to use and alter [18].

Following this rebellion in bot creation, it has multiple malware writers creating new bots that would utilize existing compulsion in software in order to generate and collect material from different infected users [19].

2.3   HOW DO BOTNET WORKS?

Botnet word itself gives sense "robot" and "network" means there is a network of robots that was controlled by the cybercriminals called botmasters to commit cybercrime. You may also say that botnet is a number of infected internet devices which have their own bot army and working together for a single unit [20].

Two basic importance for botmasters are:

- Network size and
- Infected device.

2.3.1   NETWORK SIZE

To build a botnet botmasters require as much infected bot under their control because the more bots connected to the network, the bigger the impact is. Botnet are not created to infect one individual device they are created to impact on millions or billions of devices [21]. The main strategy is to infect others bots by using email attachments, cookies, just clicking on malicious aids, through download or dangerous software from a website. After infecting device botnets are free to access their personal data, web camera and attack others network or device and do crime.

2.3.2   INFECTED DEVICE

Almost every device which is connected to internet include laptop, phone, smartwatches, kitchen appliances and security camera participate in crime but it happens before people realize [22]. They command bots to infect the device and crash them when they require [23]. The botmasters ultimate goal is to get money, by disturbing the internet world, doing illegal trades, fraud schemes or malware propagation. It can control by remote like C&C server

[24]. Mainly C&C of a botnet is centralized and controlled by one person or organization.

2.4   BOTNET ARCHITECTURE

There are many changes in the structure of botnet from late 90s [25]. It is also observed that bot programs are programed as clients which communicate to existing server, but every bot is not connected to a common server, because if the server is shut down, then the header will lose control on all devices connected to that server. Here, P2P communication plays a role which will be discussed later in the chapter.

There are two types of architecture:

- Centralized around a C&C server and
- Decentralized using peer to peer communication.

2.4.1   CENTRALIZED C&C SERVER

Here C&C server stands for "command and control server," these types of servers make bot well build than other malware [26]. Generally, botnet protocols operate on websites (like HTTP), domains, TCP, and IRC networks. These servers can also be used to carry out disturbed denial of service attacks (DDoS), deleting data and encrypting data to carry out extortion schemes. Now let us discuss in more detail about botnet protocols [27]. The client-server model botnet is like a basic network with one main server controlling the transmission of data/information from each client. As this type of bots are dependent on one server (Figure 2.2).

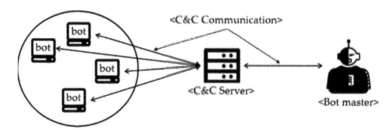

FIGURE 2.2   The client-server model botnet is like a basic network with one main server controlling the transmission of data/information from each client.

Source: https://www.researchgate.net/figure/Basic-entities-of-botnet-bots-command-and-control-C-C-server-and-bot-master_fig1_335316113. https://creativecommons.org/licenses/by/4.0/

Over a recent year C&C communication infrastructure has been rapidly derive [28]. To realize the C&C channel, several control mechanisms in terms of protocols and network architecture has been used. Botnets can be categorized as botnets with centralized, decentralized or hybrid network architecture on the basis of topology of the C&C networks [29].

2.4.2 PEER TO PEER (P2P) COMMUNICATION

Peer to peer (P2P) communication is a type of networking in which the task is distributed between peers [30]. (Peer is a system in which computers are connected via internet). P2P communication helps a user to share all types of files, network bandwidth with other computers, because of this feature, it is very hard to shut down, as this connection is not centralized every system connected to this network should be shut down to stop this network (Figure 2.3).

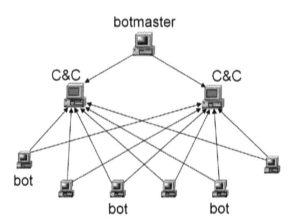

FIGURE 2.3 These P2P networks can also be divided into three types.
Source: https://www.usenix.org/legacy/event/hotbots07/tech/full_papers/wang/wang_html/.

These P2P networks can also be divided into three types, i.e., structured networks, unstructured networks, and hybrid models [31]:

1. **Structured Networks:** As the name talks about structure, it can be defined as "The structured arrangement of P2P networks in which a system can search a file/resource by working efficiently towards it, even though the file is rarely available" [32].
2. **Hybrid Models:** Models which are a combination of both P2P and Client-server model, in this the networks have a common server

which helps peer to find each other. Because of the common-server model the efficiency is higher than structured and unstructured networks.

3. **Unstructured Networks:** It is defined as "The random connection of network nodes with each other." These types of networks are easy to build and allow for localized optimization to different region of overlay.

2.5   BOTNET LIFE-CYCLE

During the botnet operation can be observed through the resolution of botnet life-cycle [33]. By utilizing specific examining of botnet behavior within the phases, the detection approaches spot specific phases of botnet life cycle [34]. Therefrom understanding of botnet life cycle is vital to the successful analysis of the existing work botnet detection. The infection phase is the first phase of the botnet cycle in which the bot malware compromised the accessible computers, thus becoming zombie within a specific botnet [35]. Usually, this phase is further classified into two sub-phases known as initial Infection and secondary Infection.

Now moving forward, the communication phase is the secondary phase of botnet life-cycle. This phase consists of botnet operational modes that entail communication between compromised computers and C&C servers. From the botmasters, the communication phase covers communication dedicated to receiving instructions as well as the reporting on the current status of bots [36]. By using C&C channel, the communication between zombie and C&C server can be realized in different ways.

From moving next attack phase is the third phase of botnet life-cycle as it includes bot operation aimed at implementing attackers' malicious agenda [37]. During the attack phase, DDoS attacks are launched by zombie computers, start e-mail campaigns, perform distributing malicious software, online reputation system being manipulated and surveys, etc.

2.6   DIFFERENT TECHNIQUES TO DETECT BOTNET

Botnet detection techniques can be categorized into two types:

*   Active techniques; and
*   Passive technique.

2.6.1 ACTIVE TECHNIQUES

Active techniques that are discussed in this chapter are:

1. **Ctu13 Datasets Detection Technique:** Ctu13 is a group of 13 datasets called scenarios which were made in CTU University in 2011 to tackle botnet traffic and find the real infected botnet traffic that is mixture of both normal and background traffic [38]. To do good verification you need three types of traffic, i.e., malware, background, and normal traffic. Firstly, Malware traffic consists of C&C (command and control) connection that helps to detect normal traffic [39]. It is also necessary to know about the performance of our machine language algorithm whereas background traffic is important to check our memory and system performance and to check if the algorithm got confused within the data [40]. All 13 scenarios in ctu13 datasets are different from each other and used to find different malware. Each scenarios have different function, characteristics, restriction, and protocol to perform in certain actions.

   ➢ **Characteristics of Botnet Scenarios:** Every scenario has been kept in a unique and different file called pcap file (.pcap extension) that contains all three types of traffic that are mentioned above [41]. All algorithms will be kept under pcap file to obtain more information about Net Flows, Weblogs, etc. [41]. First CTU report analysis was explained and published in the paper named as "An empirical comparison of botnet detection method" that explained all three traffics in one way called unidirectional Net flows to assign the labels. This will not be used so much because of the excellent performance of the bidirectional net flows file (.biargus extension) that was published after the second analysis. Bidirectional net flows have more advantage than unidirectional, some of the advantages are:

   i. Easily differentiate between user and server;
   ii Gather more information;
   iii. Gather detailed information about labels (Figures 2.4–2.6).

   Data In the second analysis of bidirectional net flows has explained about the relationship among the times taken, number of packets, net flow, and size of the pcap that is shown below.

   ➢ **Amount of Data on Each Botnet Scenarios:** After downloading bidirectional net flows file, it would be easy to differentiate between the malware and normal traffic. Nowadays this technique is used widely to find infected bot systems and network [42]. It is not easy to find infected bots with simple algorithms. The amount of data available in-network is infinite so, to obtain such information, systems of datasets need to train itself that is why it consists of machine language algorithms to detect infected networks. After downloading all 13 datasets that contain machine language algorithms you can easily detect that system, website, etc., whether it is infected or not (Table 2.1).

Table 2 – Characteristics of the botnet scenarios. (CF: ClickFraud, PS: Port Scan, FF: FastFlux, US: Compiled and controlled by us.)										
Id	IRC	SPAM	CF	PS	DDoS	FF	P2P	US	HTTP	Note
1	√	√	√							
2	√	√	√							
3	√			√				√		
4	√				√			√		UDP and ICMP DDoS.
5		√		√					√	Scan web proxies.
6				√					√	Proprietary C&C. RDP.
7								√		Chinese hosts.
8				√					√	Proprietary C&C. Net-BIOS, STUN.
9	√	√	√	√						
10	√				√			√		UDP DDoS.
11	√				√			√		ICMP DDoS.
12							√			Synchronization.
13		√		√					√	Captcha. Web mail.

FIGURE 2.4   Characteristics of the botnet scenarios.
Source: https://www.stratosphereips.org/datasets-ctu13.

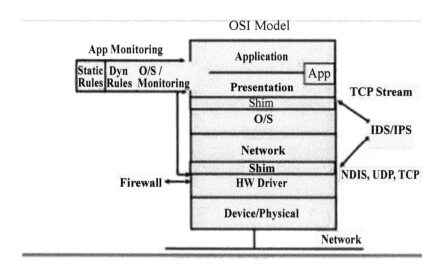

FIGURE 2.5   Host-based intrusion prevention system.
Source: https://www.sans.org/reading-room/whitepapers/intrusion/host-intrusion-prevention-systems-32824.

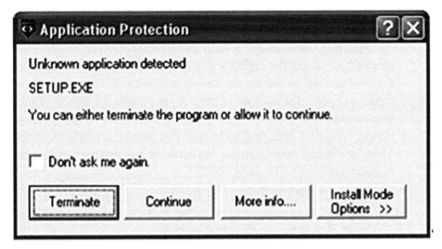

FIGURE 2.6 Application protection.

Source: https://www.stratosphereips.org/datasets-ctu13.

TABLE 2.1 The Amount of Data on Each Botnet Scenarios

Id	Duration(hrs)	#Packets	#NetFlows	Size	Bot	#Bots
1	6.15	71,971,482	2,824,637	52GB	Neris	1
2	4.21	71,851,300	1,808,123	60GB	Neris	1
3	66.85	167,730,395	4,710,639	121GB	Rbot	1
4	4.21	62,089,135	1,121,077	53GB	Rbot	1
5	11.63	4,481,167	129,833	37.6GB	Virut	1
6	2.18	38,764,357	558,920	30GB	Menti	1
7	0.38	7,467,139	114,078	5.8GB	Sogou	1
8	19.5	155,207,799	2,954,231	123GB	Murlo	1
9	5.18	115,415,321	2,753,885	94GB	Neris	10
10	4.75	90,389,782	1,309,792	73GB	Rbot	10
11	0.26	6,337,202	107,252	5.2GB	Rbot	3
12	1.21	13,212,268	325,472	8.3GB	NSIS.ay	3
13	16.36	50,888,256	1,925,150	34GB	Virut	1

2. **Intrusion Detection System:** Now a day's security is a basic necessity for any system because no any network is secure and cannot be infected by malicious objects [43]. It is not necessary that if your system has firewall protection, it is secure because firewall is basic essential

security but, its capacity is limited it cannot detect hostile intent. For detecting hostile intent in-depth, you require intrusion system that has the capacity to defense any system in-depth and to detect hostile intent. Firewall alone has the capacity to evaluate malicious intent and warn the user as well as determine the capacity of malicious network and create an option for the user to protect his system but it is not enough to protect your system for big network of malicious bots, for that you require intrusion detection technique that gives open-source options. There are many open sources available in the market but the most popular intrusion software is SNORT.

➢ **Why SNORT?:** SNORT is flexible, cost-effective, low-price, and quality security intrusion that provide us free network software. According to the snort website:

  i. It can do analysis, matching, etc.
  ii. It can detect CGI attack, buffer overflow, OS fingerprints, SMB problems, etc.
  iii. Its rules are flexible, easily handled and changed according to necessity.
  iv. It is easy for configuration.
  v. It can easily and rapidly detect the cause of alert.

➢ **Setup Required for SNORT:** The most basic and first step to install and secure any system is with the help of remote sensor and management network. Installation requires a lot of memory so, while installing both users must have to make sure that his operating system have enough storage [44]. A GNU compiler and GCC compiler is necessary to have in users' system for remote control and management network.

➢ **Management Network:** It requires installing of 8 software for better working of SNORT. After installing all 8 software's it requires OpenSSL, OpenSSH, and configure for compiling that script and file resource [45]. While doing all this, make sure to place the file outside the CS directory so that no one can access it through the server. Finally, change the settings and create SNORT data directory and databases and link all data to MySQL-P and move that data and that will complete the setup. Now you can easily insert the password and use your software.

➢ **Remote Sensor:** Till now the management network is completed now you need to setup remote sensor. In remote sensor you require to install 6 software packages for SNORT to work properly [46].

As you have installed OpenSSL, OpenSSH in management network, you have to work upon it only. Next, you have to absorb the output that SNORT uses and set the rules. Sun microsystems uses Solaris jump starts for future installation of remote sensor.

➢ **Monitoring:** Once everything is installed, setup is completed and working properly. Users need to monitor their network and make change of remote sensor configuration according to their needs [47]. In starting everything is new so it alerts more and senses more so, first sense is overwarming after that everything become normal and it finds malicious network according to their potential [48]. One thing is necessary that every user must update their machine regularly according to SNORT rule so no any problem will occur.

3. **Multi-Layer Detection Technique:** As the name "multi-layer" suggests this process is divided into four layers, i.e.:

i. **Traffic Reduction (1st Layer):** To manage a large and busy network traffic malevolent behavior should be detected. As you know that a network contains many packets, so it becomes very difficult to identify network activity by just scanning packets in each cycle. In this, you will be going to know about new theory or method that will reduce the complexity of the method that was followed before [49]. At present available methods for botnet detection many of the companies use deep packet inspection (DPI) to examine the complicated and undefined payload signatures, but there is an exception in this case, i.e., these methods will work more efficiently when the payloads are in decrypted form.

As malicious attacks are increasing day to day simultaneously level of packets in congested networks are increasing, which is not making detection processes cost-effective and the efficiency of the DPI detection system is decreasing.

In multi-layered technique, the efficiency is increased by selecting transmission mission protocol packets for botnet prototype identification [50]. Transmission traffic control packets are filtered to reduce traffic volume and increase efficiency. In this filtering process, there are two steps. Firstly, filtering the network flow linked with TCP protocol and getting access on packets link SYN Short for Synchronize, Acknowledgement packet and many more. Secondly, TCP packet header is examined and selects packets without payload data.

ii. **Classification of Peer to Peer and Non-Peer to Peer Traffic (Layer 2):** In P2P traffic detection the most used identification are port and signature identification which are based on stream feature. It is also necessary to know that port identification method is unable to identify P2P random ports applications. To detect P2P application administrators, make use of "Stream-based identification methods" which has a high false alarm rate. Therefore, the combination of non-P2P ports filtering mechanism and DNS query to filter non-P2P traffics.

The difference between port filtering and DNS query is that, to filter often used non-P2P application port filtering method is used which has the ability to filter at packet level. Whereas DNS query filtering helps in flow analysis and port judgment. When a user is using an online application he sends a service request, and with the help of multi-port, i.e., when a web application is active there are many requests at same time so the server uses parallel request connection on the page. As Peer-to-Peer communication is not centralized, network node communicates with each other using a pair of random sources. If the number of sessions exceeds the thresholds, then this situation is considered as web page traffic session.

iii. **Feature Extraction and Feature Reduction (Layer 3):** You have all experienced in our daily life that if a device has more features, it is in more user friendly than a less features device, so this may be one of the reasons behind reducing the feature is therefore one of the often-significant aspect affecting the efficiency of detection process. When you talk about feature extraction, features in detection model are designed that are able to detect the malevolent behavior of the bot.

The vision is to select a suitable set of abilities that will boost up the efficiency of detection systems and machine learning (ML) classifiers. This will also reduce the complexity of the model with constantly decreasing the accuracy. In order to increase efficiency, you need to classify a technique that will automatically enhance the feature required and will change accordingly to reduce the amount of data. The decision tree mainly consists of two types of nodes "two children's internal node" and second is "children's leaf nodes." Any type of internal node has a detection mechanism to think about the next visiting node. During the construction of the three, small groups of training sets are repetitively divided so as to decide that each resulting node got assigned to a predicted class or not.

> ➢ **P2P Traffic Classification:** According to characteristics of data, the traffic characteristics of botnets and benign are similar, therefore developers use session-based strategy for featured data extraction. As studies earlier to improve the efficiency, you have to decrease the number of stream features or synthesize a technique that will automatically enhance the requirement of features. P2P host zombies process initiate's connection by malicious code.

4. **BotFlex Tool:** There is a lot of research going on botnets and ways to detect bots. But till now there are very few open-source detection tools. BotFlex is open-source tool that helps to analyze a large amount of home traffic. Let us study about its architecture and goals.

> ➢ **Design and Properties of BotFlex:**
>
>   i. **Handling Real-Time Network Events:** Real time situation comes with malware, i.e., when a computer is infected, then the defender will have a sufficient time to react against the malware before it causes more damage.
>
>   ii. **Compliance:** Due to large increase in botnet threat, the tools that are used should be updated frequently and these tools should also sustain if there is new strategy of botnet network.
>
>   iii. **Pliability:** The tool is flexible enough to detect any type of malware and should also have an ability to work according to the user requirement.
>
>   iv. **Experiment and Analysis:** During live analysis, the tool should analysis with his past bot detection history. It should also support extensive logging.
>
> ➢ **System Architecture of BotFlex:** BotFlex was built on Bro, which is a network activity of event and has the ability to generate lots of network-based events during usual operation. To understand BotFlex, you have to first understand about the Bro-architecture.

Bro's architecture contains three layers (from bottom to top) they are Network, Event engine and Interpreter of policy script. Let us discuss all the layers. Firstly, network layer is used to analysis, store network traffic.

Secondly, Event engine are C++ program based that wrap network information in appropriate data structures. Finally, this is the top layer which gives a clear picture of for handling network information and events detected by the event engine. An alternative to this was to program this using low level language (i.e., C, C++) because this gave the developers good performance than other intrusion detection program. Developer did not use high level language program because this was not meeting the requirement or flexibility of BotFlex.

Now, let us discuss about the core architecture of BotFlex. BotFlex helps in implementation of lifecycle of bots as an event chain, wherein the several combinations of this events accelerated the final event of bots for infection declaration. (Event is defined as "In a particular time one bot infecting one device"). Placing our description in line you can divide our system into two parts they are:

a. **Sensor Module:** As you have studied about the sensor computer, sensor module also performs similar type but here sensor module scans host, C&C communication and drives to correlation module.

b. **Correlation Module:** In this step, you have to collect the information that how many number of times an event is approaching the host. And declaring the flexibility for botnet infection.

2.6.2 PASSIVE TECHNIQUES

Passive techniques that are discussed in this chapter are discussed in subsections.

2.6.2.1 ANOMALY BASED DETECTION TECHNIQUE

Despite of long presence of malicious botnet, there are only few defense systems created to solve this problem. One of them is anomaly-based technique which is used to protect the target network and system from malicious activities. The main aim is to find anomalous things also called outliers because they lie far away from other data points in a random way. First off, all Examine of the botnet is one of the big challenges of cyber security and it could be done according to the unusual increase or decrease of traffic on any website or organization. The unusual working of the system would be the first sign that your system is not in own control but rather it is affected by the malicious software or bot network. According to the traffic, you can detect the infected systems but, one of the major problems is to detection of an IRC based botnet meshes. It can be botnet because till now no one is used this technique to attack. Therefore, there are no clue of anomalies and detection of anomalies, James, and Suresh both together had made an algorithm with TCP scan detection heuristic called the TCP work weight and IRC mesh detection component called IRC tokenization that made a system to detect network of botnets. It has been developed some year ago and have been proved effective in reducing the botnet army and detecting bot networks but, botmasters can easily destroy this technique with the help of a trivial cipher. Botmasters can easily change the IRC command with the help of that trivial cipher.

Karasaridis had discover another way using an algorithm to detect with the basis of analysis, data, and flow chart in 2007 called passive analysis of data. It can be detected based on abnormal different communication and know the quality, quantity, characteristics, and analyze those botnets without joining with the network. Botsniffer observe and detect many of bots with this technique and algorithms without any negative result.

2.6.2.2 RESILIENCE TECHNIQUES

Under the radar of botnet detection and neutralization systems, the botnet operation is tried to flying is one of the primary goals of the botnet. Resilience technique have a goal of secrecy and communication integrity. The integrity of the communication and security are preserved by using these techniques. However, usage of encrypted communication channel and obfuscated communication protocol can be considered suspicious, and it can be used as a trigger for additional traffic analysis. Fast flux and domain generation algorithm (DGA) are other commonly used techniques that provide resilience of botnet operation.

2.6.2.3 HOST-BASED INTRUSION PREVENTION SYSTEMS (HIPS)

Host-based intrusion prevention system is now becoming mandatory in every device present in our environment. HIPS is an installed software which monitors a single host activity by analyzing the occurring events within the host. Firewalls also do the same thing, but here is a small difference between Firewall and HIPS, i.e., firewall regulates the traffic to and from your computer and HIPS is a solution to protect the computer against known and unknown malicious attacks. If there is a major change in the hacker's code the HIPS gives an alert to the user to make an appropriate decision (Figure 2.7).

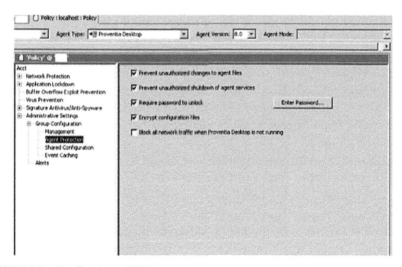

FIGURE 2.7   Configuring a HIPS.

HIPS is an installed software which uses shim functionality by inserting itself into the operating system to catch the receipts and delivery of packets on the networks (Packet is a unit of data that is transferred between origin and a destination on the internet). Then Proventia desktop executes file effectively before packets reaches to operating system. After verification of packets by Proventia desktop it will execute the command in the live environment. At this stage if anything happens out of ordinary then Blackice will raise an alert to user and stop it, if the file is further executable, then it will ask user to allow or to terminate the program. As HIPS systems are not signature-based, they have the ability to stop unknown and zero-day exploits by monitoring all traffic on host, but you cannot say that HIPS will stop all unknown program file because it depends on how the attack is been carried out and it may stop for other protective measures (Figure 2.8).

2.6.2.3.1   *Implementing and Configuring of Enterprise HIPS*

As the days are passing botnet codes are becoming more and more complicated because in maximum cases botnet code are hidden, so in order to implement and configure HIPS, a person should have enough knowledge on how the networks are designed and their functionality, if not serious problems could arise while implementing the HIPS. Proventia Desktop is managed by Site Protector and HIPS system is managed by centralized management console. There are some specific things that are essential to know before configuring the agent's rules and policies:

- What ports do applications communicate over?
- Is the communication between the clients and servers only inbound, only bound, or both?
- What protocols do the applications use-UDP, TCP, ICMP, etc.?

At last, make sure that the chosen port is flexible enough to have the ability to filter by different rules and control the agents granularly.

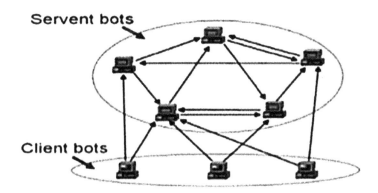

FIGURE 2.8 Bot controllers.

Source: https://www.sans.org/reading-room/whitepapers/intrusion/host-intrusion-prevention-systems-32824.

2.6.2.3.2 Configuring a HIPS

After implementation of HIPS, it is important to configure and turn on necessary precaution measures. One protection is that the unauthorized shutdown of agent services should never stop, this step will ensure that the without password no one other than administrators can shut down the HIPS system and to make changes in any setting in HIPS system agent should enter the password every time. It is also to keep in mind that implementation of more resistive policy should be allowed. After these steps configure should create and assign rules and policies of each group as per the usage of the application.

2.6.2.3.3   Things in Host-Based Intrusion Prevention Systems (HIPS) for Your Network

1. **Not Relying on Signatures:** Signatures are the primary source of antivirus and intrusion detection system. HIPS should also include (use) signature-based detection along with anomaly-based detection which will he user to establish a baseline of what the normal network activity looks like in your machine.
2. **Works with User Configuration:** Few HIPS solution may restrict in terms of what programs they are able to look into. User should find a HIPS that is capable of handling commercial packages of shelf and any home-grown basic application that you are using. If these facilities are not available, then at least HIPS will protect programs that you run.
3. **Working on User Defined Policies:** You get windows security updates or any antivirus updates once in a month or in 6 months so, in this period a user may get affected with malicious malware which HIPS is not able to detect and if the user identifies it. At those times user can create his own policies to prevent him from other attacks from the same network.
4. **Provide Centralized Reporting So That New Policies can be Provided to New Products:** While you are taking about HIPS solutions which are bit expensive, but you probably need to stand at a point a think that deploying HIPS on thousands of devices in quite impossible without any centralized report. If there is centralized report and administration when a company or individual user is going for a new product, this report will deploy new policies to all machines.

2.6.2.3.4   Honeypot Detection with Peer-to-Peer Botnets

There is much change in the structure of botnets, and identifying techniques that hackers are using is not an easy thing, but after Honey-based botnet detection has come into action, it has become easier for cyber cells to detect the malicious attacks. Now you can that detection in which a trap is created for hacker to track unauthorized or unconventional methods.

As you have studied the structure and types of bots in earlier topics, you can say that the combination of honeypots and P2P will help to create a good defense for the computer against malicious attacks. Till now, botnets are monitored by two techniques:

- Allow honeypot to mingle with other bots in the networks and these honeypots will transmit all the information to monitor as per his requirement; and
- To commandeer bot-controllers to monitor C&C communications in botnet.

As studied earlier those botnets on the internet are created and controlled by a complex network structure, and these bots try to connect one or several "bot controllers" to receive commands for further action. These commands are transmitted from a hidden computer to all the bot members; they also use multiple redundant bot controllers to prevent defenders from shutting down the network or C&C channel.

2.6.2.3.5   Detection of Honeypot Botnets

To understand this detection process lets us consider a situation in which you are starting a new project and you want some trusted members in your team so that you can attain your goal faster and in an easier way. In the same way, botmasters uses the same strategy to tag infected host as "trusted." Botmasters have remote computers which act as "sensors," if these sensors receive correct and expected information traffic from the host. Then the host is marked as trusted. And it is also not easy for honeypot administrators to detect which computer is acting remote computers for botmasters.

Procedure of honeypot detection can be performed on a newly infected computer before allowing to join the network. Botmasters uses an authorization mechanism to finalize a host or a newly infected computer to confirm that whether these host can act as defenders to honeypot administrators or not. After they pass from honeypot test, they upload key to access the host and allow them to join his botnet network.

2.6.2.3.6   Detection of Hijacked Bot Controllers

Dynamic DNS is used to detect hijacked bots, in which a sinkhole was introduced that can change the domain name of detected bot controllers to point out host machines. In this way the host receives connection request from bot networks, and truly speaking these monitors will set off a hijacked bot controller which is similar to honeypot's functionality. This was all from an administrative perspective.

Now lets us talk from the botmaster's perspective, A bot monitor is menacing because from an IP address, a security professional can learn about bots of botnet. So, there is one method that botmasters (may) use for their target called Bot controller DNS query check in which a controller is taken under control by DNS redirection process, and the Internet Protocol address that are achieve is not the real IP address. Bots can identify the actual domain names if the IP address of bot controllers is not available. After knowing all these issues, a botmaster can keep his DNS mapping updated to all the bot controllers. Here also computer (as sensor) will play a role by delivering all the DNS queries to resolve and update IP mapping to particular bot controllers and at last comparing results with known domain mappings. Beside all this, if a botmaster shifts to a new IP address, then using DNS query procedure defenders will always be checking whether it is able to detect a bot controller in present botnet network. If detected, then immediately a command will be sent from botmaster that all bots to update their domain networks.

2.6.2.4   ZEUS TOOLKIT EVALUATION

The Zeus malware software is one of the best known and widely used malware types in the history of information security was first detected in 2007. By using botnets, Zeus is a Trojan horse for windows that was created to steal bank information. It extends through email, downloads, and online messaging to users across the globe. Zeus botnets create a group of millions of zombie computers to target bank accounts, private data, and saved account passwords for his own purpose or mission. They used this data for online fraud of debit cards, identity theft and many more. In 2007 survey more than 3.6 million computers cases are reported in the United States. In the below paragraph, it will discuss about process of installation, infection, and bot building.

In addition, a detailed method to extract the encryption key from the malware binary and use that to decrypt the network communications and the botnet configuration information.

2.6.2.4.1   Issues for Builders of Collaborating Agent Systems

For any number of reasons, the need for collaboration between agents occurs; most of them rooted in the problem of scarcity of resources-information, computing, know-how, etc. Since individual agents possess to a given problem may be beyond the capabilities of any one agent, requiring that a number of agents pool their resources and collaborate with one another in order to solve the problem. It places significant demands occur when such collaboration proceeds at the knowledge level. Not least are the need for a mechanism for information discovery through which agents discover the existence, network addresses, capabilities, and roles of agent. Furthermore, for effective and coherent problem solving, the agent needs mechanisms for reasoning about their own and other agents' problem-solving capabilities and for coordinating their activities. In recent time most of the issue found in multi agent system related to Zeus have reasonable mature solution. In the following paragraphs, it reviews the main technique proposed for addressing the information discovery, communication, ontology, and co-ordination and legacy software problems.

2.6.2.4.2   The Information Discovery Issue

Name servers and facilitators are typically handled using purpose utility agents that function as society-wide white pages and yellow pages, providing look up services for agent's addresses and abilities, respectively. To become visible to the society agents only need to register their addresses with a name server and their abilities with a facilitator. In providing implementation of these utility agents, Zeus allows the developers to concentrate on building the applications agents.

2.6.2.4.3   The Communication Issue

The need for an agent-independent agent communication language (ACL) has led to the development of the knowledge query and manipulation language (KQML) and the FIFA ACL. With the rationale being that different application domains may require different content languages; most ACLs do not specify a syntax or semantics of the contents of the messages. There are a lot of content language like KIF (knowledge interchange format), FIPA SL, etc., has been developed, with the help of content language that is used in KQML and FIPA ACL, it can solve the issue of communication.

2.6.2.4.4   The Ontology Issue

If the agent uses different vocabularies for representing shared domain concepts, they communicate in a common language will still be unable to understand one another. You can map ontology issue with the help of developing specific domain for each user or achieved by general-purpose ontologies.

2.6.2.4.5   The Co-Ordination Issue

The research with many techniques in use, coordinating the behavior of multi-agent systems is an active area. The main approaches can be broadly classified as organizational structuring, contracting, multi-agent planning, and negotiation. The structure of the society is exploited for co-ordination, as typified by client-server systems is defined by organization structuring. Zeus coordination engine component handled the inter-agent coordination.

2.6.2.4.6   Integration with Legacy Software

Generally speaking, there are three possible approaches: the software could be written, but this is a costly approach. Agent must be interacting with each other because there is no replacement of legacy software so, they can solve by interacting with each other. Alternatively, a separate piece of software called a transducer could be employed to act as an interpreter between the ACL and the native protocol of the legacy system. Through which all of its internal components can be accessed or linked to external systems, Zeus uses the latter approach providing an interface.

KEYWORDS

- agent communication language
- botnets
- deep packet inspection
- disturbed denial of service
- domain generation algorithm

- **hackers**
- **honeypots**
- **host-based intrusion prevention systems**
- **intruder detection system**
- **knowledge query and manipulation language**

REFERENCES

1. Jonathan, C., (2020). *SANS Institute Information Security Reading Room*. https://www. lifewire.com/host-based-intrusion-prevention-2486685 (accessed on 10 November 2021).
2. stratosphereips.org/datasets-ctu13 URL: https://www.stratosphereips.org/datasets-ctu13 (accessed on 10 November 2021).
3. Riaz, U. K., Xiaosong, Z., Rajesh, K., Abubakar, S., Noorbakhsh, A. G., & Mamoun, A., (2021). *An Adaptive Multi-Layer Botnet Detection Technique using Machine Learning Classifiers.*
4. http://www.snort.org/about (accessed on 10 November 2021).
5. The NSS Group "Snort 1.8.1. Questionnaire" 25 November 2001 URL: http://www. modssl.org (accessed on 10 November 2021).
6. Engelschal, L., & Ralf, S., (2001). *mod_ssl: The Apache Interface to OpenSSL.*
7. URL: http://www.modssl.org (accessed on 10 November 2021).
8. Ping, W., (2010). Honeypot detection in advanced botnet attacks. *International Journal of Information and Computer Security.*
9. Maryam, F., Alireza, S., & Sureswaran, R., (2009). A survey of botnet and botnet detection. In: *2009 Third International Conference on Emerging Security Information, Systems and Technologies.*
10. Sardana, (2011). Anti-honeypot technology. *Honeypots A New Paradigm to Information Security.*
11. Ibrahim, G., & Vaclav, P., (2015). DNS traffic analysis for malicious domains detection. In: *2015 2nd International Conference on Signal Processing and Integrated Networks (SPIN).*
12. Kraemer-Mbula, E., Rush, H., Smith, C., & Tang, P., (2012). *Crime Online: Cybercrime and Illegal Innovation.* NESTA.
13. Correia, P., Eduardo, R., AntÃ³nio, N., & Paulo, S., (2012). Statistical characterization of the botnets C&C traffic. *Procedia Technology.*
14. Daniel, R., (2008). A first step towards live botmaster traceback. *Lecture Notes in Computer Science.*
15. Joseph, M. K., (2013). *Guide to Computer Network Security.* Springer Science and Business Media LLC.
16. Wang, H., Jie, H., & ZhengHu, G., (2011). Botnet detection architecture based on heterogeneous multi-sensor information fusion. *Journal of Networks.*
17. Matija, S., & Jens, M. P., (2016). On the use of machine learning for identifying botnet network traffic. *Journal of Cyber Security and Mobility.*

18. Cheng, H., Jiaxuan, H., Xing, Z., & Jiayong, L., (2019). Automatic identification of honeypot server using machine learning techniques. *Security and Communication Networks*.

19. Sean, T. M., & Busby-Earle, C., (2017). Multiperspective machine learning (MPML): A machine learning model for multi-faceted learning problems. In: *2017 International Conference on Computational Science and Computational Intelligence (CSCI)*.

20. Hyogon, K., (2007). Botnet detection by monitoring group activities in DNS traffic. In: *7th IEEE International Conference on Computer and Information Technology (CIT 2007)*.

21. Stevanovic M., & Pedersen, J. M., (2013). *Machine Learning for Identifying Botnet Network Traffic*.

22. Arash, H. L., Gerard, D. G., Jonathan, E. K., Kenneth, F. M., & Ali, A. G., (2017). A survey leading to a new evaluation framework for network-based botnet detection. *Proceedings of the 2017 the 7th International Conference on Communication and Network Security – ICCNS 2017*.

23. Schiller, C., (2007). *Botnets A Call to Action*. Botnets.

24. Sinclair, G., Nunnery, C., & Kang, B. H., (2009). The protocol: The how and why. In: *Malicious and Unwanted Software (MALWARE), 2009 4th International Conference* (pp. 69–77). doi: 10.1109/MALWARE.2009.5403015.

25. Leyla, B., Sevil, S., Davide, B., Engin, K., & Christopher, K., (2014). Exposure. *ACM Transactions on Information and System Security*.

26. https://usa.kaspersky.com/resource-center/threats/zeus-virus (accessed on 10 November 2021).

27. https://searchsecurity.techtarget.com/definition/Zeus-Trojan-Zbot (accessed on 10 November 2021).

28. https://www.enigmasoftware.com/zeustrojan-removal/ (accessed on 10 November 2021).

29. Egele, M., Scholte, T., Kirda, E., & Kruegel, C., (2008). A survey on automated dynamic malware-analysis techniques and tools. *ACM Comput. Surv., 44*(2), 6:1–6:42. doi: 10.1145/2089125.2089126.

30. You, I., & Yim, K., (2010). Malware obfuscation techniques: A brief survey. In: *Broadband, Wireless Computing, Communication and Applications (BWCCA), 2010 International Conference* (pp. 297–300). doi: 10.1109/BWCCA.2010.85.

31. Marpaung, J., Sain, M., & Lee, H. J., (2012). Survey on malware evasion techniques: State of the art and challenges. In: *Advanced Communication Technology (ICACT), 2012 14th International Conference* (pp. 744–749).

32. Stinson, E., & Mitchell, J. C., (2008). Towards systematic evaluation of the evadability of bot/botnet detection methods. In: *Proceedings of the 2nd Conference on USENIX Workshop on Offensive Technologies, WOOT'08* (pp. 5:1–5:9). USENIX Association, Berkeley, CA, USA.

33. Blunden, B., (2009). *The Rootkit Arsenal: Escape and Evasion in the Dark Corners of the System*. Jones and Bartlett Publishers, Inc., USA.

34. Arnold, T., & Yang, T. A., (2011). Rootkit attacks and protection: A case study of teaching network security. *J. Comput. Sci. Coll., 26*(5), 122–129.

35. Holz, T., Gorecki, C., Rieck, K., & Freiling, F. C., (2008). Measuring and detecting fast-flux service networks. In: *Proceedings of the Network and Distributed System Security Symposium, NDSS 2008* (pp. 8). San Diego, California, USA.

36. Antonakakis, M., Demar, J., Elisan, C., & Jerrim, J., (2012). *DGAs and Cybercriminals: A Case Study*. Tech. Rep., Damballa.

37. Zhang, L., Yu, S., Wu, D., & Watters, P., (2011). A survey on latest botnet attack and defense. In: *Trust, Security and Privacy in Computing and Communications (TrustCom), 2011 IEEE 10th International Conference* (pp. 53–60). doi: 10.1109/TrustCom.2011.11.

38. Silva, S. S., Silva, R. M., Pinto, R. C., & Salles, R. M., (2012). Botnets: A survey. *Computer Networks, 1*(0). doi: 10.1016/j.comnet.2012.07.021.

39. Hogben, G., (2011). *Botnets: Detection, Measurement, Disinfection and Defense*, Tech. rep., ENISA.

40. Kutzner, K., & Fuhrmann, T., (2005). Measuring large overlay networks â˜A the overnet example. In: MÃijller, P., Gotzhein, R., & Schmitt, J., (eds.), *Kommunikation in Verteilten Systemen (KiVS)* (pp. 193–204). Informatik aktuell, Springer Berlin Heidelberg.

41. Li, C., Jiang, W., & Zou, X., (2009). Botnet: Survey and case study. In: *Innovative Computing, Information and Control (ICICIC), 2009 Fourth International Conference* (pp. 1184–1187). doi:10.1109/ICICIC.2009.127.

42. Feily, M., & Shahrestani, (2009). A survey of botnet and botnet detection, In: *Emerging Security Information, Systems and Technologies, 2009. SECURWARE '09: Third International Conference* (pp. 268–273). doi: 10.1109/SECURWARE.2009.48.

43. Zhu, Z., Lu, G., Chen, Y., Fu, Z., Roberts, P., & Han, K., (2008). Botnet research survey. In: *Computer Software and Applications, 2008. COMPSAC '08: 32nd Annual IEEE International* (pp. 967–972). doi: 10.1109/COMPSAC.2008.205.

44. Marupally, P. R., & Paruchuri, V., (2010). Comparative analysis and evaluation of botnet command and control models. In: *Proceedings of the 2010 24th IEEE International Conference on Advanced Information Networking and Applications, AINA '10* (pp. 82–89). IEEE Computer Society, Washington, DC, USA. doi: 10.1109/AINA.2010.171.

45. Zeidanloo, H., & Manaf, A., (2009). Botnet command and control mechanisms. In: *Computer and Electrical Engineering, 2009; ICCEE '09: Second International Conference* (Vol. 1, pp. 564–568). doi: 10.1109/ICCEE.2009.151.

46. Dittrich, D., & Dietrich, S., (2008). P2p as botnet command and control: A deeper insight. In: *Proceedings of the 3rd International Conference on Malicious and Unwanted Software (Malware 2008)* (pp. 46–63).

47. Wang, P., Sparks, S., & Zou, C. C., (2007). An advanced hybrid peer-to-peer botnet. In: *Proceedings of the First Conference on First Workshop on Hot Topics in Understanding Botnets, HotBots'07* (pp. 2). USENIX Association, Berkeley, CA, USA.

48. Zhang, Z., Lu, B., Liao, P., Liu, C., & Cui, X., (2011). A hierarchical hybrid structure for botnet control and command. In: *Computer Science and Automation Engineering (CSAE), 2011 IEEE International Conference* (Vol. 1, pp. 483–489). doi:10.1109/CSAE.2011.5953266.

49. Gu, G., (2008). *Correlation-Based Botnet Detection in Enterprise Networks.* Ph.D. thesis, Georgia Institute of Technology.

50. Pouwelse, J., Garbacki, P., Epema, D., & Sips, H., (2005). The BitTorrent p2p filesharing system: Measurements and analysis. In: Castro, M., & Renesse, R., (eds.), *Peer-to-Peer Systems IV, Vol. 3640 of Lecture Notes in Computer Science* (pp. 205–216). Springer Berlin Heidelberg.

CHAPTER 3

A Survey on Opportunity and Challenges of IDS Over IoT

AMRUTANSHU PANIGRAHI,[1] BIBHUPRASAD SAHU,[2] and
SACHI NANDAN MOHANTY[3]

[1]*Research Scholar, SOA University, Bhubaneswar, Odisha, India,
E-mail: amrutansup89@gmail.com*

[2]*Assistant Professor, GIFT, Bhubaneswar, Odisha, India*

[3]*Vardhaman College of Engineering (Autonomous), Hyderabad,
Telangana, India*

ABSTRACT

IoT is becoming a prominent factor in today's scenario. It has reformed the technological aspects of the individual and industrial fields. It has converted ordinary machinery into a smart automatic one. Also, the IoT helps in making today's legacy environment into a smart environment for improvising the comfort level and efficiency of human beings. It is becoming ubiquitous in nature as it is being applied to heterogeneous devices. However, privacy and security are becoming a primary concern in the field of IoT as a large number of data has to be exchanged between smart devices and the human being. If those data are hampered due to some intentional or generic nature then the devices may perform abnormally. Though various protocols have been introduced for IoT still the security is there as the concern. During the data transfer, the primary goal, such as the CIA properties of the network needs to be constrained. But various attacks such as passive or active attacks may decrease the CIA degree. IDS is being widely used as the network security component. Intrusion Detection System for IoT can be of various forms such as host-based IDS, which monitors the system activities such as API calls, memory usage, and the network-based IDS monitors the communication and network security during the data exchange in between the user and the smart devices.

This research chapter is quite concerned with the opportunity of IDS whenever applied in IoT techniques. We have also tried to find out the challenges present of IDS over IoT. Also, in this chapter, we have analyzed the various types of available IDS techniques over IoT technology.

3.1 INTRODUCTION

The growth of the various emerging technologies such as smartphones, smart gadgets, sensors, and 4G-5G communication presage various innovative applications. These applications have been applied to various sectors such as smart cities, various industries, smart automobiles health care systems in which a very large amount of data has been adversely used. Recently the National Cable and Telecommunication Association has done a survey on the number of devices that are being used for the smart system. As per the survey, approximately 51 billion devices are used as smart ones. These devices are popularly known as the internet of things (IoT) devices which are being regularly connected to the internet for executing the user instructions for the smart work. The popularity of smart or IoT devices are subjected to the security aspect since a large amount of data is being exchanged in-between the smart device and user. This information is being passed to the other devices through the cloud which is more pruned to cybersecurity [1]. As per the research conducted by the McAfee system in 2018, there are a lot of security breaches to almost every industrial data. The higher number of IoT devices has taken the focus of various cybercriminals towards data misconduct. Along with these the degree of interconnectivity among various IoT devices even becoming more vulnerable to the security aspect. While exchanging the information, the primary objective of data communication CIA means confidentiality, integrity, availability is becoming the prominent challenge factor. In Ref. [2], it has been shown that the industries and the organization are facing a great challenge in handling and monitoring the network. So, the number of threats to the organizational data is being increased exponentially. The gadgets in an IoT system are self-ruling and associated with one another just as physical frameworks, for example, grids, and industrial frameworks joining into the digital-physical framework [3]. This makes an open design for the IoT making them an alluring objective for malevolent entertainers meaning to break the safe system framework or bargain delicate data about the conduct of the clients just as endeavoring to undermine basic national and universal foundations. These elements increase the importance of security and protection instruments for IoT frameworks and, in this manner order express endeavors to address them. A generic IoT device has some constraint on the power usage during the communication. Looking into these characteristics along with the connectivity of the devices 6LoWPAN standard has been introduced [4, 5]. This standard enables the communication between the devices with fragmentation to fit the data having packet size large into small packets so that the data can be transferred. In LoWPAN, this kind of connectivity is accomplished by utilizing an edge switch that encourages network among the gadgets taking an interest inside a LoWPAN just as with the Web. Notwithstanding, an IoT network structure is quite vulnerable against security threats due to its transparency, bigger impression, dynamically evolving topology, constant joining and leaving of hubs in the system, and absence of centralized network management process. Besides, IoT gadgets have one-of-a-kind highlights, for example, constrained power supply, restricted vitality and correspondence transfer speed, little memory size, and constrained data storage. These limitations have critical sway on the adequacy of security answers for IoT frameworks both regarding adaptability [6] just as execution effectiveness of the arrangement [7]. Thus, structuring a compelling intrusion detection framework for the IoT arrange is nontrivial rousing us to research difficulties to accomplish a compelling interruption identification framework for IoT without acquiring huge calculation and correspondence overheads. The IDS for IoT can be classified in two different ways:

1. **Standalone System:** This kind of system uses the information of a single system for detecting the intrusion present during the communication. But this kind is in less use due to the constraint in energy usage and memory overheads.

2. **Collaborative System:** This kind of IDS uses the network information from the diversified devices being connected within the same network.

By the research conducted by Cisco [8] due to the higher number of connected devices, the number of attacks on different devices also increases. The attackers to the network can be classified into two groups:

1. **Internal Attacker:** Basically, some people have the right and privilege to handle and monitor the network traffic. If those people will misuse the right to change the internal data, then they will be called internal attackers or internal intruders.

2. **External Attacker:** These are the third-party users who do not have the right and privilege in dealing with the IoT network. If these third

users want to access the network without the proper permission and privilege then they are called the external attacker or external intruders.

The threat is some kind of activity which deals with the unauthorized data access from the IoT network. The threats to the IoT network are being classified into four different groups [9]:

1. **DoS:** This kind of threat denies the user access to the corresponding resource by making some unwanted heavy amounts of traffic inside the network. So repeatedly the access to the resource is failed which decreases the performance of the IoT network.
2. **Breaches:** This is being applied to the various available data inside the network. This kind of threat generally takes the ARP packets and interrupts the secret communication.
3. **Weak Perimeter:** Basically, the connected IoT network is designed in such a manner that most of the time, it has to be connected with the cloud which indirectly makes the network and the device vulnerable.
4. **Malware:** In this threat, the intruder tried to implement some executable code at the IoT device end. Once the code is being executed by the device in the IoT network then it pruned to loss of sensitive data because by using the malware the intruder can alter the device from normal working mode to some erroneous one.

In this research chapter, we have tried to focus on the survey of various possible attacks to the IoT network and different IDS solution for preventing different types of attacks. In Section 3.2, we have focused on the IoT standard and protocols. While in Section 3.3, the detailed study of the IDS security aspect has been done. Section 3.4 provides various IDS attacks with the different security threats to the IoT network. Section 3.5 tries to bring attention to the IDS methods available to tackle different kinds of attacks. In Section 3.6, a detailed study and comparison have been drawn among all IDS techniques present in the IoT environment. Finally, the conclusion has been brought in Section 3.7.

3.2   IoT STANDARDS AND PROTOCOLS

The IoT covers almost all industries with a massive amount of devices connected with each other while connecting with the cloud system in real-time. The protocol stack for the IoT services is as follows (Figure 3.1):

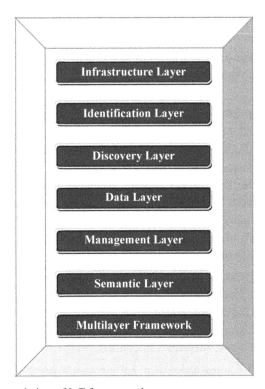

FIGURE 3.1   Layered view of IoT for protocol.

1. **Infrastructure Layer:** This layer is responsible for the interconnection of IoT devices and the cloud environment. This layer includes some well-known protocols as follows:

   i.   **IPv6:** This protocol helps in transmitting the datagrams in a switched or IP network.

   ii. **6LoWPAN [10]:** It stands for IPv6 Low Power Wireless Personal Area Network. It is a network protocol that is responsible for defining the header compression along with the encapsulation method during the communication. This protocol is free from the physical layer constraint such as frequency band and it can also be applied to the Wi-Fi and Ethernet techniques. It is specifically developed for home or small organization automation.

   iii. **UDP:** Known as user datagram protocol is used for the client-server communication based on the IP. It can act as the alternative method for TCP technique and particularly dedicated towards the real-time data.

    iv. **QUIC:** Quick UDP Internet Connection is a protocol basically used for end-to-end communication over the UDP network.

2. **Identification:** It is a critical issue in IoT as it helps in credential matching. Various protocols are available for the identification method.

    i. **EPC:** EPC stands for electronic product code is a universal identifier that provides each and every IoT device with a unique identification code. By using the code, the device can be easily recognized when it needs to be connected with the cloud service.

    ii. **uCode:** Ubiquitous code or uCode is a unique number that can be used to detect things uniquely in the real world. It is a 128-bit code used for naming convention. Unlike EPC, it can be used broadly and it cannot be dedicated to a specific application. It consists of five different elements:

        a. UCode;

        b. UCode tag;

        c. Communicator;

        d. UCoderesolution center; and

        e. UCode information center.

3. **Transport/Communication Layer:** This layer is responsible for connecting the heterogeneous devices in the IoT network. Basically, the IoT devices are operating by using the low power in the presence of noisy and lossy communication channels between the devices. Different protocols available for communication are as follows:

    i. **Bluetooth:** It is used for short-range communication purposes. In this type of communication, heterogeneous types of devices can communicate with each other by using the radio waves. The new era of Bluetooth available for the IoT network is known as BLE or Bluetooth Low Energy. The design perspective of Bluetooth is based on saving power consumption.

    ii. **Zigbee:** It is a low power having a very low data rate during the communication specially used in the smart industrial part. Dotdot is a universal language developed by the Zigbee team to enable the devices to work in any type of network.

    iii. **LPWAN:** LPWAN stands for low power wide area network (LPWAN) which is being designed for small messages over a network during the communication between the devices. In LPWAN each device will receive very less packet sized data in different time slots. These time slots may or may not frequent in nature.

4. **Discovery Layer:** As the IoT network supports heterogeneous kinds of devices, so IoT supports the discovery process as various types of devices and services. This discovery process includes the demand finding and integration of the devices. This layer will help in analyzing, visualization, and application of the existing data. For this, there are several available protocols present:

   i. **mDNS:** mDNS stands for multicast DNS which resolves the hostname to a corresponding IP address within the small network. By using this protocol, a device can be recognized within the network.

   ii. **HyperCat:** This protocol helps in driving a SIT for industrial purposes. By using the hypercat, the application can be developed in such a way that it can be executed in any device and server (Figure 3.2).

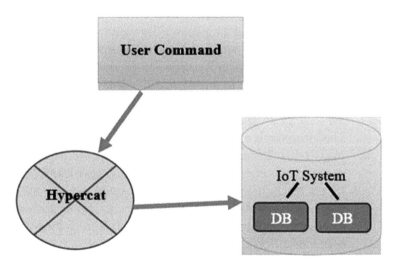

FIGURE 3.2   User interaction with IoT system through hypercat.

   iii. **UPnP:** It stands for Universal Plug and Plays which is managed by the open connectivity foundation. This protocol permits the device to be connected to the network. After the connection, the device can share the data with the other device. By using this protocol, the device is able to use the basic network features such as entertainment, communication, etc.

5. **Data Layer:** Billions and billions of devices are being connected with the IoT platform. So, this protocol will help the device to transfer the data packets to another device within the network. It just acts as a transport layer in the OSI reference model. Few data layer protocols are explained below:

i.   **MQTT:** Message queue telemetry transport popularly known as MQTT is just a messaging protocol which plays a vital role in transferring the packets from source to destination. It has been standardized by the OASIS [11] in 2013. It is only dedicated to the resource-constrained devices which use very low power bandwidth channels for communication. It is also responsible for connecting the embedded devices to the IoT-based servers for communication establishment. MQTT utilizes the send and subscriber model to give the transition facility to the depicted IoT devices. It consists of 3 basic modules subscriber, publisher, and a broker. The connected device which wants to communicate with others can act as a subscriber while the publisher will be responsible for generating the data for different the subscriber end. Finally, the broker is responsible for delivering the publisher-generated message to the interested IoT device. During transferring the data to the subscriber end, the broker also takes care of the security prospect for keeping the data safe from the intruder. The Mosquito is a very well-known broker in MQTT version 3.1.

ii. **MQTT-SN:** It stands for MQTT for Sensor Networks which is an extended version of MQTT v3.1. This specifically developed for the machine-to-machine communication and also for mobile communication. MQTT SN utilizes the encryption method which makes the communication more secure. Basically, the MQTT-SN uses four different messages for communicating messages from sender to receiver. The steps are as follows:

   a. Setup phase;
   b. Encryption phase;
   c. Communication phase;
   d. Decryption phase.

iii. **CoAP:** CoAP stands for constrained application protocol (CoAP) [12] defines a web transfer protocol that utilizes the REST. RE presentational State Transfer or REST provides a simpler path for exchanging the data between the IoT client and the servers. CoAP depends upon UDP protocol only and changes some of the http functionalities in order to match with IoT requirements. CoAP has two sub-layers, out of which one layer is dedicated for the message purpose, and another is being dedicated to receiving the response from the corresponding destination one. Like the http service, the CoAP utilizes the GET method to retrieve the message from the server, PUT method is being used to send the message by the client, PUSH method is being for updating the data during the communication and the DELETE method is being used for deleting some particular message. For messaging purpose, it utilizes four different messaging modes:

a.   **Confirmable Message:** It denotes the reliable message to be transferred from source end to destination end.

b.   **Non-Confirmable Message:** It denotes the unreliable message that is to be transferred from source end to destination end.

c.   **Piggyback Message:** It is dedicated to the client-server communication in which the server sends the acknowledgment after receiving the request from its corresponding client. But after receiving the request, the server immediately posts an ACK message to the corresponding client.

d.   **Separate Message:** This mode is being used by the server whenever the server wants to send the acknowledgment separately from the received message, but maybe some delay will be there in sending the ACK signal (Figure 3.3).

iv.   **SMCP:** It is a CoAP variant that we specifically developed for the embedded IoT environment. It supports a fully asynchronous I/O operation.

v.   **XMPP:** Extensible Messaging and presence protocol or XMPP are being used for the multimedia functionalities such as voice calling, video calling in between the smart devices. For text-based communication, XMPP uses the XML technique but the main disadvantage is that it will increase the network overhead.

vi.   **AMQP:** or advanced message queuing protocol is an application layer protocol dedicated to the message-oriented communication environment. It consists of two main things known as exchange and information queue. Exchange queue is being used in forwarding the packets from source to destination whereas the information queue contains the rules that need to be used during the communication.

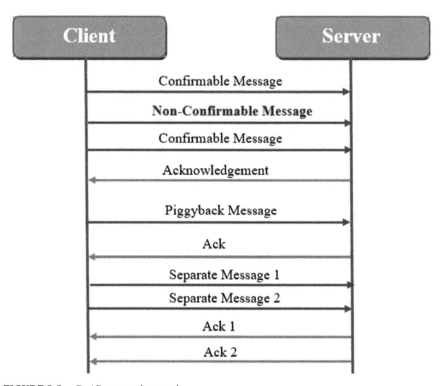

FIGURE 3.3   CoAP messaging mode.

6. **Management Layer:** The main objective of this strategy is to maintain and monitor all the available devices in the network. For this, the admin has to ensure that the devices present in the network follow the standard protocols so that the activity can be measured. For this, there are some protocols explained below:

    i. **OMA-DM:** Open mobile alliance device management or OMA-DM is quite dedicated to mobile applications. OMA is a lightweight, fast, and standardized protocol for one-to-one communication in an IoT network.

    ii. **TR-069:** Technical report 069 or TR-069 is a broadband technical specification that is being used for managing the connection to the CPE (customer premises equipment) connected within the

IoT network. TR-069 utilizes CPE WAN management protocol which facilitates the devices for auto-configuration as per the requirement.

7. **Semantic Layer:** This layer helps the user and the admin to extract the information from the network. This process is called the knowledge extraction by which the device can discover and use the resources present in the network. This layer helps the device in analyzing the data for making the smart decision within the network. It furthermore helps in maximizing the network performance by increasing the battery life, minimizing the bandwidth utilization, and optimizing the instruction optimization while communicating with the IoT server for performing the smart works. Various protocols are available as follows:

   i. **JSON-LD:** It is a lightweight data format that is being used for reading and writing the dirty data in a structured way by using some vocabulary. It allows the data to operate in a web environment whenever the device is being connected with the cloud in the IoT network.

   ii. **Web Things Model:** It provides the forum for technical aspects to identify the use cases and requirements of the application. This protocol has been adopted by various organizations for creating the application layer IoT scenarios. Web Thing Model is just like a cookbook which integrates the things with the web or internet in an IoT environment.

8. **Multilayer Framework:** This is wholly responsible for handling the interconnectivity among the devices. This layer consists of several protocols which have been explained below:

   i. **AllJoyn:** It is open-source software that helps the IoT devices to recognize each other and also helps to communicate. It is platform-independent, so it can be added with any kind of operating system present in various devices within the IoT network. These characteristics help the IoT framework more flexible in terms of interconnectivity.

   ii. **IoTivity:** It is also an open-source project whose objective is to provide a robust framework for the wired and wireless devices to be connected with each other and also to access the internet for executing the basic functionalities of the IoT system.

   iii. **Weave:** It is an application layer protocol that can be applied to the small and residential applications. The three main components of the weave are client, cloud, and smart device. The cloud helps in accessing the basic IoT functionalities. The client is a particular device that executes the command coming from the smart devices (Figure 3.4).

iv. **Homekit:** It is a lightweight protocol that is being used by establishing a common interface between the device and app. For this, it provides the API through which the device can be in touch with the cloud system.

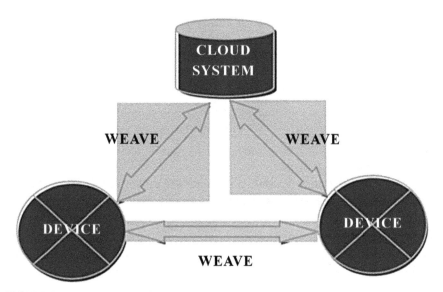

FIGURE 3.4   Weave protocol communication.

3.3 IoT SECURITY ASPECT

The previous section has discussed on the all-available protocols in different layers through which the devices will connect with the cloud. This enables all the available devices to access the basic functionalities of the IoT system. But there are several challenges and barriers are there which make the IoT system more vulnerable. In this section, we have focused on the vulnerability criteria where various attacks on the IoT system have been discussed. There are various security applications are present which makes the IoT more insecure. Some of the application areas are discussed as follows [12]:

1. **Anomaly Detection:** It is the process of detecting anomalies during communication. The anomaly is nothing but the outlier event which changes the data significantly [13]. These outliers are generated by the cyber attackers who want unauthorized access to the server. The anomaly can be categorized into the three different groups. Point anomaly who finds a normal outlier present in the data, contextual anomaly checks the abnormality of the resource whereas the collective anomaly is the combination of point anomaly and contextual anomaly. So basically, the collective anomaly is being used to detect whether any resource or context is behaving abnormally or not.

2. **IDS:** Intrusion detection system is a method to monitor the activity of the device and the network. This is an application software which scans the network and the device to find out the breach. This IDS technique is divided into two different groups:

    i. **HIDS:** Host-based IDS which aims to scan the device for finding a breach in the activity. This HIDS is deployed in the sensor device for detecting the anomaly [14].

    ii. **NIDS:** Network-based IDS is deployed to monitor the network traffic. The different layers during the communication are being analyzed by the NIDS for detecting the breaches in the network.

3. **Malware Detection:** It is the process of detecting malware. There are two different ways of detecting malware. Either the detection process is dynamic in which during the communication process the malware is being detected. But in the static analysis, the malware is being detected in the binary form [15]. These binary formats are being analyzed by the detection process for the presence of the malware.

4. **Ransom Detection:** The ransom is a kind of malware that encrypts the corrupted system along with its documents. In this process, the available systems are analyzed for the presence of the ransom [16]. This malware encrypts and publishes the affected data for use. The ransom attack is generally carried by the Trojan that is being downloaded by the device whenever dealing with the cloud for executing the task.

5. **Botnet Attack Detection:** The botnet means the internet-connected smart device which wants to perform some tasks by using the bot. This botnet uses the DDoS attack for taking the data from the user's end and also to provide an attacker a path through which the device can be accessed. The network administrator can use the C&C software for detecting the attack [17].

3.4   ATTACKS ON IoT

Based on the layers present in the IoT system the attacks have been classified into layer-wise. In IoT, the attacks have been noticed in 3 different sub-layers such as Physical Layer, Network layer, Application Layer. In Physical Layer the attacks will de be executed on the physical devices so that the smart devices which has been deployed in the IoT will show the abnormality while performing some of the tasks. In the network layer, the IoT network where the device interacts with the cloud for sharing some important data is more pruned to the attack. The attacker interferes with the network and changes the user command. Suppose the user has passed a message in the home automation system to open the door, this command has to be passed to the other device which will actually execute the command. But due to attack in the network, the command has been corrupted and the device will perform as per the corrupted command received from the cloud system. By looking into the abnormal action, the user simply discards the system as the device is performing as per the command. While in the application layer the security breaches have been found in the IoT applications. There are various well-known attacks are there to these three different layers. In Figure 3.5, the taxonomy of the available attacks on these three layers has been shown.

3.4.1   *PHYSICAL LAYER ATTACK*

In the physical layer generally, the attacker attacks the physical device and their connections. Due to this kind of attack the IoT devices act abnormally. There are various kinds of physical attacks are there which has been discussed below:

1. **Botnet Attack:** The botnet attack includes the attack on the smart device installed or deployed on the IoT network. The main objective of this kind of attack is to perform 2 different tasks. First to miscon-figure the device and secondly to target a particular server through which the IoT devices communicate with each other to execute the task. The botnet attack has 4 different components [18, 19]:

    i.   **Bot:** It is the actual malware that infects the device.

    ii.   **Centralized Interface:** It is being used to check the condition of the botnet and initiates the attack on the C&C server.

    iii. **Loader:** It just spreads malware while targeting machines and devices.

iv. **Report Server:** It is being used for preparing a log for the botnet devices.

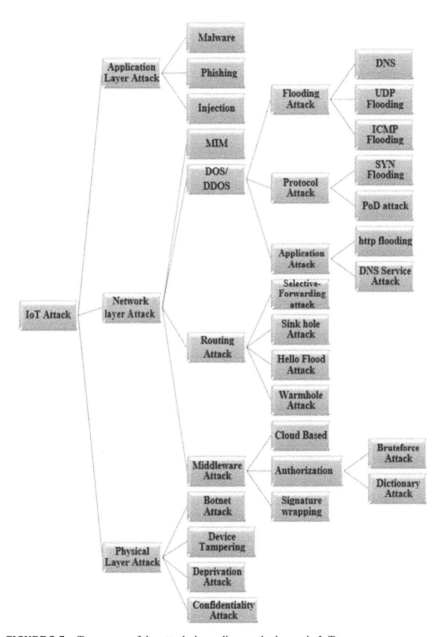

FIGURE 3.5   Taxonomy of the attack depending on the layers in IoT.

2. **Device Tampering:** This kind of attack to replace the device hardware completely for abnormal behavior in the IoT network. The tampering can also be done electronically by tackling the device's routing table, the important information, and the security keys used for the encryption process during the communication [20]. By this attack, the attacker can interfere in the radio frequency resulting in the jamming in the network, and due to jamming the delay can there during the communication.

3. **Deprivation Attack:** In this attack, the attacker focused the limited power sourced devices, i.e., the devices containing the battery. The characteristics of the energy-constrained device are that they follow the switching between the active mode and sleep mode. The attacker focuses on sleeping time. They just increase the sleep time so that the device is unable to react whenever the necessary action needs to be performed [16, 21].

4. **Confidentiality Attack:** In this attack, there is a threat to the basic characteristic of message exchange, i.e., CIA property of the communication. CIA stands for Confidentiality, Integrity, and Availability. This attack is done when communication is being done in between the sender and receiver by using some particular private channel [22].

3.4.2   NETWORK LAYER ATTACK

The network layer of the reference model generally consists of all networking components such as bridges, routers, switches. These devices are being required for establishing communication between the IoT devices and the cloud system. The network layer attack aims to damage these network layer components. Some of the well-known network layer attacks are as follows:

1. **MIM:** It stands for Man in the middle attack. In this attack, the attacker gains full access to the communication channel. After that, the attacker has not constrained to the read the message, instead, it can interfere with the message and also can modify the content resulting in the delivery of a false message to the device present in the IoT network. The attack can be achieved by performing any one of the following tasks [23]:

   i. **ARP Damage:** Address Resolution Protocol or ARP responsibility is to convert the IP address of the devices into the corresponding MAC address. So, the attacker will try to interfere with the ARP so that the actual destination can be traced out. Once the actual destination is traced out, attacker may gain complete access to the communication link [24].

ii.   **DNS Spoof:** The working of DNS is to map the names into the IP address. DNS spoof is a process of dealing with storing the false IP address against some particular symbolic names. Hence if the IoT device wants to visit the cloud then it just puts a name which will be passed to DNS for converting the name to the corresponding IP address. But the attacker has already stored the false IP address against the searched name. So, the device will receive some interpreted result which will not fulfill the original task. In this way, the network performance can be degraded [25].

2. **DDoS Attack:** This kind of attack is generally done to take the network bandwidth so that any connected device will face the problem while accessing some particular service. Due to false bandwidth utilization, the network is more pruned to the failure [26, 27]. In DDoS attacks, more number of DoS attacks are being included with a higher number of devices and networks. This attack is achieved by streaming a large number of packets in the network. A large number of devices are being included, so the number of packets will be more. A higher number of devices also increases the number of false requests to make the network busy as much as possible. One more characteristic of this attack is that multiple users or deployed devices make the resource request to the same application simultaneously, which creates the bottleneck issue at the server-side. This bottleneck issue degrades network performance. Various DDoS attacks have been discussed as follows:

i.   **Flooding Attack:** Flooding is a kind of DDoS attack in which a large number of traffic will be injected into the network which will increase the network congestion unwontedly. The traffic of the flood can full the buffer deployed at the device and server-side which decreases the performance of the IoT network. Some of the flooding attacks are as follows:

a.   **DNS Flood Attack:** In this attack, the primary objective of the attacker is to keep the DNS server as busy as possible. Then the attacker targets the device connected in the same network. Then it attempts to flood a large number of packets to the device so that the performance of the device will decrease severely [27].

b. **UDP Attack:** An UDP flood attack aims the UDP packets coming from different devices deployed in the IoT network. The objective of this attack is to flood some random available ports, which cause the device to check regularly for the various applications flooded to the particular port and replies back to false applications that have been flooded to the device port [28].

c. **ICMP Attack:** ICMP flood overpowers the objective asset with ICMP packets, for the most part sending the packets as quick as conceivable without hanging tight for replies. This sort of assault can expend both active and approaching transfer speed, since the casualty's servers will frequently endeavor to react with ICMP reply packets, coming about a critical system jam or slowdown which affects the network [29].

ii. **Protocol Attack:** This type of attack focuses on utilizing server resources such as firewalls, load balancers, etc. This attack focuses on the network layer of the reference model of communication between two or more devices deployed in an IoT network. Various protocol attacks have been discussed below [30]:

a. **SYN Flood:** This kind of attack focuses on the weakness of TCP connection. In TCP communication the device has to issue an acknowledgment message whenever one more host has issued the SYN message. Sometimes the ACK message has been released from the receiver end but could not reach the source side. This is possible if the ACK message is lost or the SYN is being delivered by a spoofed IP address [30].

b. **PoD:** Ping of Death or PoD attacks contains the method of sending a large number of malicious pings to one particular deployed device in the IoT system. The maximum size of an IP packet is 65,535 bytes, but the attacker tries to send the packets having large packet size with an intention to damage the targeted device [31].

iii. **Application Attack:** It is being designed for attacking the applications at the application layer of the reference model. Basically, it is designed for a particular application or the server. Various application attacks are discussed below:

a. **HTTP Attack:** In this attack, the http request such as http post an http get requests are manipulated. With the modified get and post method, the requesting device cannot access the particular application which will indirectly makes the system failure [32].

b. **DNS Service Attack:** The DNS helps the IoT system in converting the symbolic names of the server provided by the host to the particular IP address so that the server can be accessed for the particular application. But due to the attack the IoT system is unable to map the perfect server to which the device is looking for access which will affect the IoT system as by this attack, the requesting device will never get the proper result [32].

3. **Routing Protocol Attack:** In this type of attack generally the attacker focuses on the routing information which is used for making a successful communication. The routing information can be the routing table information where all the information regarding the sender and receiver device has been mentioned [33]. The attacker can tackle with this information for disrupting the message transfer. There are various RPL attack discusses below:

i. **Selective Forwarding Attack:** Selective repeat is a way to deal with erroneous communication. When this method is being used during the communication, the receiver will ask the sender device to forward the particular packet which has not been received during the communication. This request will have an index number the same as the lost packet number. In this attack, the receiver device will be spoofed and the send will be asked to send some particular data repeatedly so that the corresponding sending sender will be busy and will not respond to the other communication. Hence the network performance will be degraded as the other devices will guess that the sender is corrupted or dead so that it is unable to respond [33].

ii. **Sinkhole Attack:** Sink is a device which acts as a BS during a multi-hop communication. So, in this attack, a malicious device tries to deliver a huge amount of traffic to the surrounding devices. So, the network will be kept busy unnecessarily. Hence by using this attack, the attacker can disturb the entire network [34].

iii. **Hello Flood Attack:** In hello flood, a malicious device will try to broadcast a large hello message with high power to force the available devices to listen to those packets which will utilize the device power unnecessarily [34].

iv. **Wormhole Attack:** Wormhole is a high-speed link between two different devices. This can be used to send the packets faster as compared to the normal packets. This attack takes place when a malicious node interferes into the tunnel and sends high-speed packets to the connecting devices in an IoT network [35].

4. **Middleware Attack:** In the IoT, middleware refers to the component such as cloud which plays a vital role in the communication and accessing the IoT applications. Various middleware attacks have been discussed below [36, 37]:

   i. **Cloud-based Attack:** In this type of attack, the attacker focuses on the cloud for data corruption and data theft. For these, the attacker can approach to the malware injection or clouding attack to the cloud. In malware injection, the attackers get access to the device's data in the cloud and exchanges the real copy of data with a malicious one. So, whenever the device accesses the cloud data then it will have malicious one which will perform the erroneous task. Whereas in cloud flooding the attacker tries to send a huge number of data packets from a malicious device so that the traffic can prohibit the other available device from accessing the cloud service which will degrade the network performance.

   ii. **Authorization Attack:** This attack tries to break the credentials of the IoT device. These credentials are nothing but the user's name, password, and the cryptographic keys which are being used for accessing the cloud service. Various types of authorization attacks are explained below [38]:

      a. **Brute Force Attack:** Brute force attacks help the attacker in gaining cloud access by entering various combinations of credentials with the probability that the entered credential is right. This process is being continued until the correct credential has been guessed [38].

      b. **Dictionary Attack:** In this initially the attacker prepares a database of all possible passwords which is called the dictionary. Then the attacker tries to interfere with the communication channel and then enters the password as per the prepared dictionary to have access. If it matches the IoT device credentials then the attacker tackles the information which is being transferred [39].

iii. **Signature Wrapping Attack:** This kind of attack is quite similar to the masking process. Here the attacker tries to behave as a legitimate device that is authentic in the IoT environment. This can be done by putting a malicious signature just as the IoT device which has been deployed in the IoT environment and now is under the threat. When the cloud wants to send some information to the original device at that time the attacker deviates the information to the masked malicious device to hamper the IoT system performance.[40].

3.4.3 APPLICATION LAYER ATTACK

In this, the attack is done at the application itself such as smart office, smart home, and smart city, etc. This is quite related to the breaches in the IoT enabled applications. Various application-layer attacks have been discussed below [41, 42]:

1. **Malware Attack:** It is a type of attack where some malicious codes are being injected into the application. So, when the IoT device tries to access that particular malicious application inside the network, then the attackers try to gain some important information that can be used to disrupt the IoT network.

2. **Phishing Attack:** The phishing attack tries to build a false application where the device tries to put the legitimate credentials to access the service. But when it submits the id and password it is being redirected to the attacker. After obtaining the credentials, the attacker can use that information for accessing other various applications for degrading the network performance.

3. **Injection Attack:** Injection attack consists of the process of submitting some malicious code into the network space where the device has been deployed to perform various tasks. The main objective of the injection attack is to obtain an authorization on behalf of the IoT device. This injection can be done in 2 ways. Either the attackers follow the SQL injection or the entire script injection [42, 43]. In the SQL injection process, the attacker injects some malicious database SQL queries to access the server, whereas the script injection aims to inject some erroneous commands to perform malicious functionalities.

3.5   INTRUSION DETECTION SYSTEM

An IDS or intrusion detection system monitors and analyzes the network along with the deployed devices for detecting the various attacks to the network which humiliate the network performance. Due to the presence of heterogeneous devices in a network, the attacker can start attacking in a different manner. Implementing the IDS has also two challenges [44]:

1. **False Positive Approach:** In this approach, the IDS will inform the administrator by creating an action when there is no attack inside the network. This is maybe due to the abnormal activity of some devices.
2. **False Negative Approach:** In real there will be an attack on the network and its device but still, the IDS will think that it is some of the abnormal activity performed by the device. Whereas in real some kind of attack is there but a simple IDS is unable to detect that one.

By considering the above criteria, there are five different categories of IDS available for the network:

1. **Network-based IDS:** It is being placed within the network for monitoring the network traffic coming from all devices deployed within the network. Once some abnormal activity has been detected then immediately one warning message will be sent to the network administrator.
2. **Host-based IDS:** It runs on a particular device to check the activity along with the incoming and outgoing traffic. Once the HIDS detects any kind of malicious activity then it immediately alerts the administrator regarding this along with the snapshot of the activity.
3. **Protocol-based IDS:** It consists of a system that acts as a front end of a server. It will try to secure the server by constantly monitoring the http service. Since the http does follow the encryption standards, the PIDS tries to Analyze each http request and response for the deployed system.
4. **Application based IDS:** It is a system which generally stored in a group of servers. It particularly identifies malicious activity by constantly monitoring various applications being used within the server.
5. **Hybrid IDS:** It is the combination of two or more IDS for performing multiple detections within the network. By using this kind of IDS, the device, and the network along with the server can be constantly monitored.

For the above-discussed intrusion detection system, there are two different methods for detecting the intrusion to the network:

i.   **Signature-based Detection Method:** By using this method, the administrator can be able to detect the malicious activity whose definition has already been defined in the server. By looking into the pattern, the IDS detects the malicious activity. Most of the time the signature-based IDS is responsible for detecting some False-positive intrusions where upon detecting any kind of abnormal activity by which the network may not be hampered will be notified to the administration by giving a warning message.

ii. **Anomaly-based Detection Method:** This being used by the network administrator to detect any kind of malware attack which is not known to the system in prior. This detection process utilizes the ML method to obtain a trustworthy model where any incoming activity will be compared. If no match is found then immediately the deployed IDs will inform the activity along with the log containing the snapshot to the administrator for taking the appropriate step.

3.6   INTRUSION DETECTION SYSTEM IN IoT

As per the discussion in the previous section, the IDS is used to detect unauthorized and malicious activity in the network. As in IoT large number of smart devices are being connected with the cloud for executing the different applications. So, the IDS plays a vital role in the IoT network. Depending upon the architecture the IDS in IoT can be classified four different types:

1.   **Centralized IDS:** The total IDS will be deployed in a single system which will be responsible for detecting the malicious actions but within the system only.

2.   **Distributed IDS:** This kind of IDS is generally placed in all of the devices within the same IoT network for detecting malicious performance.

3.   **Hierarchical IDS:** This type of IDS works in a tree-like structure where a particular number of devices take responsibility for detecting the malicious attacks for all of the other devices.

4.   **Hybrid IDS:** This is the combination of all of the above-said IDS types where some of the nodes take the responsibility for detecting the attacks in other nodes and in some part host-based IDS is being installed in different individuals' devices.

In the chapter [44], the author tries to solve the IDS issue by developing a host-based IDS, but the main disadvantage of this IDS is that it is dedicated to the ZigBee devices. By implementing this kind of IDs in an IoT network can solve some of the issues but as its device-dependent so it cannot be applied to the IoT network.

The author in Ref. [45] has developed a HIDS which can detect the DoS attack but unable to deal with the other attacks. This HIDS can be applied to personal laptops and mobile devices but cannot be applied to the whole network. This HIDS is specially designed to detect the deprivation DoS attack.

A misuse detection system has been developed by the author in Ref. [46] which can be applied in the decentralized network in which each and every system is responsible for detecting malicious attacks of its own or some of the particular devices takes the responsibility for detecting the malicious performance for other.

A centralized anomaly detection system has been developed by the author in Ref. [47] which is utilizing the anomaly detection method for finding the malicious behavior of the devices present in the network. It is a decentralized IDS but the main disadvantage of this IDS is that it is costly in implementation as it is a hardware constraint. In Ref. [48], the author has developed a centralized NIDS which can work remotely. This characteristic makes the developed IDS stronger and the degree of implementation is more as compared to the other. The author in Ref. [49] has developed a centralized IDS which is based on the misuse detection but dedicate to the 6LowPan network. This IDS is there to detect the DDoS type of attack. The author in Ref. [50] has developed an artificial IDS which can train itself for detecting any kind of attack. It is based on a ML model. By implementing this IDS IoT network learns the self-adaption technique for detecting new attacks whose definition has not been there in the predefined database. Button et al. [51] have developed a NIDS which integrates the statistical and rule-based approach for detecting the attacks in a clustered network. The author in Ref. [52] has introduced a NIDS which uses the ML approach for the anomaly and signature-based attacks. The framework structure is intended for brilliant open vehicle applications that utilize CoAP. The fundamental highlights of this framework are its pertinence to CoAP applications and its dependence on a lightweight calculation. Jun et al. [53] has proposed an integrated IDS which uses the benefits of the CEP technique by means of which it is able to detect the different patterns through real-time data analysis. This IDS totally utilizes the rule-based approach for detecting malicious behavior. The author in Ref. [54] has developed a Network-based IDS which is based on the FCM algorithm. FCM means fuzzy c-means clustering in which the ML and the data mining approaches are integrated together to find out a better result. Liu et al. [55] has proposed an IDS for IoT network which depends upon two ML and data mining algorithm known as PCA and SFC. By using this suppressed fuzzy clustering and PCA algorithm, the accuracy in detecting the malicious attacks. In research work, the author in Ref. [56] has developed the IDS for IoT network using 6LowPAN for detecting RPL attacks. The main feature of this IDS is that it will detect the RPL attack in an energy-constrained manner.

Abhishek et al. [57] had developed a network IDS that depends upon the PDP factor of IoT device. PDP is nothing but the packet drop probability which monitors the gateways for detecting the attacks. This IDS uses the statistical approach and uses the anomaly detection method to detect the third-party user which is responsible for interrupting the communication between two different IoT-enabled devices.

In Ref. [46], the author has tried to bring a new lightweight IDS for detecting the malicious patterns but due to the energy-constrained and memory limitation, it cannot be applied to the IoT network where a huge number of the smart device are being deployed with memory and energy optimization concept. Arrington et al. [56] had developed a Host-based IDS which utilizes the machine approach for anomaly-based intrusion detection. This IDS uses some behavioral model for detecting malicious behavior.

3.7 CONCLUSION AND FUTURE WORK

Nowadays billions of devices are being connected in the IoT network. But these devices are heterogeneous in nature. One of the main constraints in the IoT network is all of the devices are energy-constrained and connected to some limited power source. These devices are connected with others and also connected to the cloud system for accessing the IoT based applications. Furthermore, different security issues to the IoT network and device make the IoT system more vulnerable. In this survey work, we have studied the IoT protocol stack and different attacks related to the IoT. Then we have concentrated on various attacks that make the network insecure. In three major layers of IoT, i.e., physical layer, network layer, and the application layer is pruned to the security aspect. Among all attacks, the Dos, DDoS, and RPL attacks are more effective attacks as these attacks totally focus on the data and the communication which plays a vital role in data communication. Then we have investigated several IDS developed for the IoT network. When dealing with the IoT network, the IDS is categorized on the basis of the type of network. Out of these categories, the hybrid IDS is the effective one. But the Host-Based IDS is the lightweight IDS but still unable to be implemented in the network because HIDS can only be implemented in the device only.

Implementing the IDS in the device itself will never solve the network issues. Implementing the NIDS will solve the issue at the network side, but the attacker can take the opportunity to make the device as the malicious one. NIDS prevents the attacker in increasing the network traffic but unable to secure the smart devices which are the key parameter to the IoT system. So, in research work, we found that the NIDS and HIDS have to be combined together to form a hybrid one to provide the security to the host devices and the IoT network which will make the IoT network more efficient.

KEYWORDS

- **API call**
- **CIA**
- **intrusion detection system**
- **IoT**

REFERENCES

1. Abomhara, M., (2015). Cyber security and the internet of things: Vulnerabilities, threats, intruders and attacks. *Journal of Cyber Security and Mobility, 4*(1), 65–88.
2. Alshahrani, M., & Traore, I., (2019). Secure mutual authentication and automated access control for IoT smart home using cumulative keyed-hash chain. *Journal of Information Security and Applications, 45,* 156–175.
3. Armando, A., Basin, D., Boichut, Y., Chevalier, Y., Compagna, L., Cuéllar, J., & Mödersheim, S., (2005). The AVISPA tool for the automated validation of internet security protocols and applications. In: *International Conference on Computer-Aided Verification* (pp. 281–285). Springer, Berlin, Heidelberg.
4. Ashibani, Y., Kauling, D., & Mahmoud, Q. H., (2017). A context-aware authentication framework for smart homes. In: *2017 IEEE 30*[th] *Canadian Conference on Electrical and Computer Engineering (CCECE)* (pp. 1–5). IEEE.
5. Chu, F., Zhang, R., Ni, R., & Dai, W., (2013). An improved identity authentication scheme for the internet of things in heterogeneous networking environments. In: *2013 16*[th] *International Conference on Network-Based Information Systems* (pp. 589–593). IEEE.
6. Vinayakumar, R., Alazab, M., Soman, K. P., Poornachandran, P., Al-Nemrat, A., & Venkatraman, S., (2019). Deep learning approach for intelligent intrusion detection system. *IEEE Access, 7,* 41525–41550.

7. Kotenko, I., Saenko, I., Kushnerevich, A., & Branitskiy, A., (2019). Attack detection in IoT critical infrastructures: A machine learning and big data processing approach. In: *2019 27ᵗʰ Euromicro International Conference on Parallel, Distributed and Network-Based Processing (PDP)* (pp. 340–347). IEEE.

8. Lu, Z., Wang, N., Wu, J., & Qiu, M., (2018). IoTDeM: An IoT big data-oriented MapReduce performance prediction extended model in multiple edge clouds. *Journal of Parallel and Distributed Computing, 118*, 316–327.

9. Berman, D. S., Buczak, A. L., Chavis, J. S., & Corbett, C. L., (2019). A survey of deep learning methods for cyber security. *Information, 10*(4), 122.

10. Wang, W., Sheng, Y., Wang, J., Zeng, X., Ye, X., Huang, Y., & Zhu, M., (2017). HAST-IDS: Learning hierarchical spatial-temporal features using deep neural networks to improve intrusion detection. *IEEE Access, 6*, 1792–1806.

11. Kozik, R., Choraś, M., Ficco, M., & Palmieri, F., (2018). A scalable distributed machine learning approach for attack detection in edge computing environments. *Journal of Parallel and Distributed Computing, 119*, 18–26.

12. Amanullah, M. A., Habeeb, R. A. A., Nasaruddin, F. H., Gani, A., Ahmed, E., Nainar, A. S. M., & Imran, M., (2020). Deep learning and big data technologies for IoT security. *Computer Communications.*

13. Karagiannis, V., Chatzimisios, P., Vazquez-Gallego, F., & Alonso-Zarate, J., (2015). A survey on application layer protocols for the internet of things. *Transaction on IoT and Cloud Computing, 3*(1), 11–17.

14. Ahmed, M., Mahmood, A. N., & Hu, J., (2016). A survey of network anomaly detection techniques. *Journal of Network and Computer Applications, 60*, 19–31.

15. Nobakht, M., Sivaraman, V., & Boreli, R., (2016). A host-based intrusion detection and mitigation framework for smart home IoT using OpenFlow. In: *2016 11ᵗʰ International Conference on Availability, Reliability and Security (ARES)* (pp. 147–156). IEEE.

16. Saxe, J., & Berlin, K., (2015). Deep neural network-based malware detection using two dimensional binary program features. In: *2015 10ᵗʰ International Conference on Malicious and Unwanted Software (MALWARE)* (pp. 11–20). IEEE.

17. Ceron, J. M., Steding-Jessen, K., Hoepers, C., Granville, L. Z., & Margi, C. B., (2019). Improving IoT Botnet investigation using an adaptive network layer. *Sensors, 19*(3), 727.

18. Deogirikar, J., & Vidhate, A., (2017). Security attacks in IoT: A survey. In: *2017 International Conference on I-SMAC (IoT in Social, Mobile, Analytics and Cloud) (I-SMAC)* (pp. 32–37). IEEE.

19. Kolias, C., Kambourakis, G., Stavrou, A., & Voas, J., (2017). DDoS in the IoT: Mirai and other botnets. *Computer, 50*(7), 80–84.

20. Andrea, I., Chrysostomou, C., & Hadjichristofi, G., (2015). Internet of Things: Security vulnerabilities and challenges. In: *2015 IEEE Symposium on Computers and Communication (ISCC)* (pp. 180–187). IEEE.

21. Vashi, S., Ram, J., Modi, J., Verma, S., & Prakash, C., (2017). Internet of things (IoT): A vision, architectural elements, and security issues. In: *2017 International Conference on I-SMAC (IoT in Social, Mobile, Analytics and Cloud) (I-SMAC)* (pp. 492–496). IEEE.

22. Hossain, M. M., Fotouhi, M., & Hasan, R., (2015). Towards an analysis of security issues, challenges, and open problems in the internet of things. In: *2015 IEEE World Congress on Services* (pp. 21–28). IEEE.

23. Barak, B., (2002). Constant-round coin-tossing with a man in the middle or realizing the shared random string model. In: *The 43ʳᵈ Annual IEEE Symposium on Foundations of Computer Science, 2002. Proceedings.* (pp. 345–355). IEEE.

24. Ramachandran, V., & Nandi, S., (2005). Detecting ARP spoofing: An active technique. In: *International Conference on Information Systems Security* (pp. 239–250). Springer, Berlin, Heidelberg.

25. Son, S., & Shmatikov, V., (2010). The hitchhiker's guide to DNS cache poisoning. In: *International Conference on Security and Privacy in Communication Systems* (pp. 466–483). Springer, Berlin, Heidelberg.

26. Sardana, A., & Joshi, R., (2009). An auto-responsive honeypot architecture for dynamic resource allocation and QoS adaptation in DDoS attacked networks. *Computer Communications, 32*(12), 1384–1399.

27. Douligeris, C., & Mitrokotsa, A., (2004). DDoS attacks and defense mechanisms: Classification and state-of-the-art. *Computer Networks, 44*(5), 643–666.

28. Bijalwan, A., Wazid, M., Pilli, E. S., & Joshi, R. C., (2015). Forensics of random-UDP flooding attacks. *Journal of Networks, 10*(5), 287.

29. Sonar, K., & Upadhyay, H., (2014). A survey: DDOS attack on Internet of Things. *International Journal of Engineering Research and Development, 10*(11), 58–63.

30. Beaumont-Gay, M., (2007). A comparison of SYN flood detection algorithms. In: *Second International Conference on Internet Monitoring and Protection (ICIMP 2007)* (pp. 1–6). IEEE.

31. Erickson, J., (2008). *Hacking: The Art of Exploitation.* No starch press.

32. Dantas, Y. G., Nigam, V., & Fonseca, I. E., (2014). A selective defense for application layer DDoS attacks. In: *2014 IEEE Joint Intelligence and Security Informatics Conference* (pp. 75–82). IEEE.

33. Kannhavong, B., Nakayama, H., Nemoto, Y., Kato, N., & Jamalipour, A., (2007). A survey of routing attacks in mobile ad hoc networks. *IEEE Wireless Communications, 14*(5), 85–91.

34. Krontiris, I., Dimitriou, T., Giannetsos, T., & Mpasoukos, M., (2007). Intrusion detection of sinkhole attacks in wireless sensor networks. In: *International Symposium on Algorithms and Experiments for Sensor Systems, Wireless Networks and Distributed Robotics* (pp. 150–161). Springer, Berlin, Heidelberg.

35. Eik, L. C., Yong, N. M., Leckie, C., & Palaniswami, M., (2006). Intrusion detection for routing attacks in sensor networks. *International Journal of Distributed Sensor Networks, 2*(4), 313–332.

36. Gruschka, N., & Jensen, M., (2010). Attack surfaces: A taxonomy for attacks on cloud services. In: *2010 IEEE 3rd International Conference on Cloud Computing* (pp. 276–279). IEEE.

37. Modi, C., Patel, D., Borisaniya, B., Patel, H., Patel, A., & Rajarajan, M., (2013). A survey of intrusion detection techniques in cloud. *Journal of Network and Computer Applications, 36*(1), 42–57.

38. Liu, J., Xiao, Y., & Chen, C. P., (2012). Authentication and access control in the internet of things. In: *2012 32nd International Conference on Distributed Computing Systems Workshops* (pp. 588–592). IEEE.

39. Chakrabarti, S., & Singhal, M., (2007). Password-based authentication: Preventing dictionary attacks. *Computer, 40*(6), 68–74.

40. Gajek, S., Jensen, M., Liao, L., & Schwenk, J., (2009). Analysis of signature wrapping attacks and countermeasures. In: *2009 IEEE International Conference on Web Services* (pp. 575–582). IEEE.

41. Kc, G. S., Keromytis, A. D., & Prevelakis, V., (2003). Countering code-injection attacks with instruction-set randomization. In: *Proceedings of the 10th ACM conference on Computer and Communications Security* (pp. 272–280).

42. Jim, T., Swamy, N., & Hicks, M., (2007). Defeating script injection attacks with browser-enforced embedded policies. In: *Proceedings of the 16ᵗʰ International Conference on World Wide Web* (pp. 601–610).

43. Kieyzun, A., Guo, P. J., Jayaraman, K., & Ernst, M. D., (2009). Automatic creation of SQL injection and cross-site scripting attacks. In: *2009 IEEE 31ˢᵗ International Conference on Software Engineering* (pp. 199–209). IEEE.

44. Raza, S., Wallgren, L., & Voigt, T., (2013). SVELTE: Real-time intrusion detection in the internet of things. *Ad. Hoc. Networks, 11*(8), 2661–2674.

45. Nash, D. C., Martin, T. L., Ha, D. S., & Hsiao, M. S., (2005). Towards an intrusion detection system for battery exhaustion attacks on mobile computing devices. In: *Third IEEE International Conference on Pervasive Computing and Communications Workshops* (pp. 141–145). IEEE.

46. Oh, D., Kim, D., & Ro, W. W., (2014). A malicious pattern detection engine for embedded security systems in the internet of things. *Sensors, 14*(12), 24188–24211.

47. Summerville, D. H., Zach, K. M., & Chen, Y., (2015). Ultra-lightweight deep packet anomaly detection for internet of things devices. In: *2015 IEEE 34ᵗʰ International Performance Computing and Communications Conference (IPCCC)* (pp. 1–8). IEEE.

48. OConnor, T., & Reeves, D., (2008). Bluetooth network-based misuse detection. In: *2008 Annual Computer Security Applications Conference (ACSAC)* (pp. 377–391). IEEE.

49. Haataja, K. M., (2008). New efficient intrusion detection and prevention system for Bluetooth networks. In: *Proceedings of the 1ˢᵗ International Conference on Mobile Wireless Middleware, Operating Systems, and Applications* (pp. 1–6).

50. Gautam, S. K., & Om, H., (2016). Computational neural network regression model for host-based intrusion detection system. *Perspectives in Science, 8*, 93–95.

51. Le, A., Loo, J., Chai, K. K., & Aiash, M., (2016). A specification-based IDS for detecting attacks on RPL-based network topology. *Information, 7*(2), 25.

52. Elrawy, M. F., Awad, A. I., & Hamed, H. F., (2018). Intrusion detection systems for IoT-based smart environments: A survey. *Journal of Cloud Computing, 7*(1), 21.

53. Arshad, J., Azad, M. A., Abdellatif, M. M., Rehman, M. H. U., & Salah, K., (2018). COLIDE: A collaborative intrusion detection framework for internet of things. *IET Networks, 8*(1), 3–14.

54. Deng, L., Li, D., Yao, X., Cox, D., & Wang, H., (2019). Mobile network intrusion detection for IoT system based on transfer learning algorithm. *Cluster Computing, 22*(4), 9889–9904.

55. Liu, L., Xu, B., Zhang, X., & Wu, X., (2018). An intrusion detection method for internet of things based on suppressed fuzzy clustering. *EURASIP Journal on Wireless Communications and Networking, 2018*(1), 113.

56. Arrington, B., Barnett, L., Rufus, R., & Esterline, A., (2016). Behavioral modeling intrusion detection system (BMIDS) using internet of things (IoT) behavior-based anomaly detection via immunity-inspired algorithms. In: *2016 25ᵗʰ International Conference on Computer Communication and Networks (ICCCN)* (pp. 1–6). IEEE.

57. Koroniotis, N., Moustafa, N., & Sitnikova, E., (2019). Forensics and deep learning mechanisms for botnets in Internet of Things: A survey of challenges and solutions. *IEEE Access, 7*, 61764–61785.

CHAPTER 4

Energy Efficiency and Resource Management in IoT

BHANU PRIYANKA VALLURI[1] and AMANDEEP SHARMA[2]

[1]*Research Scholar, Department of Electronics and Communication Engineering, Chandigarh University, Gharuan, Punjab–140413, India*

[2]*Associate Professor, Department of Electronics and Communication Engineering, Chandigarh University, Gharuan, Punjab–140413, India*

ABSTRACT

With a radical growth in population over the past few decades requires feasible, effective, and smart resolutions in all aspects. Recent studies say that all over energy sources are forced by the growth of 57% over the next 25 years. Internet of things (IoT) helps in providing modern and ubiquitous methods regarding the application. The energy demand for the IoT-based application is being increased both in requirements and needs. Effective energy management is considered as a primary criterion for the proving cost-efficient in complex energy and power modules in recent times.

IoT enables a diver's number of utilizations in various sectors. This chapter audits the current writing on the utilization of IoT in vitality frameworks, when all is said in done, and with regards to brilliant lattices especially. Moreover, we talk about empowering innovations of IoT, including distributed computing and various stages for information investigation. Besides, we audit difficulties of sending IoT in the vitality part like security, with certain answers for these difficulties, for example, blockchain innovation. This study gives vitality financial experts, and directors with a review of the job of IoT in the enhancement of vitality frameworks.

This part manages the vitality the executives, vitality strategy producers, vitality market analysts, vitality financial specialists, administrators with a review of the job of IoT in the improvement of vitality frameworks.

4.1 INTRODUCTION

4.1.1 CONCEPT

The IoT correlation computing device is a system of electromechanical devices provided with a UID (unique identifier) that enables the ability to transfer data from network to human or computer over the network without the need for human interaction. Is. Is it possible to define what the word "things" implies? Perhaps, "things" are simple or complex objects and are not directly connected to the Internet. However, they must be connected over the network.

The term IoT was coined in 1999 by Kevin Ashtonin. He edited the Internet cascade with the physical world to advance the isolation, security, and control of human life.

IoT has evolved as a result of the integration of several technologies such as sensors, ML, and embedded systems. It can also be considered as a network of things that communicate to the external environment by embedded technology. IoT mainly improves the human life-style in various aspects viz. healthcare, agriculture, and energy sector, etc. It can be enabled in real-time by facilitating automated decision making and tools to optimize such decisions. IoT has been commonly considered as a concept similar to smart home that support multiple ecosystems.

4.1.2 MOTIVATION

Global energy demand growth, industrial, and energy sector co-emissions have also increased proportionately and set a new record in 2018. At the same time, global warming has also increased. Genuine effect on the planet and human life. Other natural concerns, for example, nearby air contamination, deficiency of water assets for warm force age, and absence of petroleum derivative assets, increment the pressing requirement for progressively proficient utilization of vitality and the utilization of sustainable power sources. To improve vitality proficiency and increasingly ideal vitality the board, powerful investigation of continuous information assumes a significant job in the vitality supply chain.

Now, how is energy conservation related to IoT? In fact, a huge number of devices interact in IoT, and these devices are not powered. So, here the power factor has a significant importance in IoT. In fact, the application of IoT is widespread, so different levels of energy savings are required in

IoT-based systems to extend the life of different sensor nodes IoT uses a wide range of sensor and communication techniques to transmit and transmit real-time data, enabling faster computation and accurate decision-making. The information or data collected using Intelligent Algorithms helps us monitor energy consumption patterns, which helps us to use energy efficiently. To optimally manage energy, real-time data must be effectively analyzed [15].

The fuel supply chain consists of three main components viz. energy supply, energy conversion processes and finally management of energy demand [14] as demonstrated in Figure 4.1. Here, the authors present the implementation of IoT in the energy chain with a focus to demonstrate the contribution of IoT to energy management and RES enhancement [17]. Usage of big data acquisition and intelligent algorithms to analyze real-time data enables to monitor various devices and consumers at different time scales [19]. The application of IoT in various fields has been discussed by various authors [20–22]. Along with the widespread applications, it has several associated constraints and challenges also [23, 24, 27, 28].

Power technologies are a major contributor to clean energy development and energy improvement technologies. It provides a constant control of the efficient conversion and electrical energy. Here, power electronics converters enable to connect renewable energy sources to traditional power systems [17]. It unlocks the potential for energy savings in motor drives, buildings, transportation, and consumer electronics, etc.

4.2 INTERNET OF THINGS (IoT)

IoT utilizes the Internet and gadgets or "things" in order to give an assortment of administrations to general society. For instance, controlling the vitality utilization of structures in a savvy way can help diminish vitality costs [31–33]. IoT has been applied in a wide range of applications viz. social insurance frameworks, vitality the board in structures, and automaton [36].

When arranging an IoT application framework, IoT's segment determination, sensor gadgets, correspondence conventions, information stockpiling and calculation are proper for the proposed application. For instance, an IoT stage is made arrangements for controlling warming, cooling, and cooling (HVAC) in a structure, which requires related natural sensors and fitting correspondence innovation. Various segments of IoT are demonstrated in Figure 4.2 [38]. Different segments of IoT stages might be IoT gadgets as sensors, actuators, IoT passages, or any gadget associated with the pattern of information assortment, transmission, and handling. For instance, an IoT entryway gadget permits steering information to the IoT framework and sets up two-way correspondence among gadget and gateway.

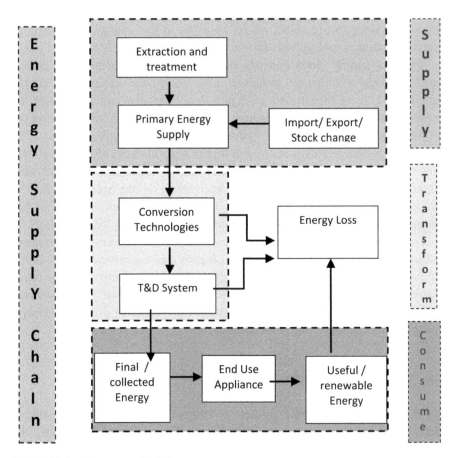

FIGURE 4.1   Energy supply chain.

The correspondence convention, the third segment of the IoT stage, permits different gadgets to impart and impart their information to controllers or choice focuses. IoT stages give the adaptability to pick the kind of correspondence innovations (each with explicit highlights) to suit the application prerequisites. Instances of these innovations incorporate [39] cell advancements, for example, 5G and LTE-4G systems [40]. Information stockpiling is the fourth piece of the IoT stage, which empowers information taking care of from sensors.

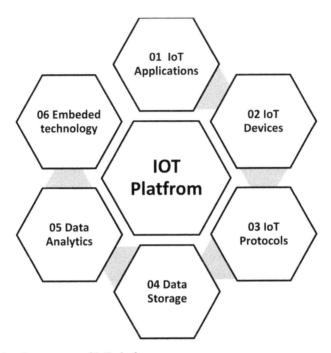

FIGURE 4.2   Components of IoT platform.

In principle, the information gathered from the hardware is huge. This requires arranging powerful information stockpiling on the cloud servers or on the edge of the IoT organization. Put away information utilized for scientific purposes shapes the fifth piece of IoT stages. Information Analytics should be possible disconnected once the information is put away, or it very well may be as constant examination. Information examination is performed to settle on choices about the activity of the application. Information investigation should be possible disconnected or ongoing relying upon need. In disconnected breaks down, put away information is first gathered and afterward envisioned nearby utilizing the representation instrument. On account of ongoing investigation, cloud or edge servers can be utilized to give perception, for example, Sector analysis [41].

4.3   UPCOMING/EMBEDDED TECHNOLOGY

IoT has objects and system components with sensors, actuators, and processors that communicate among themselves in order to confer meaningful services. Here, sensors are mainly used to collect data which is further processed and analyzed to make decision. The decision results in sending the corresponding command to the actuator. Here, the authors discuss sensors, actuators, communication technologies and data computing.

4.3.1   SENSOR DEVICE

Sensors aim to fetch real-time data, thus increasing the effectiveness and functionality of the system [42]. Several sensors are available for healthcare, environmental monitoring, and public safety, etc. [44]. In the energy sector, these sensors are deployed for fuel generation, transmission, and distribution so as to save cost and efforts. Sensors also enable to provide real-time energy optimization thus aiding energy load management [45]. Consequently, sensor devices significantly improve diagnosis, decision making, and integrated performance metrics, etc. Here, the authors illustrate some commonly used sensor devices:

1. **Temperature Sensors:** These enables to detect fluctuations in temperature of the system [46]. Temperature sensors enhance system performance when the temperature changes during normal operation and thus energy can be properly managed to save energy [42].
2. **Moisture Sensors:** These have widespread applications in the energy sector and are used to separate humidity and air humidity [17]. For instance, it can be used for wind power generation, particularly if the turbines are offshore. Moisture sensors are generally located near the bottom of the nacelle so as continuously monitor moisture.
3. **Light Sensors:** These are used to measure brightness in various scenarios. According to literature, lighting consumes 20% of electricity across the globe [49]. Hence, light sensors can be deployed to automate the brightness level to an ambient level that significantly conserves energy [19].
4. **Passive Infrared (PIR) Sensors:** These are used to detect the presence of humans in spaces. If motion is not detected in space, lights may be turned off, thus having smart control of the light thus reducing the electricity consumption [10]. It can also be applied for smart control of air conditioning systems in buildings [18].
5. **Proximity Sensors:** These detect the things in vicinity regardless of physical contact [11] and thus can be used to have reliable position sensing in wind turbines [12].

4.3.2 ACTUATOR

Actuators basically takes electrical signals from mechanization frameworks and uses the same to control gadgets and machines in IoT [13]. Actuators produce diverse movement designs, for example, straight, swaying, or rotational movement. Actuators dependent on vitality sources are named as follows [14].

Pneumatic actuators utilize packed air to deliver vibration. Pneumatic actuators are made of cylinder or stomachs to create excitation power. These actuators are utilized to control forms in light of the fact that these procedures do not require a lot of motivation vitality.

Pressure-driven actuators utilize liquid to deliver vibration. Water-driven actuators incorporate chambers or fluid engines that utilization pressure-driven capacity to give mechanical activity. Mechanical movement gives yield regarding straight and rotational movement, thus utilizing it in modern procedure control.

Warm actuators utilize a warmth source to deliver physical movement. Warm actuators convert warm vitality into active vitality or force. On the other hand, electric actuators are mechanical gadgets that can change overpower into motor vitality in a solitary straight or rotating movement. The models of these actuators rely upon the capacities planned in the methodology.

In power plants, valves are controlled through pneumatic actuators. Electric control-valve actuator innovation empowers vitality effectiveness. They are frequently utilized as a last control component in the activity of a force plant [15]. What is more, an assortment of actuators has been created for the fuel business, for instance, LINAK Electric Actuators (https://www.linak.com/business-territories/vitality/) to decrease vitality wastage when opening a bring forth. Model and slowing down on wind turbines and creating movement in sun-based following boards. There are additionally a few investigations in writing planned for portraying the uses of actuators in IoT [15]. By advancing the activity of gear and apparatus in IoT, the proposed framework accomplishes a decrease in their all-out vitality utilization over some undefined time frame.

4.3.3 COMMUNICATION TECHNOLOGY

Remote correspondence frameworks assume a key job in enacting IoT. Remote frameworks associate sensor gadgets to the IoT entryway and convey start to finish information between these components of IoT. Remote frameworks are created dependent on various remote gauges, and each relies upon the application necessities, for example, correspondence range, transmission capacity, and force utilization prerequisites. For instance, sustainable power sources, including wind and sun-based force plants, are situated in remote zones. Hence, it is trying to guarantee dependable IoT correspondence in remote regions. Utilizing IoT frameworks on these locales requires choosing proper correspondence innovation that can ensure a constant association connection and bolster continuous information move in a vitality proficient way. Given the significance of correspondence advancements in IoT, in this subsection we will survey a portion of these advances. We likewise propose a few guides to show their job in the vitality division. At that point, we give an examination in Table 4.1 to show the distinction of every strategy.

Short-go remote innovation for IoT applications in the vitality area, e.g., remote unwavering quality (Wi-Fi) (https://www.wi-fi.org/) has been generally considered. In the vitality division, the clearest situations where Wi-Fi is utilized is to manufacture vitality metering and vitality the executives [17–21]. Be that as it may, because of the powerful necessities of Wi-Fi. Low power wide area network (LPWAN) specialized strategies, Emerging LPWAN procedures [12], for example, Sigfox, Lora, and LTE-M that work in unlicensed groups [12] are acceptable arrangements utilized in the vitality segment. This is on the grounds that these rising LPWAN advances empower the establishment of dependable, minimal effort, low-power, long-go, last-mile innovation for savvy vitality the executives' arrangements [13]. In this way, in this chapter, we portray short-run and rising LPWAN strategies and survey a few instances of their applied cases in the vitality field. We additionally depict satellite innovation that assumes a significant job in giving worldwide IoT availability to modern zones situated in remote regions. Besides, highlights of these technologies is presented in Table 4.1.

Bluetooth (BLE) is a short-range remote correspondence innovation that permits information transmission utilizing shorter radio frequencies. BLE is affordable to convey with a particular scope of 0 to 30 meters, empowering a quicker close to home field arrangement [54]. BLE targets little scope IoT applications that expect gadgets to transmit little forms of low-power infor-mation. Vitality part businesses with a very much structured IoT procedure can utilize this innovation for various types of correspondences. BLE is broadly utilized in vitality use in the vitality division, private, and business structures. For instance, the creators depict a keen office vitality the board framework, which diminishes the force utilization of PCs, screens, and lights utilizing BLE. Another investigation proposes a vitality the board framework for brilliant homes that utilization BLE for correspondence between family unit apparatuses with the objective of lessening vitality in homes [7]. Similarly, a fluff-based answer for keen vitality the board has been presented in home computerization, utilizing BLE research planned for improving home vitality the executives arranging.

TABLE 4.1 Features of Various Wireless Technologies

Technology Parameters	Range (km)	Power Usage	Security	Data Rate	Application
NB-IoT	50	High	High	100 kbps	Smart grid
LoRa	50	Very low	High	0.3–38.4 kbps	Smart buildings
Sigfox	50	Low	High	100 bps	Smart buildings
LTE-M	200	Low	High	0.2–1 mbps	Smart meter
Bluetooth	50	Low	High	1 mbps	Home automation
Weightless	<5	Low	High	100 kbps	Smart meters
Satellite	>1,500	High	High	100 kbps	Renewable energy plants
Zigbee	<100	Very low	Low	250 kbps	Renewable energies metering

ZigBee is a correspondence innovation intended to assemble singular territory systems and target little scope applications. ZigBee is intended to be easy to actualize and give an exceptionally solid system to ease, low-information rates and low-power applications [18, 19]. The ZigBee Mesh likewise utilizes organize detail, where gadgets are associated with various interconnects. Utilizing ZigBee's cross-section organizing highlight, the most extreme correspondence scope of up to 100 meters is significantly improved. In the vitality division, ZigBee's IoT applications incorporate lighting (building and road lighting), savvy matrices, e.g., keen electric meters, home mechanization frameworks, and modern robotization. The reason for these applications is to give a component to vitality use in an effective way. In writing, research in Ref. [20] assesses the exhibition of a home vitality the board application by introducing remote sensor systems utilizing ZigBee, with the point of diminishing customer vitality costs. The creators likewise acquaint keen home interfaces with all the more productively separate between ZigBee gadgets, electrical gadgets, and shrewd meters gives a ZigBee-based observing framework that is utilized to quantify and move the intensity of family unit apparatuses to outlets and lights, with the point of diminishing work power utilization. Another investigation [13] gives field tests utilizing ZigBee advances for photovoltaic observing.

Long haul advancement for machine-type correspondences (LTE-M) normalization, intended to diminish the multifaceted nature of gadgets for machine-type correspondence (MTC) [14]. LTE-M bolsters secure correspondence, gives general inclusion, and gives high framework effectiveness. LTE-M additionally offers enhanced throughput and lower inactivity [15]. Likewise, this innovation gives vitality productive asset designation to little power gadgets, making it a suitable answer for brilliant meters [16] and keen lattice interchanges [17].

Weightless LPWAN is an open remote norm (http://www.weightless.org/) created to build up correspondence between an enormous number of devices. [18]. In view of the examinations in Weightless is a fitting remote innovation that can be utilized for keen metering and savvy matrix correspondence in shrewd home IoT applications. Satellite is another similar correspondence strategy that has wide zone inclusion and can bolster low information [18]. It is appropriate for IoT gadgets and machines. The examination in Ref. [19] establishes satellite correspondence as an appropriate choice to shrewd lattices, particularly in the domain of transmission and dissemination (T&D). A comparable report features the significance of utilizing satellite-based IoT correspondence in vitality fields, for example, sun-based and wind power plants [21].

4.3.4   IoT DATA AND COMPUTING

Processing and dissecting the information produced by IoT assists with increasing further bits of knowledge, exact input of the framework and fitting choices about the vitality utilization of the framework [99]. Be that as it may, IoT information calculation is a difficult issue. This is on the grounds that IoT information, otherwise called enormous information, alludes to countless organized and unstructured information, got from different parts of the IoT framework, for example, sensors, programming applications, keen or smart gadgets and correspondence systems. Because of the attributes of Big Data, which is huge volume, rapid, and high inconstancy [10], it should be prepared and investigated successfully [11]. Preparing Big Data is past the abilities of conventional techniques, for example, putting away, processing, and investigating information on nearby hard drives. Complex processing and expository methods are expected to deal with Big Data [12, 13]. In the accompanying, we depict distributed computing and haze registering, which are broadly utilized for handling and figuring enormous information.

4.3.5 CLOUD COMPUTING

Distributed computing is an information handling framework that offers types of assistance, applications, stockpiling, and figuring over the Internet and permits processing information to be transmitted from an IoT gadget. In distributed computing, the cloud speaks to the "Web" and registering alludes to the figuring and handling administrations gave by this methodology. Distributed computing comprises of two application administrations got to by means of the Internet and equipment frameworks, situated in server farms [15]. Utilizing these highlights, distributed computing permits the handling of huge information and gives complex figuring capacities [16]. The principal reason for utilizing cloud frameworks [17] is to (i) altogether diminish equipment costs; (ii) to build registering force and capacity limit; and (iii) those with multi-center engineering that encourage information the board. Moreover, distributed computing is a safe framework that gives the fundamental assets, figuring force and capacity from a geographic area [18]. These highlights of distributed computing take into consideration simple examination, control, and effective arranging of huge information coming about because of the developing utilization of IoT [19]. What is more, distributed computing disposes of the expenses of buying equipment and programming and executing calculations to process IoT information, bringing about insignificant utilization of nearby information figuring power.

4.3.6 FOG COMPUTING

In spite of the fact that distributed computing is the best figuring model for information handling for IoT applications. Because of the postponement and transmission capacity breaking point of brought together assets utilized for information handling, increasingly proficient techniques are required. Mist Computing is a dispersed model and expansion of the cloud, moving processing and examination administrations to the edge of the system. Haze tallying amplifies the cloud and can bolster a bigger outstanding task at hand [10]. In haze registering, any gadget with figuring, stockpiling, and system association capacities goes about as a mist hub. Instances of these gadgets are not constrained to PCs, mechanical controllers, switches, switches, and implanted servers. In this registering model, Fog gives IoT information preparing and capacity on IoT gadgets locally as opposed to sending it to the cloud. The upsides of this methodology incorporate numerous IoT applications and secure administrations expected to lessen organize traffic and inactivity [12]. In this manner, dissimilar to distributed computing, mist furnishes handling and figuring administrations with high security and quick reaction. This permits quicker dynamic and fitting activity.

4.4   ROLE OF IoT IN THE ENERGY SECTOR

Nowadays, the world is intensely reliant on petroleum derivatives, which represent 80% of the world's last vitality. Air contamination because of unnecessary extraction and burning of non-renewable energy sources can have unfriendly ecological, wellbeing, and monetary effects and changes to a few. Vitality productivity, that is, low vitality utilization and sustainable power source assets to offer equivalent assistance are the two primary choices to lessen the negative impacts of using petroleum derivatives [12].

In this area, we discuss the role of IoT in the vitality segment ranging from extraction to end utilization of vitality. Assumes a significant job in CO_2 emanations. A vitality the executives framework dependent on IoT can screen ongoing vitality utilization and increment the degree of mindfulness on vitality execution at any degree of the flexibly chain [13, 15]. This segment initially talks about the utilization of IoT in vitality age stages. At that point, we will proceed with the idea of brilliant urban areas, for example, shrewd networks, keen structures, savvy processing plants and clever vehicle. Next, we will talk about every one of the above independently. At long last, we sum up the consequences of this segment in Tables 4.2 and 4.3.

4.4.1   IoT AND VITALITY AGE

Computerized forms and administrative control and information procurement frameworks got mainstream in modern regions during the 1990s. By checking and controlling hardware and procedures, the beginning phases of IoT start to add to the force segment by diminishing creation or power outage misfortune. The significant difficulties are the dependability, effectiveness, natural effect, and upkeep issues of more established force plants. Age in the force part and helpless inconveniences of hardware support can prompt elevated levels of vitality misfortune and unsteadiness. Resources are now and then more than 40 years of age, over the top expensive and not effectively replaceable. IoT adds to lessening these difficulties in the administration of intensity plants [37]. By introducing IoT sensors, Internet-associated gadgets can identify any disappointment in activity or an unusual decrease in vitality proficiency, requiring support. This diminishes working expenses and builds the dependability and effectiveness of the framework [14, 15]. According to the report, the new IoT-based force plant could spare $230 million over the lifetime and $50 million if a similar size plant were outfitted with the IoT stage.

TABLE 4.2 Role of IoT in Energy Sector-1

	Applications	Sector	Description
Regulation and market	Energy democratization prosumers	Regulation	Access to the grid for end users.
		Energy market	Generation of a group of end-users
Energy supply	Preventive measures	Gas and oil industry	Fault monitoring through data analysis obtained from various sensors.
	Fault maintenance		Identifying problems in energy networks.
	Energy storage and analytics	Industrial suppliers	Analysis of market data
	Digitalized power generation	Utility companies	Analysis of big data to control generation units along various time scales.

To decrease petroleum product utilization and depend on nearby vitality sources, numerous nations are advancing RES. Atmosphere based or variable sustainable power source (VRE) assets, for example, wind, and sun powered vitality, present new difficulties to the vitality framework known as the "irregular test." In VRE's high-vitality framework, vitality coordinating is a significant generational test because of variety in flexibly and request, bringing about irregular characteristics at various time scales. IoT frameworks give adaptability in their capacity to adjust request, consequently diminishing the difficulties of executing VRE, bringing about higher joining of clean vitality and lower GHG discharges [16]. Moreover, by utilizing IoT, vitality can be utilized all the more effectively utilizing AI calculations that help decide the ideal equalization of various gracefully and request advancements [37]. For instance, the utilization of man-made consciousness calculations can adjust the warm force plant's capacity yield with inside force age sources, for example, incorporating a few little sun-oriented PV boards [17].

Table 4.3 sums up the uses of IoT in the vitality area, from vitality flexibly guideline and markets.

TABLE 4.3   Role of IoT in Energy Sector-2

Applications		Description
Transmission and distribution (T&D) grid	Smart grids	A platform to handle grid using ICT technologies.
	Network management	Uses big data to optimally manage the grid
	Integrated control of electric vehicle fleet (EV)	Analysis of charging stations and EVs.
	Control and management of vehicle to grid (V2G)	Analysis of EVs to support the grid.
	Microgrids	Helps to manage the grid.
	Control and management of the district heating (DH) network	Analysis of various parameters of network and consumers
Demand-side	Demand response	Central control
	Advanced metering infrastructure	Uses sensors to analyze the load in a consumer site
	Battery level management	Data analytics to manage battery

4.4.2   SMART CITY

Urbanization and increasing development rates nowadays have prompted numerous worldwide concerns, for example, air and water contamination [18], vitality get to and ecological concerns. Along this course, giving perfect, modest, and dependable vitality sources to urban areas is one of the fundamental difficulties. Late advancements in computerized innovations have given a main impetus to actualizing brilliant, IoT-based answers for current issues in the keen city setting [19]. In the city brilliant manufacturing plants, savvy homes, power plants, and ranches can be associated and gather information about their vitality utilization at various hours of the day. On the off chance that a segment, e.g., a local location, is found to devour more vitality toward the evening, naturally dedicate vitality to different units, e.g., processing plants, at a lower cost and danger of clog of the whole framework [20]. IoT helps to screen each thing in the city. Sensors can be associated with structures, urban foundation, transportation, vitality systems and utilities. These associations can guarantee a vitality productive keen city by continually checking the information. Also, specialists may use the data gathered and settle on progressively educated choices.

4.4.3 SMART GRID

Savvy networks are current frameworks that utilization the most reliable ICT to manage and streamline vitality creation and end-use. Smart Grid builds up a multi-faceted progression of data by incorporating different brilliant meters that can be utilized for ideal administration of the framework and proficient force appropriation [21]. The utilization of brilliant frameworks can be separately presented to different sub-fields of the vitality framework, for example, vitality creation, structures, or transport, or they can be considered in general.

In a customary lattice, the batteries are energized by connectors through an electric link and an AC/DC inverter and can be remotely charged to the shrewd lattice utilizing inductive charging innovation. Furthermore, on the savvy network, end-clients' vitality request examples can be examined by gathering information through the IoT stage, for instance, the charging time of cell phones or electric vehicles. At that point, the closest remote battery charge station rightly allots time and charge the gadget. Additionally, IoT empowers better control and checking of battery-fueled gadgets and thus force dispersion can be balanced. This fundamentally diminishes pointless vitality utilization.

Also, IoT can be actualized in separation and microgrid for certain islands or associations, particularly in each force database required no matter what. In such frameworks, all advantages associated with the matrix collaborate with one another. Additionally, information on the vitality request of any property is accessible. This collaboration can help guarantee the correct treatment of vitality dispersion when and where it is required. As far as the helpful viability of the brilliant matrix, in a shrewd city with an IoT-based savvy network, various segments of the city can be interconnected.

During synergistic correspondence between various territories, Smart Grid cautions administrators through savvy gadgets before any issues happen. For instance, nonstop checking can decide if vitality request surpasses network limit. Accordingly, by acquiring constant information, administrators can embrace various techniques and re-plan vitality utilization at an alternate time when there is less interest. In certain regions, brilliant (or dynamic) value taxes at variable fuel costs have been considered in such a manner. Constant evaluating (RTP) levies just as vitality costs are high when vitality utilization is high. Through information gathered from savvy lattice parts, vitality utilization and creation can be completely streamlined and overseen through foreknowledge systems. Diminishing transmission misfortunes in T&D systems through dynamic voltage the executives or lessening non-specialized misfortunes utilizing a shrewd meter arrange are different instances of actualizing IoT [37].

4.5   ISSUES AND CHALLENGES

Other than all the advantages of IoT for vitality sparing, conveying IoT in the vitality area speaks to moves that should be tended to. This segment tends to the difficulties and existing answers for applying IoT-based vitality frameworks.

4.5.1   *ENERGY CONSUMPTION*

In vitality frameworks, the significant undertaking of IoT stages is vitality sparing. In power frameworks, an enormous number of IoT gadgets transmit information to empower correspondence utilizing IoT. A lot of vitality is required to run the IoT framework and transmit huge vitality created from IoT gadgets [28]. In this manner, vitality utilization of IoT frameworks stays a significant test. Be that as it may, different techniques have been endeavored to decrease the force utilization of the IoT framework. For instance, by setting the sensor to rest mode and go about varying. The structure of effective correspondence conventions that permit conveyed processing strategies to empower vitality productive correspondence has been abundantly examined. Applying radio advancement strategies, for example, balance streamlining and helpful correspondence is viewed as an answer. Also, the utilization of vitality proficient directing procedures, for example, group design and multi-way steering strategies is comprehended as another arrangement [37].

IoT's integration with the subsystem, one of the main challenges is integrating the IoT system into energy system subsystems. This is because energy sector subsystems are specialized in using various devices [32–34]. Here, one approach to find solutions regarding integration challenge concerns is modeling of integrated framework considering the IoT requirements of the subsystem [32, 35, 36].

4.5.2   *USER PRIVACY*

Security alludes to one side of individual or agreeable vitality clients to keep up the classification of their own data when imparted to an organization [37, 38].

Consequently, access to proper information, for example, the number and kinds of vitality use gadgets alongside the quantity of vitality clients, gets incomprehensible. Truth be told, this kind of information can be gathered utilizing IoT, empowering better dynamic that influences vitality creation, dispersion, and utilization [39]. In any case, so as to limit purchaser protection infringement, it is suggested that vitality suppliers approach the shopper for authorization to utilize their data [40], guaranteeing that buyer data is not imparted to different gatherings. Another arrangement is the confided in security the executive's framework, where power clients have command over their data and propose protection.

4.5.3 SECURITY CHALLENGE

Integration of IoT and communication technologies escalates the threat to energy systems and cyber-attacks [42] posing as a new security challenge [44]. Moreover, IoT-based power systems span across large geographical areas and hence pose a larger risk of its impact. In order to address this challenge, encryption-based scheme may be employed [45]. Also, distributed control systems have been suggested to mitigate the risk of cyber-attacks [46].

4.5.4 IoT STANDARDS

IoT uses different devices with different technologies to connect a large number of devices from one device. Compatibility between IoT devices using different criteria is a new challenge [37]. Challenges in adopting standards in IoT include standards for dealing with structured data, privacy, and security issues apart from regulatory standards for data markets [38]. This can be addressed by defining a common system to integrate all systems. Another alternative focuses on developing open information models and standards protocols leading to publicly available standards [39].

4.5.5 ARCHITECTURAL DESIGN

IoT-enabled contains a huge variety of technologies ranging from smart interconnected devices to sensors. Resultantly, IoT systems are complex, decentralized, and designed by mobile features based on their application goals [39]. Considering the features and requirements of an IoT application, it may not only be addressed by creating a reference architecture. Hence, it necessitates different reference architectures which are open and adhere to the open standards [39, 40].

4.6 FUTURE TRENDS

Implementation of IoT systems has given several benefits as discussed in the previous sections. However, in order to improve the performance of IoT, new solutions and trends are needed as in subsections.

4.6.1 *BLOCKCHAIN AND IoT*

Existing IoT systems rely on centralized systems [41, 42] that integrates thousands of devices, thus making it difficult to synchronize the nodes. Additionally, if the server goes down, all connected things may be easily compromised in terms of security [42]. Fortunately, blockchain can be used as a promising solution to this challenge [44].

Blockchain provides a decentralized platform that does not require any third-party intervention [15–17]. In blockchain technology, the information is distributed among various participating nodes and hence IoT devices can be synced. Moreover, consensus algorithms of blockchain provides a secure database for peer-to-peer networks [43]. Software updates can also be shared among chained objects. Thus, IoT-based platforms can be easily provided with update availability and blockchain [46]. Blockchain may further boost the effectiveness of the energy sector as it provides a decentralized platform for power generation, storage, and distribution. Another advantage is that blockchain allows energy distribution by remotely controlling the energy flow in an area in response to usage statistics of an area [44]. Hence, blockchain technology can be efficiently employed towards conservation of energy [40].

4.6.2 *GREEN IoT*

The vitality utilization of IoT gadgets is a significant test, particularly in enormous scope sending of these advances in not-so-distant future. To control these gadgets, a noteworthy measure of vitality is required. Moreover, the huge number of IoT gadgets generates a plethora of electronic waste [41] thus requiring a low-carbon and proficient correspondence systems so as to maintain ecological balance, thus prompting towards green IoT (G-IoT) [42]. The key part of G-IoT is its vitality effective qualities for the duration of the existence cycle, i.e., plan, creation, sending, and at last removal [29].

G-IoT cycle can be applied in various IoT advancements. For instance, in radio recurrence recognizable proof (RFID) labels. To control the measure of material in each RFID tag, the size of RFID labels may be reduced [51, 54–58]. Green M2M interchanges is another model, which empowers changing force transmission at the base level, encourages increasingly proficient correspondence conventions utilizing algorithmic and dispersed figuring strategies [29]. In remote sensor organizes additionally the sensors hubs can be in the rest mode and simply work when fundamental. Also, radio improvement procedures, for example, balance advancement or helpful correspondence can be applied to decrease the force utilization of the hubs. In addition, vitality proficient steering strategies, for example, bunch structures or multi-way directing can give effective arrangements [30, 31]. Taking everything into account, the previously mentioned approaches and models can decrease the vitality needs of IoT frameworks.

4.7 CONCLUSIONS

Energy system is going towards a new transformation. In this direction, technological advancements in IoT can help to transform the energy sector. Here, authors present the scope of IoT in the energy sector in the context of smart grids. Employment of IoT in energy sector ensures to have optimized energy efficiency. The chapter also briefly discusses various technologies, sensors, and other components of IoT system. Cloud computing and data analytics platforms is also presented that enables to efficiently manage various applications in the energy sector. The chapter also discusses associated challenges such as big data management, lack of connectivity standards, and security and privacy issues, etc. Finally, the authors have highlighted some solutions to the challenges in terms of blockchain and G-IoT.

KEYWORDS

- **energy building**
- **energy management**
- **energy storage**
- **internet of things**
- **IoT applications**
- **resource management**
- **smart energy**

REFERENCES

1. Stearns, P. N., (2011). In: Jeff, H., Leonard, R. N., & Merritt, R. S., (eds.), *Reconceptualizing the Industrial Revolution* (p. 362). (Cambridge, Mass., The MIT Press, 2010). $24.00.
2. Mokyr, J., (1998). *The Second Industrial Revolution, 1870–1914*. Storia Dell'economia Mondiale, 21945.
3. Hossein, M. N., Mohammadrezaei, M., Hunt, J., & Zakeri, B., (2020). Internet of things (IoT) and the energy sector. *Energies, 13*(2), 494.
4. Tortorella, G. L., & Fettermann, D., (2018). Implementation of industry 4.0 and lean production in Brazilian manufacturing companies. *International Journal of Production Research, 56*(8), 2975–2987.
5. Witchalls, C., & Chambers, J., (2013). *The Internet of Things Business Index: A Quiet Revolution Gathers Pace*. The economist intelligence unit. Retrieved from http://www.economistinsights.com/analysis/internet-things-business-index15 (accessed on 10 November 2021).
6. Datta, S. K., & Bonnet, C., (2018). MEC and IoT based automatic agent reconfiguration in industry 4.0. In: *2018 IEEE International Conference on Advanced Networks and Telecommunications Systems (ANTS)* (pp. 1–5). IEEE.
7. Shrouf, F., Ordieres, J., & Miragliotta, G., (2014). Smart factories in industry 4.0: A review of the concept and of energy management approached in production based on the internet of things paradigm. In: *2014 IEEE International Conference on Industrial Engineering and Engineering Management* (pp. 697–701). IEEE.
8. Bandyopadhyay, D., & Sen, J., (2011). Internet of things: Applications and challenges in technology and standardization. *Wireless Personal Communications, 58*(1), 49–69.
9. Energy, G., (2019). CO_2 *Status Report*. IEA (International Energy Agency): Paris, France.
10. OF, I. G. W., (2018). 1.5 C| Summary for policymakers. *Intergovernmental Panel of Climate Change*.
11. Zakeri, B., Syri, S., & Rinne, S., (2015). Higher renewable energy integration into the existing energy system of Finland–Is there any maximum limit?. *Energy, 92*, 244–259.
12. Grubler, A., Wilson, C., Bento, N., Boza-Kiss, B., Krey, V., McCollum, D. L., & Cullen, J., (2018). A low energy demand scenario for meeting the 1.5 C target and sustainable

development goals without negative emission technologies. *Nature Energy, 3*(6), 515–527.

13. Tan, Y. S., Ng, Y. T., & Low, J. S. C., (2017). Internet-of-things enabled real-time monitoring of energy efficiency on manufacturing shop floors. *Procedia CIRP, 61*, 376–381.

14. Belyi, A. V., (2011). Energy economics: Concepts, issues, markets, and governance by SC Bhattacharya-book Review. *Oil, Gas and Energy Law, 9*(6).

15. Tamilselvan, K., & Thangaraj, P., (2020). Pods–A novel intelligent energy-efficient and dynamic frequency scalings for multi-core embedded architectures in an IoT environment. *Microprocessors and Microsystems, 72*, 102907.

16. Zhou, K., Yang, S., & Shao, Z., (2016). Energy internet: The business perspective. *Applied Energy, 178*, 212–222.

17. Motlagh, N. H., Khajavi, S. H., Jaribion, A., & Holmstrom, J., (2018). An IoT-based automation system for older homes: A use case for lighting system. In: *2018 IEEE 11ᵗʰ Conference on Service-Oriented Computing and Applications (SOCA)* (pp. 1–6). IEEE.

18. Da Xu, L., He, W., & Li, S., (2014). Internet of things in industries: A survey. *IEEE Transactions on Industrial Informatics, 10*(4), 2233–2243.

19. Talari, S., Shafie-Khah, M., Siano, P., Loia, V., Tommasetti, A., & Catalão, J. P., (2017). A review of smart cities based on the internet of things concept. *Energies, 10*(4), 421.

20. Ibarra-Esquer, J. E., González-Navarro, F. F., Flores-Rios, B. L., Burtseva, L., & Astorga-Vargas, M. A., (2017). Tracking the evolution of the internet of things concept across different application domains. *Sensors, 17*(6), 1379.

21. Swan, M., (2012). Sensor mania! the internet of things, wearable computing, objective metrics, and the quantified self 2.0. *Journal of Sensor and Actuator Networks, 1*(3), 217–253.

22. Gupta, A., & Jha, R. K., (2015). A survey of 5G network: Architecture and emerging technologies. *IEEE Access, 3*, 1206–1232.

23. Stojkoska, B. L. R., & Trivodaliev, K. V., (2017). A review of Internet of Things for smart home: Challenges and solutions. *Journal of Cleaner Production, 140*, 1454–1464.

24. Hui, H., Ding, Y., Shi, Q., Li, F., Song, Y., & Yan, J., (2020). 5G network-based internet of things for demand response in smart grid: A survey on application potential. *Applied Energy, 257*, 113972.

25. Luo, X. G., Zhang, H. B., Zhang, Z. L., Yu, Y., & Li, K., (2019). A new framework of intelligent public transportation system based on the internet of things. *IEEE Access, 7*, 55290–55304.

26. Khatua, P. K., Ramachandaramurthy, V. K., Kasinathan, P., Yong, J. Y., Pasupuleti, J., & Rajagopalan, A., (2020). Application and assessment of internet of things toward the sustainability of energy systems: Challenges and issues. *Sustainable Cities and Society, 53*, 101957.

27. Haseeb, K., Almogren, A., Islam, N., Ud Din, I., & Jan, Z., (2019). An energy-efficient and secure routing protocol for intrusion avoidance in IoT-based WSN. *Energies, 12*(21), 4174.

28. Zouinkhi, A., Ayadi, H., Val, T., Boussaid, B., & Abdelkrim, M. N., (2020). Auto-management of energy in IoT networks. *International Journal of Communication Systems, 33*(1), e4168.

29. Gazis, V., (2016). A survey of standards for machine-to-machine and the internet of things. *IEEE Communications Surveys and Tutorials, 19*(1), 482–511.

30. Atzori, L., Iera, A., & Morabito, G., (2010). The internet of things: A survey. *Computer Networks, 54*(15), 2787–2805.

31. Hui, T. K., Sherratt, R. S., & Sánchez, D. D., (2017). Major requirements for building smart homes in smart cities based on internet of things technologies. *Future Generation Computer Systems, 76*, 358–369.

32. Evans, D., (2011). The internet of things: How the next evolution of the internet is changing everything. *CISCO White Paper, 1*(2011), 1–11.

33. Motlagh, N. H., Bagaa, M., & Taleb, T., (2019). Energy and delay aware task assignment mechanism for UAV-based IoT platform. *IEEE Internet of Things Journal, 6*(4), 6523–6536.

34. Ramamurthy, A., & Jain, P., (2017). *The Internet of Things in the Power Sector: Opportunities in Asia and the Pacific* (Vol. 1, No. 48).

35. Jia, M., Komeily, A., Wang, Y., & Srinivasan, R. S., (2019). Adopting internet of things for the development of smart buildings: A review of enabling technologies and applications. *Automation in Construction, 101*, 111–126.

36. Karunarathne, G. R., Kulawansa, K. T., & Firdhous, M. M., (2018). Wireless communication technologies in internet of things: A critical evaluation. In: *2018 International Conference on Intelligent and Innovative Computing Applications (ICONIC)* (pp. 1–5). IEEE.

37. Burhan, M., Rehman, R. A., Khan, B., & Kim, B. S., (2018). IoT elements, layered architectures and security issues: A comprehensive survey. *Sensors, 18*(9), 2796.

38. Ala-Laurinaho, R., Autiosalo, J., & Tammi, K., (2020). Open Sensor Manager for IIoT. *Journal of Sensor and Actuator Networks, 9*(2), 30.

39. Kelly, S. D. T., Suryadevara, N. K., & Mukhopadhyay, S. C., (2013). Towards the implementation of IoT for environmental condition monitoring in homes. *IEEE Sensors Journal, 13*(10), 3846–3853.

40. Rault, T., Bouabdallah, A., & Challal, Y., (2014). Energy efficiency in wireless sensor networks: A top-down survey. *Computer Networks, 67*, 104–122.

41. Di Francia, G., (2017). The development of sensor applications in the sectors of energy and environment in Italy, 1976–2015. *Sensors, 17*(4), 793.

42. Pérez-Lombard, L., Ortiz, J., & Pout, C., (2008). A review on buildings energy consumption information. *Energy and Buildings, 40*(3), 394–398.

43. Blanco, J., García, A., & Morenas, J. D. L., (2018). Design and implementation of a wireless sensor and actuator network to support the intelligent control of efficient energy usage. *Sensors, 18*(6), 1892.

44. Riyanto, I., Margatama, L., Hakim, H., & Hindarto, D. E., (2018). Motion sensor application on building lighting installation for energy saving and carbon reduction joint crediting mechanism. *Applied System Innovation, 1*(3), 23.

45. Kim, W., Mechitov, K., Choi, J. Y., & Ham, S., (2005). On target tracking with binary proximity sensors. In: *IPSN 2005. Fourth International Symposium on Information Processing in Sensor Networks, 2005* (pp. 301–308). IEEE.

46. Buur, J., & Andreasen, M. M., (1989). Design models in mechatronic product development. *Design Studies, 10*(3), 155–162

47. Nesbitt, B., (2011). *Handbook of Valves and Actuators: Valves Manual International*. Elsevier.

PART II
IoT Applications

CHAPTER 5

Smart Agriculture Using IoT: A Survey

GAGANPREET KAUR[1] and BHANU PRIYANKA VALLURI[2]

[1]*Department of Computer Science and Engineering,*
Chandīgarh University, Punjab, India, E-mail: ghuliani04@gmail.com

[2]*Research Scholar, Department of Electronics Communication and*
Engineering, Chandīgarh University, Punjab, India,
E-mail: bhanu.priyanka1904@gmail.com

ABSTRACT

World population is increasing rapidly. Providing necessities to people in any country has become a challenging role to all developing and developed nations. The agricultural sector plays a prominent role in any country's economy. Research and development in this sector boost the development of the country. In recent times, the internet of things (IoT) has been used in the field of communication to transform things or objects into smart devices to perform specific tasks by reducing human interference or effects. Farming also needs to be smart. In this chapter, Firstly, the challenges faced by the farmers are discussed. Secondly, the benefits of smart agriculture using IoT-based techniques to improve crop yield, productivity, and to monitor and analyze the crops in many aspects such as weather forecast, Soil investigation, irrigation necessities, resource management, and disease prediction, etc., are described. Thirdly, this chapter throws light on emerging IoT tools, technologies, and their implementation in the agriculture sector to achieve a greater result than traditional farming. Lastly, the applications of IoT in agriculture are discussed in detail. Moreover, the challenges and issues in implementing smart farming are discussed which can be used as a base for research by future researchers.

5.1　INTRODUCTION

Agriculture sector is the backbone of any country's economy. The agricultural sector has large problems as it has to feed the 9.6 billion individuals by 2050. Farmers are dealing with various problems to meet the requirements of quality and quantity of the food. The agriculture sector provides jobs to over 50% of India's total workforce and contributes about 18–19% of India's GDP [1, 2].

The main motivation behind this work is half the workforce is active in this agriculture or in its related industries, high rivalry in the market, huge requirement of best products, and the shortage of resources such as soil moisture, temperature, and humidity. Agriculture is continually developing towards the adoption of new techniques like pesticides fertilizers, various irrigation methods (like ditch irrigation and drip irrigation), and enhanced seeds. However, at some places resource overuse occurs. So, the need of the hour is to replace manual methods with automated techniques in order to achieve more production. These techniques are more convenient and this will further reduce human involvement and make it easier to employ the labor force in other sectors [1]. Nowadays, IoT is introduced in almost every industrial field. Similarly, IoT technology is utilized in agriculture sector for remodeling the traditional farming system into the smart farming system with the use of sensors and networking technology and a good internet connection for interfacing. This is also known as agricultural IoT [3].

IoT investigation could be utilized as a subsequent soil checking instrument with a likely advantage of enhanced yield, less cost and least exploitation of resources. This creative methodology is known as "Precision Farming." Through the use of the new and advanced technologies to improve crop production, this method takes into account the various parameters such as soil moisture, humidity, and temperature. Through using Wi-Fi module connected to all the required sensors, which are programmed to transmit data to an IoT platform, the various parameters are continuously observed. The data can be read, analyzed, and processed at this platform. The main goal is to offer a venerable framework to the users. This framework is structured so effectively that it can be accessed through a mobile phone [1].

5.1.1　CONTRIBUTION

This chapter provides detailed insights about the smart agriculture. In this chapter, the different techniques based on IoT to improve crop yield and productivity are discussed. Moreover, smart methods to monitor and to analyze the crops in many aspects such as weather forecast, Soil investigation, irrigation necessities, resource management, and disease prediction, etc., are also described. This chapter provides insights into how IoT tools and technologies are implemented in the agriculture sector to achieve a greater result than traditional farming. Furthermore, the applications of IoT in agriculture are also discussed in detail.

5.2 CHALLENGES FACED BY FARMERS

A few common issues which the farmers face while working in farms are availability, quality, and skills of labor, investment for the resources (seeds, fertilizers, pesticides, equipment's, etc.). These problems are discussed in detail below:

1. **Lack of Education/Awareness:** The present-day Indian farmers does not have any training and they are not aware of the ways by which they can improve their way of cultivation. Moreover, they are not aware of procedures and innovations developed to grow crops faster and cheaper.

2. **Poor Infrastructure:** Approximately 70% of land is not irrigated. The road connectivity to markets is poor. Thus, it is difficult for farmers to reach markets through other means (e.g., rivers) to sell their product. Very few Agro handling components are available, so a huge amount of crops has to be sold as it is because farmers cannot delay the selling of their products to gain more profit. A thorough soil examination, fertilizer quality, and poor impacts of pesticides, etc., are hard to uncover and sometimes impossible.

3. **Absence of Financial Solutions:** Minimum prices are fixed to deal with this issue.

4. **Adopting New Mechanisms:** Mostly, Farmers cannot adopt the automatic ways of farming because they do not have enough money to pay for it. Majority of the farmers have a small agricultural area. Therefore, the land size is a limitation for running the machines in the farms. Even if any failure occurs in any tool due to any reason, then the service centers are far away from the farm, and it is difficult for them to take their tools to that service centers for repairing. Thus, it further increases problems for them [4].

5.3   BENEFITS OF IoT IN AGRICULTURE

- IoT enables the fast collection and organizing of huge data collected by sensors and can be accessed live from anywhere by integrating resources such as Agriculture maps and Cloud storage, etc. This also allows live tracking.
- Experts expect smart farming to improve food production by 70% by 2050.
- IoT lowered revenue which increased profitability and sustainability in effect.
- For IoT, the amount of productivity in the use of pesticides, soil, water, and fertilizers, etc., will be increased.
- With IoT, specific factors will also contribute to environmental security [4].

5.3.1   IRRIGATION

In India a traditional agriculture practices are in such as old irrigation, cultivation, and harvesting methods are frequently practiced in the country. Traditional Irrigation techniques can be updated by semi-automated and computerized methods. However, various issues such as the demand for agriculture produce, inadequate performance and very less supply of water for irrigation are rising day by day. These issues can be properly redressed by utilizing mechanized irrigation system.

Advantages of automatic irrigation are listed as below:

- These systems are easy to install, configure, and operate;
- Such systems save energy and resources that can be used in good quantities and methods;
- This allows farmers to harvest water at the right time;
- Water flow from the farm, after irrigation, reaching the saturation limit of the soil improves the performance of the crop;
- The automatic irrigation system uses valves to turn the engine on and off. Motors can be easily automated using controllers and do not need to turn the engine on and off;
- It is a complete irrigation method and a valuable tool for precise soil moisture control in highly specialized greenhouse vegetable production;
- Avoiding human faults by adjusting the available time soil moisture levels [5].

Karan et al. GSM technology has been used to automate irrigation systems to reduce manual participation. When the temperature and humidity of the environment change, these sensors experience changes in temperature and humidity. This represents an obstacle to the microcontroller [5].

Carlos et al. developed an IoT-based smart water management application for agricultural precision irrigation. This chapter demonstrates the SWAMP architecture, platform, and system deployment, which exposes the image of the platform and provides scalability for IoT applications, as it provides some scalability with minimal computing. Resources are required for specially designed configurations and re-engineering [6].

5.3.2 FERTILIZATION

Farmers' overuse of fertilizer is one reason for low yields. If there is a nutrient deficiency in the soil, enough fertilizer can be added. Therefore, it is necessary to test the soil for nutrients needed for plant growth before fertilization. Soil testing is usually done to determine the nutrient quality of the soil for crop growth. The primary outcome of the soil test is to determine the fertilizer recommendations for the efficient growth of the plant. Due to complex laboratory procedures, farmers rarely do soil research. Routine soil testing for nutrients in commercial plants is done manually, which is not suitable for farmers due to long term use and high cost. Some of the benefits of soil testing are to avoid unnecessary fertilizer use and reduce fertilizer costs. It also helps prevent soil erosion. Soil testing is usually performed on soil pH, nutrients such as nitrogen, potassium, and phosphorus and other minerals such as zinc, calcium, copper, and lead. Each study uses the principles of electrolysis, spectroscopy, and colorimetry and chemical analysis, etc.

Lavanya G and others have developed a novel nitrogen-phosphorus-potassium (NPK) light dependent resistor (LDR) and light-emitting diode (LED) using the IoT based system. Colorimetric theory is used for the analysis and monitoring of nutrients present in the soil. Data received from selected farms via advanced NPK sensors is sent to the Google Cloud Database to support quick data retrieval. Fuzzy logic theory is applied to distinguish nutritional deficiencies from perceived data. During dimming, the crisp value of each sensory data is divided into five fuzzy values, namely, very low, low, medium, medium, and every medium. Nitrogen (N), phosphorus (P) and potassium (K) are based on individual chemical solutions if the rules are developed. Mamdani injection technique is used to assess N, P, and K deficiencies in the soil selected for testing and a warning message is sent to the farmer about the amount of fertilizer.

In Ref. [8], a system with smart devices, WSNs, and the Internet is proposed which that can automate agricultural processes and use resources (water, fertilizers, pesticides, and manual labor) using IoT. With a smart-phone in hand, the farmer can track crops and farmland.

5.3.3   *PESTICIDES*

Pesticides are chemicals that are applied to the crop at different stages of harvest and during crop storage. The purpose of pesticide use is to prevent the destruction of food crops by controlling agricultural pests or unwanted plants and improving plant quality. The use of pesticides has contributed to the improvement of agricultural productivity in commercial farming. While the use of pesticides in agriculture has wider benefits, some incorrect applications can lead to excessive and unnecessary product users. Use of pesticides in food, use of pesticides, and proper use of washed residue before harvesting crops [9].

Excessive use of pesticides on crops increases the threat to the environment and human health. The World Health Organization (WHO) estimates approximately 220,000 deaths and 3 million pesticides each year. Farmers are not aware of the proper use of pesticides and this may adversely affect other organisms, including humans. Exposure to pesticides can have neurological effects in the form of visual acuity, loss of coordination, speed of stimulation, memory loss, and altered or uncontrolled mood. Other health problems, such as allergies, hypersensitivity, asthma, and cancer can occur as side effects of the pesticide [10].

Guo et al. introduced a Biosensor and IoT device based on acetylcholinesterase (ACHE) to determine the potential of pesticide residues and agricultural products. Pesticide removal investigation date-intended to extend remote control functionality, data processing and sharing, the ability to detect agricultural products and the benefits of such detection sites. Such detection data can be further aggregated, processed, and analyzed from devices detected by epigenetic computers to identify useful tools (detection time, detection patterns and paste residual values, etc.). It is effective in protecting the quality and health of agricultural products [9].

Archana et al. proposed IPM (integrated pest management) as a web approach language document for oncology development and how it can be made available as an IoT application to farmers.

Kajol et al. designed a system which allows the farmers to monitor soil moisture with farm soil, identify pests and recommend the best crop variety for this soil. The raspberry Pi (RPi) produces a line follower robot that uses a soil moisture sensor to monitor soil moisture, and the information collected from the sensor is sent to the cloud for storage. A camera is installed to detect pests. After a comprehensive field survey, it retrieves all data stored from the cloud and SQLite databases to provide comprehensive reports of moisture and comprehensive information about pests and advise farmers on the pesticides they need. The system operates on a battery or solar panel, and thus helps farmers effectively monitor their farms [11].

5.3.4   WEED MANAGEMENT

Monitoring weed is the first and foremost step of every weed management system. There are a large number of platforms, cameras, and sensors to detect and monitor the presence/adequate supply of weeds. Sensing with satellites or aircraft provides accurate weed maps. Cameras mounted on unmanned aerial vehicles (UAVs) have been shown to be effective in detecting early season numbers of a wide range of crops, producing images with high spatial resolution. In some cases, these ground systems are suitable for real-time weed management for the site.

Fernandez-Quintanilla et al. discussed various weed management practices; location, density, and composition in the crop area have developed site-specific weed control supported by three real people: first, the majority of the weed population is distributed throughout the crop. Installation. Second, new sensors and platforms (such as GPS and GIS) provide the tools needed to identify and map weeds with geospatial technologies, and third, new smart sprayers, mechanics, and robots can take care of weeds. Various location support [12].

The combination of observation points and traditional clinical and artificial topical surveys in the prevention of wheat diseases, pests, and weeds does not detect and manage real-time diseases, pests, and weeds. Schufen et al. designed a model which uses the ZigBee network to connect terminal sensing devices, and many links are used for big data applications. The system uses large amounts of data generated by the LOT terminal to build a large data platform based on the database and develop a smart wheat disease, pest, and weed alert system. Users can use PCs or handheld terminals to find out what is happening on wheat [13].

5.3.5   MONITOR PLANT GROWTH

The use of IoT can be very helpful with regard to plant development management. In such a situation, it is important to closely monitor plant growth and climate, as the global population moves toward volatile levels every year, and we need to increase this in order to achieve productivity rates [14].

There are a few things to note. IoT-enabled sensors can handle any farm or crop in terms of plant health and even grow under those conditions, but additionally, due to the huge data collection, processing, and visualization volume, a. Ability to accurately predict future environmental changes and plant growth. The introduction of these facilities to each existing plant development industry dramatically determines the potential for waste reduction and often uses large-scale preventive management [14].

Lakshmi and others, to the development of automated systems to the development of the proposed classification. Such knowledge can help botanists, food engineers, doctors, and entrepreneurs. This work is used to monitor the image processing plant with IoT and to collect environmental factors such as temperature and humidity. A detection system has been developed that can detect plants using images of their leaves, and pesticides can be used with the help of images. Runs the feature extraction method from the pattern matchmaker image before matching the information from the machine image to the database so that a possible match can be obtained. Various features collected and analyzed include leaf color, texture, and shape. Depending on the pattern, a leaf may be found healthy or dead. Here we merge IoT processing and image processing. In addition, our framework is user-friendly, efficient, and highly scalable [15].

5.3.6   CROP DISEASE MANAGEMENT

An important task in the field of agriculture is the detection of disease in plants manually, as disease is very common in plants. On the other hand, if the appropriate measures are not taken at the right time, this will create a real impact on the plants, causing crops and plant prices, size, or productivity to be affected. This can help detect the infection of the plant through some programed process, as it reduces the amount of work that can be done to look for products in large home spaces. In this chapter an IoT based solution is proposed [16].

A combination of observational points and traditional diagnostic and artificial topical surveys in the prevention of wheat diseases, pests, and weeds cannot identify and manage real-time diseases, pests, and weeds. This model uses the ZigBee network to connect terminal sensing devices, and many links are used for big data applications. The system uses large amounts of data generated by the LOT terminal to build a large data platform based on the database and develop a smart wheat disease, insect, and weed alert system. Users can use a PC or a handheld terminal to find out what is happening on wheat [13].

Monirul et al. proposing that it is critical to send pictures and give input utilizing IoT to distinguish and identify plant ailments. In this chapter, an IoT gadget dependent on the RPi is proposed, which sends plant pictures to group infections and update ecological boundaries, for example, soil dampness, moistness, pH, and air temperature in a continuous MySQL database. After the pre-handling step and making an interpretation of it into the L * A * B shading space, the normal bunch calculation is utilized to cut the influenced zone of the plant. Multi-class bolster vector machine (SVM) is utilized to group the malady utilizing shading, surface, and gained shape qualities. Along these lines, the investigation of illness grouping and natural boundaries empowers ranchers to successfully recognize plant development for improved creation [16].

5.3.7 FIELD LEVEL PHENOTYPE

In this part, profound learning has been fused into the field-based phenotypic examination. The wheat pictures gathered from circulated Crop Quant phenotyping workstations utilized for UK bread. Based on these arrangements of pictures, a top to bottom learning-based examination is incorporated with the spike districts portion from confused foundations. Strong estimation of key field yield qualities, a promising methodology that utilizes the fully convolution network (FCN) to perform semantic picture division in wheat spike areas, is introduced [11].

The upsides of figuring out how to move utilizing boundaries from other picture datasets. A total evolutionary model to play out a mind-boggling division task dependent on a three-year development picture arrangement to assess key yield-related phenotypes for wheat crops. Contrasted with numerous indoor phenotypic breaks down dependent on AI with perfect lighting and picture conditions, this work utilizes crop-development picture arrangement gathered in genuine horticultural and rearing circumstances where solid breezes, substantial precipitation, water system, and showering can prompt unanticipated quality issues. In any case, tests have indicated that a profound learning approach can bring about promising division execution, and the utilization of move learning could prompt better division of locales [18].

5.4   FARMING TECHNIQUES AND TOOLS

Farmers are adopting traditional farming practices. This includes methods such as labor, seed, and harvesting. On the other hand, modern farming techniques use mechanical devices for irrigation, harvesting, and harvesting of hybrid seeds [19]. In India, agricultural technology is laborious. Too much work by hand makes the work slow and imperfect. Few sequel of steps in farming are given in Figure 5.1.

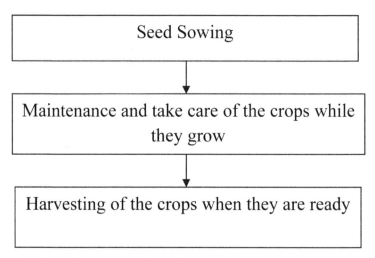

FIGURE 5.1   Steps followed in farming [22].

The most important thing a farmer should do is to take care of the crops. It determines the quality of the crop that is being cultivated:

1. **Irrigation:** It means that the plants control the water for the required period. Water is usually taken from farmers through irrigation canals or rivers and manually fed to crops or in some cases awaiting rain [34]. Farmers should maintain adequate soil moisture throughout the year. It can be detrimental to schemes if the right amount is not maintained.

2. **Fertilizer:** It is important to maintain soil quality with the minerals needed for healthy crop development. Farmers in India fertilize themselves. The quality of fertilizer is often not good or farmers are less inclined to save money. This causes the crop to decline.

3. **Crop Protection:** Many times, stray animals harm or eat the crops. Farmers should be vigilant and prevent such incidents from happening. Most farmers use enclosed bells to attach to the fence, but this is a very old practice, and animals can easily skip it [26].

Farmers rely heavily on experience gained or experience crops manually. This can lead to mistakes and losses of crops. It is important to maintain the water supply during the draft.

5.4.1 TECHNOLOGIES

For development in any field, technology plays an important role. Internet outthinks is a strong backbone with the combination various technologies, in which smart farming is one of the trending technologies in the irrigation sector [47].

So, the following are a list of few technologies that support the farming sector:

- Internet of things;
- Big data analytics (BDA);
- Wireless sensor network (WSN);
- Smart devices;
- Cloud computing;
- Robotics;
- Communication protocols;
- Embedded systems.

In this session, we discuss briefly about the contribution of each of these technologies.

5.4.1.1 INTERNET OF THINGS (IoT)

The focus on agriculture is effective agriculture to increase crop yields and increase productivity for farmers. It also uses IoT technology and provides the best solution for farmer resource management. The farmer can effectively manage crop yields, water demand, disease forecasting, and climate fore-casting [21, 41]. Smart Farming has also helped nature to conserve the environment and optimum utilization of resources. IoT Solutions in Agriculture is currently a solution:

- **Phase I:** The phase I of the internet, during which the agronomic farm receives responses via the short message service (SMS). The now-a-day correspondence medium has been replaced with portable communication de-indicators.
- **Phase II:** It is the stage of internet development. At this stage, the data is sent using, that is, the companion connection, the e-mail that matches the data and the stimulus, and the necessary results of this step [23].
- **Phase III:** It has helped the development of the Internet, e-capacity, web-based business, and similarly accurate agriculture.
- **Phase IV:** The stage IV, that is, the Internet, has helped people to have a more interactive and easier phase, and relates to different communication platforms, such as online and Google Plus Orkut, YouTube, Skype, Facebook.

5.4.1.2   BIG DATA ARCHITECTURE

Big data analytics (BDA) mainly includes all raw data stocks and expectations for cultivation. Traditional farming often makes it very difficult to tell which parameters are due to the resources or data racks required. Tools such as equipment/sensors are needed to compile and collect data and study soil analysis for crop growth, nutrient requirements, and improved crop growth [28]. Some raw data analysis is important for accurate agriculture implementation, such as climate, soil condition analysis, geographic information (GIS) information, global positioning system (GPS) data, and garden hardware analysis. Collect, compile, and analyze all necessary information.

In agricultural production and boredom, boards are currently important. Providing information from various wells of precision landscaping for presentation options is fundamental. Benefits in rural construction and management depend on climatic conditions. Hence, precision gardening can be defined as agriculture, which analyzes data provided by agriculture using precise farming techniques such as local, remote or satellite farming [29].

The day-to-day increase in population also increases the production needs of the agricultural sector. Agricultural methods are resource management and optimize farming practices to meet supply demand [39]. Agriculture is mainly based on existing climatic conditions. Adequate understanding of the current climate and climatic conditions, their analysis is a great boon for farmers to apply better methods for farming.

5.4.1.3 *WIRELESS SENSOR NETWORK (WSN)*

It is a framework that includes an assortment of hub and base stations. The hub includes a processor, memory, sensor, radio, and battery [34]. A base station receives data and the hub processes the received information. The uses of WSNs are many and fluctuating, and applications in agriculture are still relatively new. Crop conditions should be carefully considered in order to collect well.

To control and test natural components, sensors are basic. If more sensors are used in the field, plants that are indirectly identified by the actual parameters are considered [37]. WSN thus ensures better control and continuous monitoring. The WSN has two primary components:

- Information acquisition network; and
- Distribution data distribution network.

5.4.1.4 *SMART DEVICES*

The key is to apply the right thing at the right time. The use of aerial vehicles and drones in the precision agriculture sector has contributed to the development of agriculture and the implementation of smart farming in a more precise manner. These apps helped you to work remotely and analyze [35]. They helped remotely analyze soil properties over time. This has enabled remote analysis of crop erosion. The use of these tools helped to survey more land in less time with accurate data.

These will maintain distance from airborne vehicles, flood dispersion, or satellite interviews. These vehicles can lead to high maintenance costs in the initial period. They are adaptable and valuable compared to conventional farming. He also contributed effectively to precise agriculture.

5.4.1.5 *CLOUD COMPUTING*

Cloud computing has always been a reliable way of facilitating the data required for the electronic data framework. Cloud computing provides a convenient and exceptionally accessible processing step with on-demand asset allocation. This electronic gardening option helps to address the difficulties observed by psychologically assisted networks [32].

Efficiency in a farming system can only be achieved after adequate information and in-depth analysis of each of the data collected. The lack of awareness among the farmer makes it difficult to implement automation in agriculture. Once the farmers have been educated about their efficiency and productivity outcomes [31], they can work towards implementation and increase efficiency in agriculture through proper record collection. It is very difficult to analyze the records collected by the records or for the purpose of writing them through written records. So, it is important for effective communication mode between data collection and data analysis.

5.4.1.6   ROBOTICS

Most processes use the Rotate Water System Framework or the Dribble Water System Framework. However, these systems have not tried to be very successful. The most accurate response to perfect agribusiness is the robot, which specializes in water for every yield in the field. It is impossible to build an earthbound machine with this capability because it needs to be operated simultaneously with a water hose [28]. The first compelling answer is to use the Crane Robot Framework. Straight drives must be precise enough so that the Exclusive Simple Sensors Square Mean maintains the fastest possible. There should be no slip or reaction inside the drive.

It can be concluded that following are some best practices:

- Systematic monitoring;
- In-depth analysis;
- Collecting the required genotypes;
- Selecting the chemical used;
- Corrective action of enforcement;
- Preventive action through advance implementation of advance;
- Conditions monitoring weather conditions.

5.4.1.7   COMMUNICATION PROTOCOLS

They form the backbone of the IoT system to enable applications and connectivity, and these protocols facilitate data exchange over the network, as these protocols enable data exchange formats, data encoding and resolution (Figure 5.2) [29].

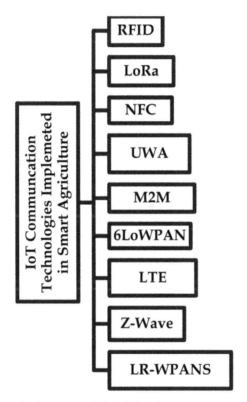

FIGURE 5.2   Communication protocols in IoT farming.

5.4.1.8   EMBEDDED SYSTEMS

It is a type of computer system that contains both hardware and software to perform specific tasks. This includes microprocessors/microcontrollers, RAM/ROM, networking components, I/O units, and storage devices (Figure 5.3).

The types of sensors that are used in agriculture are given in Figure 5.4.

5.4.2   NETWORK IMPLEMENTATION

Farmer problems are mainly structural and economic. The biggest obstacle to all of this is the lack of technical resources and education. Every day the farmer should check his crops regularly. That research includes protecting crops from crows and livestock, checking intruders, hydrating the crop regularly, spraying, and spraying water on the farm, and maintaining greenhouse crop temperatures. Most of these jobs are not manual labor that the farmer does regularly [2]. Because of physical exhaustion, a person forgets or does not care for what he deserves. With technological advances, more work can be automated, farmer reduces workload and improves some work efficiency (Figure 5.5).

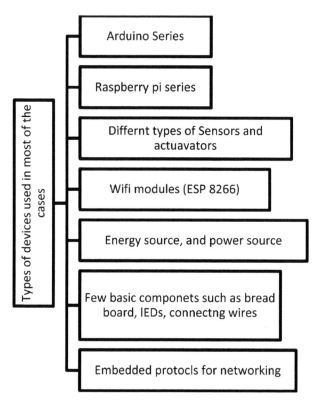

FIGURE 5.3   Types of devices used in IoT farming.

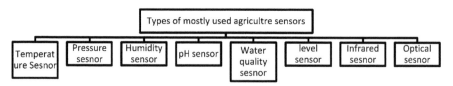

FIGURE 5.4   Types of sensors used in IoT farming.

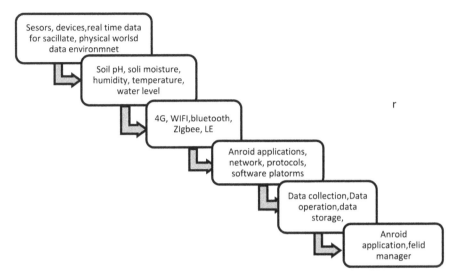

FIGURE 5.5 The flow process of IoT network layer in the field of agriculture [22].

1. **Physical Layer:** The physical layer with the catch layer is fundamentally a sensor, identifiers, and all other equipment gear (geo-stickiness, temperature, moistness, air quality, groundwater level) coupled to a microcontroller/processor to aid ongoing information assortment [31]. The sensors in this framework are increasingly reasonable for the creation of rural insights. All information gathered is first put away on the neighborhood server, blunder investigation is done and just precise, exact information is encoded and transmitted to the cloud server.

2. **Network Layer:** There are modules that help move information at the system layer. It conceals delicate data from the sensor and sends unique information to the machine's preparing unit. Its basic role is to add a layer of pressure to equipment (i.e., sensors, actuators, and so forth.) and programming. (i.e., Database, WebGIS, and so on.), and middleware layer. Sensor gadgets are associated with long-range or short-extend remote systems, for example, 4G, Wi-Fi, Bluetooth LAN, ZigBee, and that is only the tip of the iceberg. A little module can be utilized to actualize implanted frameworks and frameworks to help transmit information all the more safely to the system. Along these lines cultivating is increasingly effective. In this savvy cultivating process, a uniquely constructed framework, for example, soil dampness, temperature, moistness, air quality and groundwater level are utilized to spread data on the dirt fabricated framework. Along

these lines, the system layer assumes a significant job in moving information from sensor gadgets to programming or databases, where computations are performed based on information move [29].

3. **Middleware Layer:** The middleware acts as a layer connection between the layer of the network and the layer of the application. The middleware layer acts as a link between the various components of the IoT, allowing communication between hardware and software. This layer allows communication between hardware sensors, [34–39] operating systems and network protocols. The middleware handles layer services, resources, and operates primarily in remote databases to simplify the integration of software and hardware. In this system, a large amount of data from a remote terminal is stored in a remote layer, a remote database. A forecast analysis algorithm that can be implemented in data over time. The desired block of instruction depends on the expected values. These instructions are responsible for watering crops, automatic shading of crops, etc., in the application gateway of the system. Analytical activities play an important role [26], as the global climate is constantly changing and agriculture predicts good production. These activities allow the user to manage crop yields based on real-time changing data.

4. **Application Layer:** It includes communication protocols and interfaces. Methods used to host communication networks such as MQTT, AMQP, and CoAP. Middleware layer data is redirected to application layer devices such as websites or Android apps. These devices receive encrypted data and use internal [25] software. Decrypt and store data locally for further use. This data is used to show the tendency to use. The application monitors data and makes intelligent suggestions to gradually increase the throughput of the system.

5.4.3 APPLICATIONS

5.4.3.1 APPLICATIONS OF SMART AGRICULTURAL MODELS BASED ON IoT

*   Hardware components-based module for irrigation system:
    o   Information collection model;
    o   The site irrigation module;
    o   Irrigation controller;

o   GPRS module;
o   The central control computer;
o   The auxiliary model.

- Network constitute based module for irrigation system. This model mainly concentrates on three layers:

o   The network sensation and the key course level;
o   The monitor control for transitions layer level; and
o   Data terminating and processing level.

- Software components designed for irrigation model. This model basically concreter on five components:

o   Internet of things;
o   Lower position machine control nodes;
o   Wireless route nodes;
o   Wireless gateway nodes; and
o   Client-based data collection nodes GPRS module.

5.4.3.2   APPLICATION OF IoT IN AGRICULTURE

In 10 years, we have seen the ascent of the Internet in remote gadgets that give gadgets an interesting location over the system. The primary mainstay of IoT innovation is IPv6 (rather than IPv4), which gives a novel location to each protest world. These gadgets are associated by means of the Internet and have numerous well-known applications, and one such application is rural creation [31]. Nowadays, IoT-based Smart Living, Smart Village, Smart City, Smart Machinery are much more. Since agribusiness is the foundation of numerous nations, present day gear and innovation must be utilized to give the correct food flexibly on the planet. Numerous natural factors, for example, temperature, mugginess, saltiness, leaf wetting, soil dampness, dry spell cycle, sun powered radiation, precipitation, creepy-crawly developments, and human exercises improve rural efficiency. In the event that ranchers can see these things remotely utilizing savvy innovation, we can improve the monetary state of our nation.

Based on verifiable data on bother control, ranchers can take some preventive measures to control bugs, improve horticultural quality and increment profitability [42]. A few applications for IoT-empowered cultivating frameworks are recorded underneath. The IoT-empowered agribusiness applications are appeared in Figure 5.6.

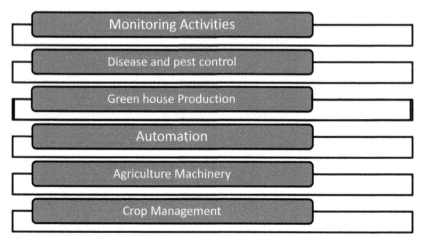

FIGURE 5.6   Applications of IoT [21].

5.4.3.2.1 *Monitoring Activities*

The most important task for a farmer today is to monitor, design, and maintain environmental standards beyond the expectations of engineers and scientists. Continuous monitoring by agronomists is essential for accurate and reliable advice on agricultural operations [32]. There are many parameters that need to be monitored, such as the environment, crop fertility and water quality for the life of the water. In this section, we present a comprehensive view of the use of IoT in climate, soil, water, and smart farm monitoring systems.

1. **Irrigation and Quality Management:** Irrigation plays a key role in achieving sustainability in agriculture. The automatic irrigation system [39] is a basic requirement for agriculture. Agriculture is therefore applied in order to understand the different parameters required for the processing of wireless sensor nodes. Soil moisture sensors and temperature sensors are used to collect readings pertaining to home gardening or fields and to inject sensory data.

   The farmer can use the data transmitted in the cloud at any time and at any time. Crop sensing is performed correctly for different parameters using the IoT technique. Remote monitoring may be carried out to monitor and control agricultural wireless adults using Wireless Senator Instruments. Ultrasound waves have been mesmerizing to monitor soil quality and groundwater levels in agricultural ultrasound. Smart drip irrigation system based on IoT (using Arduino) for optimal irrigation for the distribution of crop water [50].

In most developing countries today, water scarcity is a major challenge. Automated water monitoring and distribution systems are needed to ensure a uniform distribution of water between stakeholders. Smart water meters must be deployed on a large scale [30]. Suggested system for smart water measurement in the Indus Basin. It also requires IoT-based technology that enables demand-based distribution of water. The system has attempted to automate the irrigation network on a large scale.

Real-time water quality monitoring has been developed for the low-cost IoT environment. The usage of IoT has revolutionized the form of new technologies integrated in the web. Irrigation is the primary source of agricultural activity. WSNs are widely used for irrigation management applications.

2. **Weather Monitoring:** The significant atmosphere factors influencing agribusiness are hail, day off, dry season, and so on. It is in this manner important to have an atmosphere determining framework equipped for observing boundaries, for example, air, precipitation, temperature, light force, stickiness, speed, barometric weight, and wind course. Hence, the rancher can make appropriate arrangements for seeds, fertilizer plants, sub-soil, development, and water system. Climate conditions, for example, sun, downpour, mists, and snowfall [29]. It assists with utilizing assets. At the point when proper, atmosphere checking can be utilized to look at the possibility and economy of short-extend (Lora) ranchers.

The framework has been shown in a wide scope of horticultural sensors with numerous sensors for the assortment of physical boundaries [53]. These readings identify with the climate place and the information is accessible through the web application. LPWA interfaces this framework to LPAR-based RF handsets. During the advancement of equipment models, the Arduino NanoBoard is utilized as an open-source electronic prototyping stage that incorporates an Atmel microcontroller mounted on a circuit board. The rancher can check the latest climate conditions by visiting Ulld. Today, atmosphere observing frameworks have numerous abilities. The WSN is the correct decision for such checking applications. Since sensor hubs can be set up in remote conditions, they can revamp themselves much after the hub comes up short.

The IoT the executives program guarantees a biological equaliza-tion and improves the consistency of the ecological gauges. Contex-tual investigation Pro [32] consolidates geo-informatics, distributed computing, and data frameworks to track and handle them ideally.

A great deal of sensors is utilized in this framework to gather information and web administrations to move the data to the server. Checking and dynamic of this data framework gives information assortment, yet in addition basic information investigation, yet in addition through web administrations and distributed computing stages.

3. **Soil Monitoring:** Soil moisture is one of the primary factors deter-mining plant growth [21]. It plays an important role in providing nutrients needed for plant growth. Soil moisture and resistive sensors may be used. These sensors measure the difference of ground resis-tance between two soil moisture sensor probes. Global warming and climate have changed all at once. Due to water scarcity and necessary soil, rainfall is getting less nutrients every year. Automated irriga-tion systems [39] are essential for determining soil nutrients such as nitrogen, phosphorus, and potassium. This system saves the farmer's time, money, and energy. Many farmers have repeatedly used the manual method to perform tests requiring human intervention, and this is a laborious process. Through this automated system, farmers can get information about soil fertilization and irrigation directly via e-mail. IoT-enabled sensors have been installed on the farm to get the information regarding the soil and the environment [21].

The sensor for soil moisture refers to the amount of water in the soil. You can determine plant growth by calculating the quantity of moisture in the soil. Whenever the quantity of water exceeds the cap, a warning message is issued for the supply of water in the area. These smart devices connected using IoT can be very helpful in remote monitoring.

4. **Field Monitoring:** IoT has many innovative applications for integrated farm management systems for the agriculture industry [44–46]. Many agricultural operations need to focus on innovation and better management. Animal farms, bird farms, and bees are the most common agricultural industries. Using IoT on those farms helps the farmer achieve higher production. Not only do bees help with honey production, but beekeeping can also help with pollen crops [32]. Farmers should monitor the status of bees regularly. Therefore, the beekeeping system [35] collects both internal and external data of

the hive. The classification algorithm determines the location of the bee colony based on this data, which uses the citation algorithm based on these data. Farmers can choose to travel the hive based on sensory data directly on their smart phones. In addition, the study predicts rainfall based on bee conditions. In addition, Smart Beehive offers automated processing of honey via machinery. Therefore, it lowers the individual risk of bee sterilization. Beekeepers support farmers.

Examples of smart farming are:
- Smart cattle farming;
- Smart aquaponics;
- Smart poultry;
- Smart beehive monitoring;
- Smart hatchers.

5. **Crop Management:** Not only does sowing, watering, fertilizing, spraying pesticides and collecting large crops in cultivation requires a great deal of analysis.

At every stage of life, for example, seed germination requires soil moisture and humid weather conditions [21]. Therefore, look for a weather forecasting system during the germination stage. Likewise, fertilizer is required to grow a healthy plant. An in-depth analysis with the amount of fertilizer or pesticides is required to help manage the crop. Farmers may make decisions by keeping certain historical data or by using IoT-based methods in management. Data can be monitored or tracked remotely in real-time, via cell phones, URLs, etc.

This app provides users with different authentication levels. Smart formatting can deliver information in real-time through email notifications or SMS. Smart form net [51] is a forum for IoT-based smart farming applications to capture, analyze, and visualize data. The world's largest source of crop output data and recommendations. This framework can support any kind of IoT system and provides zero programming effort for data visualization. It offers tools to track crops rapidly and access data scalable from millions of sensor nodes [52].

5.5 CHALLENGES AND ISSUE IN SMART FARMING

The equipment must be strong enough to protect against strong rain, temperature, humidity, fluctuations, strong winds, solar radiation, and all kinds of environment (Figure 5.7).

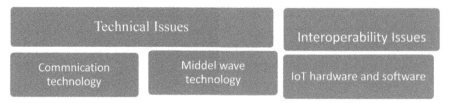

FIGURE 5.7 Challenge and issues in smart farming [21].

Changes and other dangerous activity that may damage electronic equipment. These devices are battery-powered and active for long-term battery sources. Energy-enhancing modules, such as solar panels and turbines, can help somewhat in IoT implementation. Devices must be linked to one another via an internet facility producing huge quantities of data. The small-scale architecture and low-power capabilities of the server that render compatible programming devices with hardware devices will handle this vast volume of data (big data) [43]. Additionally, IoT devices need to be deployed in an open environment that exposes devices to ever-varying environmental conditions that may affect the functioning of deployed sensors and cause failures in connections. The basic problems related to hardware/software are as below:

1. **Reliability Problem:** There is a major concern about the physical protection of the IoT devices deployed and the network systems interconnectivity so data can be transmitted to the destination [45]. Physical protection must be provided in accordance with numerous climate changes to protect costly infrastructure against natural disasters.

2. **Scalability Problem:** For billions of IoT devices installed on IoT farm networks, a significant number of IoT devices/nodes cannot be served by existing gateways and protocols. Engine and Sigfox Gateways can carry 104 and 106 nodes, respectively. This includes an intelligent/efficient IoT management framework with unique addresses as well as identities for every node.

3. **Localization:** When deploying IoT devices, there can be many factors that need to be addressed. The device's status needs to be known so it can connect with other IoT systems and gateways [21]. It provides efficient connectivity with a minimum interaction with other devices.

5.6 CONCLUSION

Mutt farming will be the future of IoT-based farming called smart farming. This term is popular and does not devote broad attention to agricultural activities. IoT leans regularly towards agricultural practices. Farmers will operate on their land by taking data from crops, machinery, and markets relating to any property in real-time. Without the farmer 's presence all can be monitored. Today's technology can display crop and soil data, assess disease, and prevent it. Furthermore, the crop can be harvested without human intervention. Important Data can be collected and stored in the cloud for convenience of farmers and retrieved from the cloud. The network is getting better and cleverer.

For two reasons, licensed low-power wireless access (LPWA) is known as a game-changer for smart agriculture. The former is its strong geographical coverage and the latter economic. While the unlicensed spectrum is readily available and appealing as a solution, in practice it has drawbacks as its ability to offer a guaranteed quality of service (QoS) lacks interference and congestion problems. Regulatory restrictions-which can differ from market to market-generate a special cultivation of resources for unlicensed spectrum solutions. As a result, the narrowband IoT (NB-IoT) has broad industry support as an important global standard for LPWA connectivity. The shifting industry understanding is a step towards smart agriculture, enabling the Internet to provide comprehensive seamless connectivity across a wide range of sensors for reliable, low-cost, secure, long-life spectrum of licensed batteries.

KEYWORDS

- **farming**
- **internet of things**
- **low power wide area network**
- **machine learning**
- **passive infrared**
- **smart**

REFERENCES

1. Mishra, D., Pande, T., Agrawal, K. K., Abbas, A., Pandey, A. K., & Yadav, R. S., (2019). Smart agriculture system using IoT. In: *Proceedings of the Third International Conference on Advanced Informatics for Computing Research* (pp. 1–7).

2. Government of India, Ministry of Finance. *Economic Survey 2019–20, 2.*

3. Park, S., Yun, S., Kim, H., Kwon, R., Ganser, J., & Anthony, S., (2018). Forestry monitoring system using Lora and drone. In: *Proceedings of the 8th International Conference on Web Intelligence, Mining and Semantics* (pp. 1–8).

4. Nayyar, A., & Puri, V., (2016). Smart farming: IoT based smart sensors agriculture stick for live temperature and moisture monitoring using Arduino, cloud computing & solar technology. In: *Proc. of The International Conference on Communication and Computing Systems (ICCCS-2016)* (pp. 9781315364094–121).

5. Kansara, K., Zaveri, V., Shah, S., Delwadkar, S., & Jani, K., (2015). Sensor based automated irrigation system with IoT: A technical review. *International Journal of Computer Science and Information Technologies, 6*(6), 5331–5333.

6. Kamienski, C., Soininen, J. P., Taumberger, M., Dantas, R., Toscano, A., Salmon, C. T., & Torre, N. A., (2019). Smart water management platform: IoT-based precision irrigation for agriculture. *Sensors, 19*(2), 276.

7. Lavanya, G., Rani, C., & Ganeshkumar, P., (2019). An automated low cost IoT based fertilizer intimation system for smart agriculture. *Sustainable Computing: Informatics and Systems.*

8. Giri, A., Dutta, S., & Neogy, S., (2016). Enabling agricultural automation to optimize utilization of water, fertilizer and insecticides by implementing internet of things (IoT). In: *2016 International Conference on Information Technology (InCITe)-the Next Generation IT Summit on the Theme-Internet of Things: Connect your Worlds* (pp. 125–131). IEEE.

9. Zhao, G., Guo, Y., Sun, X., & Wang, X., (2015). A system for pesticide residues detection and agricultural products traceability based on acetylcholinesterase biosensor and internet of things. *International Journal of Electrochemical Science, 10*(4), 3387–3399.

10. Chougule, A., Jha, V. K., & Mukhopadhyay, D., (2016). Using IoT for integrated pest management. In: *2016 International Conference on Internet of Things and Applications (IOTA)* (pp. 17–22). IEEE.

11. Kajol, R., & Akshay, K. K., (2018). Automated agricultural field analysis and monitoring system using IoT. *International Journal of Information Engineering and Electronic Business, 11*(2), 17.

12. Fernández-Quintanilla, C., Peña, J. M., Andújar, D., Dorado, J., Ribeiro, A., & López-Granados, F., (2018). Is the current state of the art of weed monitoring suitable for site-specific weed management in arable crops? *Weed Research, 58*(4), 259–272.

13. Zhang, S., Chen, X., & Wang, S., (2014). Research on the monitoring system of wheat diseases, pests and weeds based on IoT. In: *2014 9th International Conference on Computer Science & Education* (pp. 981–985). IEEE.

14. Kamruzzaman, S. M., Pavel, M. I., Hoque, M. A., & Sabuj, S. R., (2019). Promoting greenness with IoT-based plant growth system. In: *Computational Intelligence and Sustainable Systems* (pp. 235–253). Springer, Cham.

15. Lakshmi, K., & Gayathri, S., (2017). Implementation of IoT with image processing in plant growth monitoring system. *J. Sci. Innov. Res, 6*(2), 80–83.

16. Pavel, M. I., Kamruzzaman, S. M., Hasan, S. S., & Sabuj, S. R., (2019). An IoT based plant health monitoring system implementing image processing. In: *2019 IEEE 4ᵗʰ International Conference on Computer and Communication Systems (ICCCS)* (pp. 299–303). IEEE.

17. Zhou, J., Reynolds, D., Websdale, D., Le Cornu, T., Gonzalez-Navarro, O., Lister, C., & Clark, M., (2017). *CropQuant: An Automated and Scalable Field Phenotyping Platform for Crop Monitoring and Trait Measurements to Facilitate Breeding and Digital Agriculture.* BioRxiv, 161547.

18. Alkhudaydi, T., Reynolds, D., Griffiths, S., Zhou, J., & De La Iglesia, B., (2019). An exploration of deep-learning based phenotypic analysis to detect spike regions in field conditions for UK bread wheat. *Plant Phenomics, 2019*, 7368761.

19. Da Xu, L., He, W., & Li, S., (2014). Internet of things in industries: A survey. *IEEE Transactions on Industrial Informatics, 10*(4), 2233–2243.

20. Pujari, J. D., Yakkundimath, R., & Byadgi, A. S., (2015). Image processing based detection of fungal diseases in plants. *Procedia Computer Science, 46*, 1802–1808.

21. Nayak, P., Kavitha, K., & Rao, C. M., (2020). IoT-enabled agricultural system applications, challenges and security issues. In: *IoT and Analytics for Agriculture* (pp. 139–163). Springer, Singapore.

22. Verma, S., Gala, R., Madhavan, S., Burkule, S., Chauhan, S., & Prakash, C., (2018). An internet of things (IoT) architecture for smart agriculture. In: *2018 Fourth International Conference on Computing Communication Control and Automation (ICCUBEA)* (pp. 1–4). IEEE.

23. Ngu, A. H., Gutierrez, M., Metsis, V., Nepal, S., & Sheng, Q. Z., (2016). IoT middleware: A survey on issues and enabling technologies. *IEEE Internet of Things Journal, 4*(1), 1–20.

24. Liu, C. H., Yang, B., & Liu, T., (2014). Efficient naming, addressing, and profile services in internet-of-things sensory environments. *Ad. Hoc. Networks, 18*, 85–101.

25. Atzori, L., Iera, A., & Morabito, G., (2010). The internet of things: A survey. *Computer Networks, 54*(15), 2787–2805.

26. Yan-e, D., (2011). Design of intelligent agriculture management information system based on IoT. In: *2011 Fourth International Conference on Intelligent Computation Technology and Automation* (Vol. 1, pp. 1045–1049). IEEE.

27. Wu, Z., Li, S., Yu, M., & Wu, J., (2015). The actuality of agriculture internet of things for applying and popularizing in China. In: *Proceedings of the International Conference on Advances in Mechanical Engineering and Industrial Informatics* (pp. 11, 12). Zhengzhou, China.

28. Parameswaran, G., & Sivaprasath, K., (2016). Arduino based smart drip irrigation system using internet of things. *Int. J. Eng. Sci.*, 5518.

29. Muhammad, A., Haider, B., & Ahmad, Z., (2016). IoT enabled analysis of irrigation rosters in the Indus basin irrigation system. *Procedia Engineering, 154*, 229–235.

30. Fang, S., Da Xu, L., Zhu, Y., Ahati, J., Pei, H., Yan, J., & Liu, Z., (2014). An integrated system for regional environmental monitoring and management based on internet of things. *IEEE Transactions on Industrial Informatics, 10*(2), 1596–1605.

31. Dursun, M., & Ozden, S., (2011). A wireless application of drip irrigation automation supported by soil moisture sensors. *Scientific Research and Essays, 6*(7), 1573–1582.

32. Khattab, A., Abdelgawad, A., & Yelmarthi, K., (2016). Design and implementation of a cloud-based IoT scheme for precision agriculture. In: *2016 28ᵗʰ International Conference on Microelectronics (ICM)* (pp. 201–204). IEEE.

33. Kodali, R. K., & Sahu, A., (2016). An IoT based weather information prototype using WeMos. In: *2016 2ⁿᵈ International Conference on Contemporary Computing and Informatics (IC3I)* (pp. 612–616). IEEE.
34. Bing, F., (2016). The research of IoT of agriculture based on three layers of architecture. In: *2016 2ⁿᵈ International Conference on Cloud Computing and Internet of Things* (CCIOT) (pp. 162–165). IEEE.
35. Edwards-Murphy, F., Magno, M., Whelan, P. M., O'Halloran, J., & Popovici, E. M., (2016). b+ WSN: Smart beehive with preliminary decision tree analysis for agriculture and honey bee health monitoring. *Computers and Electronics in Agriculture, 124,* 211–219.
36. Chaivivatrakul, S., Tang, L., Dailey, M. N., & Nakarmi, A. D., (2014). Automatic morphological trait characterization for corn plants via 3D holographic reconstruction. *Computers and Electronics in Agriculture, 109,* 109–123.
37. Ding, Q., Ma, D., Li, D., & Zhao, L., (2010). Design and implementation of a sensors node oriented water quality monitoring in aquaculture. *Sensor Letters, 8*(1), 70–74.
38. Bang, J., Lee, I., Noh, M., Lim, J., & Oh, H., (2014). Design and implementation of a smart control system for poultry breeding's optimal LED environment. *International Journal of Control and Automation, 7*(2), 99–108.
39. Vernandhes, W., Salahuddin, N. S., Kowanda, A., & Sari, S. P., (2017). Smart aquaponic with monitoring and control system based on IoT. In: *2017 Second International Conference on Informatics and Computing (ICIC)* (pp. 1–6). IEEE.
40. Brewster, C., Roussaki, I., Kalatzis, N., Doolin, K., & Ellis, K., (2017). IoT in agriculture: Designing a Europe-wide large-scale pilot. *IEEE Communications Magazine, 55*(9), 26–33.
41. Román-Castro, R., López, J., & Gritzalis, S., (2018). Evolution and trends in IoT security. *Computer, 51*(7), 16–25.
42. Yang, K., Liu, H., Wang, P., Meng, Z., & Chen, J., (2018). Convolutional neural network-based automatic image recognition for agricultural machinery. *International Journal of Agricultural and Biological Engineering, 11*(4), 200–206.
43. Karim, F., & Karim, F., (2017). Monitoring system using web of things in precision agriculture. *Procedia Computer Science, 110,* 402–409.
44. Johannes, A., Picon, A., Alvarez-Gila, A., Echazarra, J., Rodriguez-Vaamonde, S., Navajas, A. D., & Ortiz-Barredo, A., (2017). Automatic plant disease diagnosis using mobile capture devices, applied on a wheat use case. *Computers and Electronics in Agriculture, 138,* 200–209.
45. Petrellis, N., (2017). A smart phone image processing application for plant disease diagnosis. In: *2017 6ᵗʰ International Conference on Modern Circuits and Systems Technologies (MOCAST)* (pp. 1–4). IEEE.
46. Kawakami, Y., Furuta, T., Nakagawa, H., Kitamura, T., Kurosawa, K., Kogami, K., & Tanaka, M. S., (2016). Rice cultivation support system equipped with water-level sensor system. *IFAC-PapersOnLine, 49*(16), 143–148.
47. Breivold, H. P., (2017). A survey and analysis of reference architectures for the internet-of-things. In: *ICSEA 2017* (p. 143).
48. Sarangi, S., Umadikar, J., & Kar, S., (2016). Automation of agriculture support systems using Wisekar: Case study of a crop-disease advisory service. *Computers and Electronics in Agriculture, 122,* 200–210.

49. Rodríguez, S., Gualotuña, T., & Grilo, C., (2017). A system for the monitoring and predicting of data in precision agriculture in a rose greenhouse based on wireless sensor networks. *Procedia Computer Science, 121*, 306–313.
50. Dan, L. I. U., Xin, C., Chongwei, H., & Liangliang, J., (2015). Intelligent agriculture greenhouse environment monitoring system based on IoT technology. In: *2015 International Conference on Intelligent Transportation, Big Data and Smart City* (pp. 487–490). IEEE.
51. Akkaş, M. A., & Sokullu, R., (2017). An IoT-based greenhouse monitoring system with Micaz motes. *Procedia Computer Science, 113*, 603–608.
52. Tayur, V. M., & Suchithra, R., (2017). Review of interoperability approaches in application layer of internet of things. In: *2017 International Conference on Innovative Mechanisms for Industry Applications (ICIMIA)* (pp. 322–326). IEEE.
53. Biral, A., Centenaro, M., Zanella, A., Vangelista, L., & Zorzi, M., (2015). The challenges of M2M massive access in wireless cellular networks. *Digital Communications and Networks, 1*(1), 1–19.

CHAPTER 6

A Study on IoT in the Agriculture Domain with Future Directions

RAJIV BANSAL[1] and NEHA GOYAL[2]

[1]*JMIT Radaur, Haryana, India, E-mail: rajivbansal@jmit.ac.in*

[2]*NIT Kurukshetra, Haryana, India, E-mail: Neha.goyal2309@gmail.com*

ABSTRACT

The rapid change in population is increasing, which is predicted to reach 9.6 billion people by 2050. Due to rapid change in the population, extreme weather conditions, deteriorating soil, and drying lands, collapsing ecosystems that play a crucial role in agriculture make food production harder and harder. And leading towards increasing demand for food, both in terms of quantity and quality, is a challenging task. Despite these challenges, agribusiness is to develop and deliver within the cultivate and provide it to the end consumers with the most excellent conceivable cost and best conceivable quality. The agriculture IoT market is expected to be worth USD 20.9 billion by 2024, whereas it was 12.7 billion USD in 2019. To overcome these challenges, and encouraging humans to improve agriculture yields using modern information and communication technology, IoT-based technology will turn the traditional farming to smart farming with sensor and other devices. It helps in enhancing the productivity of agribusiness, optimizes the input resources (water, fertilizers, seeds), identifying disease and infections in crops, crop growth monitoring, automated irrigation, and increased quality and reduced time and cost. Precision farming, drone-based monitoring, livestock monitoring, the smart greenhouse is the well-known application of IoT-based agriculture that aims growth not only traditional agriculture at a larger scale but also encourage the tendency of greenhouse farming, organic farming, and small-scale gardening. Apart from the services improving the agriculture with least human intervention and cost, connectivity, design, and durability of the network, and limited resources are significant issues that require closer attention. The full application of IoT in agriculture will truly achieve efficient and smart farming techniques and, notably, contribute to solving the world's food problem with an increasing population. These applications of the internet of things (IoT) in agriculture promises automated and data-driven processes. These benefits do not act as an improvement over the traditional era of agriculture, but instead, provide the solutions for the whole industry confronting the application with agriculture.

6.1   INTRODUCTION

The far-reaching of the web from the most recent two decades has brought a few advantages for varying backgrounds. Its ability to deliver information with several devices. Its ability to produce the information and send it over the system in an ongoing way is an enormous benefit taken by every single individual. It is capable of not only taking quick and correct action but also automates several processes. Internet of things (IoT) is a thing of a network that depends on the idea "connect the unconnected" or "interface the detached." It is a technology transition in which devices allow us to sense and control the physical world by making an object with the smarter concept and establish a smart and intelligent connection with the network between devices. The interconnection allows us several objects to be used more smartly; apart from the smart network, it improves the productive dependability, also mechanizes, and automates the whole process. The broad area of IoT not just confines people to think of it as a solitary innovation space. It offers numerous arrangements insightfully in various spaces, concepts, protocols, and techniques. It offers multiple solutions intelligently in different domains, i.e., healthcare, agriculture, smart cities, smart parking, precision farming, and many more.

The total populace, as announced in June 2018, is an astounding 7.6 billion. It is assessed that this number is ascending to 8.5 billion by 2030 and anticipated to contact 9.6 billion individuals by 2050. With the rapid change in the total populace, food consumption overall additionally develops quickly at a rapid rate. A fast acceleration in food creation to cater to the growing demand is not a simple undertaking. Farming being the most established industry, has developed so far to the period of what would now be able to be named as "The Third Green Revolution." The world is seeing one more major advancement in the wake of another revolution that utilizes the utilization of present-day of information and communication technologies (ICT) into farming, to deliver a sustainable agricultural production.

It includes the joining of trendsetting innovations into previously persevering agribusiness practices with the end goal of boosting quality and productivity for cultivating products. It helps in automated cultivating with the assortment of information for analysis to give the administrator with analytical information for a better dynamic to gain high-quality output of the product. It propelled cultivating the executive's framework established on watching, estimating, and reacting to entomb and intra-field changeability in items. The objective of smart agriculture research is to ground a dynamic decision making and support for farm management and other related horticulture activity. A framework that advances and inspects how cutting-edge cultivating can help the creation yield just as spotlights on the safeguarding of assets. IoT development for the agriculture domain helps in continuous monitoring and optimal resource utilization with increased productivity. The significant application of IoT with ICT in the agriculture domain involves smart farming, precision farming, livestock monitoring, smart greenhouse, smart irrigation, and many more. It is helpful in continuous monitoring of crops, yield prediction sensing the environment, optimal uses of resources, and effective management to produce the best conceivable product and its delivery to end-users.

With the advancement in the ICT sector and smart sensor, the modern agribusiness industry is information focused, exact, and more astute than at any time in recent memory. The fast development of the Internet-of-Things (IoT) modernized pretty much, which moved the business from quantifiable to quantitative methodologies. Such advanced changes are enabling the current horticulture techniques to smarter one and making new open doors along with a scope of difficulties.

A personalized landslide menace monitoring framework has been built up that permits fast executions in an intimidating environment without user intercession [2]. What is all the more fascinating about the created framework is that it manages failures of nodes and restorations of low-quality correspondence interconnection on the network without interacting with a user. An IoT based management system is proposed in Ref. [3] that examines the components, for example, wind, soil, climate, and water over a vast region. Besides, IoT-based farming checking arrangements have been recognized dependent on the sub-areas to which they have a place. The recognized sub-spaces are soil checking, air observing, temperature checking, water checking, ailment checking, area checking, ecological conditions observing, bother checking, and treatment checking.

Further, the IoT worldview improves human cooperation in the physical world through minimal effort electronic gadgets and correspondence conventions. IoT, too, observes distinctive natural conditions to make thick and continuous guides of commotion level, air, water contamination, temperature, and harming radiations [4, 5]. Moreover, information gathered about various natural boundaries is transmitted to the client by trigger alarms or sending suggestions to specialists through messages [6].

This chapter features the capability of IoT in agribusiness, different periods of IoT in horticulture, and challenges are likewise discussed. The examination covers the different parts of smart agribusiness with other related exercises that transformed into an automated procedure. It additionally covers how Data Science is starting an intelligent choice when joined with IoT devices.

6.2   BACKGROUND

Analysts have proposed distinctive IoT-based advancements in the horticulture field that are expanding the creation with less workforce exertion. Specialists have additionally dealt with various IoT-based agribusiness activities to improve the quality and increment agrarian profitability. There are many examples like wireless sensors technology is being used on plant nursery. WSN-based polyhouse checking framework has been introduced that utilizes carbon dioxide, mugginess, temperature, and light recognition modules. By utilizing GPS innovation and ZigBee convention a WSN-based framework has been suggested that screens distinctive rural boundaries. A constant rice crop checking framework has been intended to increment profitability. The harvest observing framework has been introduced which gathers the data of precipitation and temperature and breaks down it to moderate the danger of yield misfortune and upgrade crop profitability. A minimal effort Bluetooth-based framework has been proposed for checking different horticultural factors, for example, temperature by utilizing a microcontroller that functions as a climate station. The proposed framework is best for checking constant field information. Also, the burden of this framework is its restricted correspondence go and required Bluetooth setup with cell phones for persistent checking.

A keen detecting stage dependent on ZigBee has produced for observing distinctive natural conditions, for example, mugginess, temperature, daylight, and weight. The created stage gives a quick information rate, ease equipment, and a precise sensor dealing with work organize so every hub can speak with one another viably. A Global System for Mobile Communications (GSM) based water system observing framework has been built up that utilizes an android application for estimating distinctive ecological conditions, for example, mugginess, temperature, and control of the water level. The fundamental reason for this framework is to build up a minimal effort remote framework, though the negative part of the framework is to realize the working order to impel the field engine and agribusiness boundaries.

Scientists and architects around the world are proposing various strategies and models and dependent on that proposing an assortment of gear to screen and get the data with respect to trim status during various stages, considering various harvest and field types. Concentrating on the showcase request, many driving makes are giving a scope of sensors, unmanned flying vehicles (UAVs), robots, specialized gadgets, and other overwhelming apparatus to convey the detected information. Also, different commissions, food and agribusiness associations, and government bodies are creating policies and rules to watch and manage the utilization of these innovations so as to keep up food and condition wellbeing.

As of late, the Internet-of-Things (IoT) is starting to sway a wide exhibit of areas and businesses, going from fabricating, wellbeing, interchanges, and vitality to the agribusiness business, so as to diminish wasteful aspects and improve the presentation overall business sectors. On the off chance that looking carefully, one feels that the current applications are just starting to expose what's underneath and that the genuine effect of IoT what is more, its uses are not yet seen. All things considered, thinking about this progress, particularly in the close past, we can anticipate that IoT innovations are going to assume a key job in different uses of the farming division. This is a direct result of the capacities offered by IoT, including the essential correspondence foundation (used to interface the keen objects—from sensors, vehicles, to client cell phones— utilizing the Internet) and scope of administrations, for example, nearby or remote information obtaining, cloud-based astute data investigation and dynamic, client interfacing, and farming activity computerization. Such capacities can upset the farming business which is most likely one of the most wasteful divisions of our financial worth chain today [29, 30].

6.3   FRAMEWORK FOR IoT SYSTEM IN AGRICULTURE

IoT application zones are omnipresent over the existing pattern of the farming division, viz. development, water the executives, gather, stockpiling, preparing, passage, and agreements. Together with the ordinarily available sensors, an assortment of particular sensors is accessible for farming applications, for example, Soil mugginess, Moisture, Leaf Condensation, Solar Radiations, Ultraviolet Radiations, Pluviometer (Rain Gauge), Wind Vanes, and so on. In a run of the mill IoT situation, sensors can be carried in fields, fields, nurseries, seed stockpiles, cold stockpiles, horticulture apparatus, passage framework, and animals; and their information can be put away in the cloud for observing and control.

The examination and investigation of the information can direct the approaches to improve creation with upgraded utilization of assets and can connect the interest and flexibly hole of the rural produce. Preparing, relating, breaking down, and inducing the right data from the information, which is originating from an assortment of sensors, is the most testing task in any IoT framework. IoT-based farming creation framework, in light of connection investigation between the yield measurable data and horticultural condition data, to upgrade the capacity to examine current conditions and foresee the future collect. Further, Semantic heterogeneity of numerous data assets is a test for coordinating diverse horticulture IT frameworks. Numerous specialists are working toward this path.

The framework includes: Research, Prediction, Market, and economics, Monitoring, and control. The Agri-IoT information investigation stage is made out of various layers, both lower level (de-bad habit, correspondence planes), moderate layers (information, information examination), and higher layers (application, end-client planes). At each layer, different programming parts perform specific operations, identified with information procurement, demonstrating, examination, or representation. Since well-defined significant programming segments as of now exist, created in IoT and savvy city-related tasks, we have concentrated on reusing those segments, rather than re-developing the wheel, as indicated by the specific needs of brilliant cultivating, to cover most if not the entirety of the shrewd cultivating prerequisites and situations as depicted in the presentation. Every product segment goes about as a solitary substance, with its own open API, which permits us to give a flexible distributed engineering, where applications can coordinate segments from various layers dependent on their specific needs. Along these lines, segments become attachment and play and can be specifically utilized by specific farming applications' requirements. In this way we have chosen and consolidated different programming parts, suitable for the space of keen horticulture, which comprise the Agri-IoT system. Agri-IoT can coordinate, control, and procedure an enormous assortment of cross-space spilling information sources in a flexible and extensible manner, utilizing normalized techniques for information obtaining following IoT standards, utilizing semantics.

6.4   APPLICATION OF IoT IN AGRICULTURE

Smart farming using IoT innovations assists farmers with reducing field waste and improve profitability. It is a capital-intensive and hi-tech arrangement of smart devices for growing food cleanly and sustainable for the rapidly increasing populace. It is the demand of present-day using ICT into horticulture integrated with sensing devices. IoT-based smart farming is highly efficient when compared with the conventional approach. IoT-based technology is turning traditional farming to smart farming with sensors and other devices. It is a framework that is designed for monitoring the crop field with the assistance of sensing gadgets to collect information about light, humidity, temperature, soil moisture, etc., and automating the whole agriculture practice. Now, as discussed, it enables farmers to monitor the field conditions from anywhere. Additionally, it is also helpful in the irrigation system. It is also helpful in the irrigation system. The farmers can monitor the field conditions from anywhere.

6.4.1   PRECISION FARMING

Precision agriculture agribusiness can primarily be characterized as the assortment of continuous information from farm variables, i.e., and utilization of prescient examination for intelligent decisions to maximize yields, limit the natural effect and diminish cost [31, 32]. It is a procedure or training that makes the cultivating technique increasingly precise and controlled for raising livestock and developing of yields. The items like sensors, autonomous vehicles, automated hardware, control systems, and robotics, work collaboratively with ICT and control frameworks, apply autonomy, and so on in this methodology are considered as crucial components. Precision agriculture, in the ongoing years, has grown one of the most renowned uses of IoT in the agrarian part, and an immense number of associations have begun utilizing this strategy around the globe (Figure 6.1).

The services and administrations offered by IoT frameworks incorporate soil dampness tests, VRI advancement, virtual enhancer PRO. VRI (variable-rate irrigation) advancement is a procedure that augments the benefit on flooded harvest fields with soil changeability, in this manner improving yields and expanding water use proficiency [33].

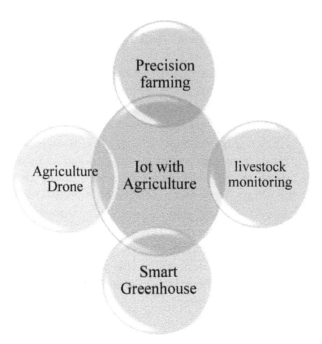

FIGURE 6.1   Application of IoT in agriculture.

6.4.2   AGRICULTURE DRONE

Technological advancements have nearly altered the rural tasks, and the presentation of farming automatons by introducing drones is the trending distraction. The Ground and Aerial drones are utilized for appraisal of yield wellbeing, crop checking, planting crop spraying, and field analysis. With legitimate methodology and arranging dependent on ongoing information, drone innovation has given a skyscraper and makeover to the horticulture business. Agriculture drones with warm or multispectral sensors recognize the regions that require changes in the water system. When the harvests begin developing, sensors show their wellbeing and ascertain their vegetation file. They are being utilized in agribusiness to upgrade different farming practices. The drone collects multispectral, thermal, and visual imagery during the flight and then lands in the same location it took off.

6.4.3 LIVESTOCK MONITORING

There is increasing global concern about the extension of agricultural production to provide enough food for the world's population. Thus, the importance of livestock management in agriculture is of the utmost value to livelihood. In this way, the significance of livestock management in agriculture holds the most extreme incentive. Yet, with ever-increasing worries regarding land and water supplies, farmers are struggling to maintain their crops and livestock. Aside from this, diminishing waste and reducing general expenses stays a need for farmers. It is essential to screen the wellbeing levels of animal livestock to prevent illness and diagnose diseases prior. IoT arrangements use wearables; for example, electronic groups with the capacity to stream information to the cloud. These wearables are mounted on the animal while the integrated sensors in them help to catch information and tell ranchers around a few factors that legitimately affect domesticated animal's wellbeing. Keeping track of an animal's regenerative cycle generally is dreary, yet with the assistance of IoT-based observing, it tends to be made simpler. Tracking location is something essential for the farmers as many grounds are spread over the homestead. It is hard to supervise numerous animals physically at a time, so wearable gadgets help farmers in getting the specific areas of their animals through the following mode.

6.4.4 SMART GREENHOUSE

To make our nurseries brilliant and smart greenhouse, IoT has empowered climate stations to consequently modify the atmosphere conditions as indicated by a specific arrangement of guidelines. Reception of IoT in Greenhouses has dispensed with the human intercession, in this manner, making the whole procedure financially practical and expanding efficiency and reliability simultaneously. For instance, utilizing sunlight-based controlled IoT sensors manufacturers present modern and cost-effective greenhouses. These sensors gather and transmit the ongoing information, which helps in checking the nursery state precisely all the time. With the assistance of the sensors, the water utilization and greenhouse state can be observed through messages or SMS cautions. Automatic and smart irrigation is completed with the assistance of IoT. These sensors help to give data on the weight, mugginess, temperature, and light levels. Greenhouse cultivating is a technique that helps in significant improvement in the total yield of vegetables, natural products, crops.

6.5   THE SUBSPACE OF IoT IN AGRICULTURE

Animal monitoring: The position of brushing creatures in vineyards requires additional assistance to the animal agronomy exercises. Such help must consolidate the checking and molding mortals' lead, particularly their taking care of bearing. With such a framework, it is conceivable to allow sheep to brush in the formed region (for example, manor, plantations) without endangering them. Accordingly, animal conduct checking stage because of IoT developments is required. It integrates an IoT neighborhood system to accumulate information from animals and a cloud stage, with getting ready and capacity abilities, to shepherd ovine inside vineyard zones self-sufficiently. The cloud stage similarity fuses AI highlights, allowing the extraction of applicable data from the information accumulated by the IoT establishments:

1. **Humidity and Temperature Monitoring:** The point of this sub-area is to assess and decide the cool to keep from damaging influences. In a research article, an IoT-based framework has been proposed for observing farming air, humidity, and temperature. This framework offers a constant microclimate detecting procedure that depends on WSNs. The framework covers of a temperature and clamminess sensor that is reinforced by a correspondence innovation called ZigBee and fueled by sun-oriented board.

2. **Soil Monitoring:** Smart Agriculture is engaged around soil, environment, and crop conditions. Given the significance of weather and water system, Soil Monitoring integrated with smart network exploits innovation to engage agriculturalists and creators to augment increasing vintage, lessen the bug and optimal utilization of resources. IoT sensors can gage soil temperature, volumetric water content, photosynthetic radiation, soil water potential and soil oxygen levels. Information from the IoT sensors is then transmitted back to an essential issue (or the cloud) for analysis, representation, and pattern examination. The resultant information would then be able to be utilized to upgrade cultivating activities, recognize patterns, and cause unobtrusive changes following conditions to boost crop profit and quality.

3. **Irrigation Monitoring and Controlling:** Brilliant farm water system structure deploy android phones for tracking and regulating of dribbles remotely by deploying remote sensors. Zigbee exploits the correspondence between sensor hubs and base station. Monitoring of field water system framework remotely not only lessens human mediation also allows distant examination and controlling on an android telephone.

4. **Precision Farming:** The IoT is helping change the way that ranchers work through exactness cultivating, a homestead the board idea that utilizes sensors, information, and system correspondence to tailor the cultivating framework to the particular states of each field. The outcome is a progressively productive framework that advances maintainable development while reducing expenses.

5. **Fertilization and Pest Monitoring:** Remotely screen for explicit vermin to comprehend their movement, area, and examples. This should be possible utilizing by associating traps to report explicit nuisance levels, along these lines computerizing checking and information assortment to take progressively exact and snappier countermeasures. One model would be an apple plantation that might need to quantify codling moth levels in various regions of the ranch so it tends to be prepared to make a move when vital.

6. **Water Resource Optimization:** Following hyper-neighborhood climate conditions can likewise add setting to help foresee the size and danger level of nuisance populaces. One model is olive ranches hoping to battle organic product flies and their hatchlings, which cause untimely falling of the natural product. Temperature and precipitation are key markers that help anticipate organic product fly movement, and whenever followed progressively, this data can illuminate what moves ought to be made.

7. **Disaster Management:** IoT advances cannot prevent debacles from occurring, yet can be exceptionally helpful for fiasco readiness, for example, forecast, and early admonition frameworks. Thusly IoT can make up for a helpless framework that places creating and rising nations in an especially defenseless position.

8. **Air Pollution Controlling and Management:** The IoT arrangement means to screen contamination levels, particularly levels present inside urban communities, by utilizing a few IoT gadgets and joined sensors. The thought includes having different stations put in a few regions of urban communities. These stations occasionally transfer and send information to the IoT cloud.

9. **Crop Yield Prediction and Management:** Utilizing the idea of IoT and wireless sensor network (WSN), a shrewd cultivating framework has been created in numerous zones of the world. The air, crop innate characteristics, crop the executives (power just as the executive's aptitude level), and the substance and physical properties of soils affect crop yield soil conditions.

10. **Greenhouse Illumination Control:** A nursery is a structure that is worked of dividers and a straightforward rooftop and is intended to keep up managed climatic conditions. IoT and Arduino based Greenhouse Environment Monitoring and Controlling Project is intended to keep up these conditions in the nursery (Table 6.1).

6.6   IoT WITH DATA SCIENCE IN AGRICULTURE

The traditional database context needs more stowage for the information gathered from the IoT sensors. Cloud-based information keeping, retrieval framework, and an end-to-end IoT platform undertake a significant job in the smart agribusiness framework. These frameworks are appraised to suppose as substantial work with the end goal that better exercises can be done. In the IoT world, sensing types of equipment are the indispensable primary source of collecting relevant data for an enormous space. The information gathered using the analytical and technical advancements and, take optimal and quick decision. With the support of the IoT devices, an individual can get information on the ongoing status of the crops by catching the data from various devices. Utilizing perceptive evaluation and predictive analytics, one can get the acquaintance to have better choices related to agriculture practice. By exploring the trends, it helps in knowing forthcoming climate conditions. The agriculturists can keep up the nature of yields and fruitfulness of the land along these lines improving the item volume and quality with IoT in the Agriculture Industry. The following benefits are target outcomes when IoT is integrated with data science and its analytical tool [33–35]:

1. **Prediction:** IoT provides comprehensive information that can be considered to approximate contemporary weather conditions. Data analysis tool and the smart programmed system can be deployed to forecast the weather changes and make available information-driven results based on data collected using various sensing devices. However, data collected through IoT devices are used to predict the various aspects of agriculture practice. It is useful in prior warning to farmers about weather changes, disease. It also estimates the crop health and growth. The whole analysis is extensively utilized for crop yield prediction, optimal utilization of the limited resource, computing the need for fertilizers, irrigation, and control other factors that affect the agriculture process [36]. In forestry, the sensing devices can be used to keep an eye on fire epidemic or locating the region in the

TABLE 6.1 Smart Phone Application for Agribusiness Using IoT Framework

Mobile Apps	Application	Features/Achievements
AgroDecisor EFC [25]	Fungicide	Essentially, this application presents a scoring framework (SS) in light of climate, infection pressure, and different components that are helpful to evaluate the likelihood of anticipated net profit for fungicide treatment. By and large, it encourages ranchers to lessen the quantity of fungicide applications by giving scoring levels to the best possible utilization of fungicide.
LandPKS [10]	Soil assessment	USDA-ARS created the LandPKS application in a joint effort with CU Boulder and NMSU with help from USAID, BLM, and NRCS. It assists clients with settling on progressively reasonable land management choices by permitting them to gather geo-found information about their soils and vegetation. It has high potential relying upon atmosphere, geography, and generally static soil properties (like soil surface, profundity, and mineralogy). This application assists with improving farmers' understanding of the land's latent capacity, just as environmental change adjustment and moderation exercises
PocketLAI [9]	Irrigation	The application gages leaf region records (LAI), a critical factor in deciding a plant's water necessities. It utilizes the portable camera and accelerometer sensor to secure pictures at 57.5° beneath the shade while the client continues rotating the sensing devices along its major axis.
PETEFA [13]	GIS	It gives data about the normalized difference vegetation index (NDVI) of different harvests at various phases of the lifecycle. Besides, it gives a geo-referenced soil investigation organized by parcels.
Ecofert [15]	Fertilizer Management	The application Ecofert assists with overseeing fertilizers for optimal utilization. It figures the best blend of fertilizers dependent on the necessary supplement arrangement and thinks about the requirements of different harvests. Besides, it considers the expense of compost dependent on current market costs
eFarm [16]	GIS	The application is a crowdsourcing and human sensing tool that collects geotagged rural land data at the land bundle level. It is exceptionally reasonable for detecting, planning, and displaying of farming area framework considers.
EVAPO [24]	Irrigation	EVAPO motive is to assess the expected evapotranspiration (PET) progressively utilizing the atmosphere lattice information from NASA-POWER. This application can be utilized for any area on the planet to improve water system proficiency through water preservation information

TABLE 6.1 *(Continued)*

Mobile Apps	Application	Features/Achievements
AgriMaps [17]	Land management	This application follows a proof-based, site-explicit way to deal with make suggestions for crop yield and land management. It gives a stage to spatial information perception with a more noteworthy scope of geo-spatial data contrasted with other comparable applications.
SnapCard [18]	Spraying applications	With the help of mobile-based sensing devices, the application helps in counting of droplet size. It was developed for analyzing the imaging-based spray in the fields.
AMACA [14]	Machinery/tools	"AMACA" (agricultural machine app cost analysis) is created for deciding the hardware cost in various field tasks and making it accessible utilizing a web portable application utilizing a cross-stage approach. The client has driven quality function deployment (QFD) approach was actualized to connect the client desires with the structural attributes of the application. The AMACA application is free, promptly accessible, and does not require any establishment on the end client's gadget. It is a cross-platform application implying that it works on any device through a web interface and is upheld by various browsers. The client can make subsequent computations by shifting the information boundaries (fuel value, loan fee, field limit, tractor power) and analyze the outcomes in an affectability examination premise. AMACA application can bolster the choices on whether to buy another hardware/tractor (vital level), the utilization of its apparatus, or to enlist a helper and to choose the economic appropriate development framework (strategic level). Equipment costs are a significant lump of harvest uses. This application is useful to appraise the expense of hardware and its usage in different field tasks. A client-driven quality capacity arrangement (QFD) approach is followed to interface the client's desires with the structural attributes of the application.
SWApp [19]	Irrigation	The main motto to develop this application is to monitor the land with dry region and where the irrigation is required more. The application provides significant and efficient solution to problem arising in area where groundwater level is low and irrigation sources are very limited. The application tends to deliver the reliable and robust solution, optimal use of resources, monitoring moisture level of soil and continuous track of weather condition.
Weedsmart [20]	Weed management	Weedsmart application is specifically focused on paddock and targets the weed management; the application is assumed to provide solution based on various questions about a paddock's farming system that user of application needs to answer.

TABLE 6.1 *(Continued)*

Mobile Apps	Application	Features/Achievements
VillageTree [21]	Pest management	The smart pest organization tool is named as "VillageTree" that provide solutions by collecting pest frequency reports from agriculturists on the basis of these reports and their analysis other landowner and farmer are informed by sending alert and location information in the surroundings.
WISE [22]	Irrigation	For optimal irrigation systems, WISE, a cloud-based irrigation tool provides a schedule for irrigation. To fulfill the objective, it uses the soil water balance method, and the user is informed about soil moisture dearth and weather condition analysis.
SafReg [23]	Forestry management	Timber construction and better organization of natural rejuvenation in agroforestry systems is the primary objective for this application is developed. With the target mentioned above, 20 agricultural land from Costa Rica, Nicaragua, and Honduras is considered. The application is not only meant to save time but also makes the system cost-effective.
BioLeaf [26]	Health monitoring	Leaves are considered using a computer vision approach to monitor the health of the plant. It identifies the damaged area in leaf, mainly because of bugs. Given the image processing approach, two methods, "Otsu thresholding and Bezier curve," are utilized to appraise the foliar misfortune in leaves with or without fringe harm.
cFertigUAL [27]	Fertigation	The app is developed to compute the essential requirement of the amount of fertilizer and water needed for specific crop types based on various harvesting systems and the variety of fertigation technologies. It is meant to help the farmers to achieve the precise application of water and other nutrients in greenhouse farming.
WheatCam [14]	Crop insurance	The "crop insurance" application is developed for improving the eminence and finding enough amount of money for insurance based on an image-based insurance approach. Smartphone camera is utilized to take pictures pre and post harmed safe region. In general, it enhances the symmetric data and minimizes the expenses of cases check contrasted with reimbursement protection strategies.

timberland that may be at high risk of fire outbreak. This information collected is useful to take the precautionary measures by firefighters in a particular position [37].

2. **Decision Making:** Data analytic requires relevant information that can be collected from sensors devices to make a better decision. The extensive data obtained offers learning prospects to expand decision making in continuously moving weather situation to automate the decision. Such automated decision varies from controlling the temperatures, taking decision regarding pest management to the irrigation system to ensure the quality of end products. The artificial intelligence (AI) algorithm enables the individual to regulate the optimal situation needed to grow crops. Data science gives a choice on the dedicated direction to farmers, microbes, and disease control and proposal from remote master direction frameworks.

3. **Storage Management:** An enormous number of agriculture products are regularly lost because of weak stockpiling system. Ecological factors like temperature, dampness extraordinarily influences the storage of food items. The utilization of IoT and Data Science administration frameworks can assist with improving horticulture items storage [38, 39]. Sensors can be sent to screen the storerooms and weather conditions. The information is sent to the cloud server to examine. An automated framework, which depends on the examined information, can be conveyed to modify the room conditions. Besides, a notice alarm can be started to farmers when extraordinary conditions are reached or if pests or insects are harming in the storeroom. In India, it is reported that about 35% to 40% of the new item is lost, subsequently due to several factors from collecting the food from agriculture lands to delivery of those items to end-users or storage rooms. In Ref. [40], a cold storage room organization framework depends on IoT innovation, to work at a controlled temperature.

4. **Farm Monitoring:** The coordinated farm management framework allows an entire farm to be observed. Information is collected through a network of sensors, counting the on-body sensors in creatures with the solitary objective of driving output. Three primary components, which includes hazard management, cost, and throughput, need to be overseen with real-time information and adequately optimized to maximize productivity [28]. Data science plays a significant role in presenting the farmers and stakeholders with valuable information that can be cautiously considered to avoid the unnecessary hazard

or implementing preventive solutions to improve yield. Data science also permits several lands to be organized on a single platform, where information on scientific advances, creation, advertising, land management, recommending the quick solution and other management, and other related topics, i.e., disease identification, insect attacks, crop yield health monitoring and many more.

6.7 VARIOUS CHALLENGES AND KEY ISSUE

By receiving IoT in the horticultural segment we get various advantages, yet at the same time, there are difficulties looked by IoT in agrarian parts. The greatest difficulties looked by IoT in the rural division are the absence of data, high appropriation expenses, and security concerns, and so forth. The vast majority of the ranchers do not know about the usage of IoT in agribusiness. Serious issue is that some of them are against new thoughts and they would prefer not to embrace regardless of whether it gives various advantages. The best thing that should be possible to bring issues to light of IoT's effect is to exhibit ranchers the utilization of IoT gadgets like automatons, sensors, and different advances and they could give them ease at work and joined by certifiable models.

There are many open issues and difficulties that are related with the execution of IoT applications. A portion of the difficulties that are distinguished from the writing have been examined in this area:

1. **Cost:** Gear expected to execute IoT in farming is costly. Anyway, sensors are the most economical part, yet furnishing the entirety of the ranchers' fields to be with them would cost in excess of 1,000 dollars. Robotized apparatus cost more than physically worked hardware as they incorporate expense for ranch the executives programming and cloud access to record information. To gain higher benefits, it is huge for ranchers to put resources into these advancements anyway it would be hard for them to make the underlying speculation to set up IoT innovation at their homesteads.

2. **Scalability:** Scale, by definition, alludes to "the capacity of a framework, system, or procedure to deal with a developing measure of work, or its capability to be amplified so as to oblige that development." It has its own difficulties.

3. **Security and Privacy:** Since IoT gadgets collaborate with more seasoned gear they approach the web association, there is no assurance

that they would have the option to get to ramble planning information or sensor readouts by taking advantage of open association. A huge measure of information is gathered by IoT agrarian frameworks which is hard to ensure. Somebody can have unapproved get to IoT suppliers' database and could take and control the information.

4. **Reliability:** In the field of agribusiness, IoT gadgets are conveyed in an open domain because of which brutal ecological conditions may cause correspondence disappointment and the embarrassment of sent sensors. Thusly, it is essential to guarantee the physical wellbeing of conveyed IoT gadgets/sensors to shield them from extreme atmosphere conditions.

5. **Localization:** There are numerous variables that should be thought of while conveying gadgets/sensors. Such gadgets ought to be able to give usefulness and backing to the remainder of the world without conveying extra gadgets with overhead design. Also, it is imperative to choose the best arrangement position so gadgets can convey and trade data with no obstruction.

6. **Interest of Farmer in Agribusiness:** The cost, lack of awareness, scalability, reliability, etc., all affect the interest of farmers in this business.

7. **Interoperability:** There are billions of IoT gadgets, guidelines, and conventions that are expected to interoperate. Interoperability includes semantic, syntactic, specialized, and hierarchical approach. Semantic interoperability is the capacity to manage the understanding of substance traded among people. Linguistic interoperability is identified with information groups, for example, JavaScript object documentation (JSON), information exchanged electronically, extensible markup language (XML), and factors isolated by a comma. Specialized interoperability is related with the improvement of framework, conventions, and equipment/programming parts that empower the IoT gadgets' correspondence. Hierarchical interoperability is identified with strategies for conveying and moving information adequately over the distinctive geographic locales and foundation.

6.8 FUTURE SCOPE AND CONCLUSION

The chapter deals with demystifying IoT in agriculture practice and smart practices in land management. The chapter focus on background details and the necessity of network and ICT in agriculture. Various trends of IoT are introduced for the successful deployment of IoT in agriculture is discussed. The work is representing how several small things can be connected efficiently to avail substantial benefits, and one can get benefitted from their interdependency. IoT in Agriculture applies from garden farming to large scale agriculture practice. It is helpful in all practices from precision farming, animal monitoring, optimizing the resources, i.e., water, fertilizers, transportation, storage room, crop health monitoring like their growth, yield, diseases, insect attack, and several other factors that may affect plantation. Several mobile-based and web-based applications also introduced to take care of farming culture. Identifying weather conditions, soil moisture, humidity, fire outbreak, natural disasters management, and similar things are nowadays significant benefit any individual farmer is getting on-site. The significant operational efficiency and various key issues are also discussed when IoT is integrated with data analytics. In the future, there is a scope to manage more activities simultaneously and reduce the several factors that are limiting smart farming.

KEYWORDS

- **agri-business**
- **data analytics**
- **light-emitting diode**
- **livestock monitoring**
- **precision farming**
- **sensors**

REFERENCES

1. Farooq, M. S., Riaz, S., Abid, A., Umer, T., & Zikria, Y. B., (2020). Role of IoT technology in agriculture: A systematic literature review. *Electronics, 9*(2), 319.
2. Giorgetti, A., Lucchi, M., Tavelli, E., Barla, M., Gigli, G., Casagli, N., & Dardari, D., (2016). A robust wireless sensor network for landslide risk analysis: System design, deployment, and field testing. *IEEE Sensors Journal, 16*(16), 6374–6386.
3. Zheng, R., Zhang, T., Liu, Z., & Wang, H., (2016). An EIoT system designed for ecological and environmental management of the Xianghe segment of China's grand canal. *International Journal of Sustainable Development & World Ecology, 23*(4), 372–380.

4. Torres-Ruiz, M., Juárez-Hipólito, J. H., Lytras, M. D., & Moreno-Ibarra, M., (2016). Environmental noise sensing approach based on volunteered geographic information and Spatio-temporal analysis with machine learning. In: *International Conference on Computational Science and its Applications* (pp. 95–110). Springer, Cham.

5. Hachem, S., Mallet, V., Ventura, R., Pathak, A., Issarny, V., Raverdy, P. G., & Bhatia, R., (2015). Monitoring noise pollution using the urban civics middleware. In: *2015 IEEE First International Conference on Big Data Computing Service and Applications* (pp. 52–61). IEEE.

6. Liu, Z., Huang, J., Wang, Q., Wang, Y., & Fu, J., (2013). Real-time barrier lakes monitoring and warning system based on wireless sensor network. In: *2013 Fourth International Conference on Intelligent Control and Information Processing (ICICIP)* (pp. 551–554). IEEE.

7. Song, Y., Ma, J., Zhang, X., & Feng, Y., (2012). Design of wireless sensor network-based greenhouse environment monitoring and automatic control system. *Journal of Networks, 7*(5), 838.

8. Sakthipriya, N., (2014). An effective method for crop monitoring using wireless sensor network. *Middle-East Journal of Scientific Research, 20*(9), 1127–1132.

9. Camacho, A., & Arguello, H., (2018). Smartphone-based application for agricultural remote technical assistance and estimation of visible vegetation index to farmer in Colombia: AgroTIC. In: *Remote Sensing for Agriculture, Ecosystems, and Hydrology XX* (Vol. 10783, p. 107830K). International Society for Optics and Photonics.

10. Andriamandroso, A. L. H., Lebeau, F., Beckers, Y., Froidmont, E., Dufrasne, I., Heinesch, B., & Bindelle, J., (2017). Development of an open-source algorithm based on inertial measurement units (IMU) of a smartphone to detect cattle grass intake and ruminating behaviors. *Computers and Electronics in Agriculture, 139*, 126–137.

11. Azam, M. M., Rosman, S. H., Mustaffa, M., Mullisi, S. S., Wahy, H., Jusoh, M. H., & Ali, M. M., (2016). Hybrid water pump system for hilly agricultural site. In: *2016 7th IEEE Control and System Graduate Research Colloquium (ICSGRC)* (pp. 109–114). IEEE.

12. Herrick, J. E., Beh, A., Barrios, E., Bouvier, I., Coetzee, M., Dent, D., & Matuszak, J., (2016). The land-potential knowledge system (LandPKS): Mobile apps and collaboration for optimizing climate change investments. *Ecosystem Health and Sustainability, 2*(3), e01209.

13. Morales, G., (2018). *PETEFA: Geographic Information System for Precision Agriculture.* 10.1109/INTERCON.2018.8526414.

14. Ayaz, M., Ammad-Uddin, M., Sharif, Z., Mansour, A., & Aggoune, E. H. M., (2019). Internet-of-things (IoT)-based smart agriculture: Toward making the fields talk. *IEEE Access, 7*, 129551–129583.

15. Bueno-Delgado, M. V., Molina-Martínez, J. M., Correoso-Campillo, R., & Pavón-Mariño, P., (2016). Ecofert: An Android application for the optimization of fertilizer cost in fertigation. *Computers and Electronics in Agriculture, 121*, 32–42.

16. Jordan, R., Eudoxie, G., Maharaj, K., Belfon, R., & Bernard, M., (2016). AgriMaps: Improving site-specific land management through mobile maps. *Computers and Electronics in Agriculture, 123*, 292–296.

17. Ferguson, J. C., Chechetto, R. G., O'Donnell, C. C., Fritz, B. K., Hoffmann, W. C., Coleman, C. E., & Hewitt, A. J., (2016). Assessing a novel smartphone application–SnapCard, compared to five imaging systems to quantify droplet deposition on artificial collectors. *Computers and Electronics in Agriculture, 128*, 193–198.

18. Freebairn, D., Robinson, B., McClymont, D., Raine, S., Schmidt, E., Skowronski, V., & Eberhard, J., (2017). SoilWaterApp-monitoring soil water made easy. In: *Proceedings of the 18th Australian Society of Agronomy Conference*.

19. Scholz, M., (2018). Enhancing adoption of integrated weed management-an Australian farmer's perspective. *Outlooks on Pest Management, 29*(2), 66–69.

20. Suen, R. C. L., Chang, K. T., Wan, M. P. H., Ng, Y. C., & Tan, B. C., (2014). Interactive experiences designed for agricultural communities. In: *CHI'14 Extended Abstracts on Human Factors in Computing Systems* (pp. 551–554).

21. Bartlett, A. C., Andales, A. A., Arabi, M., & Bauder, T. A., (2015). A smartphone app to extend the use of a cloud-based irrigation scheduling tool. *Computers and Electronics in Agriculture, 111*, 127–130.

22. De Sousa, K., Detlefsen, G., Rivera, O., De Melo, E., Tobar, D., Castaño-Quintero, M. E., & Casanoves, F., (2015). Using a smartphone app to support participatory agroforestry planning in Central America. In: *Annals of World Forestry Congress (XIV)*. Durban, South Africa.

23. Júnior, W. M., Valeriano, T. T. B., & De Souza, R. G., (2019). EVAPO: A smartphone application to estimate potential evapotranspiration using cloud gridded meteorological data from NASA-POWER system. *Computers and Electronics in Agriculture, 156*, 187–192.

24. Carmona, M. A., Sautua, F. J., Pérez-Hernández, O., & Mandolesi, J. I., (2018). AgroDecisor EFC: First Android™ app decision support tool for timing fungicide applications for management of late-season soybean diseases. *Computers and Electronics in Agriculture, 144*, 310–313.

25. Machado, B. B., Orue, J. P., Arruda, M. S., Santos, C. V., Sarath, D. S., Goncalves, W. N., & Rodrigues-Jr, J. F., (2016). BioLeaf: A professional mobile application to measure foliar damage caused by insect herbivory. *Computers and Electronics in Agriculture, 129*, 44–55.

26. Pérez-Castro, A., Sánchez-Molina, J. A., Castilla, M., Sánchez-Moreno, J., Moreno-Úbeda, J. C., & Magán, J. J., (2017). cFertigUAL: A fertigation management app for greenhouse vegetable crops. *Agricultural Water Management, 183*, 186–193.

27. Ceballos, F., Kramer, B., & Robles, M., (2019). The feasibility of picture-based insurance (PBI): Smartphone pictures for affordable crop insurance. *Development Engineering, 4*, 100042.

28. Wang, N., Zhang, N., & Wang, M., (2006). Wireless sensors in agriculture and food industry—recent development and future perspective. *Computers and Electronics in Agriculture, 50*(1), 1–14.

29. Shannon, D. K., Clay, D. E., & Kitchen, N. R., (2020). *Precision Agriculture Basics* (Vol. 176). John Wiley & Sons.

30. Pathak, H. S., Brown, P., & Best, T., (2019). A systematic literature review of the factors affecting the precision agriculture adoption process. *Precision Agriculture, 20*(6), 1292–1316.

31. Tejada-Castro, M., Delgado-Vera, C., Garzón-Goya, M., Sinche-Guzmam, A., & Cárdenas-Rosales, X., (2019). Trends in the use of webapps in agriculture: A systematic review. In: *2nd International Conference on ICTs in Agronomy and Environment* (pp. 130–142). Springer, Cham.

32. Mendes, J., Pinho, T. M., Neves, D. S. F., Sousa, J. J., Peres, E., Boaventura-Cunha, J., & Morais, R., (2020). Smartphone applications targeting precision agriculture practices—A systematic review. *Agronomy, 10*(6), 855.

33. Elijah, O., Rahman, T. A., Orikumhi, I., Leow, C. Y., & Hindia, M. N., (2018). An overview of internet of things (IoT) and data analytics in agriculture: Benefits and challenges. *IEEE Internet of Things Journal, 5*(5), 3758–3773.

34. Chen, C. P., & Zhang, C. Y., (2014). Data-intensive applications, challenges, techniques and technologies: A survey on big data. *Information Sciences, 275*, 314–347.

35. Hong, S., & Kim, H., (2009). An analytical model for a GPU architecture with memory-level and thread-level parallelism awareness. In: *Proceedings of the 36th Annual International Symposium on Computer Architecture* (pp. 152–163).

36. Lee, H., Moon, A., Moon, K., & Lee, Y., (2017). Disease and pest prediction IoT system in orchard: A preliminary study. In: *2017 Ninth International Conference on Ubiquitous and Future Networks (ICUFN)* (pp. 525–527). IEEE.

37. Xu, G., Gao, S., Daneshmand, M., Wang, C., & Liu, Y., (2016). A survey for mobility big data analytics for geolocation prediction. *IEEE Wireless Communications, 24*(1), 111–119.

38. Godfray, H. C. J., Beddington, J. R., Crute, I. R., Haddad, L., Lawrence, D., Muir, J. F., & Toulmin, C., (2010). Food security: The challenge of feeding 9 billion people. *Science, 327*(5967), 812–818.

39. Nellemann, C., & MacDevette, M., (2009). *The Environmental Food Crisis: The Environment's Role in Averting Future Food Crises: A UNEP Rapid Response Assessment.* UNEP/Earth print.

40. Venkatesh, D., Tatti, M., Hardikar, P. G., Ahmed, S. S., & Sharavana, K., (2017). Cold storage management system for farmers based on IoT. *Int. J. Recent Trends Eng. Res.* ISSN, 2455-1457.

Role of the Internet of Things and Wireless Sensors in Agriculture Management

RAJAT TIWARI

Department of Electronics and Communication Engineering, Chandigarh University, Punjab–140413, India, E-mail: er.rajattiwari@gmail.com

ABSTRACT

In agriculture production, weed control is a time-consuming and expensive process. The differentiation of seeds in the field in which crops and weeds intermingle is of great value for weeding and spraying pesticides. Weed monitoring in crop production can be carried out using various techniques, including manually surveys, sensors on land vehicles, or remote sensing. Weed labeling and identification for a region-specific weed control are one of the basic and essential steps. It eliminates the potential risk and adverse effect on human health and crops from the use of excessive pesticides. Because uniform spraying process of pesticides is the prevailing technique. This method wastes the pesticides by spreading it to the areas where no weeds exist. The creation of an online weed detector sensor is a progressive step towards the application of variable pesticide level. To deal with the traditional pesticides, non-chemical weed control method must be focused towards a specific weeding technique. The primary concern is to measure the accuracy of a ground-based weed tracking system that would include optoelectronic weed tracking sensors and to determine the sampling details needed for effective weed maps. A large number of sensors are available with the advancement in remote sensing technologies, which provides the various number of bands with various spectral resolutions. Segregation between the different plants could be carried out from the basis of spectral reflection of both the plants. The impact of this variability on identification of weeds are analyzed. The sensor uses laser as an illumination source to monitor the relative value of reflected light in narrow wavebands. The optical characteristics of the source of light have been modified to get a more even illumination around the sensor's viewing platform. An optic mechanical system has developed and installed with the reliability needed to operate the weed sensor under the outside area.

7.1 INTRODUCTION

The Indian economy depends on agricultural production. For more than half of the population is the source of revenue. Agricultural production is the major issue in today's world, with the growing demand for agricultural goods and need to upgrade the plantation system. One of the major problems in the agriculture is the control of rising weeds among all the crops. A weed is a plant in the wrong spot. The weed is the plant that developed forcefully. Many plants that people see this is as weeds are intentionally grown in agriculture, where they are referred to as useful weeds [1]. Sometimes weeds are useful as weeds maintain the nitrates in the soil when no crop for a long time as in barren conditions. Another way where weeds are useful when green manure plowed down these weeds trowel up and vanish in the soil eventually blend in the soil and boost it in different ways. Weeds also make a good compost when collected in piles and blended with the soil and a bit of lime. Weeds act as the host for the crop parasites that infect and degrade the crop quality. Many weeds can also harm ground surface, drain pipes [2]. Weed restricts crops growth by interfering with the crops for nutrients, sunlight, and water, resulting in noxious impact on agricultural production. With the incorporation of new weed control approach such as crop rotation, physical removal and mechanical separation, application of pesticides remains the most extensively used form of weed control. Farmers can cut the weeds manually, but it is big time consumable task other method is to use pesticides and other fertilizers to kill weeds but they have negative impact on living beings. So, one of the biggest obstacles is to aim of the sustainability is to reduce the number of pesticides used to control excessive weeds in the farm. Pesticide weed control is applied uniformly across the field, and the strength or volume of weeds are random across the whole field. So, if the use of pesticides is applied according to the weed density, then the cost of pesticides and the negative impact of pesticides on the environment can be reduced to some extent. For this type of implementation information about weed distribution across the field is required. Weed monitoring exercises are costly and can make agriculture financially infeasible. Agricultural weed control raises crop production expenses by investing in tools and equipment and pesticides expenses. Figure 7.1 shows various traditional methods for weed control [3].

FIGURE 7.1   Traditional weed control methods.

7.2   WEED MANAGEMENT TECHNIQUE

The weed control in agriculture is mechanized by cultivation or using pesticides. Weed management system includes directly to kill weeds, biological control of weeds and selection of crops, including the use of cover crops to suffocate the weed growth through condition. Weed Management tries to sustain plant densities at reasonable rates while avoiding shifts in weed community to harder to control plant population. The weed management techniques are chosen in such a way that how much crop production, availability of pesticides, cost of pesticides, climate is required. The best method is understanding of all these facts with climate conditions to each farm and area with in the farm. This data can be used in crop yield that direct crop management with an integrated weed control approach (Figure 7.2) [4].

Other problem faced in agriculture is temperature of climate, soil condition, irregular rainfall, and humidity. From these results, it is difficult for them to determine the threats that crop faced. That will be the serious implications.

Use of modern technologies such as cloud computing, IoT, big data that predict the hazards that crop will face in future. This would substantially reduce the burden and increase the yield productivity. Figure 7.3 shows the plant leaf disease.

FIGURE 7.2 Numerous parts of developed weed management combine to create an efficient weed management strategy.

FIGURE 7.3 The plant leaf disease.

Various approaches for visual diseases detection are to take digital copies of plant and perform preprocessing. The preprocessing method can be any of one textural feature's, edge detection and color space [5].

Various techniques used in smart agriculture for weed detection and disease detection are:

- Weed detection using support vector machine (SVM) method;
- Weed mapping using neural network;
- Weed mapping using ground-based sensors;
- Weed mapping using optoelectronic sensors;
- Weed mapping using optical sensors;
- Weed mapping using laser-based spectroscopy;
- Weed mapping using image processing;
- Weed detection using IoT.

7.3 ROLE OF IoT IN SMART AGRICULTURE

IoT interconnects human beings to things and things to things and things to humans. IoT aims to build a massive network by integrating various forms of connected devices. The three aims of the IoTs are: Communication, cost-saving, and automation. When the data is processed, when it enters the network, the program processes data obtained. Figure 7.4 shows the role of IoT in agriculture. Figure 7.4 describes a classification of major products, utilities, and wireless sensor used for developments in smart agriculture [6].

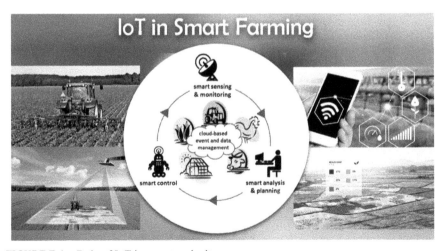

FIGURE 7.4 Role of IoT in smart agriculture.

Creating an IoT framework includes the correct selection and combination of sensors, networks, and modules of communication. Following IoT components used in IoT system tells how IoT works (Figure 7.5) [7]:

- Sensor device;
- Connectivity;
- User interface;
- Data processing.

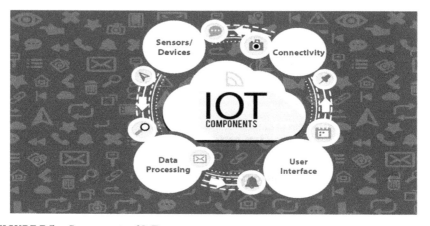

FIGURE 7.5   Components of IoT.

Sensors are used to collect very minute data from the environment. And the collected data is sent to a database network but requires a transport medium. Transport communication medium such as:

- Wi-Fi;
- Bluetooth;
- WAN;
- Zigbee;
- Z-waves;
- NFC;
- LoRaWAN;
- Cellular.

7.3.1   ZIGBEE

ZigBee is built specifically for a wide variety of applications in general to replace existing nonstandard technologies. The device based on this protocol can be one of three types based on application specifications: router, controller, and end-user. ZigBee networks called star, Mesh, and cluster Tree different topologies (Figure 7.6) [8].

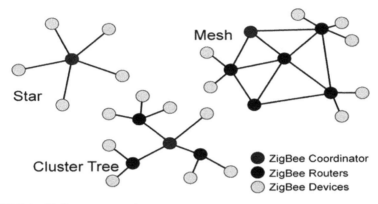

FIGURE 7.6 ZigBee representation.

7.3.2 BLUETOOTH

Bluetooth is a wireless transmission protocol that links tiny heads devices over shorter distances that typically operate in close proximity to one another. This technology is used in many smart farming applications thanks to its advantages of low power requirements, simple to use and low cost. In addition, Bluetooth makes advances with the introduction of Bluetooth in many IoT systems.

7.3.3 LORAWAN

The long range, low power wireless qualities of Lora WAN technology allow low-cost sensors to send data from the farm to the cloud where it can be examined to enhance operations. It allows farming companies to deliver numerous services using a common IoT enabler platform, providing LoRaWANTM network server and software for managing private or public networks under a unified, SCALab. Advantages of LoRaWAN are (Figure 7.7) [9]:

- Total cost of ownership low network;
- Versatility in mode of network deployment;
- Battery life optimization;
- High safety;
- Fast-growing open ecosystem of producers of original equipment.

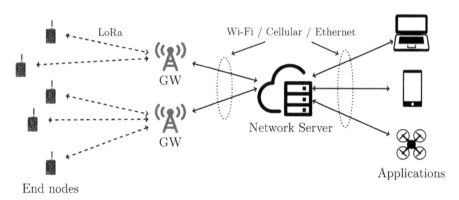

FIGURE 7.7   LoRaWAN representation.

7.3.4   *Z WAVES*

It is a low power frequency technology mainly proposed for home automation, including the control lamp and many sensors. Z waves used for trustworthy communication among small data packets. It capable the topology of complete mesh networks without the necessity for a coordinator node and could manage up to 232 devices. Sigma designs is still the only one Z-wave creator as opposed to ZigBee and others that have several manufacturers. This system of communication consists of multiple devices that are marked by specific network ID. Identification of all multiple nodes that are part of a single logical Z-wave network is the network Id (Figure 7.8) [10].

7.3.5   *NFC*

The NFC tags are used as the key identifier of different elements of agricultural management. The in-field service node, which is focused on a programmable system-on-chip with IP core, supports device management activities in distributed agricultural (Figure 7.9).

7.3.6   *WI-FI*

Wi-Fi is the most frequent alternative for developers. It is also called wireless LAN. Wi-Fi is technology in which is necessary for data transmission from one location to another high frequency RF waves are used. Wi-Fi range between two places is approximately 50 m. The Wi-Fi system only works with high frequency radio signaling. It flops to work properly in low frequency. Now it is used in home network, IoT application, office, college, and also in many boarding such as Yun, and raspberry pi (RPi) Arduino. The common standard used is 802.11n, which is generally found in homes and other IoT applications consisting of remote various sensors connected to the microcontroller. It delivers fast data transfer speeds in hundreds of Mbps which are higher than Bluetooth. Wi-Fi operating frequencies vary between 2.4 GHz and 5 GHz. It can effectively duplex links over 50 m. Wi-Fi l data rate is from 150–200 Mbps, but maximum speed is 600 Mbps.

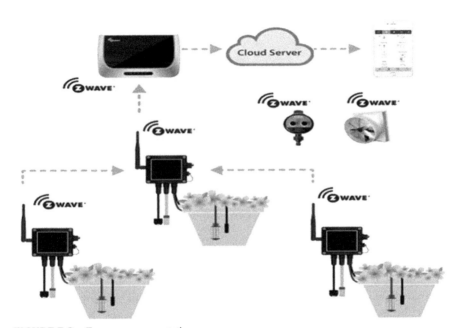

FIGURE 7.8   Z waves representation.

7.3.7   *CELLULAR*

Technology enables connection between IoT devices, i.e., GAN-Generic Access Network and Unlicensed Mobile Access. Unlicensed Mobile Access provides services to the network through Unlicensed Mobile Access technologies such as the wireless network. Initially, Unlicensed Mobile Access was designed for the use of GSM/EDGE cellular technology through various Unlicensed Mobile Access points. It is now being developed under the name of generic network of access. Unlicensed Mobile Access also offers faultless switching between Wi-Fi protocol and cellular network. It connects different technologies such as Wi-Fi, 802.11 and Bluetooth to the cellular network. So, it is very supportive where it can connect sensor directly to the cellular base station of the many spectrum businesses. Mobile use and other various application have developed rapidly across the world. Effective and short-range wireless communication with links from the cellular network to wireless network would be possible.

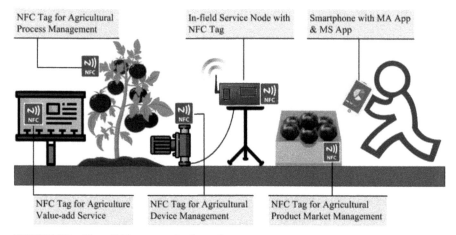

FIGURE 7.9   Near field communication role.

7.4   VARIOUS SENSORS USED IN SMART AGRICULTURE

In smart farming, known as precise farming, helps farmers to increase yields using limited resources including seeds, pesticides, water. By the use of sensors, farmers will start understanding the crops on a local scale, conserve resources. In precision agriculture, arrange of sensing technologies are used to provide the data that help the farmers to track and optimize crops and respond to various environmental factors [12].

7.4.1   LOCATION SENSOR

It uses the signals from GPS satellite to determine longitude, latitude. Examples a LIKENJRNJG1157PCD-TE1.

7.4.2 OPTICAL SENSORS

It is used to measure soil properties. Optical sensors are developed to determine moisture of soil, organic matter, and clay. Following Figure 7.10 shows a basic structure block for light sensors.

FIGURE 7.10   Photo IC sensor.

7.4.3 MECHANICAL SENSORS

These sensors measure the mechanical resistance. The sensor used probe that enters the soil and monitors resistive pressure using pressure gauges. It is also used to forecast the dragging conditions for ground engaging equipment's (Figure 7.11).

FIGURE 7.11   Mechanical sensor.

7.4.4 DIELECTRIC SOIL MOISTURE SENSORS

The total water content in soil is measured by moisture sensors. The dielectric constant of the soils, an electric feature that is majorly dependent on the moisture content, is measured by dielectric soil moisture sensors. Dielectric soil moisture sensors measure the level of humidity by calculating the dielectric constant in the soil.

7.4.5 AIRFLOW SENSORS

These sensors are required to measure the permeability of soil air. Different types of soil properties, including soil erosion, moisture of soil create specific signatures.

The output of these sensors is used for yield mapping, weed mapping, variable rate pesticides, variable spraying, salinity mapping.

Use of Sensors for Weed Detection: Ground-based tools are fully climate independent conditions and can be used to classify weed species and its density [13]. Commonly used sensors categorized as:

1. **Non-Imaging Sensors:** Non-imaging sensors yields advert in the field. The identification is done by following steps:
    i.   First identification is the spectral characteristics of emitted light, reflected light;
    ii. Second identification is height above the ground.
2. **Imaging Sensors:** Image taken with a video camera, and more recently from a high-resolution digital camera, can achieve higher spatial resolution. Contrast enhancement is used to increase the image's quality before it is processed further. As a consequence, output is a new image with improved edges, contrast, color, or other aspects of image quality.

7.4.6 SPECTROMETRIC SENSORS

The spectrometer technique is to calculate luminous intensity as wavelength function. It is achieved by the diffracting the beam into wavelength range, measuring the intensities with charge-coupled devices and showing the graph on detector and display the value at digital display (Figure 7.12).

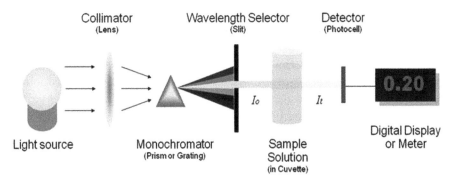

FIGURE 7.12   Principle of spectrometer.

Common sensors will deliver information to distinguish vegetation from the soil, but they are unable to distinguish between various plant types. Needed green leaves are distinguished by high green and lower reflectance in blue and red spectra. Spectrometer will provide the details to distinguish plants from the soil, but they are not capable of distinguishing between different plant types. The spectrometer, providing the certain measuring the depth of field, bends into area of region and thus obtained signal is the mixture of various plant species and soil quantities. The spectral characteristics of various plants and weeds species examined and used in controlled circumstances of their segregation, which cannot be directly translatable to field conditions. Because specular refection can change rapidly in field conditions because of general climatic conditions such as climatic variances and clouds the observations must be resolved as per the daytime and annual periods of light from the sun. Furthermore, spectrometric sensor efficiency is based on the combination of all entities in the visual field. Micro weeds that can be observed by an imaging sensor because of its higher spatial resolution, can therefore slip unnoticed and unappreciated [14].

7.4.7   OPTOELECTRONIC SENSOR

Sensors that concentrate on very few spectral bands are known as optoelectronic sensors. These are mainly concentrated on near-infrared/red bands. By calculating indices associated with plant coverage value, non-imaging optoelectronic sensor can distinguish between plant absence and presence. But they cannot find the difference between crop and weed. However, they are useful to find weed between rows in row crop. To map weed distribution inside the crop, ground-based weed mapping along with optoelectronic sensor with personal information can be used. The tracking system consists of three key points: sensors for plant detection, data collection, and DGPS receivers. Place of optoelectronic detectors in the crop row, the position of the DGPS transmitter and the viewing area of the detector in the center for each inter-row region (Figure 7.13) [15].

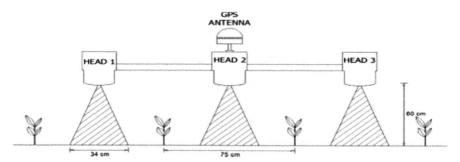

FIGURE 7.13   Optoelectronic sensor location.

7.4.8   TELEMATICS SENSORS

Telematics includes precision farming solutions by remotely automating decisions or actions. The wise machinery of farmers will use seeds and pesticides at interest rates based on soil requirements. Telematics sensors are more effective in promoting telecommunications between two locations between two automobiles when considering application focused on agriculture. Telemetry sensors are used to collect data from remote locations and report how well the components operate and position and travel routes to avoid the same patch being visited. Figure 7.14 shows how telematics used in agriculture [16].

7.4.9   MASS FLOW SENSORS

The mass availability sensor is the most important component, but ultimately the yield surveillance system consists of many other components such as the grain humidity sensors, information storage until an internal data analysis program.

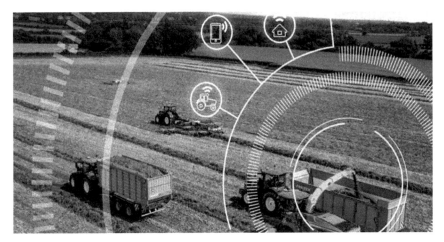

FIGURE 7.14   Telematics used in agriculture.

7.4.10   *LIDAR*

LIDAR is light detection and ranging. This system is used in a number of agricultural applications, such as land modeling and segmentation, soil type determination, 3D field mapping, erosion control and soil monitoring and yield forecasting. LIDAR is widely used to collect complex calculation information about the area of the fruit-tree leaf, it can generate a 3D map when combined with the GPS. Figure 7.15 shows LiDAR usage in agriculture.

FIGURE 7.15   Use of LIDAR in agriculture.

7.5 AGRICULTURAL LARGE DATA PROCESSING PLATFORM

The smart farming method produces a great deal of information in the crop cycle all the time and requires the smart farming system to make suitable reactions permitting to this information in a short period, attaining real time observing of growing crops, improving crops quality and enhance production rate. Big data processing stage that built on STORM and Cassandra according to the real requirement of the smart farming method and the characteristics of large field data. Big data analytics (BDA) stage puts together Storm's excellent real-time handling capabilities and excellent distributed storing information capabilities from Cassandra, and it is an important consequence for growth of smart farming system [17].

Big data knowledge is widespread technology after the cloud computing and IoT. It is extensively used in many areas like e-commerce, and financial analysis, social platform social platform, and so on. Smart farming will generate large quantities of complex structure data in the course of the project, and it will be very important to fully leverage the values of these data for the advancement of agriculture.

7.6 CONCLUSION

Deploying sensors and taking images services linked to the internet in the crop area sufficient IoT decisions may be taken. Effective use of IoT can be used to produce fertilizers and pesticides. Ultimately conclude that optimal agri-IoT development is required Architecture with low cost, low power interfaces application usage, efficient decision-making process, QoS support goals performance and it is easy to recognize the farmer without familiarity. IoT enables the agriculture crop observing easy and resourceful to enhance the output of the crop and hence gives profit to the farmer. WSN and various types of sensors are used to gather the data about crop condi-tions and changes in environment and this information is communicated to the farmer or to devices that initiates accurate actions through network. Various communication technologies and system provide independent deci-sion without human involvement. LoraWAN N/W protocol provides long distance communication with less energy consumption. Farmers are linked at any moment or anywhere in the world, and conscious of the conditions of the agricultural sector. Communication disadvantages have to be overwhelmed by progressing the technology to consume less resources also make user interface user friendly.

KEYWORDS

- **global system for mobile communications**
- **internet of things**
- **internet of things**
- **sensors**
- **unmanned flying vehicles**
- **weed**

REFERENCES

1. Lottes, P., Hoeferlin, M., Sander, S., M¨uter, M., Schulze, P., & Stachniss, L. C., (2016). An effective classification system for separating sugar beets and weeds for precision farming applications. In: *ICRA* (pp. 5157–5163).

2. Milioto, A., Lottes, P., & Stachniss, C., (2018). Real-time semantic segmentation of crop and weed for precision agriculture robots leveraging background knowledge in CNNS. In: *ICRA*, (pp. 2229–2235).

3. Lottes, P., Behley, J., Milioto, A., & Stachniss, C., (2018). Fully convolutional networks with sequential information for robust crop and weed detection in precision farming. *IEEE Robotics and Automation Letters (RA-L), 3*, 3097–3104,

4. Ronneberger, O., Fischer, P., & Brox, T., (2015). U-net: Convolutional networks for biomedical image segmentation. In: *International Conference on Medical Image Computing and Computer-Assisted Intervention* (pp. 234–241).

5. Aichen, W., Wen, Z., & Xinhua, W., (2019). A review on weed detection using ground-based machine vision and image processing techniques. In: *Proc. of the Elsevier Computers and Electronics in Agriculture.*

6. Nikesh, G., & Kawitkar, R. S., (2016). IoT based smart agriculture. *International Journal of Advanced Research in Computer and Communication Engineering.*

7. Varghese, R., & Smarita, S., (2018). Affordable smart farming using IoT and machine learning. In: *2018 Second International Conference on Intelligent Computing and Control Systems (ICICCS)* (pp. 645–650).

8. Gerhards, R., & Oebel, H., (2006). Practical experiences with a system for site-specific weed control in arable crops using real-time image analysis and GPS-controlled patch spraying. *Weed Res., 46*, 185–193.

9. Slaughter, D. C., Giles, D. K., & Downey, D., (2008). Autonomous robotic weed control systems: A review. *Comput. Electron. Agric., 61*, 63–78.

10. Balaji, B., Raghava, R., Ramesh, J. V. N., & Mohammed, A. H., (2014). Agriculture field monitoring and analysis using wireless sensor networks for improving crop production. *Eleventh International Conference on Wireless and Optical Communications Networks (WOCN).*

11. Liu, D., Cao, X., Huang, C., & Liangliang, J., (2015). Intelligent agent greenhouse environment monitoring system based on IoT technology. *International Conference on Intelligent Transportation, Big Data & Smart City.*

12. Joseph, H., & Kisangiri, M., (2014). Deployment of wireless sensor networks (WSN) in automated irrigation management and scheduling systems: A review. *Science, Computing and Telecommunications (PACT), Pan African Conference.*

13. Vijayakumar, S., & Nelson, R. J., (2011). Preliminary design for crop monitoring involving water and fertilizer conservation using wireless sensor networks. *Communication Software and Networks (ICCSN), IEEE 3ʳᵈ International Conference.*

14. Nisha, G., & Megala, J., (2014). Wireless sensor network based automated irrigation and crop field monitoring system. *Sixth International Conference on Advanced Computing (IcoAC).*

15. Ji-Hua, M., Bing-Fang, W., & Qiang-Zi, L., (2006). A global crop growth monitoring system based on remote sensing. *IEEE International Symposium on Geoscience and Remote Sensing.*

16. Alan, M., Joseph, P., Robert, S., David, C., & John, A., (2002). *Wireless Sensor Networks for Habitat Monitoring.* International Conference.

17. Lei, X., & Lejiang, G., (2010). The realization of precision agriculture monitoring system based on wireless sensor network. *International Conference on Computer and Communication Technologies in Agriculture Engineering.*

18. Ling-Ling, L., Shi-Feng, Y., Li-Yan, W., & Xiang-Ming, G., (2011). The greenhouse environment monitoring system based on wireless sensor network technology. *Proceedings of the 2011 IEEE International Conference on Cyber Technology in Automation, Control, and Intelligent Systems.* Kunming, China.

19. Chun-Ling, F., & Yuan, G., (2013). *The Application of a ZigBee Based Wireless Sensor Network in the LED Street Lamp Control System.* College of Automation & Electronic Engineering, Qingdao University of Scientific & Technology, Qingdao, China embedded technology, Consumer Electronics-China, 2014 IEEE International Conference.

20. FuBing, (2012). Research on the agriculture intelligent system based on IoT. *International Conference on Image Analysis and Signal Processing.*

21. Wen-Yao, Z., Miguel, C. J., Pedro, C., & Kam-Weng, T., (2011). Flood monitoring of distribution substation in low-lying areas using wireless sensor network. *Proceedings of International Conference on System Science and Engineering.* Macau, China.

22. Lin, Z., Min, Y., Deyi, T., Xia, O., Xiang, Z., & Yuanyuan, Z., (2010). Design and implementation of granary monitoring system based on wireless sensor network node. *International Conference on Measuring Technology and Mechatronics Automation.*

23. Yunseop, K., Member, IEEE, Robert, G. E., & William, M. I., (2008). Remote sensing and control of an irrigation system using a distributed wireless sensor network. *IEEE Transactions on Instrumentation and Measurement, 57*(7).

24. Balamurali, R., & Kathiravan, K., (2015). An analysis of various routing protocols for precision agriculture using wireless sensor network. *IEEE International Conference on Technological Innovations in ICT for Agriculture and Rural Development (TIAR 2015).*

25. Giuseppe, A., Orazio, F., Giuseppe, L. R., & Marco, O., (2009). Monitoring high-quality wine production using wireless sensor networks. *Proceedings of the 42 Hawaii International Conference on System Sciences.*

26. Rwan, M., Tasneem, Y., & Fadi, A., (2015). Internet of things (IoT) security: Current status, challenges and prospective measures. *Internet Technology and Secured Transactions (ICITST), 10th International Conference*.

27. Dragoş, M. O., Bogdan, A. O., & Dragoş, I. S., (2010). Improved environmental monitor and control using a wireless intelligent sensor network. *Electrical and Electronics Engineering (ISEEE), 3rd International Symposium*.

28. Cardell-Oliver, R., Keith, S., Mark, K., & Kevin, M., (2004). *Field Testing a Wireless Sensor Network for Reactive Environmental Monitoring.* IEEE International Conference.

29. Yan-E, D., (2011). Design of intelligent agriculture management information system based on IoT. *Fourth International Conference on Intelligent Computation Technology and Automation*.

30. Fiona, E. M., Emanuel, P., Adraig, W. P., & Michele, M., (2015). Development of heterogeneous wireless sensor network for instrumentation and analysis of beehives. *Instrumentation and Measurement Technology Conference (I2MTC), IEEE International Conference*.

31. Sandeep, V., Lalith, G. K., Naveen, S., Amudhan, A., & Kumar, L. S., (2015). Globally accessible machine automation using raspberry pi based on internet of things. *Advances in Computing, Communications and Informatics (ICACCI), 2015 International Conference*.

32. Nguyen, T. K. D., Nguyen, D. T., Tra, H. S., & Luong, H. D. K., (2015). Automated monitoring and control system for shrimp farms based on embedded system and wireless sensor network. *Electrical, Computer and Communication Technologies (ICECCT), 2015 IEEE International Conference*.

33. Zulhani, R., Hizzi, H. M., & Shahrieel, M. A., (2009). Application and evaluation of high-power ZigBee based wireless sensor network in water irrigation control monitoring system. In: *2009 IEEE Symposium on Industrial Electronics and Applications (ISIEA 2009)* (p. 138). Kuala Lumpur, Malaysia.

34. Weimin, Q., Linxi, D., Haixia, Y., & Fei, W., (2014). Design of intelligent greenhouse environment monitoring system Based on ZigBee and embedded technology. *IEEE International Conference, 139*.

35. Sonal, V., Nikhil, C., & Dhananjay, V. G., (2008). Wireless sensor network for crop field monitoring. In: *2010 International Conference on Recent Trends in Information, Telecommunication and Computing*.

36. Elias, Y., Abdullah, K., Mohammed, M., & Abu-Dayya, A., (2013). Air quality monitoring and analysis in Qatar using a wireless sensor network deployment. In: *9th International Wireless Communications and Mobile Computing Conference (IWCMC)*.

37. Jinhu, L., Qingyong, Z., Yang, F., & Xuegang, X., (2015). The remote monitoring system design of farmland based on ZigBee and GPRS. In: *4th International Conference on Mechatronics, Materials, Chemistry and Computer Engineering (ICMMCCE 2015)*.

38. Nelson, S., Orlando, R., & Artur, A., (2015). Wireless sensor and actuator system for smart irrigation on the cloud. *Internet of Things (WF-IoT), IEEE 2nd World Forum*.

39. Chen, X., Jin, Z. G., & Yang, X., (2013). Design of tropical crops pests monitoring system based on wireless sensor network. *Consumer Electronics, Communications and Networks (CECNet), 2012 2nd*.

40. Narut, S., Panwadee, T., Panu, S., & Preesan, R., (2014). An agricultural monitoring system: Field server data collection and analysis on paddy field.' *International Symposium on Communications and Information Technologies (ISCIT)*.

41. Sivasankari, A., & Gandhimathi, S., (2014). Wireless sensor based crop monitoring system for agriculture using Wi-Fi network dissertation. *International Journal of Computer Science and Information Technology Research, 2*(3), 293–303. ISSN 2348-120X (online).

42. Wang, W., & Cao, S., (2009). Application research on remote intelligent monitoring system of greenhouse based on ZIGBEE WSN. *Image and Signal Processing, CISP '09: 2nd International Congress.*

CHAPTER 8

Design of 7 GHz Microstrip Patch Antenna for Satellite IoT (SIoT) and Satellite IoE (SIoE)-Based Smart Agriculture Devices and Precision Farming

MANVINDER SHARMA,[1] BIKRAMJIT SHARMA,[2] ANUJ KUMAR GUPTA,[1] HARJINDER SINGH,[3] and DISHANT KHOSLA[1]

[1]*Chandigarh Group of Colleges, Landran, Mohali, Punjab, India, E-mail: manvinder.sharma@gmail.com (M. Sharma)*

[2]*Thapar Institute of Engineering and Technology, Patiala, Punjab, India*

[3]*Punjabi University, Patiala, Punjab, India*

ABSTRACT

Focused on increase in agriculture production of good grain, the global agriculture revolution was started from 1930s to 1960s whereas in India green evolution commenced in 1958. But after 60 decades of global agriculture revolution, still there are so many people who do not have enough food to eat and about 815 million people are undernourished. By 2050, the global population will reach 9.8 billion, to tackle this food production should increase by 70%. For this, the farmers should be equipped with digital technologies, big data, IoT, and artificial intelligence (AI) which will lead farmers to 'agriculture 4.0' and enables automatic irrigation, pesticide sprays, weather forecast, selection of crop according to current soil and weather conditions, etc. The great challenge for IoT systems for agriculture application is the availability of internet over remote areas. To counter this problem for remote areas, the IoT/IoE devices can be so fabricated that it can be connected with satellite, eliminating the risk of link breakage with the internet. For the all-round connectivity, cognition, and intelligence, any device can be integrated with digital features and connected to the internet. The global satellite IoT (SIoT) and M2M device market will reach 5.96 million by 2020. Both machine and human can communicate, sense, and trigger via IoT based frameworks over a large or remote geographical area using satellite communication. The signal can be sensed at a remote location and can be uplinked to satellite and can be provided to a central control station. Another challenge for this is the IoT devices should be compact in size so that they can be mounted easily farming devices and equipment. Microstrip patch antenna (MPA) is having advantage of compact design, light in weight, low profile, can be fabricated easily and inexpensively as compared to other conventional antennas. Due to their planar structure MPA are widely used in wireless communication, satellite communication and in many areas where electromagnetic waves are used. In this chapter, inset fed MPA is designed and analyzed for 7 GHz frequency band for satellite communication which can be used to be mounted on IoT/IoE based smart agriculture devices. The size of the proposed antenna is 5.3 × 5.2 cm. The electric field norm plot, radiation pattern is analyzed. Directivity is approx. 12.016 dB and return loss (S11) calculated is –20.5 dB and front to back ratio is calculated as 19 dB.

8.1   INTRODUCTION

In today's world, the internet has spread all over and has reached almost every corner of the globe. Internet connectivity is affecting life of humans. In the next coming decades, IoT is definitely going to gear up. As the IoT gadgets are surpassing the mobile devices, IoT will spread through consumer, industrial, and commercial applications. First IoT based device which is mostly used even now a days is ATM machine. The era is moving toward in Better than IoT which only provide machine to machine (M2M) communication, Internet of Everything (IoE) includes machine to people (M2P) and technology-supported people to people (P2P) communication. Rather than only communicating, network intelligence, ML and artificial intelligence (AI) is used in IoE [1]. For the proper implementation of (internet of things (IoT)) IoT and IoE ecosystem over a large area and remote areas, satellite services have inimitable and required characteristics [2]. United Nation's Food and Agriculture Organization (FAO) predicted that the population will reach 9.8 billion by 2050. Other than combating challenges like rising climate change, extreme weather conditions and farming's environmental impact, this is another big challenge for the agriculture industry to feed 9.8 billion across the world [3, 4]. For this the global agriculture production should increase by 70%. Over the last decades, the agriculture industry has witnessed many technological transformations and become more technology-driven and industrialized. To meet increasing needs, the agriculture industry has to turn to IoT/IoE based smart farming which enables farmers to reduce waste, choosing fertilizers and pesticide spray to increase productivity. In smart farming, IoT-based sensors (humidity, soil moisture, light, temperature, pesticide detection, etc.), and weather forecast based automatic irrigation systems are used which optimizes water usage and eliminates wastage of water. An optimized amount of water is provided to crop which is actually needed by a particular type of crop [5]. As compared to conventional approach, IoT based smart farming has higher efficiency and production rate and this system takes input from sensors placed in farm and on vehicles and place the data on cloud from internet on mobile, farmer can monitor his farm and vehicles from anywhere [6, 7]. Figure 8.1 shows various applications of IoT in the agriculture industry. IoT based systems can also guide the vehicle for the best route to save fuel. Drones connected with internet services are used to monitor field's condition, pests or other animal invasion and can also trigger some pesticide spray or other device automatically using image processing algorithms and deep learning. The prediction about the use of agriculture-based IoT devices will reach 75 million by the end of 2020 and will grow 20% annually [8]. By 2025, smart device agriculture market is expected to be triple ($15 billion) as compared to 2016 which was $5 billion.

A method or practice which makes farming process more controlled and accurate and which will lead to raise livestock and production of crop is known as precision farming. The key component of this is the use of internet-based devices like connecting sensors, automated hardware, robotics, autonomous vehicles and control system with internet and cloud. Figure 8.2 shows a method of precision farming and its connectivity with satellite for brakeless connectivity [10]. The steps included in smart farming and precision farming is monitoring, sensing, and uploading data of field condition on cloud then according to data provided the smart analytics is done and planning is done and this system can trigger a smart robotic control of any device. For example, in first step the monitoring of soil moisture is done by sensor the data is uploaded on cloud, when the soil moisture decreases as per crop need, the smart analysis step will first check weather condition like prediction of rain, if there is no prediction of rain it will automatically trigger sprinkler or watering device using smart control [11–13]. The smart

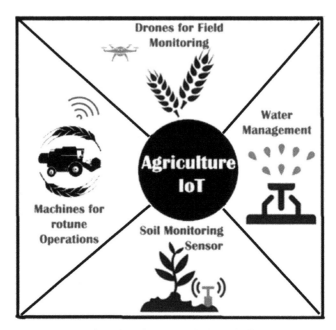

FIGURE 8.1   Applications of IoT-based smart agriculture devices [9].

Source: Reprinted from Ref. [9]. https://technofaq.org/posts/2018/05/the-impact-of-iot-on-agriculture/

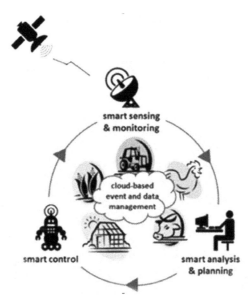

FIGURE 8.2   Precision farming and connectivity via satellite communication [14].
Source: Reprinted from Ref. [9]. https://technofaq.org/posts/2018/05/the-impact-of-iot-on-agriculture/

agriculture sensors can collect tons of data about type of soil, weather conditions, type of invasion by pests' animals, irrigation water availability and other conditions so that it can be analyzed and proper solution can be done by farmer in real-time so as to increase productivity.

But for real-time monitoring and triggering of event, the devices must be connected with internet all the time. Farms that are located at remote locations or hilly areas suffer from break-in connectivity due to insufficient coverage by landline internet device. One solution to this is connecting the devices with satellite for seamless connectivity with the internet. For the services "smart farming," satellite technology can provide a variety of frequencies, speeds, and orbits [15]. With the global broadband connectivity via satellite networks satellite IoT (SIoT) provides IoT solutions in remote locations which cannot be reasonably accessed due to cost of terrain. Figure 8.3 shows satellite-based IoT system. People and things will intelligently connect in industry, 'business 4.0' and 'agriculture 4.0.' Majority of IoT based network is terrestrial with geostationary satellite (GEO), low earth orbit (LEO) and highly elliptical orbit (HEO) are optimized for the IoT market. GEO satellites provide high-capacity data (terabytes) and used for internet over satellite connection [16]. For this, the antenna should be directive so that it should not interfere with nearby satellite communication system. While LEO and HEO operate much closer to earth and requires antenna with high directivity [17].

FIGURE 8.3 Satellite-based IoT (SIoT) system for precision farming [14].

8.2   IoT/IoE ARCHITECTURE

IoT is basically defined as the network devices which have the capability of sensing, accumulating, and transferring the data on the internet with any interference of humans. There are various functional blocks in the IoT system which facilitate different kinds of utilities. The first component of IoT system is the device. The devices present in the IoT system can sense, actuate, control, and monitor the activities. The IoT devices and other connected applications can exchange collect data from one another through applications based on cloud network [18]. Various interfaces are present in the IoT device so that it can communicate with other wired and wireless devices. These interfaces are for sensors, connectivity with the internet and for audio/video. All these interfaces are shown in Figure 8.4. The second functional block in the IoT system is the communication [19]. The remote servers and the devices communicate in this block. The communication protocols in IoT work under the data link, network, application, and transport layer. The third functional block is service. Different functions are served by IoT system in this block, such as modeling and control of device, publishing, and analyzing the data and discovering the device. The fourth functional block is of management. Different functions are provided by the management block to govern the IoT system. The fifth functional block of IoT system is security. Various functions such as authorization, integrity of message, authentication, privacy security of data is provided by this block to secure the IoT system. The last functional block of the IoT system is the application layer. It provides the module by the interface through which various aspects of IoT system are controlled and monitored. This also allows the visualization and analysis of the status of system in present stages and in future prospects [16].

An object which is equipped with sensors is termed as a "thing." The data is gathered and transferred in the network with the help of sensors which can be connected with humans, and these things are allowed to act with the help of actuators. Figure 8.5 shows IoT/IoE architecture model. Many objects which are used in the daily use are included in this concept, such as buildings, automobiles, fridges, street lamps, production machinery and so on. It is not necessary that the sensors are attached physically to the object; sensors can also be needed to monitor the things. Gateways are used to move the data from things to the cloud and vice versa. The things and the cloud are connected through gateways. The preprocessing and the filtering of the data is done in the gateways before the data is moved to the cloud. This is done for the volume reduction of the data so that it can be easily processed and stored further. Then the control commands from the cloud to the things

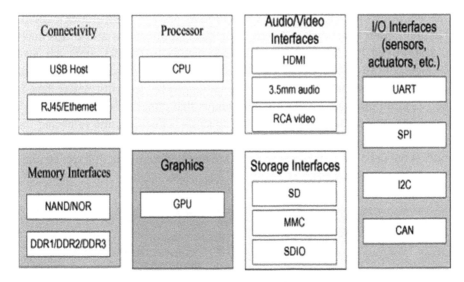

FIGURE 8.4 Various interfaces in device component of IoT [14].

are transmitted. The commands are then executed by things with the use of their actuators [21]. The data compression is facilitated by cloud gateways. Cloud gateways also ensure the secure transmission of data between cloud IoT servers and field gateways. The various protocols need to be compatible so that the communication with the field gateways is supported by the protocols depending upon the gateways. The input data is effectively translated to the data lake through streaming data processor. This also ensures control applications so that no data is lost or corrupted. The connected devices generate the data in its natural format which is stored in the data lake. The data is extracted from the data lake when it is needed for insights. The data is then loaded to the warehouse of big data (batches and streams). Big data warehouse stores the data that is extracted from the data lake for meaningful insights. This data is preprocessed and filtered. Only the matched and structured data is present in the big data warehouse, unlike the data present in Data Lake, which contains all types of sensors generated data. The information related to the things and sensors are also stored in big data warehouse. The application sent to the things is controlled by commands. The data from the big data warehouse can be used by the data analytics, which use the data to analyze the performance of the devices, which further help in identifying the inefficiencies and then to work out the ways for improving IoT system [22]. This makes the system reliable and customer-oriented. This can also contribute to control applications by creating algorithms. ML helps creating opportunities for efficient and precise models used in control applications. The new models are tested based upon their applications and efficiencies and approved by data analysts. The commands to the actuators are sent through control applications. The big data warehouse stores the commands sent to actuators through control applications. The security of the data is also ensured through the storing commands that come in big amounts [23]. In rule-based control applications, the specialists decide some rules and the control apps work according to these rules. In ML control applications, the models are used by control apps which are updated regularly that can be once in a week or month [24].

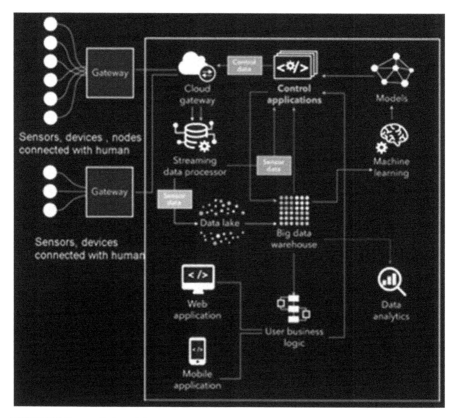

FIGURE 8.5   IoT/IoE architecture.

The models are updated using the data stored in the big data warehouse. The users should always have an option to influence the nature of the application through the better automation of IoT systems is ensured by control apps.

The IoT systems and the users are connected through software components called user applications. The user can control and monitor the smart things through user applications [25]. The state of the things can be monitored using the web or mobile app. Users can also send commands for controlling the applications and set their behavior.

Installing the app is not enough for the IoT devices to function sufficiently. The performance of the devices also needs to be managed through certain procedures. This includes the interaction between the devices and the data transmission to be secure. The identity of the device is established through device identification which ensures that the device has the software that transmits the data reliably. The devices are tuned through control and configuration according to the IoT system. Some parameters are written on the device after installing and some may require updates. The devices are diagnosed and monitored to ensure the performance of the device to be smooth and secure. The risk of breakdowns is therefore reduced. The functionality and security vulnerabilities are added to the devices through software updates and maintenance [26].

There are various utilities of IoT. The IoT devices are self-adapting and dynamic. With the changing contexts, these devices adapt dynamically, and the actions are taken according to the environment being sensed. The IoT devices and systems have the capability to self-configure which allows various devices to work together so that a proper functionality can be attained. They have the capability to upgrade the latest software and networking setup with minimal user interference. Various communication protocols are supported by IoT devices which are interconnected to each other and with the infrastructure as well. A unique identity is processed by each IoT device [27]. The interface in IoT device allows user for status monitoring, remote control, and infrastructure management. The integration of IoT devices with information network allows them to communicate with other systems and exchange files with them. The knowledge of the surrounding nodes can be gained through the sensor nodes present in the IoT devices.

8.3 MICROSTRIP PATCH ANTENNA (MPA) FOR AGRICULTURE SIOT-BASED DEVICES

For the antennas to be integrated for communication on "thing," the size of the antenna should be small and inexpensive. Microstrip patch antenna (MPA) is very easy to build and has low production cost, which makes it a very good choice in a large number of applications [28]. These applications include wireless LAN, mobile satellite communication, and global system for mobile communication, missile, and so on. All these applications owe to certain advantages of MPA such as low profile, low cost, low mass and very easy to integrate [29, 30]. The resonance of this antenna can be achieved at any frequency by varying various antenna parameters and shape of the patch. Figure 8.6 shows MPA physical geometry and Figure 8.7 shows the microstrip antenna radiation pattern.

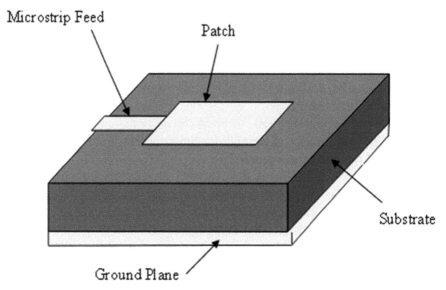

FIGURE 8.6   Structure of microstrip patch antenna [31].

Source: Reprinted from Ref. [31].

The conducting material constitute the patch in MPA. The patch can be of any shape such as circular, rectangular, elliptical or any other shape. The photoetching of the feed line and radiating patch is done on the dielectric substrate. There are fringing fields present between the ground plane and the edge of the patch which are the primary cause for radiations in MPA. For antenna to have high performance, the dielectric substrate should be thick. It is desired to have a low dielectric constant for better efficiency, radiation, and increased bandwidth. But the antenna of larger size is required for such configuration. Now if we use the MPA of compact size then then the efficiency and bandwidth will be lowered because of high dielectric constant used in the substrate. So, there is always a tradeoff between the dimensions and performance of the antenna. The electromagnetic energy is guided to the patch through excitation due to which negative charges are generated in the feed point, and at other parts of the patch, positive charges are generated [33].

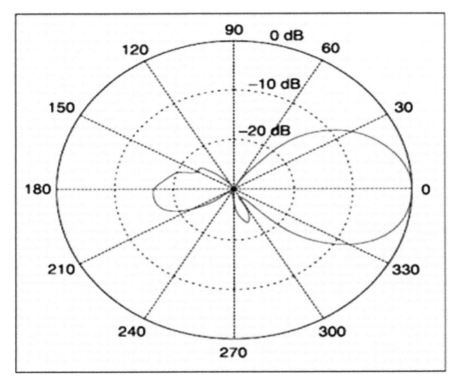

FIGURE 8.7 Typical radiation pattern of microstrip patch antenna [32].

Source: Reprinted from Ref. [32].

The radiated electromagnetic waves are of three types. The first type of wave is the useful radiation since it is radiated into the space. The diffracted waves are the second type of electromagnetic radiation which results in the true power transmission as these waves are reflected in the space present between the ground plane and patch of the antenna. The waves which are trapped inside the dielectric substrate are the third type of electromagnetic radiation and are usually undesirable.

The dimensions and shapes vary in various kinds of antenna. There are four subtypes of microstrip antenna which are: MPA, microstrip traveling-wave antenna, printed slot antenna and microstrip dipoles [34]. When the radiation of the wave in a specific direction is similar to the electric field direction then the antenna polarization is determined. A figure is traced at a time through the vector of instantaneous electric field. The antenna can be linearly polarized or circular polarized. The linear polarization has further two subtypes: horizontal polarization and vertical polarization. When the electric field vector and earth are perpendicular to each other, then there is vertical polarization of electromagnetic wave, and when the electric field vector and earth are parallel to each other, then there is horizontal polarization of electromagnetic waves [35].

Microstrip antenna have wide applications including the one based on communication, radio frequency identification (RFID) fields, in healthcare, mobile communication, telemedicine application, communication equipment based on WiMAX, satellite communication and global positioning satellite systems (GPS). The radiation patterns which are circularly polarized are used in the satellite communication which is realized by using the MPA (circular or square) [36].

8.3.1   DESIGN OF INSET FEED

Due to sinusoidal distribution in current as shown in Figure 8.8, moving along distance R, from the ends, the value of current is increased by:

$$I = Cos\pi \left(\pi \times \frac{R}{L} \right) \tag{1}$$

If the wavelength is 2L, the phase difference is given by:

$$\Phi = \left(\pi \times \frac{R}{L} \right) \tag{2}$$

As the current increases, there is a decrease in the magnitude of voltage using Z=V/I. [37]. The input impedance is given as:

$$Z_m(R) = cos^2 \left(\frac{\pi R}{L} \right) Z_m(0) \tag{3}$$

where $Z_{in}(0)$ is the impedance if fed from end [38].

8.3.2   DESIGN OF MICROSTRIP

The width of Patch Antenna can be calculated with [29]:

$$W = \frac{v_0}{2f_r} \sqrt{\frac{2}{\varepsilon_r + 1}} \tag{4}$$

The length of Antenna can be calculated with [20]:

$$L = \frac{v_0}{2f_r\sqrt{\varepsilon_{reff}}} - 2\Delta L \tag{5}$$

and

$$\varepsilon_{reff} = \frac{\varepsilon_r + 1}{2} + \frac{\varepsilon_r - 1}{2}\left[1 + 12\frac{h}{W}\right]^{-1/2} \tag{6}$$

$$\Delta L = 0.412h\frac{\left(\varepsilon_{reff} + 0.3\right)\left(\dfrac{W}{h} + 0.264\right)}{\left(\varepsilon_{reff} - 0.258\right)\left(\dfrac{W}{h} + 0.8\right)} \tag{7}$$

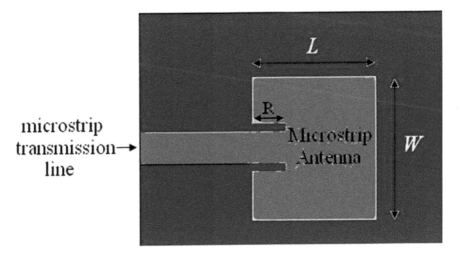

FIGURE 8.8   Inset fed microstrip antenna.

8.4   MODELING AND ANALYSIS OF PROPOSED DESIGN

The design is modeled in COMSOL Multiphysics using the equations in software environment for analysis. Electromagnetic frequency domain was used to model the design with 7 GHz frequency which was applied on the lumped port. The analysis of design was done. Table 8.1 shows the design values used for the model. The Model design is shown in Figure 8.9. The design structure of MPA is shown in Figure 8.10.

TABLE 8.1   Description of Model

Description	Value
Substrate thickness	0.1524 cm
50-ohm line width	0.32 cm
Patch width	5.3 cm
Patch length	5.2 cm
Tuning stub width	2 cm
Tuning stub length	1.2 cm
Substrate width	5.3 cm
Substrate length	5.3 cm

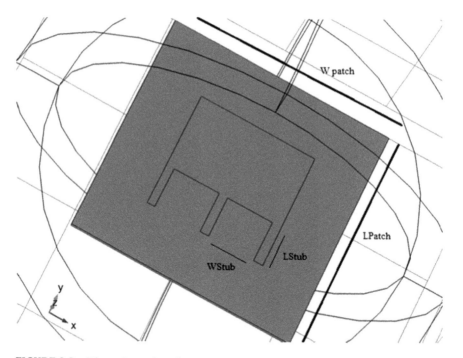

FIGURE 8.9   Dimensions of patch antenna with inset feed.

Tetrahedral meshing is done. There are five elements per wavelength in the meshing in meshing 155,109 tetrahedron values, 22,940 prisms, 15,596 triangles 1,140 quad, 1,002 edge elements and 52 vertex elements are used. Inside design of patch maximum element size of 6.6620 is taken with curvature factor of 0.6. The meshed structure is shown in Figure 8.11.

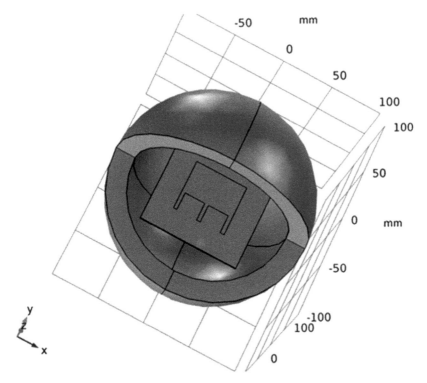

FIGURE 8.10 Structure of microstrip patch antenna.

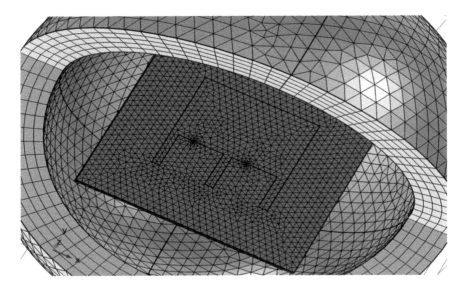

FIGURE 8.11 Meshing of design.

8.5   RESULT AND DISCUSSION

The modeling and simulation of design is done on 4×2.60 GHz processor speed. The simulation used physical memory of 3.6 GB. The frequency 7 GHz is fed to lumped port of antenna as discussed which is in center of patch. Figure 8.12 shows the electric field distribution plot and shows the current distribution over the patch.

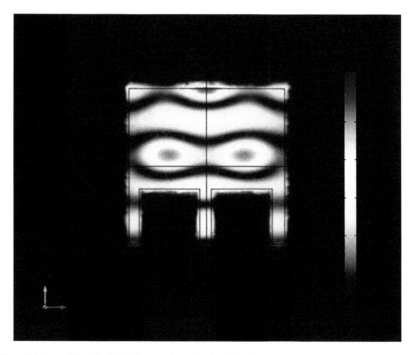

FIGURE 8.12   Electric field distribution plot for 7 GHz.

Figure 8.13 shows the 2D radiation pattern in H Plane and E plane. The radiation patterns show directive beam due to ground plane which block radiation towards backside. The calculated antenna directivity is 12.016 dB and the front to back ratio in radiation pattern is more than 19 dB. It can be observed from the radiation pattern that the antenna is radiating like a directional antenna which is good for satellite communication. The calculated S_{11} parameter is −20.5 dB which is much better than desired −10 dB. The 3D radiation pattern is shown in Figure 8.14.

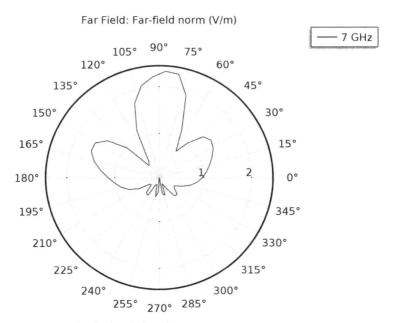

FIGURE 8.13   2D far-field radiation plot.

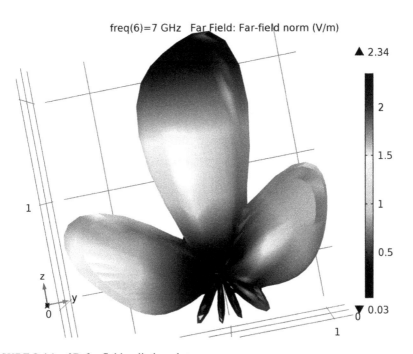

FIGURE 8.14   3D far-field radiation plot.

8.6 CONCLUSION

With several new applications emerging for satellite-based IoT and IoE devices in field of smart agriculture industry the devices "things" will be connected to internet for real-time monitoring of crop health, invasion by pests or animals and automatic smart triggering of events on devices. For the all-time connectivity of remotely located "things" to internet satellite communication plays a vital role. In this chapter, four-layer IoT architecture system is presented and a MPA is designed and modeled for 7 GHz satellite communication. With the advantages of compact size, inexpensive design, and low profile, the MPA can be mounted on "things" easily. The designed antenna is analyzed for parameters like electric field intensity, directivity, front to back ratio, Insertion loss S_{11} and radiation far filed plot were calculated for 7 GHz. The design showed directional antenna radiation pattern which is good for satellite communication.

KEYWORDS

- **internet of energy**
- **internet of things**
- **mechanical sensors**
- **microstrip patch antenna**
- **near field communication**
- **satellite-based IoT device**
- **smart agriculture device**
- **spectrometer**

REFERENCES

1. Gineste, M., Thibault, D., Michel, C., Nicolas, C., Visvesh, S., Valerio, F., Markus, M., et al., (2017). Narrowband IoT service provision to 5G user equipment via a satellite component. In: *2017 IEEE Globecom Workshops (GC Wkshps)* (pp. 1–4). IEEE.
2. Yang, Z., Yingzhao, Y., Yu, Y., Yufeng, P., Xiaobo, W., & Wenji, L., (2011). Study and application on the architecture and key technologies for IoT. In: *2011 International Conference on Multimedia Technology (*pp. 747–751). IEEE.

3. Jernigan, V. B. B., Kimberly, R. H., Jimmy, V., & Vanessa, W. S., (2017). Food insecurity among American Indians and Alaska natives: A national profile using the current population survey-food security supplement. *Journal of Hunger & Environmental Nutrition, 12*(1), 1–10.

4. Jen-Hu, C., (2017). *Climate and Agriculture: An Ecological Survey.* Routledge.

5. Baranwal, T., & Pushpendra, K. P., (2016). Development of IoT based smart security and monitoring devices for agriculture. In: *2016 6th International Conference-Cloud System and Big Data Engineering (Confluence)* (pp. 597–602). IEEE.

6. Abagissa, A. T., Ashutosh, B., & Santosh, K. P., (2018). IoT based smart agricultural device controlling system. In: *2018 Second International Conference on Inventive Communication and Computational Technologies (ICICCT)* (pp. 26–30). IEEE.

7. Rajeswari, S., Suthendran, K., & Rajakumar, K., (2017). A smart agricultural model by integrating IoT, mobile and cloud-based big data analytics. In: *2017 International Conference on Intelligent Computing and Control (I2C2)* (pp. 1–5). IEEE.

8. Sohraby, K., Daniel, M., Benedict, O., & Wei, W., (2018). A review of wireless and satellite-based m2m/IoT services in support of smart grids. *Mobile Networks and Applications, 23*(4), 881–895.

9. https://technofaq.org/posts/2018/05/the-impact-of-iot-on-agriculture/ (accessed on 10 November 2021).

10. Minoli, D., (2015). *Innovations in Satellite Communication and Satellite Technology.* Wiley.

11. Kozlov, D., Jari, V., & Yasir, A., (2012). Security and privacy threats in IoT architectures. In *Proceedings of the 7th International Conference on Body Area Networks* (pp. 256–262). ICST (Institute for Computer Sciences, Social-Informatics and Telecommunications Engineering).

12. Ramnath, S., Abhishek, J., Bhumika, N., Pallavi, M., & Sudhir, K. R., (2017). IoT based localization and tracking. In: *2017 International Conference on IoT and Application (ICIOT)* (pp. 1–4). IEEE.

13. Miraz, M. H., Maaruf, A., Peter, S. E., & Rich, P., (2015). A review on internet of things (IoT), internet of everything (IoE) and internet of nano things (IoNT). In: *2015 Internet Technologies and Applications (ITA)* (pp. 219–224). IEEE.

14. Gottiz, J.A. Seguridad en Internet de las Cosas: Honeypot to Capture IoT-Attack Methods. http://openaccess.uoc.edu/webapps/o2/bitstream/10609/89027/6/jarminanaTFM1218 memoria.pdf

15. Kaur, S. P., & Manvinder, S., (2015). Radially optimized zone-divided energy-aware wireless sensor networks (WSN) protocol using BA (bat algorithm). *IETE Journal of Research, 61*(2), 170–179.

16. Desai, P., Amit, S., & Pramod, A., (2015). Semantic gateway as a service architecture for IoT interoperability. In: *2015 IEEE International Conference on Mobile Services* (pp. 313–319). IEEE.

17. Ren, J., Hui, G., Chugui, X., & Yaoxue, Z., (2017). Serving at the edge: A scalable IoT architecture based on transparent computing. *IEEE Network, 31*(5), 96–105.

18. Wang, C., Mahmoud, D., Mischa, D., Xufei, M., Rose, Q. H., & Honggang, W., (2013). Guest editorial-special issue on internet of things (IoT): Architecture, protocols and services *IEEE Sensors Journal, 13*(10), 3505–3510.

19. Kraijak, S., & Tuwanut, P., (2015). A survey on IoT architectures, protocols, applications, security, privacy, real-world implementation, and future trends. In: *11th International Conference on Wireless Communications, Networking, and Mobile Computing (WiCOM 2015)* (pp. 1–6). IET.

20. Sokhi, I. K., & Ramesh, R., (2017). Design of microstrip patch antenna with polarization diversity for wireless applications. *International Journal of Applied Engineering Research, 12*(21), 11345–11349.

21. Castellani, A. P., Nicola, B., Paolo, C., Michele, R., Zach, S., & Michele, Z., (2010). Architecture and protocols for the internet of things: A case study. In: *2010 8th IEEE International Conference on Pervasive Computing and Communications Workshops (PERCOM Workshops)* (pp. 678–683). IEEE.

22. Karagiannis, V., Periklis, C., Vazquez-Gallego, F., & Alonso-Zarate, J., (2015). A survey on application layer protocols for the internet of things. *Transaction on IoT and Cloud Computing, 3*(1),11–17.

23. Lloret, J., Jesus, T., Alejandro, C., & Lorena, P., (2016). An integrated IoT architecture for smart metering. *IEEE Communications Magazine, 54*(12), 50–57.

24. Li, H., Kaoru, O., & Mianxiong, D., (2018). Learning IoT in edge: Deep learning for the Internet of Things with edge computing. *IEEE Network, 32*(1), 96–101.

25. Tang, J., Dawei, S., Shaoshan, L., & Jean-Luc, G., (2017). Enabling deep learning on IoT devices. *Computer, 50*(10), 92–96.

26. Ziouvelou, X., Panagiotis, A., Constantinos, M. A., Orestis, E., Joao, F., Nikos, L., Frank, M., et al., (2017). Crowd-driven IoT/IoE ecosystems: A multidimensional approach. In: *Beyond the Internet of Things* (pp. 341–375). Springer, Cham.

27. Wang, T., Guangxue, Z., Anfeng, L., Md. Zakirul A., & Qun, J., (2018). A secure IoT service architecture with an efficient balance dynamics based on cloud and edge computing. *IEEE Internet of Things Journal, 6*(3), 4831–4843.

28. Sharma, M., & Harjinder, S., (2018). SIW based leaky-wave antenna with semi C-shaped slots and its modeling, design and parametric considerations for different materials of dielectric. In: *2018 Fifth International Conference on Parallel, Distributed and Grid Computing (PDGC)* (pp. 252–258). IEEE.

29. Shackelford, A. K., Kai-Fong, L., & Kwai, M. L., (2003). Design of small-size wide-bandwidth microstrip-patch antennas. *IEEE Antennas and Propagation Magazine, 45*(1), 75–83.

30. Boon-Khai, A., & Boon-Kuan, C., (2007). A wideband E-shaped microstrip patch antenna for 5-6 GHz wireless communications. *Progress in Electromagnetics Research, 75*, 397–407.

31. Singh, S., Neelesh, A., Navendu, N., & Jaiswal, A. K., (2012). Design consideration of microstrip patch antenna. *International Journal of Electronics and Computer Science Engineering, 2*(1), 306–316.

32. Patil, S.A., Dhanawade, P.C. Microstrip Antenna and Their Applications. Electronicsforu. com. **2019.** https://www.electronicsforu.com/technology-trends/microstrip-antenna-applications (accessed on 10 November 2021).

33. Menzel, W., & Wilfried, G., (2008). *A Microstrip Patch Antenna with Coplanar Feed Line, 1*(11), 340–342.

34. Mak, C. L., Luk, K. M., Lee, K. F., & Chow, Y. L., (2000). Experimental study of a microstrip patch antenna with an L-shaped probe. *IEEE Transactions on Antennas and Propagation, 48*(5), 777–783.

35. Khosla, D., & Amandeep, K., (2012). Design of hybrid compression model using DWTDCT-Huffman algorithms for compression of bitstream. *International Journal of Engineering Research & Technology (IJERT), 1*(5), 1–7.
36. Singh, S., Sumeet, G., Manvinder, S., & Rahul, K., (2018). *Waveguide Diplexer Design and Implementation in Communication Systems, 1*(1), 40–43.
37. Sharma, M., & Harjinder, S., (2019). Design and analysis of substrate integrated waveguide for high frequency applications. *Recent Trends in Programming Languages, 6*(1), 1–5.
38. Sharma, M., Sohni, S., Dishant, K., Sumeet, G., & Anuj, G., (2018). Waveguide diplexer: Design and analysis for 5G communication. In: *2018 Fifth International Conference on Parallel, Distributed and Grid Computing (PDGC)* (pp. 586–590). IEEE.

CHAPTER 9

Health Monitoring System for Cancer Care Using IoT

BIBHUPRASAD SAHU,[1] AMRUTANSHU PANIGRAHI,[2] and
SACHI NANDAN MOHANTY[3]

[1]*Assistant Professor, Department of CSE, Gandhi Institute for Technology, Bhubaneswar, Odisha, India*

[2]*Research Scholar, Department of CSE, SOA University, Bhubaneswar, Odisha, India*

[3]*Department of Computer Science & Engineering, Vardhaman College of Engineering (Autonomous), Hyderabad, Telangana, India*

ABSTRACT

We are living in a new era of computing technology named the internet of things (IoT). It is also known as the Universal Neural Network of smart sensing devices. This enables interoperability, sensor-to-sensor communication, exchange of information, and data movement to build up a trustworthy patient glance framework. The goal is that social insurance expert can easily monitor their patients, who are either hospitalized or executing their regular day-by-day life exercises. In the present scenario, the whole world is facing serious healthcare challenges with the rapid increase of population, which leads to different chronic diseases like cancer due to poor living style, poor sanitation, polluted water, and air. The cancer disease spread throughout the society which high demands the medical facility during the last several years. All healthcare systems are hospital-centric where the patient has to visit the hospital to check the status of the disease at regular intervals, which is a physician and disease-centric where the patient has no direct involvement except the physical presence for clinical observation. The basic challenges found such as: (a) patient/doctor limited time interaction; (b) adherence monitoring; (c) larger geriatric population; (d) urbanization; (e) healthcare work staff shortage during the emergency; and (f) increase medical expenses. To achieve success against the above challenges, the application of IoT may be used to provide seamless communication among the patient/doctor with communication objects. This will enhance the eminence of human life with smart connected sensors and it will play an important role to save the precious life of the human being. Sensor readings can be used effectively in diagnosing a cancer patient with its severity during the critical stage, and it will help the doctor to reduce the interconnectivity gap between hospital and patient. A health monitoring system for cancer care using cloud-based IoT with a wireless sensor network (WSN) is proposed to enhance the healthcare solution. Here cloud services are used to achieve transmission of data accurately, a good decision-making environment to enhance the cancer treatment facility.

9.1   INTRODUCTION

In the modern age, people having a great potential to live a smarter life, in this regard, IoT became a great witness to enhance life from smart to smarter than smartest. IoT is a union of telecommunication networks, sensors devices, actuators, various applications, cloud computing, and Big Data through the Internet to provide precise services. As an IoT-based environment is the collection of heterogeneous devices and applications, protocols, architectures, wired/wireless, frequency bands should be maintained for smooth communication or data exchange [1]. Healthcare is always a serious concern, So IoT should be customized according to the need to achieve the target. There are three basic areas to access healthcare such as (1) hospitals (large clinical healthcare); (2) clinics and pharmacies (medium clinical healthcare); and (3) patient homes, communities, rural areas (non-clinical healthcare). To understand the impact of IoT in healthcare we have to analyze two major areas such as (1) understanding the area of operation; and (2) patient monitoring. To enhance the style of living, pervasive healthcare promotes proactive healthcare services and experience. Here we have presented a concept by incorporating cloud services with cancer care delivery. It provides a framework architecture model, with a solution through the make use of WSN concept, smart sensing devices, and data analytic tools/techniques to develop monitor, and improve cancer treatments [2]. This healthcare solution not only provides a better smart life at the same time healthcare provides service to exchange the intelligent, healthcare insight decision into streams of data to well recognize the disease in a good manner. IoT-based healthcare system added an extra feature to provide a quality healthcare service without the conscious knowledge of the patient because of smart sensors attached to the IoT model [25]. The main aim of this chapter is to provide a smart healthcare service framework, which can be adopted in the future with better suitable modifications on a certain scale. The designed framework may be validated in three ways: (a) pre-implementation; (b) go live; and (c) post-implementation. From these three validation approaches, we can easily find out which approach meets our fundamental design to achieve specific design goals such as connectivity, inter-connectivity, inter-operability, reliability, scalability, network tolerance, security tolerance, redundancy, performance, maintainability, etc. [4]. Even if most of the authors used IoT-based approach to explain healthcare but no such paper was found related to the topic of health monitoring for cancer care. Figure 9.1 presents the architecture of Patient-Centric IoT healthcare.

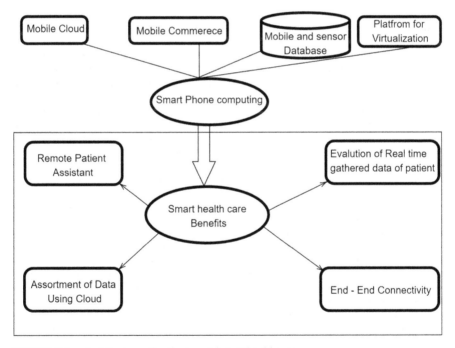

FIGURE 9.1 Architecture of patient-centric IoT healthcare.

9.1.1 MOTIVATION

The burden of the cancer disease grows globally, which increases not only physical, emotional but also financial strain. In low and medium-class countries, many health systems are not ready to manage the burden. Due to this large no of people in this world do not have financial access to appropriate eminence diagnosis and treatment. Cancer is the main cause of death globally. Around 9.6 million peoples died in 2018 due to various cancers [9]. The type of cancer in the case of the male is Lung, prostate, colorectal, stomach, and liver cancer, whereas the female cancer types are breast, colorectal, lung, cervical, and thyroid cancer. According to information provided by World Health Organization (WHO) presently, 10 million new malignant patients are diagnosed every year in the universe except if there is a productive prevention campaign among society, then it may be a serious concern for the world and disease rates are set twofold by 2020. If we consider the case country India, as per the report stated by WHO 1.16 million new cancer cases found from this more than 50% of patients are female. So, it is necessary to study the present status of cancer in India so that advanced steps may be taken to reduce the affected ratio.

Cancer death ratio increases due to the ignorance of the patient at the early stage and the people staying in rural are not aware of the early symptoms of the disease. This problem motivates us to develop a healthcare system for cancer patients. Nowadays, IoT plays an important role in healthcare. Combining both traditional healthcare systems and IoT to develop a user-friendly IoT framework with a combination of wearable sensors which will enhance the clinical diagnostics using various applications. IoT-based healthcare systems will easy and convenient access to access the data of the patient on a routine basis, who are suffering from different types of cancers like breast, lung, and colorectal cancer. It will provide an easy way to provide a better diagnosis from the routine based generated data recovered from embedded smart connected devices and sensors [3]. IoT-WSN approach is accepted by most of the researchers to enhance the healthcare system but also it reduces the cost of the diagnosis. This approach is adopted in many fields of IoT. Inclusion of RFID and Wi-Fi network, cancer diagnosis with Cloud computing, healthcare-associated with GPS for location tracking. Practically these approaches improve the clinical job such as Pulse rate of heart, ECG, EKG, etc. Application is not limited to Clinical and Hospital centric but also its focus on remote monitoring system (RMS), Auto emergency service system, old age patient care, remote medical treatment as per the clinical report, etc. [5] After reviewing different articles related to healthcare using IoT we find out the gap that only a few papers only focus on cancer diagnosis. And this motivates us to develop a framework for health monitoring for Cancer care using IoT. In this chapter, we provide a framework, instead of keeping the data as hospital-centric we have used a wireless sensor approach to connect different hospitals for easy access to data among them [6]. So not only it will improve the treatment but also it will provide easy access to the patient document during the transfer from one hospital to another.

9.2 WHY IoT HEALTHCARE?

With the help of IoT healthcare, the routine check-up of the patient is done remotely by the wearable sensor and wireless sensor network (WSN). Through this, the doctor can receive various information such as a patient's physical health history, for example, age, weight, height, and gender and other clinical information can be gathered which are time-stamped, location-tagged, and tagged with data on the testing environment and other situational pieces of information [7]. In short, we can conclude that healthcare using IoT enables the hospital to enhance the diagnosis of the patient in a convenient manner. The advantages of IoT-based healthcare is stated in Figure 9.2.

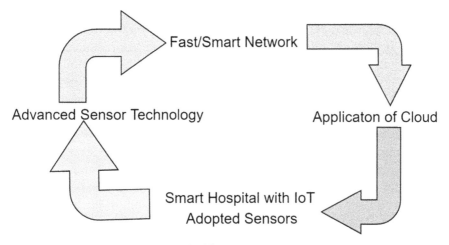

FIGURE 9.2   Basic components IoT healthcare.

9.2.1   MOTIVATION

- Solution for every patient;
- Resiliency;
- Enable diverse technologies;
- Massive data processing and analytic;
- Personalized healthcare;

- Lifetime monitoring;
- User friendly;
- Reduction of Clinical Test Cost;
- Clinical efficiency improved;
- Patient data remote action;
- Online solutions;
- Efficient resource management.

9.3 BENEFITS OF IoT IN SMART HEALTHCARE SYSTEM

The smart healthcare system related to e-resource management, e-health, m-health, managing medical devices, and smart home services. IoT focuses on the gathering of real-time patient details with less interaction of the human Smart healthcare system focus on the improvement of different health policies including Medicare and Medicaid coverage, divergence in exploitation, and admittance of care. So, the IoT healthcare system provides remote healthcare services for cancer patients. In traditional hospital-centric, if there should arise an occurrence of an urgent situation, when a patient gets seriously ill, in that time instant arranging an ambulance and rush to the hospital for treatment is a critical situation, where is always a risk to the life of the patient. But adopting a smart healthcare system using IoT is a better and suitable option for saving lives because the time-stamped data of the patient is collected by the IoT connected sensors such as oxygen level, sugar level, heart pulse rate, weight, ECG plot already available at the hospital end. Which provides a better option to choose the doctor can guess the vital information of the patient and can provide medicine details over the Smartphone. So, for the minor health issue, the cost of travel may be avoided. Here Figure 9.3 presents the applications of IoT/WSN cancer healthcare. Various healthcare devices are used to gather patient data remotely as per the need such as HEARTFAID, ALARM-NET, CAALYX, Tele-CARE, CHRONIC, My Heart, OLDES, SAPHIRE, Mobi-HEALTH, SAPHE, DITIS, AXARM, Virtual E Care, Sense mother, etc. With the help of the IoT devices interaction between the patient and doctor, the same can be shared with the cloud for easy assessment of data over the network [23, 24]. The sharing of the resource includes oncology, doctor, clinical staff, nurses, and other related staffs within the circle with care in charge, medical staff, ambulance, emergency staff, cloud work-station server, and smart devices like Mobile phones, Tablets. Various sensors are connected in the heterogeneous network should work as per the network standard. In IoT-based networks we consider all fundamental sensors are connected with the internet, so all are known as things. Various constraints of sensors are to be taken for consideration, such as range, power consumption, the topology of the network, frequency bands of individual sensors, constrained node/devices, and constrained networks. Sensors are used to measure the physical phenomenon from the outside world and then represent it in some physical presentation. Limitations with sensors enable network is lack of power supply. So related to this sensor are classified into various types active/passive, invasive/non-invasive; contact/no-contact and absolute/reactive.

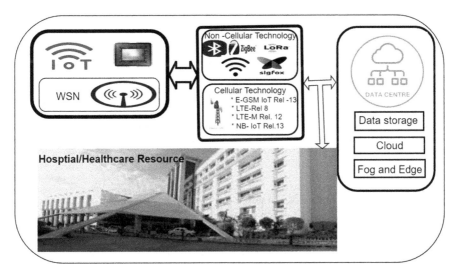

FIGURE 9.3   Architecture IoT/WSN related healthcare.

As we are adopting WSN architecture for establishing a network with easy access to patient data storage, the basic WSN consists of followings units such as processor or processing unit, power source, sensor/Actuator, communication unit. Various access technologies are used to connect the heterogeneous sensors with the internet, these technologies are plenty used everywhere. Some technologies are Wi-Max, IEEE 802.11 (wireless LAN), Area (LPWA); IEEE 802.15.4, 802.15.4e, 802.15.4g, 1901.2a standards, Area (LPWA); IEEE 802.15.4, Wireless cellular-2G, 3G, LTE, 4G, 5G. The various technologies related to healthcare are coupled with one of the data management layers of the repository (Figure 9.4) [11].

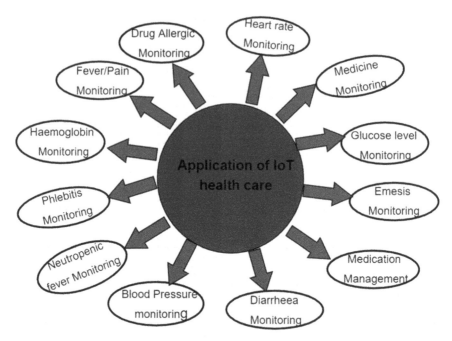

FIGURE 9.4   Applications of IoT/WSN cancer healthcare.

9.4   CANCER AND ITS NATURE

It is necessary to understand the cancer types and nature of the disease before implementing an IoT-based healthcare system. In this section, we have briefly discussed cancer types, its classification, impacts on human life. Cancer itself is a broad term. When the cellular changes in the human body cause uncontrolled growth and division of the cell occur. It leads to a Tumor. In the tumor, some cell division grows rapidly whereas some go very slow. So, the classification of the tumor depends on various parameters such as growth size, growth shape, and location of the tumor in the body. Three basic categories of tumors are named as benign, pre-malignant, and malignant [9]. The cancer cells first appear in the area of the body, then it spread to other parts by lymph nodes. No treatment is required for the benign tumors, but the doctors keep under watchful waiting treatment to confirm that this should not cause any serious problem in health conditions [29]. The patients are advised for radiation or medication. Surgery is the common approach used by the doctors to remove cancer-affected areas without damaging outlier tissues of the affected area. Benign tumor growth depends on reasons such as Environmental toxins, Genetics, Diet, Stress, Local trauma or injury, and inflammation or infection. Some common types of benign tumors are Adenomas, Fibromas, Hemangiomas, and Lipomas. Pre-malignant not cancerous but may lead to developing the properties of cancer, so close monitoring is done to prevent all chances of development. Different types of pre-malignant tumors are actinic keratosis, cervical dysplasia, Leukoplakia. Malignant is a cancer affected area of the body with an increase rapidly by cell division approach called metastasis. Different types of malignant tumors are originated as per the types of a cell of the human being such as Carcinoma, Sarcoma Germ cell tumor, Blastoma. Various treatment methods like MRI are used to detect the lump. A biopsy is an approach adopted to identify cancer [10]. There are a lot of treatment methods are available such as chemotherapy, immunotherapy, radiotherapy, and surgery. Chemotherapy is one of drug therapy to destroy the rapidly growing cells in the body. But this method is only an option left during the advanced stage of the patent. Immunotherapy is the biological therapy used as cancer therapy which helps the immune system of the body to fight with the cancer cell. Surgery is the option for doctors to remove the cancer cell from the body. In Radiotherapy, radiation is applied to the cancer cell to disable the metastasis. Even if different treatment options are available, this research we have proposed an IoT-based healthcare framework to augment with the current one. Because from the patient feedback it is clear that Cancer treatment causes different side effects include trouble in eating, tiredness, constipation, diarrhea, edema, fatigue, appetite loss, delirium, etc. So, the addition of smart sensor devices with the current method will add an extra feature to improve the life of the patient.

9.4.1 LAYERED ARCHITECTURE OF IoT HEALTHCARE FRAMEWORK FOR CANCER CARE

Figure 9.5 represents the framework of the proposed model where various devices are interconnected and interdependent with each other as per the adopted network topology. The framework defines how integration, interface, the transmission of various sensing devices occurs to achieve interconnectivity and inter-operability [11]. The proposed framework is divided into 5 layers which provides a better solution for cancer care.

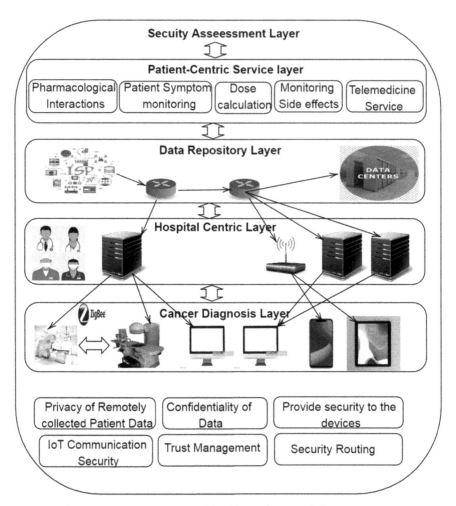

FIGURE 9.5 Layered architecture of IoT healthcare framework for cancer care.

9.4.1.1 *PATIENT-CENTRIC SERVICE LAYER*

The patient-centric service layer deals with the collection of various smart sensor devices for gathering the data from the IoT/WSN to enhance cancer detection, diagnosis, and better treatment. Smart sensors are embedded with various machines to estimate different parameters to optimize cancer care services. The report is generated the corresponding course of action such as which treatment option may be chosen.

9.4.1.2 DATA REPOSITORY LAYER

Data collected through the machine and IoT-based sensor devices are stored in the data repository layer. As per the data collected, this is analyzed by the doctor, and it provides an easy way to decide for the patient betterment. It is safe with less resource utilization. The data repository layer is linked with the cloud, which improves if a patient moves from one hospital to another in an emergency. By this data visualization and cloud service repeat symptom information gathering can be avoided.

9.4.1.3 HOSPITAL-CENTRIC LAYER

Hospital centric layer allows communication of various healthcare centers, clinics to share the healthcare results like lab work, pathos-lab, scan reports (CT, RT, and MRI. This layer provides an access layer for physicians, doctors, oncologists to go through the report by utilizing the cloud service and choose appropriate treatment program which can be adopted in the daily routine of the patient. Hospital centric layer is complex as the layer enables the communication and collaboration of various community centers, patient homes, clinics, rehabilitation centers, physician practices, insurance providers, ambulance services, blood banks transversely the healthcare system.

9.4.1.4 CANCER DIAGNOSIS LAYER

This layer ensures the application of various smart sensor devices connected via IoT technologies should be used efficiently. The application method chosen may be remotely or on-site as per the demand. This layer establishes a platform where cancer patients, drug administration, treatment machines can interactively interact with the smart sensor devices. Symptom information of the patient can be passed to the oncologist, which enhances the communication and data visualization between both. It leverages the cancer diagnosis later to ensure the condition to choose the preeminent smart sensor as the need of the patient.

9.4.1.5 SECURITY ASSESSMENT LAYER

The security assessment layer revolves around the protection of patient data from unauthorized people. Here cloud is the main repository of patient information, security plays a major concern as it is shared among various hospitals and different health organizations. Malicious activists continue giving their luck on each growing technology for satisfying their exceptional acts. So, there is maybe a chance of theft, modification, and misuse of patient data. As IoT-based network is a collaboration of heterogeneous sensor devices there may be involvement of risks and vulnerabilities. There are different types of attacks such as IoT, Botnet attacks, IoT devices sending spams, Shodan IoT Search Engine, Privacy Leaks, Unsecured Devices, Home Intrusions, and Remote Vehicle Hijacking can be avoided with secure assessment layer [12]. The goals of a security mechanism in an IoT framework are to: provide patient data privacy:

- Confidentiality of patient data;
- Security to the end-users of each layer;
- Security to the sensor devices;
- Assurance of the accessibility of the services presented by the system.

9.5 NETWORK TOPOLOGY AND ITS DESCRIPTION

For successful implementation of any network is depends on accurate network design. To provide the network fully reliable and efficient we have paid concentration regarding various parameters such as the size of the organization, no health work resource, and other relevant major necessities as per the project expected. Before designing the network, the requirement analysis is mandatory. We have analyzed both technical and non-technical for a good design. The complications of the network are avoided by considering the requirement analysis in a better way. Various types of network architectures are used in WSN like architecture and hierarchical architecture. Here we preferred hierarchical one because it is easy to manage and expand the network as per the need. The main criteria behind choosing hierarchical architecture, small issues that occur in the network can be easily detected and solved with our disturbing other operations. Besides, it can efficiently balance the load between the sensor nodes via conveying different tasks for each one sensor node according to its capabilities. The architecture of IoT is not the same as the architecture of the Internet and Telecommunication Networks. Three diverse architectures of IoT are not appropriate for IoT applications, even though they have some familiar features. They do not perform the necessities of security and privacy and are exaggerated by numerous security attacks. To prevail over the worry of security, we propose and ascertain a novel standard six-layered architecture of IoT. It can be effortlessly and efficiently unmitigated to fundamental functions along with the modest impact on IoT open layered architectures to impose the security attacks and maintain a strategic distance from IoT applications from attackers. In general, hierarchical architecture has six layers: The perception layer (lower one), the observer layer or the monitor layer, processing layer, security layer, network layer, or transmission layer, the application layer (upper one). When data is over, it sends the data to the observer layer to get approval regarding authentication for the sensor and the devices.

The monitor layer receives data from the perception layer. The main function of this layer to authenticate whether the gathered data of the patient is free from intruder and virus or not. Authentication of the object and security of the data from the unauthorized person is a major concern of this layer. The processing layer gathers information from the observer layer with a trust that it should be safe and protected from viruses and intruders. Unnecessary information is deleted in this layer. By this original data recovered from the patient maintained with safe custody. It uses various data processing modules, databases, and cloud computing concepts to extract the necessary information. Network traffic can be eliminated by removing unnecessary pieces of information. The security layer is designed to maintain a secure IoT (SIT)/WSN based network. In this layer, it assembles data from the processing layer and encrypts it using some key. And the forward it through the network with a key. At the receiver end using the same key information of the patient which was received from the processing layer can be generated. Advanced encryption and decryption techniques are used in this layer. The key role of the network layer is interconnection, interoperability between various sensors. The transmission medium may be wired/wireless as per the need of the user. The responsibility of the application layer is to provide conveyance of various applications to different users [26].

9.6 WIRELESS SENSOR NETWORK (WSN) AND ITS IMPACT ON HEALTHCARE

In the case of IoT application for healthcare WSN plays a major role. The implementation and deployment of smart connected sensor devices are done through WSN. As per the requirement of the patient instead of using all sensing devices few required sensors are implanted with the body of the human being the human body for data collection. The collected information can be stored in a cloud and with doctors, supervision diagnosis can be done for the betterment of patient health. After deployment, the independent sensor node is attached to the main network for further processing. Patient data is routed through the data center with the help of the cloud via a WSN. During data dissemination from one sensor node to another, it is dependent on the routing protocol architecture [21]. The consideration of routing protocol depends on IoT/WSN network to achieve both optimality and efficiency in intercommunication and high computation between the things. Various types of routing protocols are adopted in WSN, but here we are focusing on the location-based routing protocol. The location-based routing also known as geographic-based routing. The geographic location of the destination sensor is tracked by the source node and sends a message to the destination sensor. The basic idea about this protocol is there is no need for flooding so it minimizes the control overhead. Route discovery and packet forwarding are done based on location information. With less maintenance, scalable, requirement of less memory space, less energy consumption, it provides opportunity including different routing algorithms for data dissemination. The communication and interoperability between various nodes within the WSN in a healthcare system present in Figure 9.6.

9.7   OUR PROPOSED METHOD FOR IoT-BASED HEALTHCARE SYSTEM FOR CANCER CARE

IoT-based system is a collaboration between various smart sensor devices and machines. All things in the network are coordinate with each other through forwarding data packets from one node to another. Heterogeneous devices use the diversity of network topologies for network communication. Since the location-based routing concept is adopted using GPS to track the position and timestamp of the patient, So the message passes from one node to another to provide a better solution. Every node in the network has a connection to each of the other nodes even if one link fails, the patient data will transmit through another link, for this reason, we have considered full mesh topology in the proposed method. The proposed healthcare system comprises with series of services and applications under the treatment of the doctor administrative team. Various methods like chemotherapy, radiation therapy, immunotherapy, hormone therapy, targeted drug therapy, and cryoablation coupling with various applications as per the necessary conditions, here we have used a variety of smart sensor devices to monitor the progress and side effects of the approaches and forward the same to cloud center for proper investigation of the medical team. The proposed architecture is presented in Figure 9.6.

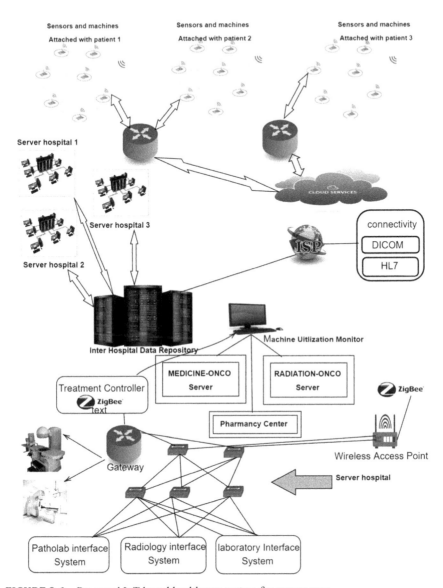

FIGURE 9.6 Proposed IoT-based healthcare system for cancer care.

9.8 NETWORK TOPOLOGY FOR CANCER CARE SERVICE

In the proposed architecture for cancer care, we are mainly focusing on cancer instead of benign. When the tissues of the body start to grow the uncontrolled way, it shows the primary symptom of cancer disease. Cancer creates abnormal growth in the tissue that is called malignant tumors. Due to this loss of the normal organ function of the body occur. The cancer cells spread to different nearby organs or it spread through the bloodstream to all organs of the body, as per the type of cancer and severity of cancer. This is called metastasize. Not only it causes changes and damaging the position wherever it is in progress, cancer frequently causes additional symptoms, such as tiredness, weight loss, anemia (low blood count), tenderness, weakness, despair, and shortness of breath, and associated with contamination. As per the WHO report, 12 million patients are diagnosed everywhere. Healthcare professionals involved in cancer care include oncologists and hematologists classify the difference between normal cell, cancerous cell, and frequency of multiplication of normal cells in the context of appearance and nature at microscopic view called grading. Treatment or cancer services of cancer depend on the type of cancer, involved organ, and the extent of nature and health status of the patient. The treatment of cancer comprises chemotherapy, radiation therapy, surgical procedure, blood transfusions, bone transplantation, etc. Surgery is the common approach used by the doctors to remove cancer-affected areas without damaging outlier tissues of the affected area. Two basis treatments adopted by such as chemotherapy (part of medicine approach oncology (MEDICINE-ONCO) treatment) and radiotherapy (part of radiation oncology (RADIATION-ONCO). To monitor the health condition and improve the quality of cancer care of the patient before or after treatment, chemotherapy or radiotherapy, smart sensor devices with WSN can be adopted. Remotely patient care, monitoring, follow up, report alert) can be done at patient home by the sensing devices with the patient body and improved quality of patient service can be provided [19]. With the help of IoT devices using WSN process automation and remote monitoring can be done as per the physical report of the patient. IoT can be used to identify the position of the tumor and later treatment Smart sensors should be programmed in such a way it should work as per the reasonable adverse side effect of the patient's health in case of immunotherapy. Immunotherapy will as per the parameter generated by the smart sensors. In the absence of the physical presence of doctor high-level treatment can be provided and monitored at the patient end remotely. By IoT/WSN healthcare improves the patient-centric treatment [32].

9.9 THE ARCHITECTURE OF CANCER-BASED HEALTHCARE SYSTEM USING IoT WITH CLOUD

This section provides a brief discussion about the architecture of how various sensors and interconnected with each other and the data flow between them.

The connected device's description and working principle in this architecture are stated below. Practically the implementation of IoT-based cancer care is quite different from the natural way how the doctors prescribe the dose to the patient as per the report of radiotherapy or chemotherapy. This network architecture expresses a visual version of the pretend model for the future generation. This architecture consists of a machine (radiotherapy machine, printer) Software (Servers (MEDICINE-ONCO, RADIATION-ONCO)/ Client interface of different machines), ISP, WAP, Gateways, and Remote Access VPN [20].

Digital imaging and communications in medicine (DICOM) communicate with various machines like path lab interface system (PI), radiology interface system (RI), laboratory interface system (LI) to gather the patient information to understand the condition if the disease. The pathology lab is embedded with PI to observe the stage of cancer. The observation of the stage can be found out by comparing the tissues with normal tissues. This will help the oncologists to apply differentiation therapy for a fast recovery. LI is the repository connected with the blood bank to detect the symptom and component issues during and after treatment. RI interface gathers the report of CT, ST, MRI results. PI, RI, LI results help for easy prediction of towards better treatment. DICOM and semantic XML are connected with ISP, machines, servers through gateways, and all interfaces are connected with a wireless access point (WAP) for remote patient treatment. Eclipse stores the CT and RT profile of the patient and is connected with the DICOM for easy access from the cloud. Prescribed medicine dose mentioned and update regularly at Dose-volume history. Other body war sensors can be used to identify various factors of the patient such as hemoglobin level, fever, and pain monitoring, emesis monitoring, glucose level monitoring, heart rate monitoring, drug allergic monitoring. All the mentioned information provides the oncologist for convenient treatment with less resource utilization.

9.9.1 CLOUD SERVICES FOR CANCER CARE

The implementation of cloud technology has been increasing at a frenetic pace. For behavioral healthcare organizations, cloud computing solutions can frequently provide better levels of service as compared to their internal IT efforts. For behavioral healthcare organizations, cloud computing solutions can frequently provide better levels of service as compared to their internal IT effort. A high volume of patient medical data generated from WSN and machine physical characteristics that are attached to the patient.

The data are collected for various needs such as research, disease analysis, report generation, gaining intelligence, streamlining operations, etc. Cloud service provides a platform where the patient data availability and access can be done remotely from the real-time continuous basis. It is a difficult job to store a high volume of patient data in a physical server. So, the preference of cloud plays important roles where the ever-increasing data can be stored and managed remotely between the healthcare networks. Benefits of cloud computing in healthcare are stated below:

- Streamline collaborative patient care;
- Decreases data storage costs;
- Superior data security;
- Data storage/big data applications;
- Flexibility and scales easily;
- Enhances patient safety;
- Enhance medical research;
- Drive data interoperability.

The relayed data generated from the machines and various sensors are stored in the cloud as patient identity. The data format may vary from machine to machine (M2M) and sensor to sensor, such as text, visual, multimedia. All formats of data are routed through the cloud. With the presentation of cloud computing, the entirety of the information inaccessible in filing cabinets can be searched through and analyzed utilizing the most complex computer algorithms available. This will empower healthcare providers to distinguish and react to public health threats that would beforehand have been undetectable until some other time in their life cycle. This architecture has reporting capabilities for the immediate generation of the consolidated dashboard for not only better treatment as well as it helps to analyze the disease by understanding epidemic patterns, patient monitoring, and optimization using data analytical tools. This gathered data helps the healthcare providers to enhance patient hospitality and also improve the working efficiency of the clinical experts and oncologists. The repository may be utilized for research with keeping an eye on the privacy policy of the patient to enhance the approach of treatment. Data gathered from various machines are text, image, video in nature, so in this architecture we have adopted PACS systems (picture archiving and communication system). PACS, frameworks that electronically process, store, distribute, and recover computerized clinical images in a portion of, or throughout, a health insurance endeavor. PACS epitomizes the incorporation of clinical, computer, and communication innovations with its prerequisites for high amounts of storage, sophisticated databases, and large-bandwidth based networks, computational power at the desktop, convenience, for an assortment of individuals, and specific clinical application software. PACS can improve the imaging department workflow contrasted with film-based technologies and underlines that the practical implementation of PACS requires a high degree of integration with the radiology information system (RIS) and/or the hospital information system (HIS) for sequence execution of the task, resource management, and generation of radiology reports [27]. PACS minimizes film use, film processing, and storage costs, as well as the number of lost films and retakes. We have proposed an appropriate strategy to accumulate and dissect data as gathered over the network and communications framework through secure transmissions from one end to another.

9.9.2 HADOOP/SQOOP DEPLOYMENT IN CLOUD SERVICE

Numerous tools are available to store the high volume of patient data generated from the healthcare systems for easy and efficient data management. Apache Hadoop/scoop is the most well-known data repository and processing engine used in the big data industry with its enormous capability of handling data. So, we have chosen the Hadoop/scoop framework for the cancer care solution. In the framework in Figure 9.7, the Hadoop cluster head is used for predictive analysis using its ML algorithm and data mining approach. This framework runs in parallel on a cluster and can allow us to process patient data across all nodes. Hadoop distributed file system (HDFS) is the storage system of Hadoop which splits big data and distributes across many nodes in a cluster [28, 31]. To guarantee that, it prevents data loss by replicating data on servers [15]. The biggest advantage of considering Hadoop is its very low response time and capability of time alert as compare to other tools available. Hadoop is considered for the following features like fault tolerance, reliability, high availability, economic, easy to use, data locality, data value, schema, workload, data source, and security. Sqoop tool is used to design to route the data between Hadoop and relational database servers like My SQL, Oracle.

Here we have used the Sqoop concept between NoSQL databases and Hadoop cluster for conducting disease, genomics, and epidemic pattern research; patient-disease tracking and monitoring; patient sentiment analysis; risk, and quality of care analysis, etc.

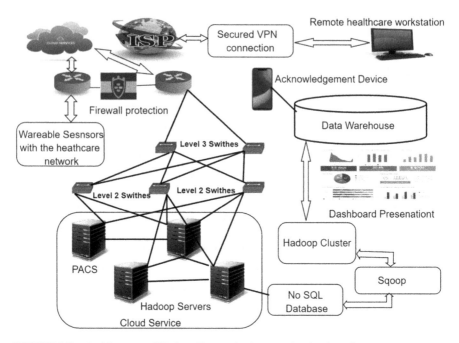

FIGURE 9.7   Architecture of Hadoop/Sqoop deployment in cloud service.

9.10   SOLVING SECURITY ISSUES OF PATIENT DATA IN IoT/WSN BASED HEALTHCARE SYSTEM

IoT/WSN adopted the healthcare system consists of heterogeneous sensors, a variety of mobile devices and applications, machines interconnected with each other with different network access technologies. During communication, every machine face with various operational challenges and security issues [14]. So, issues with security are the biggest challenge in IoT-based architecture. Privacy and confidentiality of patient reports have a concern without expressing the personal demographic information to the research group. Protections of sensitive information of the patient should be encrypted and stored in the Hadoop server. Based on the application of the healthcare system the security issues are classified into following types such as data confidentiality, data authentication, strong user authentication, data integrity, key distribution, access control, data availability, data freshness, secure localization, forward, and backward secrecy, communications, and computation cost, patient permission, etc.:

1. **Data Confidentiality:** Patient health information is commonly held under the legal and ethical responsibility of confidentiality. This health information ought to be private and accessible to the approved specialists or persons involved in the healthcare system. Hence, it is fundamental to keep the individual health Report secret, with the goal that an enemy cannot snoop on the patients. Information spying may make damage to the patient as an unauthorized user can utilize the data for any illicit purposes and thus, the patient's protection is penetrated.

2. **Data Authentication:** It is the common ethics of security in the WSN/IoT healthcare application framework. Here the enemy tries to change the packet or add the additional packet, which is sent by a source to destination nodes. It makes sure that the data comes from the exact source, as these data are carried out in different valuable activities. Thus, every sensor node needs to identify the actual sender's identification. Otherwise, the wrong action will be performed. Authentication can be maintained by the use of message authentication code (MAC).

3. **Strong User Validation:** The difficult issue in a remote health-care environment is the vulnerability of remote messages to an unapproved client, so it is highly profoundly exceptionally that strong user verification should be thought of, whereby user client must their validness before getting to any patient physiological information.

4. **Data Integrity:** It makes sure that any received message has not been modified by illegal parties either by force or choice. Here the enemies try to alter the data during the transmission from source to a destination node. Data integrity gives the assurance to the sensor networks that the packets used by sensor nodes are unaltered and genuine. To achieve data integrity, the best way is the practice of message integrity code [33].

5. **Key Distribution:** During information exchange between two sensor nodes, for privacy point of view, a session key must be shared between them. A secure session key helps secure subsequent communication and safeguards data against various security attacks. In this manner to protect the patient's security, and proficient key distribution scheme is a significant prerequisite in wireless health-care applications.

6. **Access Control:** In healthcare application, many users (such as doctors, nurses, pharmacists, insurance companies, lab staff, social workers, etc.), are always directly involved with the patient's physiological data, so a role-based access control mechanism should be implemented in real-time healthcare applications that can restrict the access of the physiological information, as user's roles [34]. For example, the HL7 Standard Development Organization uses a role-based access control model.

7. **Data Availability:** This means the services and patient information only can be accessed during the time required only. Sensor node availability must ensure constantly forwarding of data to the caregiver like oncologists and other staff. If a sensor hub is caught by an enemy, at that point its information accessibility will be lost, in this manner, it is required to keep up consistently on the activity of the healthcare applications on account of the loss of accessibility.

8. **Data Freshness:** It makes sure that no previous data have been repeated. Here the enemy can catch a packet from the existing network, clutch that packet for some instant, and then rejoin it to the network. So, by using the outdated message, the entire network becomes at risk, and the products used in the system display the wrong result. To achieve data freshness, a packet uses timestamp. A delivery sensor node knows how to evaluate the timestamp appended in the packet through its timer and check the validation of the packet.

9. **Secure Localization:** Geographical position tracking of the patient is significant in real-time based healthcare applications, otherwise, an absence of keen patient following permits the attacker to send incorrect position by utilizing bogus signals.

10. **Forward and Backward Secrecy:** In a constant healthcare services application, when a sensor gets fail to provide the health-related data due to some reason new sensors may be deployed at the same position of the body. In WSN/IoT each deployed sensor must follow forward and backward secrecy. This secrecy states that after a sensing node gets dead, then it cannot read the transmitted message at that timestamp, similarly when a new sensing node joins to the network cannot peruse any recently transmitted messages.

11. **Communication and Computation Cost:** Considered Security schemes should be efficient in terms of communication and computational cost because sensors are resource-inhibited in nature and require a room for executing their tasks.

12. **Patient Permission:** Without the permission of the patient, a health-care provider never disseminates his/her health records to another. For example, a medical researcher, the insurance company, etc.

9.10.1   *APPROACHES TO PREVENT IoT DEVICES/SERVICES FORM ATTACK OF INTRUDER*

Security is a major concern in the IoT cancer care system as no patients and no devices (wearable and machine) attached increase as per the patient demand. So, it is necessary to maintain security in each level of solution. This section talked about different security approaches embraced identified with healthcare. The working principles of every attached thing are classi-fied into three types such as Data gathering, distribution, and access [37]. In WSN each and sensor work sense the data with a routing protocol which should be should be made secure using RFID devices [16]. Trust manage-ment and distribution management is the two major approaches used in WSN to maintain data routes between different sensors in the healthcare network. In modern networking, all devices are connected with IPv6 which protocol is safely secure. IoMT (Internet of medical things) devices aimed at increased non-intrusive access or efficient remote health monitoring [18]. As per the internet of health things Survey 2017 done by Accenture 18% of the healthcare organizations sell their patient confidential data in unauthor-ized parties which leads to cyber exploitation by enabling the attack on the network using denial of service attack (DDoS) and also interfere with the safety of the IoT device. From a security point of view, both manufactures of the device and healthcare organizations are accountable to protect health data at rest, use, in transit. IoT devices are controlled by public key infra-structure with Digital signature to accept a secure connection for software security updates. Zero trust architecture is the best security policy "Never Trust, always verify." The following are some solutions to provide IoT/WSN healthcare system secure:

- Dedicated gateway and staff;
- Use of enterprise applications;
- Always follow the security recommendations from the manufacture;
- Denial of unauthorized IP access;
- Awareness among the staff that is a part of this healthcare network;
- Regular update of IoT device patches.

In WSN all the sensing devices are working with low power mode so the privacy and security mechanisms should use low power Ipv6 architecture.

9.10.2 PROPOSED VS. EXISTING SIMILAR APPROACHES IN HEALTHCARE

For understanding the novelty of the proposed approach for cancer healthcare, we have compared the proposed solution with the exiting solution from the literature survey mentioned in the reference. From the comparative study, we found the following parameters better as compared to others. The framework or the architecture design for cancer healthcare is a promising one. Most of the papers presented health is a framework with mobile applications with IoT for various diseases like diabetes, etc. All the symptoms are controlled with the help of the application based on mobile [36]. Although the different author has a different notion to provide a solution using IoT. We have focused on utilizing the IoT enabled heterogeneous devices to work under a single platform with compatibility protocol mode to provide a robust service. The major advantage of the proposed one we have used GPS for online position tracking of the patient to alert the hospital, clinical, and other related staffs like ambulance, etc. [17]. The main motto of this architecture is to provide a solution for cancer patients. It is optimized care as compared to the hospital-centric traditional approach. Not only improves the quality of the treatment at the same time it creates a platform where the patient can move one healthcare institute to others without carrying the patient report [35]. Cloud service provides an easy and convenient method to provide better treatment with fewer human resources with the help of wearable sensors and cloud Computing.

9.11 CONCLUSION

A well-designed healthcare system for cancer care is proposed. It is a framework with IoT that enables a medical system and provides easy and efficient cancer diagnosis, detection, and other cancer care services with the help of cloud service. Health solution work is done with the help of various smart sensors. WSN plays an essential role in establishing a communication path for routing the data from source to destination within the healthcare environment. To maintain the security and privacy point of view, we have considered various encryption-based cryptography techniques. This architecture is not a complete solution for physical cancer but this IoT-based framework may provide a better solution to improve the levels for diagnosis.

KEYWORDS

- **cancer care services**
- **Food and Agriculture Organization**
- **healthcare system**
- **internet of things (IoT)**
- **smart sensing devices**
- **wireless sensor network (WSN)**

REFERENCES

1. Allareddy, V., Rengasamy, V. S., Nalliah, R. P., Caplin, J. L., & Lee, M. K., (2019). Orthodontics in the era of big data analytics. *Orthodontics & Craniofacial Research, 22*, 8–13.
2. Gu, D., Li, J., Li, X., & Liang, C., (2017). Visualizing the knowledge structure and evolution of big data research in healthcare informatics. *International journal of medical informatics, 98*, 22–32.
3. Bains, J. K., (2016). Big data analytics in healthcare-its benefits, phases, and challenges. *Advanced Research in Computer Science and Software Engineering, 6*(4), 430–435.
4. Acharjya, D. P., & Ahmed, K., (2016). A survey on big data analytics: Challenges, open research issues, and tools. *International Journal of Advanced Computer Science and Applications, 7*(2), 511–518.
5. Balamurugan, S., Madhukanth, R., Prabhakaran, V. M., & Shanker, R. G. K., (2016). Internet of health: Applying IoT and big data to manage healthcare systems. *International Research Journal of Engineering and Technology, 310*, 732–735.
6. Sonnati, R., (2017). Improving healthcare using big data analytics. *International Journal of Scientific & Technology Research, 6*(03), 142–146.
7. Das, N., Das, L., Rautaray, S. S., & Pandey, M., (2018). Big data analytics for medical applications. *International Journal of Modern Education and Computer Science, 11*(2), 35.
8. Chang, B. R., Lee, Y. D., & Liao, P. H., (2017). *Development of Multiple Big Data Analytics Platforms with Rapid Response.* Scientific Programming.
9. Sahu, B., Mohanty, S., & Rout, S., (2019). A hybrid approach for breast cancer classification and diagnosis. *EAI Endorsed Transactions on Scalable Information Systems, 6*(20).

10. Sahu, B., (2018). A combo feature selection method (filter+ wrapper) for microarray gene classification. *International Journal of Pure and Applied Mathematics, 118*(16), 389–401.

11. Chauhan, R., & Jangade, R., (2016). A robust model for big healthcare data analytics. In: *2016 6th International Conference-Cloud System and Big Data Engineering (Confluence)* (pp. 221–225). IEEE.

12. Mehta, N., & Pandit, A., (2018). Concurrence of big data analytics and healthcare: A systematic review. *International Journal of Medical Informatics, 114*, 57–65.

13. Ambigavathi, M., & Sridharan, D., (2020). A survey on big data in healthcare applications. In: *Intelligent Communication, Control, and Devices*, (pp. 755–763). Springer, Singapore.

14. Ficco, M., & Palmieri, F., (2017). *Security and Resilience in Intelligent Data-Centric Systems and Communication Networks*. Academic Press.

15. Farahani, B., Firouzi, F., Chang, V., Badaroglu, M., Constant, N., & Mankodiya, K., (2018). Towards fog-driven IoT eHealth: Promises and challenges of IoT in medicine and healthcare. *Future Generation Computer Systems, 78*, 659–676.

16. Adame, T., Bel, A., Carreras, A., Melia-Segui, J., Oliver, M., & Pous, R., (2018). CUIDATS: An RFID-WSN hybrid monitoring system for smart healthcare environments. *Future Generation Computer Systems, 78*, 602–615.

17. Pramanik, M. I., Lau, R. Y., Demirkan, H., & Azad, M. A. K., (2017). Smart health: Big data-enabled health paradigm within smart cities. *Expert Systems with Applications, 87*, 370–383.

18. Carney, T. J., & Kong, A. Y., (2017). Leveraging health informatics to foster a smart system's response to health disparities and health equity challenges. *Journal of Biomedical Informatics, 68*, 184–189.

19. Vippalapalli, V., & Ananthula, S., (2016). Internet of things (IoT) based smart healthcare system. *International Conference on Signal Processing, Communication, Power, and Embedded System (SCOPES)*, (pp. 1229–1233). IEEE.

20. Patel, P., Ali, M. I., & Sheth, A., (2017). On using the intelligent edge for IoT analytics. *IEEE Intelligent Systems, 32*(5), 64–69.

21. Zuhra, F. T., Bakar, K. A., Ahmed, A., & Tunio, M. A., (2017). Routing protocols in wireless body sensor networks: A comprehensive survey. *Journal of Network and Computer Applications, 99*, 73–97.

22. Rath, M., & Solanki, V. K., (2019). Contribution of IoT and big data in modern healthcare applications in smart city. *Handbook of IoT and Big Data*, 109–124.

23. Dimitrov, D. V., (2016). Medical internet of things and big data in healthcare *Healthcare Informatics Research, 22*(3), 156–163.

24. Jagadeeswari, V., Subramaniyaswamy, V., Logesh, R., & Vijayakumar, V. J. H. I. S., (2018). A study on medical internet of things and big data in the personalized healthcare system. *Health Information Science and Systems, 6*(1), 14.

25. JYuehong, Y. I. N., Zeng, Y., Chen, X., & Fan, Y., (2016). The internet of things in healthcare: An overview. *Journal of Industrial Information Integration, 1*, 3–13.

26. Alaba, F. A., Othman, M., Hashem, I. A. T., & Alotaibi, F., (2017). The internet of things in healthcare: An overview. *Journal of Network and Computer Applications, 88*, 10–28.

27. Onasanya, A., & Elshakankiri, M., (2018). Secured cancer care and cloud services in IoT/WSN based medical systems. In: *International Conference on Smart Grid and Internet of Things* (Vol. 88, pp. 10–35). Springer, Cham.

28. Kumar, S., & Singh, M., (2018). Big data analytics for the healthcare industry: Impact, applications, and tools. *Big Data Mining and Analytics, 2*(1), 48–57.

29. Sahu, B., & Panigrahi, A., (2020). *Efficient Role of Machine Learning Classifiers in the Prediction and Detection of Breast Cancer.* Available at SSRN 3545096.

30. Sahu, B., (2019). Multi filter ensemble method for cancer prognosis and diagnosis. *International Journal of Engineering Applied Sciences and Technology [Online], 4,* 105–109.

31. Hassan, M. K., El Desouky, A. I., Elghamrawy, S. M., & Sarhan, A. M., (2018). An intelligent hybrid remote patient-monitoring model with a cloud-based framework for knowledge discovery. *Computers & Electrical Engineering, 70,* 1034–1048.

32. Ondiege, B., Clarke, M., & Mapp, G., (2017). Exploring a new security framework for remote patient monitoring devices. *Computers, 6*(1), 11.

33. Mikalef, P., Pappas, I. O., Krogstie, J., & Giannakos, M., (2018). Big data analytics capabilities: a systematic literature review and research agenda. *Information Systems and E-Business Management, 16*(3), 547–578.

34. Marjani, M., Nasaruddin, F., Gani, A., Karim, A., Hashem, I. A. T., Siddiqa, A., & Yaqoob, I., (2017). Big IoT data analytics: Architecture, opportunities, and open research challenges. *IEEE Access, 5,* 5247–5261.

35. Wang, Y., Kung, L., & Byrd, T. A., (2018). Big data analytics: Understanding its capabilities and potential benefits for healthcare organizations. *Technological Forecasting and Social Change, 126,* 3–13.

36. Kankanhalli, A., Hahn, J., Tan, S., & Gao, G., (2016). Big data and analytics in healthcare: Introduction to the special section. *Information Systems Frontiers, 18*(2), 233–235.

37. Hu, J., & Vasilakos, A. V., (2016). Energy big data analytics and security: Challenges and opportunities. *IEEE Transactions on Smart Grid, 7*(5), 2423–2436.

CHAPTER 10

GRAD-Grape Disease Management with IoT

SUSHOPTI GAWADE,[1] UMESH KULKARNI,[2] and PRAMOD SHITOLE[3]

[1]*Pillai College of Engineering, Panvel, Mumbai, Maharashtra, India, E-mail: sgawade@mes.ac.in*

[2]*Vidyalankar Institute of Technology Wadala, Mumbai, Maharashtra, India, E-mail: umesh.kulkarni@vit.edu.in*

[3]*Adarsh Institute of Technology and Research Center, Vita, Maharashtra, India, E-mail: mail2pramodshitole@rediffmail.com*

ABSTRACT

Pests, soil moisture, and weather conditions affect grape plants, resulting in different diseases that affect plant stem, leaves, flowers, and berries' quality. It causes considerable losses to the farmers and can be avoided using smart farming methods and IoT based on plant disease management systems. Timely information about the weather conditions, the likely pest attacks, and the required pesticide used at vital for the farmers as misinformation leads to excessive use of pesticides resulting in a loss in both the quantity and the quality of the grapes. The proposed system makes use of wireless sensor networks (WSN) that collect data from different sensors deployed at various identified nodes in the field and communicate it through a wireless protocol. In the application developed, we use a large number of small and low-cost sensor nodes powered by small batteries, equipped with various sensing devices to collect field information such as soil moisture, Temperature, and Humidity and plant-related information from the images of plant leaves of the grape. This raw information collected through the WSN then sent to the webserver, where the suggestion for remedies with the help of agriculture experts. This provides a solution for a farmer in less time and reduces the use of pesticides.

10.1   INTRODUCTION

Wireless sensor network (WSN) consists of a low-cost sensor node in large numbers, which are powered by small batteries, which are equipped with different sensing devices. Once a WSN deployed, probably in an inhospitable area, say for 4-year required data is collected. Each sensor has limited energy, they usually put to sleep to save the energy, and this helps to extend the network lifetime [16]. In the Proposed System, the basic information collected from the field, such as diseases, soil moisture, Temperature, Humidity. Disease management generally uses pesticides frequently during the growing season. The farmers cultivating grapes have no clear ideas about the weather condition, and sometimes they are ignorant about the effect of pests on the crops. As result of it, use of pesticides are on a large scale, which results in the loss in both ways as the quantity as well as the quality of the grapes. High cost and frequent use of pesticides that have motivated the development of such monitoring systems that predict all the basic information and provide the effective solutions to farmers in less time. We proposed the novel approach with a sensor node having solar-powered and managing the data using a data server. The tree is rooted in the sink node. Data transfer from the leaf node to the sink node done using distance vector routing and link-state and EIGRP routing protocol logic. We construct a computer application such that they can take raw information from the field through a wireless network and send it to the webserver. The server side calculates the remedies with the help of agriculture and weather experts, which is sent to the farmer. That will be providing a better solution for a farmer in minimum time and reduces the use of pesticides. As a result, crops will be healthy, and the quality and quantity of the crop will increase.

   The main cause of the disease depends on the environmental conditions, which favors the pathogen growth infection upon the susceptible plant. Weather conditions play a vital role in spreading the infection in the plant, which lead to a disease. Other major environmental conditions such as humidity, moisture of the soil, and wetness of the leaf that stimulate the fungal infection in a plant. For fungal infection, pathogens need a plant's leaf surface to germinate using their spores and it needs suitable temperature and a thin coating of water on the leaf. Due to dew wetness is produced on the surface of the leaf is one of the significant factors for promoting pests. The pests are increasing in number as long as the leaf is in wet condition. The duration of the wetness on the leaf is directionally proportional to the increase in number of the pests. Hence there would be a greater risk of infection on the plant.

The common diseases named downy mildew important fungal diseases of the grape worldwide. The leaf and fruit berry are worst affected by this disease. This kind of infection reduces the size of the berry small or produces a flavorless one. Fungicides many times applied to manage the disease while growing the plants. In India, many farmers liberally select the grape farm and use large amounts of pesticides to lay on their hands. Hence, the grapes, is produced through this process, become very toxic and reduce the strength of the soil and on top of that, it is a very expensive one. The main aim is to limit the pesticide spray and is used as and when required. That is if the plant is in high risk, then the spray must be used in a limited and recommended quantity. Some considerable efforts are been taken to reduce the cost of applying pesticides often and to reduce the level of the pesticide in the field. Hence, a prediction system is been developed which predicts the disease accurately and lacks consistency on the field.

This system mainly implemented to predict the impact of the disease, lack of consistency, managing the evolution of space-time on the grape field. WSNs with solar-based are used to find the ambient temperature, humidity, and soil moisture and in addition to this wetness of the leaf is collected for cultivation in the areas such as Sangli, Maharashtra. Using real time data, a strategy planned for pesticide application from the index values, computed by the system. The system notifies the framers about the infected crop and the absolute need of pesticide application. WSN consists of a large number of small and low-cost sensor nodes powered by small batteries, equipped with various sensing devices. Every sensor node has limited energy, and hence the other nodes are usually in sleeping mode when not in use to save the power, and this helps to prolong the network lifetime. Overcome this problem; the Proposed System is a good approach.

The proposed system is collecting field information in a different form. Disease management center because the farmers cultivating grapes have no clear ideas about the weather, and sometimes they are ignorant about the effect of pests on the crops. As a result of it, the use of pesticides on a large scale, which results in the loss in both ways as the quantity as well as the quality of the grapes. Hence, developing such monitoring systems to predict all the factors and effective solutions, made available to farmers in less time.

We proposed the novel approach with a sensor node, which has a solar-powered and data server for data management. Data is transferred from the leaf node to the sink node is done using broadcast tree construction, data compression algorithm, routing distance vector, and link-state algorithms. We construct a computer application such that they can take raw information from the field through a wireless network and send it to the webserver. The server side calculates the remedies with the help of agriculture and weather experts and sends them to the farmer. That will be providing a better solution for a farmer in minimum time and reduces the use of pesticides on a large scale. As a result, crops will be healthy, and quality and quantity increased.

10.2   LITERATURE SURVEY

This section covers literature referred to as understanding the need for the proposal. This chapter uses the Broadcast Tree Algorithm in which each node sends one broadcast message to all other nodes to decide whether the node is an internal node or leaf node [1]. Hop count differs from protocol to protocol, e.g., EIGRP and OSPF [2, 8]. The sensor information uses a data compression algorithm and soli, and lethal cell sensors collect the data related to soil and send the data to a data server [16]. This provides a data-centric routing approach where the data is identified using high-level descriptors or metadata [17]. Based on probability a set of path selection done. The probability value depends on the low energy consumption on each path. The complex method of addressing is problems with this protocol and communication overhead during the setup phase [8, 11].

Different power-aware metrics can be used to increase energy efficiency, such as minimizing the energy consumed/packet, maximize time to a network partition, minimize variance in node power levels, cost/packet, maximum node cost. Rather than using usual metrics such as hop count or delay for finding roots, it is important to use metrics [12]. The pinpoint idea in this approach is to identify and to retrieve information about the occurring events, rather than flooding the entire network only the queries to the nodes that have observed a particular event are to be flooded. The rumor routing algorithm employs long-lived packets, called agents through the network. When a node detects an event, that event gets added into the local table, called events table, and generates an agent. Agents travel the network in order to populate the information about local events to distant nodes. When a node generates a query for an event, the nodes that know the route may respond to the query by inspecting its event table. There is no necessity of flooding the whole network, which reduces delivery costs [13]. The algorithm for Energy-saving is used to initiate the sleep mode in the network. Due to which the energy consumption of the system be reduced, and the network lifetime can be extended. The idea behind is to employ the sleep mode based on probabilistic and to decide whether a node should become inactive for the next period of cycle It shows that with a specific value of sleep probability P, gossip, and under dense topology, the network remains connected and works well [13]. For computing the infection for downy mildew, the logistic infection model was used [7]. For calculating the temperature infection index, the initial model is used [15].

10.3 SYSTEM DESIGN

Graduate system architecture is given in Figure 10.1.

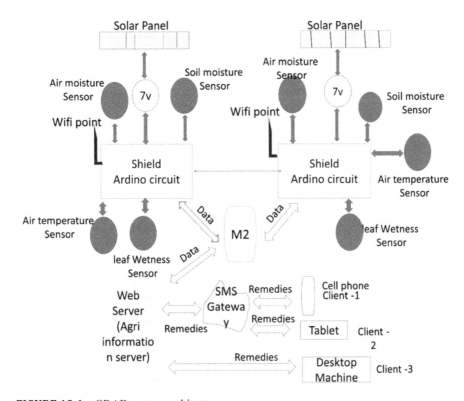

FIGURE 10.1   GRAD system architecture.

The WSN system deployed at cultivating commercial grape farms consisted of the solar-powered nodes equipped with sensors for continuously monitoring agricultural parameters, i.e., air temperature, air relative humidity, soil moisture, rainfall, and leaf wetness. Each node can transmit/receive packets to/from another node in every five minutes over a transmission range of 54 m. Data collected by the sensors wirelessly transferred in a multi-hop manner to a centralized processing unit. Each sensor mote contains the solar-based power supply in the proposed system and sends power to each sensor periodically whenever a sensor requires. For adjusting the strategies for the crop, real-time information about the fields provided to the farmer. This helps enable early alertness for any eventual pests, disease of the crop, etc., which will facilitate the control action first.

10.3.1   SENSOR SYSTEM SETUP

In the proposed GRAD system, each sensor node develops by using a transceiver (nRF24L01) wireless point. Four sensors, i.e., Air Moisture, Soil Moisture (YL69), Temperature, and Humidity (DHT11), Leaf wetness (Y.L. 83), one microcontroller (Arduino ATmega 328) and one 9v energy generate solar panel, and this sensor node is connected to other sensor nodes or the cluster head for data sending. The microcontroller using, distance-vector, and link-state algorithm for transmitting the data from one node to another node or the sink node and one group of nodes.

10.3.2   NETWORK SYSTEM SETUP

In the proposed system, each sensor node connected with another sensor node through a transceiver (nRF24L01) wireless point. Data to convert from analog form to digital, each sensor node connected to the raspberry microcontroller through a transceiver (nRF24L01). Finally, for data storing, raspberry pi (RPi) connects through the wireless point (M2) or wireless router to the database application. Each sensor node has the capacity to transmit and receive the data from itself or from the different sensor nodes, and it transmits to the sink node for clustering.

10.3.3   SOFTWARE CONFIGURATION

In the software configuration, every sensor node contains the sensor interface program, timer program, and the different supporting software to handle the data, which is coming from the field. On the server-side, for Wi-Fi setting, a virtual network connection is setup through putty software for that P.I. The operating system installed on the controller (raspberry). Configure the P.I. Operating system Wi-Fi setting to digital router program and accessing the sensor node information. The raspberry application, interface program for storing information in a database for further calculation.

10.3.4 USER AUTHENTICATION

In the user authentication, the server application designed, which completes the authentication process. Authentication provided to the username and password to the user through an SMS and mail alert system for account access. With the help of the communication, the facility server will store the expert suggestion in database application for server maturation through feedback.

10.3.5 FEEDBACK COLLECTION AND ANALYSIS

In the proposed system, a communication model used to collect feedback from users in terms of massage, email, and remedies. All this information is stored in the remedy database. For future calculation, this infection index and risk factor feedback are used, and always it compares with expert's suggestions. This will improve the application extension, inquiring about the quality, performance, and usability of the system.

Here, users can see evaluated values and acknowledgment from experts or from the system in its web panel account as shown in Figure 10.2.

FIGURE 10.2   Communication module.

10.4   DETAILS OF COMPONENTS USED TO SET-UP GRAD

This section describes the sensor setup and network setup and components used for it.

10.4.1 SENSOR NETWORK SETUP

In the proposed system GRAD, each sensor node is made by one transceiver (nRF24L01) wireless point, four sensors, i.e., air moisture, soil moisture (YL69), temperature, and humidity (DHT11), leaf wetness (Y.L. 83), one microcontroller (Arduino atmega 328) and one 9v energy generate solar panel. The sensor node connected to each other through the transceiver (nRF24L01) wireless point or to the cluster head of data communication. The microcontroller contains distance vectors and link-state algorithm logic using RF24. H library header files for data sending from one node to another node or to the sink node. With the help of this network, all sensor nodes acting as cluster points and sink nodes act as a cluster head. This cluster head can connect to the webserver application through the virtual wireless network (Figure 10.3).

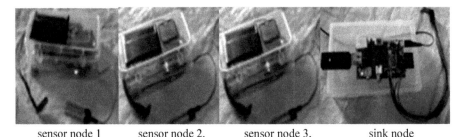

    sensor node 1   sensor node 2,   sensor node 3,   sink node

FIGURE 10.3   A sensor node mote structure.

10.4.2 NETWORK SYSTEM SETUP

In proposing, a system, to develop a cluster of sensor nodes, connected to each other through a transceiver (nRF24L01) wireless point network. For the cluster or tree, each sensor node acts as the internal node or source node, and the sink node is the head node or the root node. Based on the algorithm applied, all source nodes are sending information to the root (cluster head) node. The root node connected to the server application. The source data are in analog form. For digital conversion, sensor nodes are wirelessly connected to the raspberry microcontroller (sink or root node) through transceiver (nRF24L01). Finally, with the help of wireless routers and its software root node or sink node (raspberry) is configured to the agri server application. Each sensor node has the capacity to transmit and receive the data from itself or from the different sensor node and send to the sink node for clustering. Figure 10.4 represents the same.

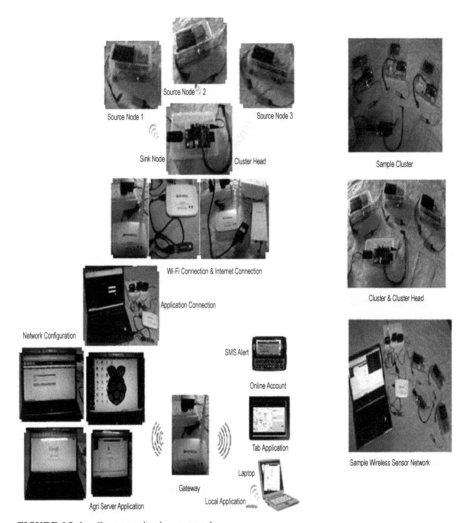

FIGURE 10.4 Crop monitoring network.

10.5 EXPERIMENTAL SETUP

10.5.1 GRAPHICAL USER INTERFACE (GUI)

Using Figure 10.5 with the help of username and password system entered into the design panel. The design panel divided into three modes, i.e., administrator mode, expert mode, and user mode. The administration panel use to design the logic part, which is required for the application.

An expert panel is used for calculating the remedies with a solution and sending the calculated remedy to the proper user using different alerts system facilities. Through the user panel, the user can see the current situation of its farm and discuss the suggestions with expert's panel for calculation.

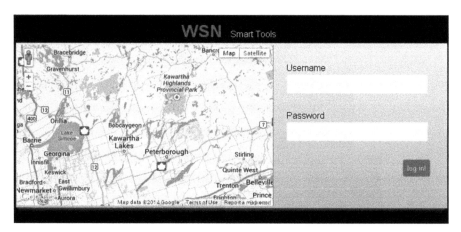

FIGURE 10.5   Login page.

10.5.1.1 ADMIN PANEL

Using a communication model, Figure 10.6 represents the administrator panel; used for sending the messages to experts and users of data sharing with each other. The administration panel provides the sensor node registration for configuring the sensor node with the network. Using user registration for accessing the correct information on its farm securely. Admin panel can generate the log reports for particular users with individual parameters and dates.

Figure 10.7 shows the design of the registration form of sensor nodes with a machine address, and Figure 10.8 shows the list of registered sensor nodes with the name, its I.P. address, and the machine address.

Figures 10.9 and 10.10 show the user registration form that will allocate the password and sensor node to its farm and the identities to allocate sensor nodes.

Figures 10.11 and 10.12 provide the different parameter and unit registration option with proper units for the calculation.

Figure 10.13 is used for government standard method registration.

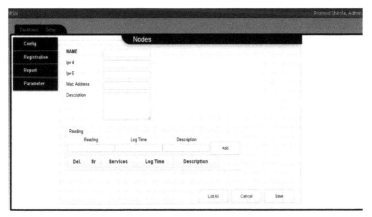

FIGURE 10.6 Administrator panel.

FIGURE 10.7 Sensor node registration panel.

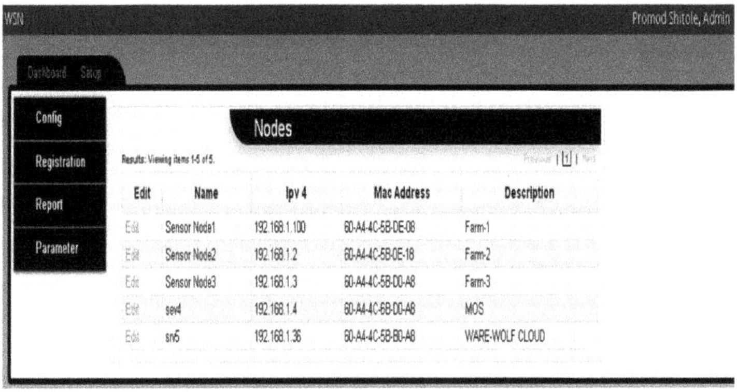

FIGURE 10.8 List of sensor nodes.

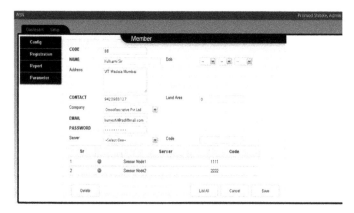

FIGURE 10.9   User registration form.

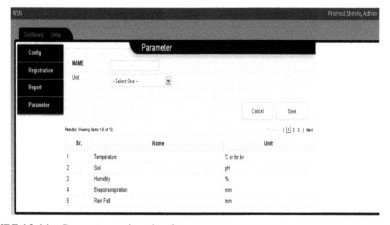

FIGURE 10.10   Registered user list.

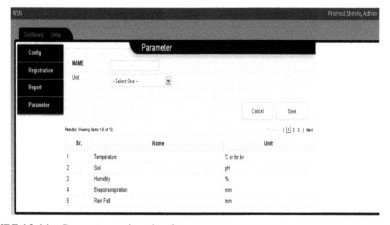

FIGURE 10.11   Parameter registration form.

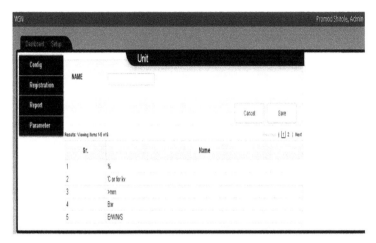

FIGURE 10.12 Unit registration form.

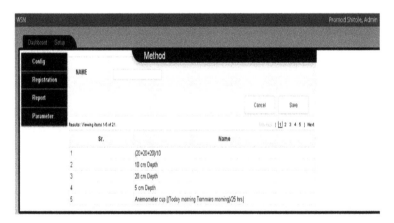

FIGURE 10.13 Method registration form.

With the help of Figure 10.14, methods and parameters result are stored in the database, and with the help of Figure 10.15, remedies are created and stored in a remedies database.

10.5.1.2 DATABASE

Figures 10.16 and 10.17 show the system design, database tables for user registration, and value storing tables in the database. Figure 10.18 shows the table which stores the sensor allotment list with the user.

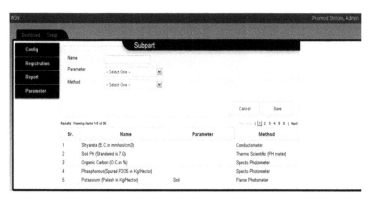

FIGURE 10.14   Result registration form.

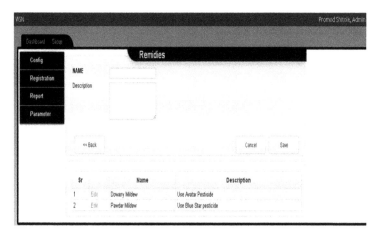

FIGURE 10.15   Remedy registration form.

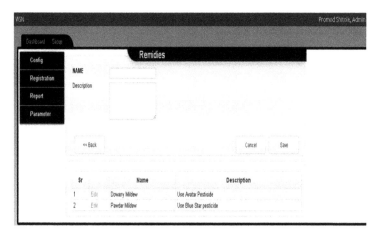

FIGURE 10.16   User registration database.

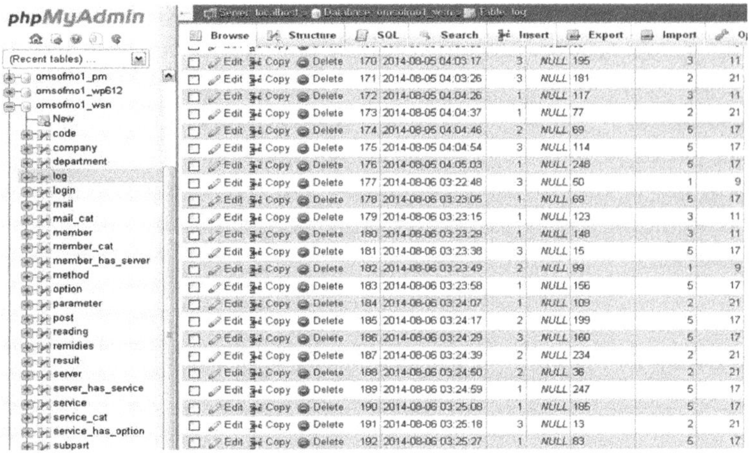

FIGURE 10.17 Parameter values database.

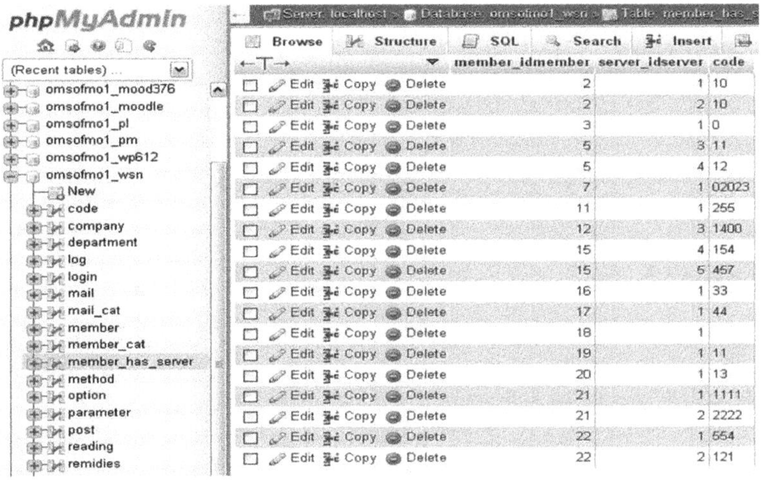

FIGURE 10.18 Sensor node allotment table.

10.6 CONCLUSION

Grape disease management system (GRAD) is WSN system developed for farmers. Used as a real-time application to collect different parameters like soil moisture, air temperature, humidity, and rainfall collection. With the help of today's weather situation, farmers can easily understand the accurate weather situation of their farms and different modes of the power supply so that it will manage the pesticide levels, which will increase the quality and productivity of the grapes. The proposed system, GRAD WSN system provides a solid base for farmers to adjust strategies at any time and efficient way to get accurate information in less time considering the weather and pest management for crops. With a sensor network, this system provides information in several ways to the server application and energy-efficient modes of power supply like solar, battery, and D.C. current. It also provides the communication network and message alert facility to users in favorable crop situations.

KEYWORDS

- **grape diseases**
- **Hadoop distributed file system**
- **humidity**
- **pesticides**
- **soil moisture**
- **wireless sensor networks**

REFERENCES

1. Amulya, R. S., & Hansdath, R. C., (2010). An energy routing protocol with sleep scheduling for wireless sensor network. In: *24ᵗʰ IEEE International Conference on Advanced Information Networking and Application*, 1550-445X/10 IEEE.
2. Ayub, N., et al., (2011). Performance analysis of OSPF and EIGRP routing protocol with respect to the convergence. *European Journal of Scientific Research, 61*(3), 434–447. ISSN 1450-216X.
3. Hou, X., & Tipper, D., (2004). Gossip-based sleep protocol (GSP) for energy-efficient routing in wireless ad hoc networks. *Wireless Communication and Networking Conference, 2004* (Vol. 3, pp. 1305–1310). IEEE.
4. Shah, R., & Rabaey, J., (2002). Energy-aware routing for low energy ad hoc sensor networks. *Wireless Communication and Networking Conference, 2002* (Vol. 1, pp. 350–355). IEEE.
5. Wang, L., &. Xiao, Y., (2006). A survey of energy-efficient scheduling mechanism in sensor networks. *Mob. Netw. Appl., 11*(5), 723–740.
6. Ruizhon, L., Zhi, W., & Youxian, S., (2004). Wireless sensor network solution for real-time monitoring of nuclear power plant. *Proceeding of the 5ᵗʰ World Congress Control and Automation*. Hangzhou, P.R.China. 0-7803-8273- 0/04/$20.00 2004. IEEE.

7. Broome, J. C., English, J. T., Marois, J. J., Lotoroe, B. A., & Aviles, J. C., (1995). Development of an infection model for botrytis branch rot of grapes based on wetness duration and temperature. *Phytopathology, 85*, 97–102.

8. Pramod, T. S. (2012). Auto monitoring energy-efficient wireless sensor network system for a grape farmland. *International Journal of Advanced Research in Computer Science and Electronics Engineering (IJARCSEE)* (Vol. 1, No. 3). (ISSN: 2277-9043).

9. Shitole, P. T., et al., (2014). Embedded based monitoring and controlling energy-efficient wireless sensor network system using distance vector protocol. *International Journal on Recent Trends and Innovation in Computing and Communication. (IJRITCC)* (Vol. 2, No. 7). (ISSN: 2321-8169).

10. Komal, R., Sushopti, G., et al., (2017). Usability improvement with crop disease management as a service. *International Conference on Recent Innovations in Signal Processing and Embedded Systems (RISE).*

11. Sushopti, G., & Varsha, T., (2017). Analysis of digital media compatibility with framers in Maharashtra and recommendation of service provider design framework E-Krishimitra. *International Journal of Applied Agricultural Research* (Vol. 12, No. 1).

12. Komal, R., & Sushopti, (2017). Review of usability and digital divide for ICT in agriculture. *International Journal of Advanced Research.*

13. Hou, X., & Tipper, D., (2004). Gossip-based sleep protocol (GSP) for energy-efficient routing in wireless ad hoc networks. In: *2004 IEEE Wireless Communications and Networking Conference (IEEE Cat. No. 04TH8733)* (Vol. 3, pp. 1305–1310). IEEE.

14. Singh, S., Woo, M., & Raghavendra, C. S., (1998). Power-aware routing in mobile ad hoc networks. In: *Proceedings of the 4th Annual ACM/IEEE International Conference on Mobile Computing and Networking* (pp. 181–190).

15. Enriclk, O., & Modden, L. V., (2003). Temperature and wetness duration parameter for grape leaf and cane infection by *Phomopsis viticola. Plant Disease, 87*(7), 832–840.

16. Ruirui, Z., Liping, C., Jianhua, G., Zhijun, M., & Gang, X., (2010). An energy-efficient wireless sensor network used for farmland soil moisture monitoring. In: *IET International Conference on Wireless Sensor Network 2010 (IET-WSN 2010)* (pp. 2–6). IET.

17. Sangwan, A., & Bhattacharya, P. P., (2018). Reliable energy efficient multi-hop routing protocol for heterogeneous body area networks. *International Journal of Sensors Wireless Communications and Control, 8*(1), 47–56.

18. Telosb Data Sheet. https://www.willow.co.uk/ (accessed on 10 November 2021).

CHAPTER 11

An Overview of IoT in Financial Sectors

P. S. SHEEBA

Department of Computer Science & Engineering (IoT & Cyber Security including Blockchain Technology), Lokmanya Tilak College of Engineering, Navi Mumbai, Maharashtra, India,
E-mail: sheebaps@gmail.com

ABSTRACT

Internet of things (IoT) enables humans to transfer the data over a network using connected devices without human-to-human or human to computers interaction. With the growing demand for technology in vast areas of everyday life, IoT is widely been used in several fields, including home automation, health care and fitness, automated machines, agriculture, smart cities, etc. Apart from this, there are wide applications of IoT in financial sectors. A lot of technological advancements were seen in financial sectors in the last decade. The advancements in technology lead to several new dimensions to conventional banking. More and more financial organizations are getting adopted to new technologies which in turn increases their operational efficiency and user-friendliness. IoT in financial sectors can be explored much to minimize the risks involved owing to the rapid increase in digitalization and mobilization of those sectors. Use of IoTs in banks can help them to improve the decision-making process and to gather information about customers and provide personalized services. It has been estimated that 40% of the financial sectors are now experimenting with IoT and big data. This chapter gives an overview of IoT in financial sectors and the various risks involved in it. Proper use of IoT in financial sectors can lead to various growth opportunities.

11.1 INTRODUCTION

Internet of things (IoT) is a network of connected devices, both mechanical and digital which transfers data over a network with unique identifiers without human interaction. It has become so popular that we can see it almost everywhere. It has wide range of applications in every sector of life. IoT is one of the biggest innovations of this century for the technological advancement.

Several researches are going on in this field of connected devices. As the application of IoTs is not limited, it can be applied to digital services, weather applications, GPS systems, various sensors used for collecting data, smart gadgets, industrial applications, finance, etc., as discussed in Ref. [1]. It also discusses about the various security threats that can arise in such connected networks.

Impact of digital trends in banking sectors using IoT is discussed in Ref. [2]. How the traditional banking is impacted by the use of IoTs in finance sectors is analyzed by the authors. Banking processes are changing due to the new digital developments which will benefit the society at large.

By 2025, it is been estimated that the total number of IoT connected devices will grow to 25 billion [3]. The future World will be a place where communication can happen between objects, and these objects also can communicate with its users by various communication means and the internet.

The major challenges faced by financial sectors are fraud and thefts. As per the reports in Ref. [4], the banking and finance industries have prevented 1.66 billion pounds of unauthorized frauds in the UK. Fraudsters and criminals get the personal data of customers and they use it to exploit them.

Digital transformations are happening at an exponential rate. We can see connected devices everywhere. The benefits of IoTs are highly utilized by the financial sectors. The transfer of data is happening autonomously and instantly, hence financial organizations can pave the way for new business opportunities and intelligent services using the connected devices [5].

In Ref. [6], authors discuss about various ways to predict and tackle financial frauds by using behavior-based analogy. It also discusses about designing a solution to detect vulnerable or malicious activity.

Virtual money concept will happen due to the block chain technology. It can be used to transfer assets, enhance traceability, automatic contract execution, etc. It will help IoT in many ways as it can track the data records by analytical models and provide instant payments for better security and customer satisfaction [7].

How IoT can be used for finance and accounting is studied in Ref. [8]. The development of IoTs is through advancements in wireless communication, RFIDs (radio frequency identification), microelectromechanical systems which is called MEMS. In this study, it has been found that communication between objects can be made possible with IoT, which in turn can be used for various financial services including accounting due to the automation of data it creates.

A study on complex network construction for financial risk is discussed in Ref. [9]. In this study they have found that by using IoT in a proper manner can reduce the risks in lending or borrowing the money substantially by collecting accurate information. Government authorities also should look into various means by which the risks can be eliminated.

In a recent article [10], the use of Neural networks in the field of digital financing is explored. It has been found that by using this new technology, risks in business can be eliminated. It suggests the managers of various firms, including marketing and finance sectors to make use of this technology to reduce the risks involved in the business.

How financial data can be streamed using digital simulation is explored in Ref. [11]. This also enables the financial service organizations to predict their production and the performance. This can be used by financial services to increase their business capacity. Hence by using digital platforms, the firm's performance behavior can be predicted, which in turn can be used to minimize the cost of business operations.

Another article [12] explores the way how traditional banking operation has changed owing to the IoT use in financial technology (FinTech). FinTech improves the performance and can make powerful business plans. Financial sectors can make use of FinTech to promote more innovative business.

11.2 COMPONENTS OF IoT

IoT is a network of connected devices which communicate with each other by transfer of data [13]. Sometimes it is also called the Internet of Everything. The major components used by IoT are shown in Figure 11.1.

Sensors play an important role in collecting complex data from the environment. Multiple sensors are required in a device to sense various types of data. Once the data is collected, it needs to be communicated to the cloud known as IoT platforms by various communication mediums like satellite networks, Wi-Fi, Cellular networks, etc. So IoTs should have proper connectivity. After transferring the data to the cloud, it has to be processed. Proper software is required for data processing. This processed data should be sent to the user by means of a user interface. For example, mobile phones can act as a user interface.

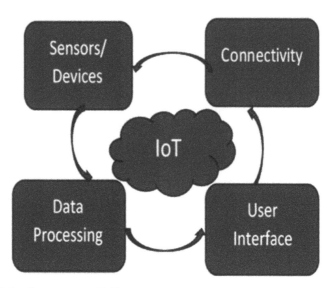

FIGURE 11.1   Components of IoT.

11.3   CHALLENGES FACED BY THE FINANCIAL SERVICES

As the technology is growing at a faster pace, the financial services are facing several challenges which have to be addressed in an efficient manner. The challenges faced by the financial sectors are:

- Customer demand for better services;
- Faster transactions;
- Data security and privacy;
- New technology adoption;
- Efficiency and cost reduction;
- Management of risks;
- Competition from new market players;
- New revenue stream exploration;
- Acquisitions and merger;
- Cyber security;
- New regulations;
- Economy.

Today, most of the customers have gone digital irrespective of the age. Consumers need to get time to time instructions from financial sectors whenever a new technology is being implemented. If the customers are not satisfied with the services provided by their bank, then they prefer to choose another service provider where they feel the services are much better.

11.4 OBJECTIVE OF FINANCIAL SECTORS

Without making the customers happy, the business will not be growing hence the prime objective of financial services is to address the customer needs. Finance sectors need to adapt to new technologies, thereby making convenient transactions for customer needs so that they can retain the customers.

To know the customer needs the service providers should understand the customers and also the infrastructure should be modified to meet the customer needs. This has been taken care of by most of the financial services now.

11.4.1 KNOW YOUR CUSTOMER

Financial services should know about the personal levels of a customer to remain competitive among the other market players. For getting more information of a customer on a time-to-time basis, financial services should adapt to new technologies like IoT.

With the use of IoTs huge amount of data can be generated. Research states that majority of the customers prefer mobile banking or payment gateways over conventional banking systems.

Due to the digitization of various sectors, customers also understand the need to share their information to the service providers.

Insurance sectors are optimizing business by using customer data generated by various digital means, for example, health monitored by wearable devices, driving habits by GPS enabled devices, etc. Such personal data collected from the customers are beneficial to the customers as well as the service providers by giving the right policy at the right price.

11.4.2 INFRASTRUCTURE

With the increase in data collected through connected devices, there should be a proper infrastructure in place to store and analyze the data. For managing the huge data larger workforce is required.

As handling the data is of utmost importance, use of IoTs plays a significant role here. Most of the service providers will make use of IoTs to gather the enormous data, which in turn requires the storage space. Consequently, data centers will also grow tremendously. IoT in Financial sectors is shown in Figure 11.2.

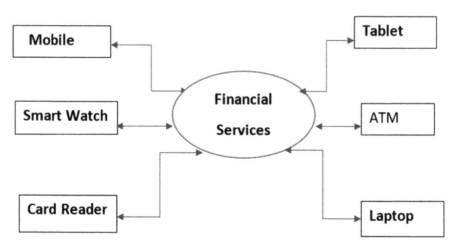

FIGURE 11.2   IoT in financial services.

By making use of IoTs banks can make their services completely digitized thereby transforming from the age-old paper-based system and can make their customers satisfied with the easiness of the services. With the digitization of financial services, efficiency will be increased and risks can be minimized.

A report states that, by 2023 the Banking and Financial Services market will be grown to 2030 million USD from 249.4 million USD in 2018 at a Compound Annual Growth Rate of 52.1% during the forecast period.

11.5   DIGITALIZATION IN VARIOUS FINANCIAL SERVICES

Let us look in to the various changes happening in various financial services due to digitalization.

11.5.1   BANKING SECTOR

Due to the digitization, more innovations are happening in banking services. The mode of operation itself is totally transforming due to the easy access to mobile devices. According to a study, 86% of the population, irrespective of the generations, use mobile devices for banking. Banking sectors will totally change from the traditional mode of operation using papers to paperless transactions. It is been reported that "Global mobile wallet market (Remote wallet and NFC) is expected to reach USD 3142.17 billion by 2022, growing at a CAGR of 32% between 2017 and 2022."

For the majority of the customers, mobile wallets are the most preferred transaction now owing to the increase in E-commerce markets. For example, Google Pay is one of the most popular payment gateways around the world in addition to various payment wallets which is country-specific viz., PayPal, Paytm, Yandex, Alipay, etc. In addition to this, mobile companies are also proving digital pay schemes based on the operating system they are using, like iOS or Android.

Due to the growing demand for technology Banking sectors have to utilize IoT and make innovations for better customer experience.

11.5.2 INSURANCE SECTOR

Due to the awareness about the insurance policies in various sectors like vehicle, life, health, travel, liability, etc., the demand for this has increased in the recent past. It is basically a risk management process to protect against financial losses.

As per Insurance Information Institute, "The U.S. Insurance industry is the world's largest insurance market where 6,118 companies employing 2.5 million people, have net annual premiums of USD 1.1 trillion.

With IoT, the risk management becomes much easier which be beneficial to both the customers and the insurance companies. Adopting to IoTs enable the insurance companies to take up challenges and minimize the risks involved.

11.5.3 STOCK MARKET

Individual or corporates invest in the stock market to get maximum profit. To achieve this the knowledge of the company's share in the stock exchange is required for selling or buying the shares. IoT plays a major role in determining the risks involved in an investment and help the investors to take the right decision at the right time.

11.5.4 INVESTMENT BANKING

The purpose of investment banking is to provide financial assistance to individual or various businesses. Due to the various new businesses available in the market, knowledge of the risks involved and decision making becomes more difficult.

Investments done by banks heavily depends on the market survey on projects, stocks, or business. They will be heavily investing on the businesses with growing markets. By making use of IoTs banks can easily determine the risks involved in a business and can make the investment decisions wisely.

11.5.5 FOREIGN EXCHANGE

Forex or Foreign Exchange is used for exchanging the currencies or buying and selling them. Time to time update of the currency value is essential for the Foreign Exchange market. Hence time is the major factor which determines the value of currency. With IoT it becomes easier for Foreign Exchanges to keep track of the exchange rates globally.

11.6 BENEFITS OF IOT IN FINANCIAL SERVICES

By adopting to IoTs, there are various benefits for financial sectors which can win them over their competitors. Benefits of IoT in Financial Sectors is shown in Figure 11.3.

11.6.1 TRANSPARENCY

As the complete real-time data about a customer or business is easily available through connected devices, risk management becomes much easier.

For example, in automobile insurance services, the insurance companies have a clear data about the customer's driving habits. Based on study of this data, the insurance amount can be fixed. Studies revealed that the driving habits determine the insurance amount rather than the type of car.

The companies also can optimize the management system and expenses based on the data received from smart sensors.

Banks can also get details about the customers who default in paying their credit card bills. Using appropriate data from the IoT devices, it will be easier for financial services to evaluate the creditworthiness of a customer.

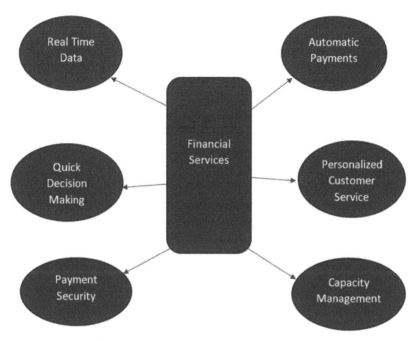

FIGURE 11.3 Benefits of IoT in financial sectors.

IoTs can be used in an efficient manner to increase the business and also can bring growth in the business.

11.6.2 AUTOMATION

One of the happening business in the finance sector is trading and investment activities. For this, one should have a real-time analysis of the stock market value or trader's activities. Based on the real-time value one can invest or sell or buy the shares/businesses.

With the adoption of IoT and ML the whole financial process can be automated. By automation, the future value of market can be predicted and also the whole transaction process can be automated.

Even some of the banks have implemented beacon system for customers to unlock ATM doors using smartphones.

Cashless payments can be automated through IoTs. For example, if a customer wants to buy a product, then the smart sensors will calculate the amount and communicated to the smart wallets which will automatically do the payment. Hence, the whole payment process is automated and customers do not need to carry any form of currency with them. Further, the efficiency of the services can be greatly improved by automation through IoT.

11.6.3 SECURITY

As the transactions through mobile devices are increasing in the recent past, the security of payment transactions is very important. Mobile devices are providing their own security features to its customers, for example, finger-print enabled devices. Apart from this PIN authentication is also available for various financial services to guard the security for transactions.

With IoTs, security can be increased even more by using innovative technologies. Instead of PIN, some real-time personal data generated by wearable devices can also be used for security purpose. Such innovative ideas will be developed from time to time depending on the customer needs or what technology demands in future.

IoT enabled security system can prevent misuse of ATM debit and credit cards by means of more secured personal authorization methods.

IoTs can track a person's activity and their mobile location which can be used for additional security purposes. In future IoTs will give rise to innovation of more security tools to enhance prevention of frauds.

Some of the financial services have already implemented biometric authentication by means of a customer's heartbeat recorded through wearable smart gadgets. This is the most efficient and secure way of wireless payment.

11.6.4 CUSTOMER SERVICES

To retain the customers, the financial services should provide better customer support to satisfy them. By making use of IoTs, the financial services can provide better facilities to the customers through their smart gadgets.

As the real-time data and credit history of customers are available to the financial sectors, they can easily arrive at a decision to provide loans/investments or other banking needs.

Financial services can provide incentives to the customers in terms of reward points which they can redeem it in a useful way. By making use of IoTs, intelligent reward points can be given to the customers based on their personal preferences.

Hence the reward points may vary from customer to customer, and the ultimate goal is to make the customers satisfy with the current financial services experience and show loyalty towards them.

Beacon system for notification of a customer's arrival is being implemented in a few financial services wherein the financial services can act quickly and save customer's time thereby giving complete support to the customers.

By adopting to IoTs, the queues in banks can also be easily managed by allocating a representative to the customer based on their needs before they arrive at bank premises.

Thus, by using IoTs customer service can be improved in an efficient manner by giving proper instructions through personalized messages and welcoming them on arrival.

11.6.5 CAPACITY MANAGEMENT

With the use of IoTs, financial services can monitor real-time data of customers thereby they can track the number of customers visiting a branch and the purpose of visit. By knowing this data, optimum workforce management and infrastructure is possible.

Through IoTs, even the decision regarding the opening of new ATMs or new branches and the locations can also be easily determined by making use of customer data.

Apart from workforce management, IoTs also can be used to access the amount of cash which needs to be deposited in the cash vending machines at various locations.

11.6.6 VOICE ASSISTANTS

Everyone is familiar with the voice assistants like Alexa and Siri in smart gadgets. Similarly, such voice assistants can be made available to the customers in real-time by means of IoT.

Use of voice assistants in real-time will help customers to gather information about the financial services including their credit balance and loan status. They can also use the voice assistant to know the dates of payment of bills and the outstanding amount.

11.6.7 DECISION MAKING

IoTs give the real-time data of customers; hence decision making regarding a business or investment will be much easier. Also, the risk involved can be reduced. Hence faster decision making is possible by means of IoTs. These are the various benefits financial sectors can achieve by adopting to IoTs. Now, let us have a look on to the use cases of IoT.

1.7 USE CASES OF IoT

Various use cases of IoT are shown in Figure 11.4.

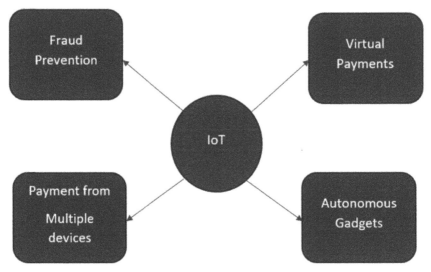

FIGURE 11.4 Use cases of IoT.

1. **Fraud prevention:** It can be done by properly combining artificial intelligence (AI) with IoT. This can also prevent security issues and help in preventing cybercrimes.
2. **Virtual Payments:** which are done using wearable gadgets will become very common. In future, due to the proper use of IoT invisible payments will be possible without physically touching the mobile phones.
3. **Payments from Anywhere:** It will be possible with the use of IoTs. With smart appliances at home, sensors can determine whether groceries need to be purchased, and depending on the purchase requirements payments will be done automatically.
4. **Autonomous Gadgets:** These are what all the financial sectors will be looking for in future. With the invention of more smart wearable

gadgets and IoT, payments can be done without the use of mobile phones too.

11.8   CHALLENGES OF IoT

We have seen that there are many benefits to the financial sectors by adopting to IoT. At the same time, they also have to address a few challenges that may arise due to the use of IoTs. Various challenges of IoT are shown in Figure 11.5:

1. **Privacy:** As the financial services are dealing with enormous data of customers from different devices, proper care should be taken for data theft. Hacking should be prevented by using various security measures.
2. **Failure of Equipment:** This will be a major issue which needs to be considered. IoT devices may be manufactured by different companies and the quality of the products may vary. There are no uniform standards available common to all manufacturers. Failure of the hardware equipment needs to be addressed as it may affect the functionality of IoTs.
3. **Complexity:** of the networks used for the functioning of financial sectors is high. As the complexity of the network increases, it will be difficult to troubleshoot the faults which may occur in a network link. This will disrupt the functioning of financial services, which in turn affects the business. Hence while implementing IoTs, proper care should be taken to use good quality hardware and trustworthy software.
4. **Unemployment:** This will increase due to the automation of financial services by the use of IoTs. Some of the current jobs will disappear in future owing to the increased use of IoTs. Unemployment may affect the economy and the society.

11.9   ISSUES TO BE ADDRESSED

People often go behind new technologies without properly understanding them. They will invest on IoTs before doing a thorough study about it. In addition to the purchase cost of IoT devices, additional costs may incur once they start using it. This they will experience only after implementing IoT for their personal use.

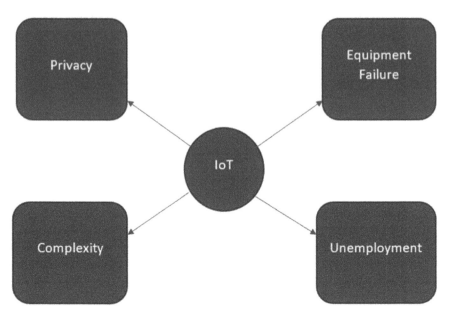

FIGURE 11.5   Challenges of IoT.

For example, the batteries of IoT devices may wear out after a certain amount of time, similar to any other electronic product which uses rechargeable batteries. In addition to dealing with battery issues, there may be other issues due to the failure of equipment. There may be additional expenses for proper maintenance of the equipment. So, it is not only the cost of IoT devices there may be additional expenses which may incur to the owners of IoT devices.

As IoT gives data from different devices, an enormous amount of data will be generated. There should be proper infrastructure to store and analyze these data. There may be errors in the data or the data may be incomplete. There should be a proper mechanism to identify these errors. It is a complex task to deal with such a high amount of data and complete error correction may not be possible. Hence, these data may not be as reliable as we may think. Proper care should be taken to analyze and handle the data. Security of the data should be of utmost importance.

A prediction by Gartner states that the amount spend for IoT security will reach USD 3.1 billion by 2021. Naturally spending will increase once the companies are aware of the risk involved and the importance of data security.

Since the financial services have the complete personal data of the customers and they are dealing with the transfer of cash, hackers will be targeting financial sectors on a priority basis. Majority of the cybercrimes may happen in financial sectors as the data is not originating from such organizations but from some other organizations which provide IoT services to them. The data in such organizations may not be well protected as in the case of financial sectors. Hence hackers will be targeting them. To avoid this, it must be communicated properly what type of data is collected from the customers and for what purpose it is used.

For the proper management of data, financial organizations should think of integrating AI along with IoT. IoT alone may not be that effective in certain cases but the inclusion of AI along with IoT can extract the most appropriate data. Studies found that only a few of the organizations found that IoT is beneficial to them, but the inclusion of AI along with IoT proved beneficial to most of the organizations.

11.10   HOW TO INTEGRATE IoT DEVICES?

While integrating IoT devices in financial sectors, the following points have to be taken care of:

- Identify the IoT devices which are part of the infrastructure of the respective organization. Always keep monitoring these devices and identify the purpose of the device and the accessibility of the devices.
- Try to integrate IoT with artificial intelligence for efficiency and better business opportunities.
- If the authentication of the access is granted only to a few people, then identify how to monitor those people for enhanced security. They should not misuse the data.
- The integrated IoT devices should be updated regularly whenever there is an update and security patch available. For proper update management ensure that the existing IoT devices are compatible with the new ones.
- Be always aware of the new threats emerging for IoT devices. There should be a proper plan in place about handling the threats and malicious activities that may affect your IoT devices.
- Ensure that the IoT product you purchased have identity and access management (IAM) support.
- Make sure to integrate IoT to the organization's security management programs.

- Thus, IoT devices needs to be dealt with very carefully as it handles massive data which may be vulnerable to cyber-attacks. Just purchasing and implementing is not the end of it. It has to be continuously monitored throughout and proper maintenance should be provided.

11.11 IoT AND MARKET DYNAMICS

Many new advancements have happened in this century, but IoT has been emerged as the best technological innovation in this century. It is estimated to have at least 50 billion IoT devices by 2020. Due to the popularity of these connected devices, every sector of the industry, both Government and non-Government organizations with see advancements in digital services. In case of banking and other financial sectors like insurance, IoT plays a major role in terms of planning, health, and fitness.

Moreover, in financial services, IoT tracks the personal data of their customers through sensors and keep them updated about the life events of customers. Hence financial services can offer individual based insurances and help them make decisions regarding financial investments.

IoT in banking and financial services is expected to grow to USD 2,030.1 million by 2023, as shown in Figure 11.6. This is due to the increasing use of connected devices in finance sectors. This may give rise to some new opportunities in service industries.

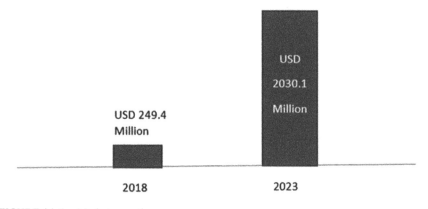

FIGURE 11.6   Market growth.

More opportunities will arise in the markets owing to the growth rate and economy. As the number of IoT devices increase, the monitoring of data of such devices also naturally increase so as to make the data more accurate, which in turn result in the growth of monitoring sectors. Market growth on various sectors is shown in Figure 11.7.

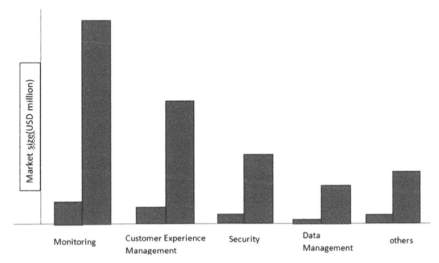

FIGURE 11.7 Market growth on various services.

11.11.1 DRIVING FORCE

Smart financial decisions by banks can be made through IoT devices by the data collected from the connected devices which in turn satisfy the customer needs. By monitoring the data, the banks can make financial decisions and provide services tailor made for a particular customer.

In this way, banks can reduce operational costs and get the skills required for next-generation banking with innovative technologies.

11.11.2 CONSTRAINT

Currently, there exists no global standards in terms of connecting IoT devices to the products. This is one of the major restraint industries are facing today. Another constraint is the inter-operability of the products and services which is required for the growth of the business.

Since financial sectors are dealing with vulnerable data, they need to look for standardized IoT protocols. Interoperability and interconnectivity between different hardware and software platforms in the financial sectors can be achieved by using standardized protocols for communication.

11.11.3 OPPORTUNITY

The surge in use of smart gadgets which is connected to IoT devices results in generation of huge data. These data which is been generated continuously are real time data which needs to be stored and processed. These data have to be analyzed to get the outputs. Those industries which are doing business on data processing has to increase its business by increasing the productivity. These generated data can be used for doing research and development, thereby creating solutions to various problems. Financial sectors can use this data to study risk analysis and ways to improve the business. This can also be used to analyze the transaction costs and stock market values.

11.11.4 CHALLENGE

Whenever an organization implements new system, every data in the old system has to be integrated or migrated to the new system. Migrating to a new system is not an easy task as huge amount of data has to be handled. So, data handling expenses will increase. If standards are not followed properly, then the migration of data creates serious issues. Migrating unstructured data will be difficult as it needs to be reviewed and then processed. There should be an estimated time for migrating in to a new system. When the process becomes complicated, it will be difficult to keep up with the deadlines, and there will be a delay in the whole process. Proper care should be taken that the migration process should not be affecting the quality of data. For this proper IoT planning is required before the implementation of the new system.

These are the market dynamics a financial organization should look for before implementing IoT system for their businesses.

11.11.5 DEVELOPMENTS

Key players in the current market are IBM (USA), Microsoft (USA), SAP (Germany), Oracle (USA), Infosys (India).

Now we will look into some of the recent business developments which happened in the market. C3 IoT is a company which provides full-stack IoT developments that enables the design, development, and deployment of large-scale data and IoT applications for any business value chain. C3 IoT offers new smart, real-time applications by overcoming the development challenges which blocked the companies to explore IoT. Microsoft made a partnership with C3 IoT in April 2018 to deliver new technological developments. This partnership benefits the financial organizations to implement new IoT platforms integrated with AI for customer engagement, investment planning and fraud detection.

Indosuez Wealth Management is the global wealth management brand of Credit Agricole group. They offer a systematic approach which enables customers to manage, protect and pass on wealth according to their specific needs. It offers a wide range of services for management of both personal and business assets. This group is one of the global leaders in wealth management. Capgemini partnered with Indosuez Wealth Management in March 2018 to develop a new platform for banking operations. With this partnership, Capgemini could provide IT solutions and digital services to Credit Agricole group for further developments.

Banco Atlántida is a company operating in the banking sector. It is a branch of the Honduran firm Grupo Financiero Atlantida established in 1913 to provide banking services. SAP partnered with Banco Atlantida in February 2018 to provide digitalized banking model. With this partnership now Banca Atlantida is benefitted by implementing the performance management of SAP for financial services to obtain greater insights for performance indicators like branch level profitability.

To speed up the digitalization in the Grand Duchy of Luxembourg, Cisco signed an agreement with the Government of Luxembourg in January 2018. With this agreement, Cisco will be able to provide financial service providers with highly secured systems to reduce the risk of cyber-attacks and improve customer experiences.

Vivant Digital is an Australian-based digital and innovation agency. The company is a developer for Artificial Intelligent systems. It uses insights from behavioral science, data, and technology to assist start-ups primarily in financial services and distribution industries. And it has a robust track record in financial services and distribution industries. IBM acquired Vivant Digital in November 2017 which enabled IBM to blend industry expertise, technology, and experience to reinvent digital experience design to consumers in financial sectors and distribution industries.

It is been observed that in recent past people spending time on smart devices has drastically increased which also means that the connected devices have increased to multiple folds from millions to billions. It is been estimated that around 75% of the world's population has internet access and hence increased use of connected devices, which is more than 6 million devices. In 2019 around 4.5 billion people accessed connected devices through the internet which indicates that IoT will be more trending in coming years.

Moreover, the developers of IoTs are supporting financial sectors to make use of the opportunities of IoT by developing new apps for better customer experience.

From Figure 11.8 we can observe how the connected devices are increasing year by year. With the increase in IoT connected devices along with AI and big data analytics (BDA) will totally change the way how companies are operating now and it will give rise to a technological digital revolution. This integration of AI and big data is essential to improve the efficiency and get the real-time data.

By 2025, it is estimated that the number of IoT connected devices will be approximately amount to 75.44 billion.

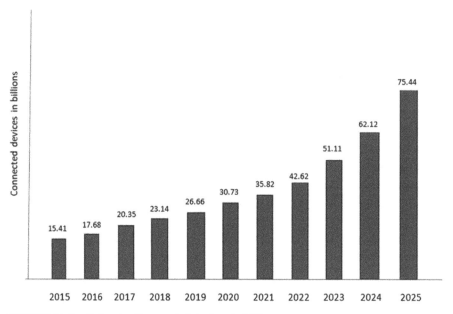

FIGURE 11.8   Estimate of connected devices in billions.

11.12 RISKS INVOLVED IN USAGE OF IoT FOR FINANCIAL SERVICES

Majority of the financial organizations now depend on IoT for their services. There are several benefits of using IoTs similarly there are drawbacks too.

Since the financial services always deal with customer's real-time personal data and money transfer, they are the target for fraudsters and cyber-attacks.

There should be a proper security system in place to protect the data theft. Organizations started realizing the importance of security system for IoT and they are keeping funds to meet the expenses. It is been estimated by Gartner that the total spending for IoT security will amount to 3.1 billion dollars by 2021.

Financial organizations should always be alert about the latest threats for IoT devices and should be ready with the solutions to handle it.

Integrating IoT with AI can collect financial information and help to prevent fraud activities. Now financial organizations have started using biometrics instead of PINs or passwords for increased security.

11.13 CONCLUSION

It is no doubt that IoT is the most trending innovations in the last decade. Digitalization of the financial services gives new dimensions to the traditional business. Use of IoT enabled networks by the financial services are giving better customer experience. As the competition is increasing day by day, every organization is trying to keep it up to date with the latest technologies to satisfy the needs of the customers. This in turn increases the operational efficiency and the business. By updating to the latest technology and integrating IoT with AI in financial organizations, helps to minimize the risks involved owing to the rapid increase in digitalization and mobilization of those sectors. Use of IoTs in banks can help them to improve the decision-making process and to gather information about customers and provide personalized services. It is also very important to have proper standards for IoT maintenance and compliance for security. Adoption of IoTs by financial organizations will give rise to automation, new business opportunities, better user experience and smart future.

KEYWORDS

- **artificial intelligence**
- **banking**
- **finance**
- **internet of things**

REFERENCES

1. Val, S., (2016). *The Internet of Things and the Financial Services Industry*. A quick look blog.
2. Fadoua, K., Azdine, B., & Mohamed, T., (2019). Impact of digital trends using IoT on banking processes. *Procedia Computer Science, 151*, 77–84.
3. GSMA, The Mobile Economy, (2018). https://data.gsmaintelligence.com/api-web/v2/research-file-download?id=28999769&file=The%20Mobile%20Economy%202018.pdf (accessed on 10 November 2021).
4. (2018). https://data.gsmaintelligence.com/api-web/v2/research-file-download?id=28999769&file=The%20Mobile%20Economy%202018.pdf (accessed on 10 November 2021).
5. Winderlich, N. V., Wangenhein, F. V., & Bitner, M. J., (2013). High-tech and high touch: A framework for understanding behaviors related to smart interactive services. *Journal of Service Research, 16*(1), 3–20.
6. Hoballah, et al., (2019). Electronic financial fraud: Abstract, definitions, vulnerabilities, issues and causes. *Proceedings of POM Beirut*, 9–14.
7. Mckinsey, (2018). *Transforming a Bank by Becoming Digital to the Core*. McKinsey and company. https://www.mckinsey.com/industries/financial-services/our-insights/transforming-a-bank-by-becoming-digital-to-the-core (accessed on 10 November 2021).
8. Nurgun, K. Y., & Hulya, B. H., (2019). *The Rise of Internet of Things (IoT) and its Applications in Finance and Accounting, 10*, 32–35. Press Academia Procedia (PAP).
9. Xu, Mi, Mierzwiak, & Meng, (2020). Complex network construction of internet finance risk. *Physica A: Statistical Mechanics and its Applications, 540*(C).
10. Qi, Jin, Li, & Qian, (2020). The exploration of internet finance by using a neural network, *Journal of Computational and Applied Mathematics, 369*.
11. Murphy, Taylor, Acheson, Butterfield, Jin, Higgins, & Higgins, (2020). Representing financial data streams in digital simulations to support data flow design for a future digital twin. *Robotics and Computer-Integrated Manufacturing*.
12. Suseendran, Chandrasekaran, Akila, & Kumar, (2020). Banking and fintech embraced with IoT device. *Data Management Analytics and Innovation*.
13. Sharma, S., Nanda, M., Goel, R., Jain, A., Bhushan, M., & Kumar, A., (2019). Smart cities using internet of things: Recent trends and techniques. *International Journal of Innovative Technology and Exploring Engineering (IJITEE), 8*(9S), 24–28.

PART III

Integration of IoT with Blockchain and Cloud

CHAPTER 12

Integrating Cloud with IoT-Cloud IoT

SAKSHI KAPOOR and SURYA NARAYAN PANDA

Chitkara University Institute of Engineering and Technology, Punjab, India, E-mails: sakusakshi100@gmail.com (S. Kapoor), snpanda@chitkara.edu.in (S. N. Panda)

ABSTRACT

Cloud computing is expanding continuously due to its high-performance computational services at an economical rate. Internet of things (IoT) is an innovation widening rapidly in the field of media communications and wireless broadcast communications. The combination of IoT and cloud is progressively valuable for experiencing boundless abilities like storage as well as processing power. Both IoT as well as cloud have a correlative connection among them. In this way, they build the effectiveness of regular work. The principle objective behind the association or collaboration among objects via wireless networks is to assure the objective set to them as a joined entity. Because of the approval in accepting cloud-IoT, the evaluation of cloud become very scientific. For the assessment of the performance, the two things simulation and modelling are viewed as the most appropriate. In this chapter, a review on Cloud computing as well as IoT with attention on the need for the convergence of both innovations as well as security issues of their integration is presented. The limits of storage and processing power, security and privacy are limited in IoT. Thus, the blend of both the technologies IoT and cloud is necessary. Cloud can broaden its points of confinement with real-world objects in increasingly powerful as well as disseminated way, also transfers huge services in real-time. The two different technologies are combined to find common attributes or features between them. Concluding, the chapter presents a cloud-based IoT framework for dealing with the complex nature of object-based IoT.

12.1   INTRODUCTION

Technologies are extending with inclusions to them consistently. Cloud computing and IoT have turned out to be two most intently connected technologies with one giving the other a stage to progress and success [1]. IoT may be defined as an arrangement of structures, gadgets, automobiles, and various things which can be inserted with different types of sensors, hardware, and software. Data can be switch from one gadget to another through IoT [2]. IoT is the next significant advance in the new technology sector, yet with the incredible contrast that it conveys huge changes in business performance. The idea behind IoT is the huge effect that it will have on daily existence as well as the behavior of potential clients [2, 3]. The impacts of IoT would be noticeable by both workings as well as domestic fields. Enhanced learning, e-health are some scenarios where IoT plays a major role in the future. The same consequences are observed by the business client which are traceable in fields like process management, logistics, automation, and industrial manufacturing [4].

Industries like healthcare, building management, transportation have practically taken by IoT [6–8]. Cloud computing, the latest generation technology with a big IT infrastructure provides the ways by which clients can access applications and services over the internet [9, 10]. Cloud implies web and therefore Cloud computing is web-based computing. Cloud computing empowers a client to effectively get to applications and programming from wherever they need whenever while it is being facilitated by some outside party in the cloud [11]. Clients just appreciate the final product without worrying about the storage, power as well as maintenance issues of original resources. Google apps, allow us to access services over the browser is also an instance of Cloud computing that can be installed on various machines over the net. Cloud is proved to be attractive to the Industrial world due to its usage-based pricing, quick resource elasticity, location free resource pooling, transfer of risk, on-demand self-service, the ability, and efficiency to handle the large amount of work without influencing the execution of framework, reduced IT costs, scalability, flexibility of work, access to automatic updates. These reasons cause the rapid growth of the cloud in the business [11, 12].

CC delivery models are Software-as-a-service, Platform-as-a-service, and Infrastructure-as-a-service. The on-demand service, includes pay-per-use of application software to the clients or users is SaaS. It is platform-free and the installation of software is not required on the user computer. PaaS includes database, OS, web server as well as coding execution environment [1, 14]. It provides an environment where a user can compile or run programs easily without concerning the basic or underlying infrastructure. IaaS provides hardware, storage, server, data center space. Only authorized users are permitted to use services from provider, and therefore, it is most suitable for a single organization, whereas the public cloud allows anyone to access the services. Hybrid cloud is the mix of the public as well as a private cloud [12].

Popular IT companies like Google, Microsoft, Salesforce, Amazon, and IBM supports cloud services over the Internet. Information technology relies on the idea of using the infrastructure without managing it. Google delivers Google docs and many other services including document applications, maps, email access to its users by using a private cloud, whereas Microsoft office 365 online service allows business tools to be moved into the cloud. Cloud computing has many advantages over the traditional IT model. Although Cloud computing is beneficial to a large extent, there are still some barriers to its adoption. Data security is the most significant barrier [4, 9].

IoT and Cloud computing together have a correlative relationship between them thus increasing the efficiency of everyday work. Loads of information are generated with IoT while Cloud computing clears path for the ease in traveling this information from one location to another. With the advantage of this, cloud providers provide pay-as-you-go services where the client has to pay only for those services that they have utilized and no other extra cost will be taken by the client [15–17].

Due to the remote storage, the developers can easily implement their projects without any kind of delay. A large amount of big data can be accessed by the IoT companies which use the cloud for the storage of data [17]. Table 12.1 describes how IoT and cloud are fit with each other. Cloud is fabricated on the tenets of scale and pace and IoT applications are fabricated based on mobility and broad networking. Therefore, for cloud-based IoT applications, it is necessary for both cloud as well as IoT to collaborate thus, contributes towards the success of the IoT [7, 17]. Figure 12.1 shows convergence of Cloud and IoT.

12.2 INTERNET OF THINGS (IoT)

Internet of things (IoT) is made up of three primary parts: the "things," the communication networks that associate them, the computer frameworks utilizing information spilling from, and to objects. IoT is an organization of associated or connected computing gadgets, automated, and advanced progressive machines, objects, creatures, or individuals having exclusive identifiers with facility for transmitting information above system devoid of expecting any human-to-PC communication [16]. We can relate this technology with a person with an implanted heart screen or any automobile that has worked in sensors which warns the driver of forthcoming risk. Any man-made or natural object having an IP addressable to transfer or transmit information over the system goes under IoT [19]. IoT has developed with higher propagation of information. There is redundant communication among modest sensors in the IoT because of IoT cloud services which imply that with higher connectivity; tons of closely associated machines are soon joined human users [17].

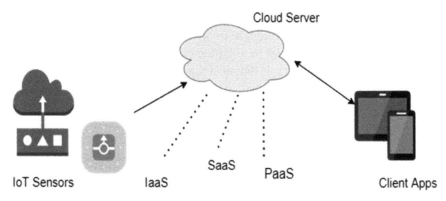

FIGURE 12.1 Convergence of cloud and IoT.

12.2.1 INTERNET OF THINGS (IoT): ADVANTAGE OF DATA [15–18]

What will happen when sensors and devices are connected and communicate with one another? How IoT influence our everyday life? Constant information is being sent and received by alarm systems, GPS systems to the monitors. Thus, automate all the activities of everyday life. Furthermore, ordinary items like garments, cups can likewise join the network to send and get information over the Internet. For encouraging positive variations or augmenting existing services, all the chances or opportunities where the streaming information will make new markets are explored by businesses [17]. Sectors which are the soul of these advancements are as follows:

1. **Quick Resolution in the Bucket of Transport:** Set priorities in vehicle repair programs, and save lives. With quick resolution, there is a decline in the consumption of fuel as well as traffic seen on the road. By setting priorities in automobile repair programs, thousands of lives get saved.

2. **Smart Power Frameworks Including more Inexhaustible or Renewable:** The system's authenticity or accuracy gets improved by smart power frameworks including more inexhaustible and renewable. Also, there is a reduction in the charge's consumers, which helps in providing electricity at a cheap price.

3. **Remote Monitoring:** Patients are accessible to health care services easily which promotes or enhances the aspect of services. There is an increment in the count of people and money gets saved [17].

4. **Use of Sensors Everywhere:** Sensors, anywhere indoors, homes, or shoes helps in improving safety by transmitting a signal when not in use for a long time or use in false time.

12.2.2 IoT SECURITY

IoT security is regarding the attempt to achieve something concerned with safeguarding associated devices as well as systems in the IoT. It promotes the growing popularity of entities referred to as things. The entities are given exclusive identifiers and the capacity to consequently move information over a network. A huge portion of IoT originates through embedded sensors as well as computing devices utilized in M2M communication [15, 17].

In product designing, security has not generally been examined or considered because of the notion that network devices or gadgets are moderately new, which is the biggest problem. IoT items are frequently sold with the old embedded OS as well as software. Moreover, buyers are unable to change passwords which are by default on smart devices, and if they do modify them, still not be able to choose a more secure password. To boost or enhance security, there is a need that all the IoT devices that should be straightforwardly feasible over the internet, ought to be divided into its very own system and have system access limited. There should be proper monitoring of network divisions for identifying potential peculiar traffic as well as implementing actions to cope up with detecting problems (Figure 12.2) [19, 20].

12.3 CLOUD COMPUTING

Cloud computing works as a utility model [9] because of its zero-maintenance cost as a service provider is available for providing services and on the other hand, clients remain free from the worries about management and maintenance issues. The cloud develops coordinated effort, deftness, accessibility, versatility, and also capacity to adjust to changes as per the requests quickens the progression work and brings the potential for cost diminish through improved and compelling computing. Cloud is expanding continuously due to its high-performance computational services at the economical rate [14, 19].

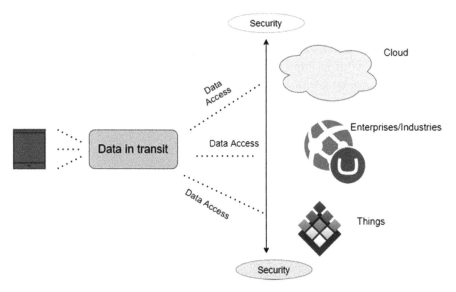

FIGURE 12.2   IoT security.

12.3.1   *CLOUD COMPUTING ARCHITECTURE [2, 9, 10, 15]*

12.3.1.1   *LAYERED ARCHITECTURE*

1. **Hardware Layer:** Physical assets, for example, switches, power frameworks, physical server, and test systems are overseen by this layer. This layer is commonly used in Datacenters. Issues found are an adaptation to fault-tolerance, Hardware arrangement, and traffic management [9, 22].
2. **Infrastructure Layer:** With the use of virtualization technologies, the layer partitions physical resources in order to create storage as well as computing resources. So, it can be called a virtualization layer, ended up being an essential part of distributed computing as just virtualization is in charge of the dynamic resource assignment.

3. **Platform Layer:** The operating system and application framework are under the platform layer. In order to reduce all the heavy load which is due to execution of applications, this layer focuses on VM containers. Example for providing API support, Google App Engine performs at this layer to enable storage.

4. **Application Layer:** The topmost in the model, which has actual cloud applications for improved performance, availability as well as reducing operating cost.

12.3.1.2 BUSINESS MODEL

1. **SaaS (Software as a Service):** A software distribution architecture where provider helps in providing various applications over a network mostly the Internet. It is on-demand software and based on pay-per-usage. The operation and installation of application software in the cloud will be done by cloud providers and the clients of the cloud will be responsible for providing the software to the users. There is no need for installing and running the software application on the user's computer as the user does not require to handle the platform and infrastructure of the cloud where the application executes [1, 9, 11]. SaaS services are highly scalable which provide their customers with choices to access more or fewer services-on-demand. There is no need for purchasing new software; Customers can depend on SaaS providers for automatic updates. SaaS services are easily accessible for any user having an internet-enabled device and location. Google Docs where documents can be obtained by using a browser and can be shared on any number of computers via the Internet and Salesforce. com are some prominent examples. Due to the limited control over security, SaaS users face many security issues [12, 23]. Distributed computing operates an administration driven model, which we call the cloud business model. Hardware as well as platform-level resources are served on-demand basis. Each layer of the can be accomplished as a utility to the layer above. This suggests each layer goes about as a client of the layer underneath [24].

2. **PaaS (Platform as a Service):** It provides a PaaS for the customers to develop, run, and handle applications with no need of constructing. PaaS provider is responsible for hosting hardware and software on its infrastructure and makes the user focused only on creating and running

applications rather than building and maintaining the underlying infrastructure including operating system, server, network, storage [23, 25]. Its convenience and simplicity make it more beneficial for the users. With a web browser, users can have access to infrastructure and other IT services which are supplied by PaaS provider. Examples are Microsoft Windows Azure which is associated with software development, delivers a robust platform, and allows all users to test, create, and deploy applications easily [11, 22].

3. **IaaS (Infrastructure as a Service):** For the execution of services, hardware resources are shared using the virtualization technology. The main goal is to make resources like servers, storage, and network available and accessible to software applications as well as an operating system. So, infrastructure services are provided on-demand. Fundamental resources namely networks, processing, storage is authorized to all the consumers by the IaaS provider [23]. Further, consumers can convey and run arbitrary software that contains the operating system, administrations, and applications. The operating system, storage, deployed applications, are under the supervision of the client [23]. It provides more adaptability as compared to PaaS. Due to the smaller degree of abstraction, it provides great customer control over security in comparison to both PaaS and IaaS. EC2, S35, Amazon web service are some of the examples which are using IaaS services [12].

12.3.1.3 DEPLOYMENT MODEL

1. **Private Cloud:** Services are provided to the authorized people within a specific boundary or organization [23]. It may be possessed, handled, and operated by the organization itself. Big organizations mostly prefer this model for the provision of a private network to the customers within the organization. Higher Security and privacy, improved reliability, and coast energy efficiencies are some of the benefits of the private cloud [22, 23].
2. **Public Cloud:** General public used this type of cloud. It is possessed, handled by government organizations, businesses. Google, Amazon, IBM are some of the companies providing public cloud facilities. It is highly scalable, flexible, location-independent, and reliable [24–26].
3. **Hybrid Cloud:** It is a mixture of both above clouds. It gives benefits like security, versatility, adaptabilities, and cost efficiencies [14].

12.4   NEED BEHIND INTEGRATION OF IoT AND CLOUD

IoT has restricted capacities of processing power as well as storage likewise considerable issues including security, privacy, the combination of IoT and cloud is progressively valuable to experience boundless abilities-storage as well as processing power. Cloud can broaden its points of confinement with real-world objects in increasingly powerful as well as disseminated way, also transfers huge services in real-time [4, 8, 16, 19]:

1. **Computational Resources:** Due to restricted processing capabilities, on-site data processing is not granted in IoT. Due to inappropriate framework, scalability is found to be a challenging thing in IoT, its on-request paradigm permits the unlimited abilities of a cloud. The vast majority of processing requirements of IoT are fulfilled and engaged investigation of remarkable complexities. The integration of data-driven decisions with predicted algorithms is possible at a low rate and hazard is diminished. Different undertakings can be accomplished in real-time processing to cover all sensor-driven applications adaptability, also dealing with immense tasks [31].

2. **Communication Resources:** To analyze objects, IoT is IP-empowered hardware for interacting with objects that are generally costly. Cloud is beneficial in solving this kind of issue, which offers an economical and efficient solution for associating, handling, and tracking anything from anyplace and whenever utilizing customized portals and applications and permits constant approach to created information. Remote objects are been observed as well as restrained [20].

3. **Storage Resources:** IoT incorporates by separating total of data sources, which can be called things that makes a huge proportion of semi-organized or non-organized, with some qualities ordinary of Big Data speed (data generation frequency), volume (data measure), variety (i.e., information type). Consequently, it infers gathering, preparing, imagining, accomplishing, sharing, and seeking enormous information. All the information is treated in a consistent and compatible manner over API standards and can be ensured by implementing high-level security [11, 19].

4. **New Abilities:** IoT means structure of gadgets, sensors, and vehicles. Therefore, it is extremely hard to acquire interoperability, versatility, security, accessibility, efficiency. The integration with cloud takes care of the greater part of these issues likewise gives extra highlights like reduction in deployment cost, ease of use as well as access.

5. **New Models:** It allows different scenarios for smart objects dependent on the improvement of the cloud through objects:

   i. **SaaS or Sensing-as-a-Service:** Universal approach to different type of sensors is provided by SaaS.

   ii. **EaaS or Ethernet-as-a-Service [4]:** Universal associability is provided to different gadgets on different places using EaaS.

   iii. **SAaaS or Sensing-and-Actuation-as-a-Service:** Automated control logics or reasoning resolved in SAaaS.

   iv. **IPMaaS or Identity and Policy Management as a Service:** Universal approach for describing supervision capabilities supported.

   v. **VSaaS or Video Surveillance as a Service [4]:** Infinite access to taped or listed videos and of complicated analysis or investments.

   vi. **DBaaS or Database as a Service:** Universal management and handling of the database system are under this service.

   vii. **SEaaS or Sensor Event as a Service:** Texting facilities which are generated through sensors are dispatched by this service.

   viii. **SenaaS or Sensor as a Service:** Universally handling different gadgets.

   ix. **DaaS or Data as a Service:** Universal approach to any type or kind of data is provided by this service.

12.5 CLOUD-BASED IoT FRAMEWORK

IoT is turning into the next cloud revolution [7]. Various devices are interconnected with the use of IoT. IoT devices prefer to transfer control information as well as ongoing sensor information in different messages rather than filtering data. Cloud services handle all the data from a large number of gadgets or devices and to help enormous scale IoT Applications.

Architecture based on the CoAP [8] or constrained application protocol for cloud-IoT services is utilized for low-cost systems as well as resource compelled IoT devices. The efficient execution of various applications are assessed in the cloud through this framework. Here, different types of sensors are joined with the data system. They are efficient in taking part in businesses at whatever point they are required. Now, at various stages of abstractions, it becomes a challenge that heterogeneous IoT segments should assist themselves with traditional IT foundations.

12.5.1 CLOUD-ASSISTED AND AGENT-ORIENTED FOR IoT REFERENCE ARCHITECTURE [4]

It is presented to deal with the complex nature of Object-based IoT. The architecture is composed of various segments described below:

1. **Smart Interface Agent:** In this, mediators, wrappers as well as brokers are interfacing agents which interact with the external IT system [4].
2. **Smart User-Agent:** Services are requested by users as well requests are assigned through GUI or graphical user interface (GUI) features. Users are modified in the framework of any particular smart system.
3. **Smart Object Agent:** Agents are entrenched in physical as well as logical parts or elements. Physical Environment is being modeled by the smart object agents. According to the coordination model, Agents will also collaborate. There is full support of the Cloud computing Platforms in case of smart agents. Agent-oriented as well as cloud-assisted objects develop large or big scale IoT applications. The implementation of this architecture is beneficial in adopting as well as integrating an effective cloud platform [4, 16].

12.6 SECURITY ISSUES IN IoT AND CLOUD INTEGRATION

The IoT innovation stretches out its extension to manage things in a progressively dynamic way by conveying latest services in various situations, may be useful in the utilization of Cloud. Mostly in different scenarios, the cloud usually acts as middle layer among objects and applications, concealing all the functions important to execute last. With integrating IoT with Cloud computing, the researchers observed that the cloud can load a few holes of IoT like limited apps over the web. On considering the security issues of both the technologies, some drivers for their integration can be known. A serious problem in the security issues of the integration is found [15, 32].

Due to the integration, some major concerns emerge due to less knowledge of the Service Level Agreement or SLA [11] as well as the physical location of the data. Security is compromised by multi-tenancy which creates a risk for leaking confidential or sensitive information. These are instances that are at present under scrutiny [15, 33]:

1. **Performance:** Due to the convergence of both the technologies, the introduction of QoS specifications and requirements at several

dimensions, e.g., for correspondence, calculation. In some situations, it is very difficult to achieve meeting requirements easily [1].

2. **Heterogeneity:** The wide heterogeneity of operating systems, gadgets, or devices, working frameworks, platforms, as well as all the services available at that time utilized for latest or enhanced, improved applications.

3. **Reliability:** It concerns normally emerge when IoT and cloud combination is followed for mission-critical applications for example, vehicles are frequently progressing, and vehicular communication is discontinuous with regards to smart mobility. At the point when applications are conveyed in resource compelled environments, various issues or difficulties which are regarding failing or declining of devices exists.

4. **Big Data:** It is expected that near about 50 billion devices, proper protection is needed over the access, and handling, transportation, stockpiling in huge amount of material delivered. The universality of cell phones and sensor inescapability, in reality, calls for adaptable computing platforms.

5. **Monitoring:** According to the literature, it is a fundamental operation in the cloud to manage assets, SLAs, execution, security, privacy, capacity planning as well as for troubleshooting.

12.7   MODELING AND SIMULATION OF CLOUD IoT

Simulations are crucial to promote research experiments and analysis in cloud systems. There are various simulation tools in cloud computing that are beneficial not only to the customers but also for the providers. By using these simulators, services can be easily tested by the customers in a controllable environment with no cost and performance can be inquired before issuing to the real cloud [34]. These tools allow providers to check various leasing according to distinct price and load, which in turn, supports resource optimization. In short, simulator tools are found to help model distinct cloud applications by designing VM's, constructed properly, makes it so simple and accessible to examine [15, 25, 27, 29].

12.7.1   CLOUD SIMULATORS

1. **CloudSim:** A setup, and expandable simulator gives consistent modeling, experimentation, and simulation of creating a cloud

system, its framework, and application condition for single and also inter-networked clouds. Existing simulators were not discovered pertinent for the cloud environment as they end up troublesome for them to make sense of the execution of cloud provisioning approaches, application workload, administrations, models under various user requirements. So, to vanquish this issue, CloudSim is used [35–38].

In 2009, the GRIDS Laboratory invented CloudSim as a Cloud-Bust project. The system as well as behavior modeling of data centers, virtual machines, and other cloud system elements like resource planning policies are also approved [36, 38].

There is no need for researchers and developers to get low-level information regarding cloud-based infrastructure and services, which in turn become beneficial for them to target on particular system designing issues very easily. CloudSim proves to be beneficial in three ways: (a) time effectiveness: Less time and limited efforts are needed for performing various tests; (b) Adaptability: With minimal programming and development efforts, developers, and researchers test the accomplishment of services in an assorted environment; and (c) easy to learn: Basics of OOPS and JAVA is enough to learn and use CloudSim [38].

Some of the peculiar features of CloudSim are: (a) full-scale cloud computing environment; (b) the simulation of network links between simulated systems elements is supported by CloudSim; (c) user-defined policies for allocating hosts to VM's are supported; (d) modeling federated clouds, data center network topology, energy-aware computational resources, message passing applications are also supported. Some of the main entities in CloudSim are shown in below:

i. **Cloudlets:** In data centers, any task which is carried out by VM's are Cloudlets [33].
ii. **Service Broker:** Compliance of Cloudlets to a particular data center are decided by service broker.
iii. **Data Center:** Host as well as virtual machines are included under data center. Allotted Cloudlets are executed by VM's [41].
iv. **Cloud Information Service (CIS):** For the registration of all entities in a cloud environment, CIS is accountable layered.

The communication between different components in CloudSim occurs by message passing. The layered architecture of CloudSim have a lowest layer which is accountable for communication among components, and the second layer contains sub-layers that have sensors and other cloud components in it.

2. **CloudAnalyst:** A new simulator, known as CloudAnalyst having CloudSim toolkit as an underlying platform was developed by Wick-remasinghe et al. For the evaluation of accomplishment of wide-scale distributed applications that have enormous workload dispersed over various data centers, CloudAnalyst is used [42].

   In Contrast to CloudSim, CloudAnalyst is graphical with superior visualization [28] results. The simulator is beneficial to analyze the nature of huge web applications. Because of its GUI feature, the researchers and developers can set up simulations without any need of getting details about underlying programming. It is an open-source tool developed using java. Source code can be altered and entities can be added or removed according to the demand.

   The underlying platform for CloudAnalyst in CloudSim toolkit. Above CloudSim toolkit, there are CloudSim extensions which make researchers target only simulation exercise without worrying about the programming. GUI capability is beneficial for researchers to perform various simulation experiments with minor parameter deviation in an informal way. Output generated by CloudAnalyst is either in chart or table format which summarizes a large number of users at the time of modeling [3].

3. **GreenCloud:** It is an extension on network simulator NS2. It is planned with the goal that it can figure energy consumption at any specific parts like a gateway, switch, link, and so forth and correspondence between the packet levels. It can be utilized to create novel arrangements in observing, workload scheduling [43]. This simulator empowers the datacenter administrator to create the energy profile of the data center and bring choices to let down the energy utilization and create eco-friendly datacenters. It likewise permits the examination of workload disseminations. It is the utilization of planning, assembling, and use of figuring assets with the least environmental harm. It can diminish power utilization by solidifying workloads with data center virtualization [38, 39].

4. **iCloud:** A simulator focused on those clients who bargain intimately with those sorts of systems. This simulator is dependent on SIMIAN [38]. The fundamental objective is to anticipate the tradeoffs amongst cost and execution of various applications which are in execution

mode. The full GUI encourages the simple design and implementation of experiments [36, 44].

Key highlights of iCloud are as follows:

- iCloud gives an easy-to-understand GUI for generating huge distributed models and is particularly valuable for dealing with a repository of preconfigured VMs, cloud frameworks and experiments, propelling investigations from GUI, and making graphical reports. Be that as it may, analyzes can be executed likewise by utilizing traditional command-line scripts [36–39].
- Easy to use GUI to encourage the generation as well as customization of expansive distributed models [28].
- For modeling and simulation, it gives a POSIX-based API and other few techniques for demonstrating applications can be utilized as a part of iCanCloud: utilizing hints of genuine applications; utilizing a state chart; and programming new applications straightforwardly in simulation platform. Thusly, the end goal to model whole cloud computing frameworks, iCloud architecture has been composed in light of this guideline [38].

5. **SPECI:** or Simulation Program for Elastic Cloud Infrastructures permits investigating and investigation of features of extensive data center behavior under configuration approach as well as the size of middleware as inputs. Discrete event simulations (DES) are a kind of simulation where events are requested in time kept up in a line of events by the simulator [38] and each prepared at a given simulation time. SPECI utilizes a current package for DES in Java [15].

6. **DCSim:** This simulator is popular for creating data center management techniques [39]. It focuses on transactional and persistent workloads as well as virtualized data centers. It gives an extra ability of modeling replicated VMs sharing approaching workload.

7. **CloudReports:** A graphical model of CloudSim with an adaptable environment with customizability and repeatability. Distributed computing environments depending on cloud computing are simulated using this simulator [36].

8. **EMUSIM [39]:** It is not just a simulator; it has capabilities of both emulator and simulator. This is particularly helpful when the analyzer has no clue on the execution of the software under various levels of simultaneousness and parallelism, which hinders the use of

simulation. All VM related data like location of VM, different VMs is not needed by this simulator [35, 36, 39]. It has some limitations regarding adaptability due to either troubles in producing extensive and reasonable workloads or hardware constraints. EMUSIM, naturally extricates data from application behavior.

12.7.2   IoT SIMULATOR (IOTSIM)

Illuminated with the performance of CloudSim [34], IoTSim is structured with layered architecture and support for big data processing systems. It can be depicted as general layered architecture for IoTSim [21, 34, 40, 46, 47]:

1. **CloudSim Core Simulation Engine Layer:** Core functionalities like association among components, processing the events, ordering the events, designing cloud system entities like virtual machines, brokers, etc., as well as proper handling of the simulation clock, is supported by bottom-most layer or the simulation engine.

2. **CloudSim Simulation Layer:** It has many sub-layers with the purpose of modeling core components of the cloud. There is full support for modeling and simulating virtual cloud-based environments as well as interfaces for storage and virtual machines. Issues like managing the execution of the application, checking, or auditing dynamic system state, supplying hosts to VM's are all handled and managed properly by this layer. Network topology and datacenter are modeled by the bottom-most layer. IaaS environments are designed with these elements.

3. **Storage Layer:** Modeling of storage like Azure Blob Storage is supported by the storage layer, where huge datasets produced from gadgets or devices are to be stored. In run time, All the data files are moved from these storages and written to these storages through IoT-based applications when needed. A delay in storing the files will be acquired at this layer [5, 7, 13].

4. **Big Data Processing Layer:** Two sub-layers are included. One is the Map-Reduce sublayer whose function is supporting applications only when there is a requirement of batch-oriented information. Another one is the Streaming Computing sublayer for handling those applications that need an ongoing processing paradigm. Based upon the nature of IoT-based applications that the clients utilize, it can handle enormous information that is produced or created from

IoT sensors utilizing either MapReduce or streaming computing layers. CloudSim has some drawbacks which in turn makes Big Data Processing Layer more popular and demanded [5, 13].

5. **User Code Layer:** Top-most layer uncovered all the fundamental entities for hosts such as the count of machines and IoT-based applications' designs, virtual machines, number of customers, their application types, as well as planning paths or ways. It encourages clients to characterize setups for approving their calculations [5].

12.8   CONCLUSION

CC offers numerous potential outcomes along with few restrictions also. IoT is developing quickly in the field of wireless broadcast communications. In this chapter, an overview of IoT Technology with its characteristics and convergence with cloud technology is presented. Besides, we also present the architecture of Cloud with its models. The principle objective behind the association or collaboration among objects through wireless system is to satisfy the target set to them as a joined thing. Based on wireless networks, both IoT, as well as the cloud, grows very quickly. The combination of IoT and cloud is progressively valuable for experiencing boundless abilities like storage as well as processing power.

In the chapter, a review on Cloud computing as well as IoT with attention to the security issues of the integration of both is also presented. With the secure convergence of cloud with IoT, an improvement in the functionality of IoT is found. Security issues of the integration are also mentioned. Additionally, IoT can fill a few holes in Cloud computing such as the primary issue of limited scope. Due to the expansion in the acceptance of this innovation, the evaluation of the performance of cloud computing becomes analytical. To evaluate performance, simulation, and modeling are found to be suitable. So, at last, the solution is to simulate the real cloud environment with the use of simulators. Simulators can model many cloud applications by making data centers, virtual machines that can be arranged properly, in this way making it easier to analyze. These days, an increase in cloud-based IoT applications to run big data platforms for processing huge data from various devices or gadgets as well as conducting analytics for the abstraction of knowledge. However, it looks very challenging and costly too. To overcome this, IoTSim Simulator comes into existence. IoTSim is an extension of CloudSim, discussed in the chapter.

KEYWORDS

- **cloud computing**
- **cloud simulator**
- **internet of things**
- **radio frequency identification**
- **smart environment**
- **virtual machine**

REFERENCES

1. Biswas, A. R., & Giaffreda, R., (2014). IoT and cloud convergence: Opportunities and challenges. In: *2014 IEEE World Forum on the Internet of Things (WF-IoT)* (pp. 375–376). IEEE.

2. Radanliev, P., De Roure, D. C., Nurse, J. R., Burnap, P., Anthi, E., Ani, U., & Montalvo, R. M., (2019). *Definition of Cyber Strategy Transformation Roadmap for Standardization of IoT Risk Impact Assessment with a Goal-Oriented Approach and the Internet of Things Micro Mart*. University of Oxford.

3. Lakhwani, K., Gianey, H., Agarwal, N., & Gupta, S., (2019). Development of IoT for smart agriculture a review. In: *Emerging Trends in Expert Applications and Security* (pp. 425–432). Springer, Singapore.

4. Gubbi, J., Buyya, R., Marusic, S., & Palaniswami, M., (2013). Internet of things (IoT): A vision, architectural elements, and future directions. *Future Generation Computer Systems, 29*(7), 1645–1660.

5. Ta, D. T., Khawam, K., Lahoud, S., Adjih, C., & Martin, S., (2019). Lora-MAB: A flexible simulator for decentralized learning resource allocation in IoT networks. In: *2019 12th IFIP Wireless and Mobile Networking Conference (WMNC)* (pp. 55–62). IEEE.

6. Lee, I., & Lee, K., (2015). The internet of things (IoT): Applications, investments, and challenges for enterprises. *Business Horizons, 58*(4), 431–440.

7. Sun, E., Zhang, X., & Li, Z., (2012). The internet of things (IoT) and cloud computing (CC) based tailings dam monitoring and pre-alarm system in mines. *Safety Science, 50*(4), 811–815.

8. Catarinucci, L., De Donno, D., Mainetti, L., Palano, L., Patrono, L., Stefanizzi, M., & Tarricone, L., (2015). An IoT-Aware architecture for smart healthcare systems. *IEEE Internet Things J., 2*(6), 515–526.

9. Sayginer, C., & Ercan, T., (2020). *Benefits and Challenges of Cloud Computing in Production and Service Sector in Izmir, the city of Turkey*.

10. Pearson, S., & Benameur, A., (2010). Privacy, security and trust issues arising from cloud computing. In: *2010 IEEE Second International Conference on Cloud Computing Technology and Science* (pp. 693–702). IEEE.

11. Wang, C., Chow, S. S., Wang, Q., Ren, K., & Lou, W., (2011). Privacy-preserving public auditing for secure cloud storage. *IEEE Transactions on Computers, 62*(2), 362–375.

12. Tari, Z., (2014). Security and privacy in cloud computing. *IEEE Cloud Comput., 1*(1), 54–57.

13. Mellino, J. A. Z., Luján, E., Otero, A. D., Mocskos, E. E., Vega, L. R., & Galarza, C. G., (2019). lite NB-IoT simulator for uplink layer. In: *2019 XVIII Workshop on Information Processing and Control (RPIC)* (pp. 286–291). IEEE.

14. Rong, C., Nguyen, S. T., & Jaatun, M. G., (2013). Beyond lightning: A survey on security challenges in cloud computing. *Computers & Electrical Engineering, 39*(1), 47–54.

15. Wang, C., Bi, Z., & Da Xu, L., (2014). IoT and cloud computing in automation of assembly modeling systems. *IEEE Transactions on Industrial Informatics, 10*(2), 1426–1434.

16. Gubbi, J., Buyya, R., Marusic, S., & Palaniswami, M., (2013). Internet of things (IoT): A vision, architectural elements, and future directions. *Future Generation Computer Systems, 29*(7), 1645–1660.

17. Stergiou, C., Psannis, K. E., Kim, B. G., & Gupta, B., (2018). Secure integration of IoT and cloud computing. *Future Generation Computer Systems, 78*, 964–975.

18. Kong, L., Khan, M. K., Wu, F., Chen, G., & Zeng, P., (2017). Millimeter-wave wireless communications for IoT-cloud supported autonomous vehicles: Overview, design, and challenges. *IEEE Communications Magazine, 55*(1), 62–68.

19. Doukas, C., & Maglogiannis, I., (2012). Bringing IoT and cloud computing towards pervasive healthcare. In: *2012 Sixth International Conference on Innovative Mobile and Internet Services in Ubiquitous Computing* (pp. 922–926). IEEE.

20. Chang, C. C., Wu, H. L., & Sun, C. Y., (2017). Notes on Secure authentication scheme for IoT and cloud servers. *Pervasive and Mobile Computing, 38*, 275–278.

21. Chen, G., Dong, W., Qiu, F., Guan, G., Gao, Y., & Zeng, S., (2020). Scalable and interactive simulation for IoT applications with TinySim. In: *IEEE INFOCOM 2020-IEEE Conference on Computer Communications Workshops (INFOCOM WKSHPS)* (pp. 1296–1297). IEEE.

22. Armbrust, M., Fox, A., Griffith, R., Joseph, A. D., Katz, R., Konwinski, A., & Zaharia, M., (2009). *Above the Clouds: A Berkeley View of Cloud Computing.* EECS Dept. Univ. California, Berkeley, No. UCB/EECS-2009-28.

23. Dillon, T., Wu, C., & Chang, E., (2010). Cloud computing: Issues and challenges. In: *2010 24ᵗʰ IEEE International Conference on Advanced Information Networking and Applications* (pp. 27–33). IEEE.

24. Knorr, E., & Gruman, G., (2008). *What Cloud Computing Really Means* (Vol. 7, p. 20). InfoWorld.

25. Buyya, R., Ranjan, R., & Calheiros, R. N., (2009). Modeling and simulation of scalable cloud computing environments and the CloudSim toolkit: Challenges and opportunities. In: *2009 International Conference on High Performance Computing & Simulation* (pp. 1–11). IEEE.

26. Youseff, L., Butrico, M., & Da Silva, D., (2008). Toward a unified ontology of cloud computing. In: *2008 Grid Computing Environments Workshop* (pp. 1–10). IEEE.

27. He, W., Yan, G., & Da Xu, L., (2014). Developing vehicular data cloud services in the IoT environment. *IEEE Transactions on Industrial Informatics, 10*(2), 1587–1595.

28. Xu, X., (2012). From cloud computing to cloud manufacturing. *Robotics and Computer-Integrated Manufacturing, 28*(1), 75–86.

29. Subashini, S., & Kavitha, V., (2011). A survey on security issues in service delivery models of cloud computing. *Journal of Network and Computer Applications, 34*(1), 1–11.

30. Yang, G., Xie, L., Mäntysalo, M., Zhou, X., Pang, Z., Da Xu, L., & Zheng, L. R., (2014). A health-IoT platform based on the integration of intelligent packaging, unobtrusive bio-sensor, and intelligent medicine box. *IEEE Transactions on Industrial Informatics, 10*(4), 2180–2191.

31. Nurmi, D., et al., (2009). The eucalyptus open-source cloud-computing system. In: *2009 9ᵗʰ IEEE/ACM Int. Symp. Clust. Comput. Grid, CCGRID 2009* (pp. 124–131).

32. Kelly, S. D. T., Suryadevara, N. K., & Mukhopadhyay, S. C., (2013). Towards the implementation of IoT for environmental condition monitoring in homes. *IEEE Sensors Journal, 13*(10), 3846–3853.

33. Chiang, M., & Zhang, T., (2016). Fog and IoT: An overview of research opportunities. *IEEE Internet of Things Journal, 3*(6), 854–864.

34. Zeng, X., Garg, S. K., Strazdins, P., Jayaraman, P. P., Georgakopoulos, D., & Ranjan, R., (2017). IOTSim: A simulator for analyzing IoT applications. *Journal of Systems Architecture, 72*, 93–107.

35. Zhao, W., Peng, Y., Xie, F., & Dai, Z., (2012). Modeling and simulation of cloud computing: A review. In: *2012 IEEE Asia Pacific Cloud Computing Congress (APCloudCC)* (pp. 20–24). IEEE.

36. Byrne, J., Svorobej, S., Giannoutakis, K. M., Tzovaras, D., Byrne, P. J., Östberg, P. O., & Lynn, T., (2017). A review of cloud computing simulation platforms and related environments. In: *International Conference on Cloud Computing and Services Science* (Vol. 2, pp. 679–691). SCITEPRESS.

37. Núñez, A., Vázquez-Poletti, J. L., Caminero, A. C., Castañé, G. G., Carretero, J., & Llorente, I. M., (2012). iCanCloud: A flexible and scalable cloud infrastructure simulator. *Journal of Grid Computing, 10*(1), 185–209.

38. Suryateja, P. S., (2016). A comparative analysis of cloud simulators. *International Journal of Modern Education and Computer Science, 8*(4), 64.

39. Malhotra, R., & Jain, P., (2013). Study and comparison of cloudsim simulators in the cloud computing. *The SIJ Transactions on Computer Science Engineering & Its Applications, 1*(4), 111–115.

40. Yugha, R., & Chithra, S., (2020). A survey on technologies and security protocols: Reference for future generation IoT. *Journal of Network and Computer Applications,* 102763.

41. Kephart, R. W., Sanchez, H., & Abruzere, E., (2016). *U.S. Patent No. 9,529,348.* Washington, DC: U.S. Patent and Trademark Office.

42. Wickremasinghe, B., Calheiros, R. N., & Buyya, R., (2010). Cloud analyst: A cloudsim-based visual modeler for analyzing cloud computing environments and applications. In: *2010 24ᵗʰ IEEE International Conference on Advanced Information Networking and Applications* (pp. 446–452). IEEE.

43. Liu, L., Wang, H., Liu, X., Jin, X., He, W. B., Wang, Q. B., & Chen, Y., (2009). GreenCloud: a new architecture for green data center. In: *Proceedings of the 6ᵗʰ International Conference Industry Session on Autonomic Computing and Communications Industry Session* (pp. 29–38).

44. Ahmed, A., & Sabyasachi, A. S., (2014). Cloud computing simulators: A detailed survey and future direction. In: *2014 IEEE International Advance Computing Conference (IACC)* (pp. 866–872). IEEE.

45. Lin, Y. W., Lin, Y. B., & Yen, T. H., (2020). Simtalk: Simulation of IoT applications. *Sensors, 20*(9), 2563.

46. Sadeghi, P., & Ejlali, A., (2020). A new analytical simulator for the provisioning stage of IoT-based WSNs. In: *2020 CSI/CPSSI International Symposium on Real-Time and Embedded Systems and Technologies (RTEST)* (pp. 1–5). IEEE.

47. Sharma, S., Nanda, M., Goel, R., Jain, A., Bhushan, M., & Kumar, A., (2019). Smart cities using internet of things: Recent trends and techniques. *International Journal of Innovative Technology and Exploring Engineering (IJITEE), 8*(9S), 24–28.

CHAPTER 13

Framework for Video Summarization Using CNN-LSTM Approach in IoT Surveillance Networks

CHAITRALI CHAUDHARI[1] and SATISH DEVANE[2]

[1]Lokmanya Tilak College of Engineering, Koperkhairane, Navi Mumbai, Maharashtra, India, E-mail: chaitralichaudhari13@gmail.com

[2]Principal, Maratha Vidya Prasarak Samaj's Karmaveer Adv. Baburao Ganpatrao Thakare College of Engineering, Gangapur Road, NashikMaharashtra, India, E-mail: srdevane@yahoo.com

ABSTRACT

The surveillance industry is rapidly changing and growing. Processing of surveillance videos to maintain useful information is a challenging and time-consuming task. This work proposes a framework for the effective summarization of surveillance videos by combining the advantages of deep learning to the internet of things (IoT). A convolutional neural network (CNN) is used for the selection of significant video features from the selected video frames and a long short term memory network (LSTM) is used for the generation of video summary in the compact from preserving the salient information. Summarization of the videos can be sent to the receiver over a network providing benefits of reduced bandwidth utilization and transmission cost. The proposed framework has the benefits of autonomous operations without the need for human intervention. Since the time consumed to analyze the summarized text is comparatively less than for the video, quick decision making and faster action in case of emergency is possible increasing the efficiency at crucial situations.

13.1   INTRODUCTION

The information in a visual format is rich and vastly available over the internet. Visual representation has the potential to effectively convey the information which can be memorized longer, but it suffers from some disadvantages. Raw visual data utilize huge storage space. To execute a query of a certain event, or to carry out tasks like extraction of similar visual representation, requires a large amount of visual data analysis. In any certain specific video-based applications, transmission, and analysis of full videos are time-consuming and impractical. In such situations, the summarization of videos before transmission is required. Video summarization generates the summary of a whole video consisting of selected and representative scenes from the video reflecting continuity, avoiding repetition, and also redundancy. It gives the user a core idea about the video without watching it fully. This summarization can be used for carrying out various tasks like pattern analysis, strategic decision making, and so on. It is useful for easy retrieval, browsing, and matching the visual contents in various domains where videos and images play a critical role, like summarizing day-long indoor/outdoor/industrial surveillance videos, summarizing movies, various events, and ceremonies, etc.

Besides these applications, video summarization has an important role in the field of surveillance. The today surveillance industry is providing solutions far beyond basic functionalities like generating alarms. Organizations can access live streaming of surveillance videos and able to provide immediate protective or security actions to safeguard their infrastructure and people.

The field of surveillance with IoT and deep learning is the futuristic technology which opens many new perspectives. This work proposes a surveillance framework by merging this powerful medium of 'smart things' with another emerging and powerful area of artificial intelligence (AI) and suggest making the use of lightweight CNN and LSTM network in the IoT environment for video summarization. The visual data collected during surveillance should be processed, and only the informative data should be recorded for future usages, such as abnormal event detection, case management, data analysis, and video abstraction. It is impractical to send the unprocessed video and/image data over because of energy and bandwidth limitations. Also, it is comparatively difficult and time-consuming for an analyst to efficiently extract actionable intelligence from the sheer volume of surveillance data. Video summary can be used instead of lengthy videos, to efficiently browse similar contents and perform effective analysis for many applications. Thus, the proposed system is the best fit for industrial as well as general surveillance scenarios.

13.1.1 SUMMARY OF CONTRIBUTIONS

Our contributions in this chapter are as follows:

- Reviewed the IoT and deep learning techniques to process videos and images in various application areas;
- To use the technique of deep learning in IoT framework, we researched the literature deeply to identify the key features of IoT and a deep learning environment;
- Proposed a four-layer framework for video summarization;
- The challenges and future research directions in merging the fields of deep learning and IoT are presented.

The remainder of this work is organized as follows. The survey of literature in presented Section 13.2, the background is discussed in Section 13.3, the overall framework is proposed in Section 13.4, materials, and methods are discussed in Sections 13.5 and 13.6 concludes the chapter with some limitations of the current framework and future plans for a better surveillance framework.

13.2 LITERATURE SURVEY

Various approaches towards the summarization of videos are presented by different authors. We surveyed the literature and present our findings as follows:

- Various approaches used for video summarization are discussed by Refs. [1–4]. Ajmal et al. [5] have categorized different video summarization methods and discuss their advantages and disadvantages.
- In the surveillance domain, the video is captured after the motion is detected. Recent developments in computer vision have led to various ways of motion recognition. The robustness of Visual sensors like cameras is often compromised due to human or technical error which can be avoided by using the multi-view cameras as stated in Ref. [6]. But multiview cameras suffer from the drawback of redundant data generation, resulting in unnecessary resource utilization, processing, and transmission of data. Authors have suggested the use of improved

storage and processing capabilities of the visual sensor networks to discard irrelevant and redundant visual data, thus minimizing the bandwidth requirements. The informative frames are extracted from the surveillance video data and to avoid the threat of frame modification during transmission, an intelligent algorithm to increase robustness and security is proposed.

- Manzanera and Richefeu [7] used an estimation technique based on Sigma-Delta background and proposed an algorithm to detect motion. Cedras and Shah [8] provided the review of computer vision aspects of motion-based recognition and described various recognition schemes for objects and motions and also methods designed to recognize human motion.

- Datta, Joshi, Li, and Wang [9] extracted visual features such that the feature extraction is expected to discriminate between esthetically pleasing and displeasing images. Whereas Li, Yao, Ling, and Mei [10] presented a keyframe selection and video summarization framework, and proposed a boundary detection algorithm, that learns a dictionary from the given video and updates atoms in the dictionary, with the philosophy that different shots cannot be reconstructed using the learned dictionary. After the shot boundaries are detected, representative keyframes are selected and concatenated to construct the video-based summary. Priya and Domnic [11] presented a method for keyframe extraction to cluster the frames sequentially into shots to provide efficient representation and indexing of video sequences. They proposed a block similarity-based feature, containing characteristics of both color and edge-based information and used for calculating the similarity between consecutive frames. For extracting the representative keyframes, Gianluigi and Raimondo [12] analyzed the complexity of the frame sequence in terms of changes in the visual contents between two consecutive frames of a video expressed by different frame descriptors.

- Fei, Jiang, and Mao [13] used the concept of image memorability and image entropy to propose a Memorability-Entropy-based video summarization framework aiming to maintain the diversity of the video summary. Ejaz, Tariq, and Baik [14] used an aggregation mechanism to combine the extracted visual features and an adaptive formula is used to combine current and previous iteration to reduce the redundancy. Divakaran, Radhakrishnan, and Peker [15]; Borth, Ulges, Schulze, and Breuel [16]; Ciocca and Schettini [17]; and Li,

Wu, Yu, and Chen [18] also presented a notable contribution towards the keyframe extraction approaches.

- Neural network architectures like CNN and LSTM are used for video summarization in IoT based environments. Deep CNNs have been used on computer vision datasets for their improved accuracy. Iandola et al. [19] proposed SqueezeNet architecture with few parameters and equivalent accuracy. Hochreiter and Schmidhuber [20] discusses the LSTM Network in detail with advantages and disadvantages. Muhammad et al. [21] used a CNN framework for feature extraction and shot segmentation. Feature extraction uses the memorability, entropy, and esthetics of each frame of the shot. Hierarchical weighted fusion is used to obtain an aggregated score for each frame for an intelligent fusion of extracted features using which, an attention curve is constituted, which in turn is used for the representative frame selection. No sequence learning mechanism like LSTM is used. Lawrence and Zhang [22] developed an architecture called IOTNET consisting of groups and blocks. A group is a logical collection of a block which contains metadata and a block is a collection of operations such as convolutions. The architecture is shown to improve the trade-off between accuracy and computational cost over existing approaches typically used in efficiency-focused models. Redmon et al. [23] presented YOLO, a faster approach towards object detection to predict what objects are present where. YOLOv3 tiny object detection model is presented in Ref. [24] with some updates to YOLO to make it more accurate and fast.

- IoT frameworks are developed for various application areas. Akter et al. [25] developed an IoT-based Doorbell to enhance the security of home or office using Raspberry Pi (RPi). Whereas, Lee et al. [26] proposed an IoT-based visitor detection system using RPi to detect human visitors by minimizing the blind spots of the camera. Gowtham, Nazeer, and Saranya [27] presented a drone design using IoT. Ansari et al. [28] discussed and developed an IoT-based application to get notifications when motion is detected using low processing power chips.

- Muhammad et al. [29] used coarse redundancy removal through the comparison of low-level features on the captured video. Selected frames are sent to the cloud for detailed analysis, where sequential features are extracted for the selection of candidate keyframes. These keyframes are refined to discriminate those with maximum information as part of the summary. Fu et al. [30]; and Li and Merialdo [31] presented a method for summarizing multi-view videos. Hussain et al. [32] discussed the advantages of installing an embedded multi-view camera to get the advantages like reduced cost, processing time, difficulties in installation, and connection with computers through wires.

13.2.1   DATASETS

Khosla et al. [33] introduced a procedure to objectively measure human memory, by building LaMem (Large-scale Memorability Dataset), the largest annotated image memorability dataset containing 60,000 images from diverse sources. De Avila et al. [34] created a new database composed of videos collected from websites like YouTube. Several other datasets also exist.

13.3   BACKGROUND

13.3.1   KEY FEATURES OF IoT

IoT is the wireless network connecting the things which are everyday objects. The objects enabled with sensors are connected to each other and the network and hence always able to communicate and transfer data. IoT has enormous applications in various domains where it provides assistance to humans to ease and simplify life. Since it is continuously connected to the network, it can communicate instantly. In emergencies like fire, earthquakes, accidents, etc. IoT can be used effectively to provide help in rescue and search operations in time. Also, necessary action can be taken in a short time in the case of emergency conditions such as in the medical and health sector to monitor blood pressure (BP), heartbeat, and various other medical instrument readings, in applications at industries, offices, military areas, smart homes, the elderly person falling sick, etc.

The applicability and availability of IoT architecture are vast and varied according to the requirement to serve the purpose. Low to high-cost IoT devices are available with limited to vast computing power and low to high power consumption needs, to use in a limited to major impact environment. The user has a choice to select from a range of lightweight to heavyweight frameworks. Smart environments are created using IoT and it can get expanded with the addition of devices by fulfilling the requirement of connectivity and security aspects. Thus, in the field of security and surveillance IoT based applications serve as a perfect choice.

13.3.2   KEY FEATURES OF DEEP LEARNING

Deep learning is a technique of ML which has a powerful feature to deal with the unstructured data. Deep learning is based on artificial neural networks (ANNs), which is a layered framework combining the ML algorithms. The word "deep" refers to the number of layers of transformations through which the input passes and the network finds the correct mathematical manipulation to derive the output by calculating the probability of each output. Various deep learning architectures exist such as recurrent neural networks (RNNs), LSTMs, CNNs, deep belief networks (DBN), and deep stacking networks (DSNs), etc., which have applications in various domains including computer vision, ML, natural language processing (NLP), speech processing, medical imaging, bioinformatics, drug design to name a few. We propose to make the use of CNN and LSTM architectures in IoT based surveillance framework due to their specific features as discussed ahead.

13.3.3   CNN

CNN is a class of *deep neural networks*. Unlike the fully connected networks, CNN exhibits the property of local connectivity where each neuron is connected only to a small subset of the input, decreasing the total number of parameters. CNN is an important variant of neural network framework in which the first layer is a convolutional layer. Convolutions are the filters or a mechanism for feature selection. After the convolutional layer, the pooling layer simplifies the data by reducing the dimensionality. Next, the fully connected layer generates a single vector of output probabilities. Due to its architectural features, CNN is a top choice to handle image data and has exhibited good performance in applications involving image classification. Hence, most of the CNN applications are in the field of computer vision. CNN architectures are also investigated for a variety of application scenarios that involve image capturing and processing using IoT devices equipped with cameras, such as flood or landslide prediction through drone images, plant disease detection using plant pictures on smartphones, and traffic sign detection using vehicles cameras.

13.3.4   LSTM

RNNs are used to process variable-length sequences of inputs and encode the extracted sequential features. They are used to analyze the hidden sequential patterns. A video is consisting of many frames that carry visual information through which the context present in the video is conveyed. RNNs can interpret such sequences but suffer from problems like vanishing and exploding gradients which are overcome by LSTMs when trained with backpropagation through time. LSTM is a special kind of RNN architecture with a gating mechanism capable of learning long term dependencies and preserve sequence information over time. They are created as the solution to short-term memory and can learn long-term contextual information from temporal sequences. A common architecture of LSTM consists of cell memory and three gates, an input gate, an output gate and a forget gate adjusted by a sigmoid unit. Its special structure control long-term sequence pattern identification.

13.3.5   CNN-LSTM ARCHITECTURE

CNN-LSTM architecture consists of LSTM that use CNN as a front end. This architecture has the flexibility to be used in a variety of tasks involving sequence prediction problems with spatial inputs, like images or videos. This architecture extract features using CNN layers and LSTM is used to perform sequence prediction on the feature vectors. CNN-LSTM models are spatially and temporally deep and used in applications involving fields of Computer Vision and NLP. These models have enormous potential and are increasingly used for tasks such as text classification, video conversion, image captioning, etc. Captioning images represent the story behind the picture or image in a single sentence, i.e., converts the image into text. Vast research is ongoing in this area. Bernardi et al. [35] presented a detailed survey of Models, Data-sets, Evaluation Measures, and classified existing approaches based on how they conceptualize this problem. Following the work of Ref. [35], a detailed survey of various approaches towards captioning images is presented in Ref. [36]. Authors have also suggested a framework for image captioning using CNN and LSTM. Kulkarni et al. [37] developed a system which detects the objects in the image and processes it to generate a sentence based on the labeling of the graph. A huge amount of multimedia data in the form of images and videos are uploaded daily on the internet and research is ongoing for effective retrieval and processing of this vastly available information which is a challenging task. Techniques such as image captioning and video summarization can be seen as one of the solutions to this problem.

13.4   PROPOSED FRAMEWORK

After extensively reviewing the literature and following the key Refs. [21, 32, 39], we propose a framework that generates a summary for videos captured using the IoT-enabled video capturing device and also sends prompt notifications when motion is detected.

13.4.1   *FRAMEWORK COMPONENTS*

We propose a four-layered architecture:

- **Layer 1:** Data acquisition layer;
- **Layer 2:** Feature extraction layer;
- **Layer 3:** Summarization layer;
- **Layer 4:** Transmission layer.

The data acquisition layer and feature extraction layer are functional at the client RPi whereas the summarization layer and transmission layer are functional at the server RPi.

Figure 13.1 shows the proposed framework for video summarization using CNN-LSTM approach in IoT surveillance networks.

13.4.2   *ALGORITHM*

1. **Initialize Camera:** The data acquisition layer at client RPi consists of a multi-view camera to capture the image. Initialize camera.
2. **Detect Motion:** Various ways of motion-based recognition techniques are available which help to disambiguate between possible or allowable types of motion from a non-desirable type of motion in a particular scene. If the last frame is different from the current frame, video recording is triggered, and a notification e-mail/message is sent to the recipients.
3. **Capture Video:** When the motion is detected, capture video using the camera.
4. **Feature Extraction:** Extract features using CNN.
5. **Summarization:** Summarize using LSTM.

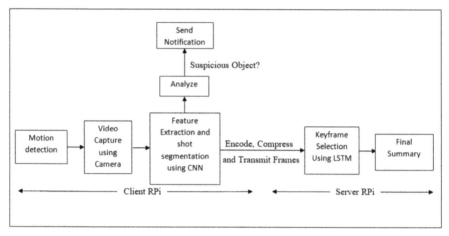

FIGURE 13.1 Proposed framework for video summarization using CNN-LSTM approach in IoT surveillance networks.

13.5 MATERIALS AND METHODOLOGY

13.5.1 CONTROLLER/PROCESSOR/RPI

RPi client can be used as a controller or processor with an embedded multiview camera to capture the video. Frames captured per second are set such as to make the process online and efficient. RPi detects targets in frames using the CNN model and analyzes these targets for suspicious objects like guns or knives, vehicles, persons, etc. It sends a notification on the detection of motion to the recipient in the IoT network. The frames of client RPi are encoded, compressed, and transmitted to the RPi server over the wireless network getting the advantage of saving communication bandwidth. Video streaming can be seen in the monitor connected to RPi via the HDMI-VGA connector. Multiple client RPis can also be used if required.

13.5.2 GSM (GLOBAL SERVICE FOR MOBILE COMMUNICATION) MODEM

GSM is the means to initiate communication among the stakeholders and emergencies. A SIM (subscriber identification module) card operating over a subscription to a mobile operator is required. GSM modem comes with a serial, USB (universal serial bus), or Bluetooth association, or it can be a regular GSM mobile.

13.5.3 VISUAL SENSORS

A client RPi module embedded with a multiview camera act as a vision sensor, to capture the videos for 24 hours which are transmitted to the server RPi periodically over a wireless network. Motion detectors are used to trigger a camera to start recording after the motion is detected. Many modern motion detectors use combinations of different technologies available with variable cost and detection ranges. PIR (passive infrared sensor) technology can be paired with another model to maximize accuracy and reduce energy use.

The multiview camera has a built-in SD (secure digital) card. It supports remote viewing and stores the video on the SD card, which cannot be easily damaged. The main properties required for visual sensors are good design, low energy consumption, stable transmission. It should have enough power to last until the users are available for charging. There is also a requirement of a stable transmission method to transmit data to the server for processing and storage. Some IoT architectures give customization ability to users such that the users can set attributes like frames per second, resolution, brightness, contrast saturation, save the video locally, or send it to server or services like Dropbox. The frames are transferred to CNN for further processing.

13.5.4 FEATURE EXTRACTION AND SHOT SEGMENTATION USING CNN

Salient feature and keyframe extraction from the video and shot segmentation is an important task since it directly affects the summarization, i.e., meaningful summary generation. In the surveillance domain, the length of the video is generally comparatively longer hence summarization is required. Since this summary of a video is used for analysis purposes, it should be precise. To capture the gist of the videos and to summarize it more precisely, significant features from the video keyframes are extracted using CNN. A video sequence is a set of frames or groups of shots and each video frame corresponds to several low levels and semantic descriptions. In IoT based resource-constrained environments like surveillance, the use of specifically designed neural network architectures is a good choice. Large models that are available mainly focus on performance but they are difficult to scale down. Also, since the objects are far in the surveillance domain, fine-tuning

CNN is required. Fine-Tuning is a multi-step process that is required to learn new or intended object classes. The different models are discussed in the literature survey.

The captured video frames are processed by a suitable and trained fine-tuned CNN at client RPi. Features are extracted and video is segmented in shots to remove the redundancy from the captured video. Thus, the deep features extracted using CNN are encoded and compressed and transmitted over a network to the server RPi. The server RPi and the IoT enabled devices are also connected to the same wireless network. If the network is not available, then the resulting video frames are stored locally on client RPi or in a storage device such as an SD card and sent when the association resumes.

13.5.5   SUMMARIZATION USING LSTM

LSTM Network provides an effective means of summarization as it encodes the varying input lengths into a predetermined dimensional vector, and it further deploys this demonstration to "decode" it to the exact output sentence. At the server RPi, the compressed and encoded video frames are received in the form of a vector and inputted to the LSTM.

LSTM is used for summary generation using sequential learning. LSTM decodes the frames to restore the original frames and learns whether the sequence of frames is informative or not. Image entropy indicates the amount of information inside a frame. The complexity of a frame is also computed. The higher value of entropy and complexity indicates a high amount of information present in the frame. Also, if the objects identified near the camera indicate they are important and need to be considered for the final summary. If the amount of information is low and objects are far from the camera, the complexity and entropy values are lower. A refinement process is carried out by storing the frames with the highest value of sum for complexity and entropy as keyframes and the rest of the redundant frames are discarded. A high compression rate shows that the frame has little visually important information and vice versa. Thus, the final summary is generated.

13.5.6   TRANSMISSION OVER A NETWORK

The output of the final state of LSTM is sent to the smart device connected to the wireless network; which facilitates access anytime and anywhere. The transmission layer utilizes a 4G (Fourth Generation) router to connect the data acquisition and feature extraction layer with the server, thereby achieving real-time information surveillance. The transmission layer uses a wide area network (WAN) and local area network (LAN) to provide basic network transmission for the surveillance system. The application layer can be a service window for users consisting of web pages and mobile apps.

13.5.7 PROPERTIES

1. **Cost-Effective:** Most of the current surveillance systems are costly as a certain amount of money must be paid to store the recorded video despite the fact that there is no human movement is recognized. Also, there is no need to avail surveillance manned by security professionals. IoT based video surveillance and summarization can overcome the drawbacks of the traditional system and make it cost-effective due to its features.

2. **Storage Space:** An intelligent surveillance system can start recording video only after a motion is detected which minimizes the required storage space. Also, the use of the web ensures less storage space.

3. **Security:** The framework is secure due to the choice and features of components. More security features can be added with the assistance of the web.

4. **Availability:** Now, at most of the places like buildings, houses, offices, malls, roads, schools, temples, and many other locations, closed-circuit televisions are installed. Surveillance is a need everywhere to ensure security and availability at a very low cost.

5. **Real-Time Monitoring:** The real-time monitoring technology makes the user able to act instantly if required after the reception of a notification which is always better than checking the videos as proof after the mishap or an event has occurred.

13.6 CONCLUSIONS AND FUTURE TRENDS

The proposed framework enables total autonomous operations, reduces the need for human involvement, and increases efficiency in crucial situations. Although the proposed system still needs improvement, it does show a great potential application in capturing personal life-long or indoor/outdoor/industrial surveillance in real-time. We have proposed a framework with restricted devices having short design and low energy consumption which is a need of time. The proposed framework will encourage the research towards manufacturing the low-cost and energy-efficient hardware for IoT.

Muhammad et al. [29] explored several limitations of existing visual summarization methods, such as computational complexity, no domain specificity, use statistical features, or computationally expensive deep learning models for video summarization and use frame-level strategy for redundancy removal which ignore the importance of events that occur in the sequence of frames. Also, the existing methods focus more on entertainment and news, than on industrial surveillance, which limits their usefulness for specific indoor or outdoor surveillance scenarios. Also, surveillance data of a whole day is transmitted over wireless networks without any special mechanism to reduce the network traffic and bandwidth. They have also identified that the resource-constrained devices are not explored in existing approaches for video capturing and preprocessing, for making the summary. Summarization using multi-view camera is challenging because it has both inter- and intra-view correlations to be considered while generating a summary. Another challenge is the variation of light conditions among different views. Furthermore, synchronization among different views also makes the summarization process a difficult one.

For future research, the proposed framework can be extended with more domain knowledge to further improve the quality of video summarization. Security features can also be considered. To find a balance between framework accuracy and computational cost and to ensure the functioning within resource-limited environment also gives a future work direction that will serve the purpose of overall improvement of the quality and capabilities.

We have presented a detailed review of the work done by different researchers in the field of video summarization to remove redundancy and preserve consistency and saliency of visual contents. We have also reviewed the application domain of image data, i.e., image captioning, where much work is done and research is still ongoing. Similar to image captioning, video captioning is also an emerging and challenging area of research. Chen, Chen, and Chen [38] proposed an encoder-decoder RNN framework that generates a captioned video summary for a given video in the test phase. There is a scope to use more complicated structures such as hierarchical RNN or bi-directional RNN or LSTM to improve the performance. Also, different types of attributes can be considered to generate more meaningful summaries. As a future direction, image-based video summarization can be clubbed with text-based video captioning considering multiple research dimensions.

KEYWORDS

- **Cloud information service**
- **Infrastructure as a service**
- **Internet of Things**
- **Platform as a service**
- **Surveillance network**
- **Video summarization**

REFERENCES

1. Khan, S., & Pawar, S., (2015). Video summarization: Survey on event detection and summarization in soccer videos. *International Journal of Advanced Computer Science and Applications, 6*(11).

2. Del, M. A. G., Tan, C., Lim, J. H., & Tan, A. H., (2016). Summarization of egocentric videos: A comprehensive survey. *IEEE Transactions on Human-Machine Systems, 47*(1), 65–76.

3. Sebastian, T., & Puthiyidam, J. J., (2015). A survey on video summarization techniques. *Int. J. Comput. Appl., 132*(13), 30–32.

4. Murugan, A. S., Devi, K. S., Sivaranjani, A., & Srinivasan, P., (2018). A study on various methods used for video summarization and moving object detection for video surveillance applications. *Multimedia Tools and Applications, 77*(18), 23273–23290.

5. Ajmal, M., Ashraf, M. H., Shakir, M., Abbas, Y., & Shah, F. A., (2012). Video summarization: Techniques and classification. In: *International Conference on Computer Vision and* Graphics (pp. 1–13). Springer, Berlin, Heidelberg.

6. Muhammad, K., Hamza, R., Ahmad, J., Lloret, J., Wang, H., & Baik, S. W., (2018). Secure surveillance framework for IoT systems using probabilistic image encryption. *IEEE Transactions on Industrial Informatics, 14*(8), 3679–3689.

7. Manzanera, A., & Richefeu, J., (2004). A robust and computationally efficient motion detection algorithm based on sigma-delta background estimation. In: *Indian Conference on Computer Vision, Graphics and Image Processing (ICVGIP'04)*.

8. Cedras, C., & Shah, M., (1995). Motion-based recognition a survey. *Image and Vision Computing, 13*(2), 129–155.

9. Datta, R., Joshi, D., Li, J., & Wang, J. Z., (2006). Studying aesthetics in photographic images using a computational approach. In: *European Conference on Computer Vision* (pp. 288–301). Springer, Berlin, Heidelberg.

10. Li, J., Yao, T., Ling, Q., & Mei, T., (2017). Detecting shot boundary with sparse coding for video summarization. *Neurocomputing, 266*, 66–78.

11. Priya, G. L., & Domnic, S., (2014). Shot based keyframe extraction for ecological video indexing and retrieval. *Ecological Informatics, 23*, 107–117.

12. Gianluigi, C., & Raimondo, S., (2006). An innovative algorithm for keyframe extraction in video summarization. *Journal of Real-Time Image Processing, 1*(1), 69–88.

13. Fei, M., Jiang, W., & Mao, W., (2017). Memorable and rich video summarization. *Journal of Visual Communication and Image Representation, 42,* 207–217.

14. Ejaz, N., Tariq, T. B., & Baik, S. W., (2012). Adaptive key frame extraction for video summarization using an aggregation mechanism. *Journal of Visual Communication and Image Representation, 23*(7), 1031–1040.

15. Divakaran, A., Radhakrishnan, R., & Peker, K. A., (2001). Video summarization using descriptors of motion activity: A motion activity based approach to key-frame extraction from video shots. *Journal of Electronic Imaging, 10*(4), 909–917.

16. Borth, D., Ulges, A., Schulze, C., & Breuel, T. M., (2008). *Keyframe Extraction for Video Tagging & Summarization* (pp. 45–48). In: Informatiktage.

17. Ciocca, G., & Schettini, R., (2005). Dynamic key-frame extraction for video summarization. In: *Internet Imaging VI: International Society for Optics and Photonics* (Vol. 5670, pp. 137–142).

18. Li, C., Wu, Y. T., Yu, S. S., & Chen, T., (2009). Motion-focusing key frame extraction and video summarization for lane surveillance system. In*: 2009 16*[th] *IEEE International Conference on Image Processing (ICIP)* (4329–4332). IEEE.

19. Iandola, F. N., Han, S., Moskewicz, M. W., Ashraf, K., Dally, W. J., & Keutzer, K., (2016). *SqueezeNet: AlexNet-Level Accuracy with 50x Fewer Parameters and< 0.5 MB Model Size*. arXiv preprint arXiv:1602.07360.

20. Hochreiter, S., & Schmidhuber, J., (1997). Long short-term memory. *Neural Computation, 9*(8), 1735–1780.

21. Muhammad, K., Hussain, T., Tanveer, M., Sannino, G., & De Albuquerque, V. H. C., (2019). Cost-effective video summarization using deep CNN with hierarchical weighted fusion for IoT surveillance networks. *IEEE Internet of Things Journal, 7*(5), 4455–4463.

22. Lawrence, T., & Zhang, L., (2019). IoTNet: An efficient and accurate convolutional neural network for IoT devices. *Sensors, 19*(24), 5541.

23. Redmon, J., Divvala, S., Girshick, R., & Farhadi, A., (2016). You only look once: Unified, real-time object detection. In: *Proceedings of the IEEE Conference on Computer Vision and Pattern Recognition* (pp. 779–788).

24. Redmon, J., & Farhadi, A., (2018). *Yolov3: An Incremental Improvement*. arXiv preprint arXiv:1804.02767.

25. Akter, S., Sima, R. A., Ullah, M. S., & Hossain, S. A., (2018). Smart security surveillance using IoT. In: *2018 7*[th] *International Conference on Reliability, Infocom Technologies and Optimization (Trends and Future Directions) (ICRITO)* (pp. 659–663). IEEE.

26. Lee, H. R., Lin, C. H., & Kim, W. J., (2016). Development of an IoT-based visitor detection system. In: *2016 International SoC Design Conference (ISOCC)* (pp. 281–282). IEEE.

27. Gowtham, S., Nazeer, A., & Saranya, G., (2017). Surveillance drones imparted with optimized cloud server techniques. In: *2017 International Conference on Innovations in Green Energy and Healthcare Technologies (IGEHT)* (pp. 1–3). IEEE.

28. Ansari, A. N., Sedky, M., Sharma, N., & Tyagi, A., (2015). An Internet of things approach for motion detection using Raspberry Pi. In: *Proceedings of 2015 International Conference on Intelligent Computing and Internet of Things* (pp. 131–134). IEEE.

29. Muhammad, K., Hussain, T., Del, S. J., Palade, V., & De Albuquerque, V. H. C., (2019). DeepReS: A deep learning-based video summarization strategy for resource-constrained

industrial surveillance scenarios. *IEEE Transactions on Industrial Informatics, 16*(9), 5938–5947.

30. Fu, Y., Guo, Y., Zhu, Y., Liu, F., Song, C., & Zhou, Z. H., (2010). Multi-view video summarization. *IEEE Transactions on Multimedia, 12*(7), 717–729.

31. Li, Y., & Merialdo, B., (2010). Multi-video summarization based on video-mmr. In: *11*th *International Workshop on Image Analysis for Multimedia Interactive Services WIAMIS 10* (pp. 1–4). IEEE.

32. Hussain, T., Muhammad, K., Del Ser, J., Baik, S. W., & De Albuquerque, V. H. C., (2019). Intelligent embedded vision for summarization of multi view videos in IIoT. *IEEE Transactions on Industrial Informatics, 16*(4), 2592–2602.

33. Khosla, A., Raju, A. S., Torralba, A., & Oliva, A., (2015). Understanding and predicting image memorability at a large scale. In: *Proceedings of the IEEE International Conference on Computer Vision*, 2390–2398.

34. De Avila, S. E. F., Lopes, A. P. B., Da Luz, Jr. A., & De Albuquerque, A. A., (2011). VSUMM: A mechanism designed to produce static video summaries and a novel evaluation method. *Pattern Recognition Letters, 32*(1), 56–68.

35. Bernardi, R., Cakici, R., Elliott, D., Erdem, A., Erdem, E., Ikizler-Cinbis, N., & Plank, B., (2016). Automatic description generation from images: A survey of models, datasets, and evaluation measures. *Journal of Artificial Intelligence Research, 55*, 409–442.

36. Chaudhari, C. P., & Devane, S., (2019). Captioning the images: A deep analysis. In: *Computing, Communication and Signal Processing* (pp. 987–999). Springer, Singapore.

37. Kulkarni, G., Premraj, V., Ordonez, V., Dhar, S., Li, S., Choi, Y., & Berg, T. L., (2013). Babytalk: Understanding and generating simple image descriptions. *IEEE Transactions on Pattern Analysis and Machine Intelligence, 35*(12), 2891–2903.

38. Chen, B. C., Chen, Y. Y., & Chen, F., (2017). Video to text summary: Joint video summarization and captioning with recurrent neural networks. In: *BMVC*.

39. Hussain, T., Muhammad, K., Ullah, A., Cao, Z., Baik, S. W., & De Albuquerque, V. H. C., (2019). Cloud-assisted multi view video summarization using CNN and bidirectional LSTM. *IEEE Transactions on Industrial Informatics, 16*(1), 77–86.

CHAPTER 14

Blockchain of Things: Benefits and Research Challenges

SANGITA CHAUDHARI, RASHMI DHUMAL, and TABASSUM MAKTUM

Department of Computer Engineering, Ramrao Adik Institute of Technology, Nerul, Maharashtra, India

ABSTRACT

Internet of things (IoT) provides an infrastructure where ubiquitous things are connected to each other in a decentralized fashion. Technologies such as cloud computing, data analytics and ML are an integral part of IoT and plays a major role in information exchange, modeling, and analytics. In recent years, IoT has been used by a variety of applications ranging from wearable smart gadgets to precision agriculture, E-healthcare, smart city, smart industry, etc. IoT has tremendous potential and it has changed the business processes completely in industry 4.0. The primary objective of IoT is to improve the efficiency of operations by reducing the downtime of ubiquitous devices. However, it results in some challenges including interoperability issues, heterogeneity of devices, network complexity, resource constraints, privacy, and security of devices and information. Physical security of the devices as well as security and privacy of information cannot be achieved using traditional cryptographic techniques alone. Even though cloud services are an integral part of IoT, these services fail to provide the expected trust, integrity, and availability of data. These services are not robust enough against data leakage and sometimes vulnerable to server failure. The adoption of the blockchain technologies has the potential to beat the security challenges posed in IoT infrastructure.

Blockchain is the recent disruptive technology, which is based on tamper resistant distributed ledger spreading over distributed systems ensuring privacy, scalability, and reliability. It allows recording and transmission of events in trust-based distributed peer to peer (P2P) network. In IoT, blockchain can be utilized for recording the events (change in location, temperature, moisture, water level, etc.), and creating immutable ledger readable by authorized IoT components only. Various important characteristics of blockchain are immutability, decentralization, transparency, anonymity, traceability, and non-repudiation. Combination of blockchain and IoT will not only overcome the challenges of IoT but also provide a seamless and autonomous computing environment by providing reliability, interoperability, and traceability. This convergence of blockchain and IoT is retitled as blockchain of things (BCoT). Although the benefits of BCoT are multifold, there are few challenges as well which need to be addressed to fully utilize the strength of blockchain and IoT in BCoT.

14.1 INTRODUCTION

In recent years, we have witnessed tremendous growth in IoT applications ranging from military applications to smart homes. "IoT is a ubiquitous and intelligent network connecting various physical objects, called Things," and people over communication networks. In today's era, almost everything can be connected to the Internet making IoT as IoE. It facilitates the service to connect, transmit, and translate data sensed by ubiquitous devices into voluminous information repositories. IoT ecosystem is making use of many modern tools and techniques in the field of networking, information modeling and analytics to handle these repositories efficiently. The incredible development in the field of IoT is causing growth and opportunities in industry and business arenas.

With an ever-expanding visibility of IoT in enormous applications over the Internet triggered the concern of privacy and security. Even though lots of innovations are happening in sensors and ubiquitous devices, damage of individuals and property can happen due to lack of security measures in these smart systems. Centralized servers used to store the sensed and processed data are likely to be on the radar of the attacker and may lead to a breach of privacy. The challenges faced by IoT industry are security, privacy, and interoperability of the connected devices [1].

Currently, blockchain technology is seen as sufficiently matured technology providing promising solutions to achieve the laid security goals for a variety of applications including IoT. Blockchain is referred to as secure by design system that relieves the risk associated with security while satisfying the properties like immutability, transparency, auditability, persistence, and encryption.

Blockchain and IoT both can complement each other to provide benefits of both the technologies while suppressing each other's limitations. This convergence is named as blockchain of things (BCoT). It provides an autonomous and seamless environment with enhanced interoperability, improved security, reliability, and traceability. The proposed architecture of BCoT presents blockchain composite layer in the existing IoT layered architecture and serves as middleware or blockchain as a service to the end applications of IoT systems.

This chapter gives an insight of state of the art for Blockchain and IoT. The chapter addresses research challenges, issues, and the concept of convergence of blockchain and IoT as BCoT. It also discusses the architecture, deployment, benefits, and challenges of BCoT. Section 14.2 presents an overview of blockchain technology. Section 14.3 gives a complete insight into IoT and associated security challenges. The convergence of IoT and Blockchain as BCoT is proposed in Section 14.4. It also highlights the benefits and research challenges of BCoT. Finally, the chapter is concluded in Section 14.5.

14.2 BLOCKCHAIN

Blockchain is the disruptive technology providing a seamless and autonomous environment for sharing and maintaining business ledgers in digitized form among various parties involved in the application. It is defined as "Blockchain is a decentralized computation and information sharing platform which enables multiple authoritative domains who do not trust each other to cooperate, coordinate, and collaborate in a rational decision-making process" [2]. It is thought of as a decentralized database facilitating cooperating environment between multiple authoritative domains. Blockchain network consist of various nodes over peer-to-peer network. Each node maintains a local copy of the global data sheet in blockchain network. It is the responsibility of the system to ensure that all these individual copies are in a consistent state. This individual/local information is called a public ledger and it can be utilized for future computation. Whenever blockchain is utilized as a public ledger, different aspects like protocol of commitment, consistency maintenance, integrity, privacy, and authenticity need to be ensured.

14.2.1 CHARACTERISTICS OF BLOCKCHAIN

Blockchain is characterized by various characteristics [3, 4]. Some of the common characteristics are:

1. **Decentralization:** This is one of the important characteristics of blockchain making it as a popular component in various applications. Central trusted agency performs validation of every transaction in centralized transaction systems resulting in the cost and the performance bottlenecks at the central servers. In blockchain, a transaction can be completed by participation of peer-to-peer nodes without intervention of central authority for completing the authentication process. Each node stores a local copy of the transaction and no one can modify it. This feature also enables transparency and security.

2. **Persistency:** In blockchain, a transaction is spread across the network instead of lying at a single node making it highly impossible to tamper the contents. Also, every broadcasted block is validated by other nodes, recorded, and checked. Therefore, it would be easy to detect falsification if any in the transaction.

3. **Anonymity:** Over the blockchain network, each user is identified by a specific address. In the course of time, the user can generate multiple such addresses to avoid identity reveal. Users' private information will not be made available to any of the other parties. It will help to preserve the privacy of the transactions which are part of the blockchain. However, due to some intrinsic constraints, perfect privacy is not always guaranteed.

4. **Auditability:** On blockchain, every transaction is validated and recorded with a timestamp. It became easy to verify and trace the previous records by accessing any node in this distributed network. It is possible to trace the transactions iteratively which enhances transparency and traceability of user data stored on the blockchain.

5. **Immutability:** In public blockchain, transactions are stored on different nodes over distributed blockchain network making it impossible to tamper blockchain. However, if maximum members of the consortium or dominant organization aims to manipulate the blockchain, then the private and consortium blockchain could be overturned and tampered.

6. **Smart Contract:** It is one of the fascinating aspects of blockchain. "Smart contracts are digital contracts allowing terms contingent on decentralized consensus that are self-enforcing and tamper-proof through automated execution" [5]. It normally releases digital assets to involved parties once some predefined condition is met. It does not rely on trusted third parties for its operation and thus results in

low transaction costs. It is tamper proof and does not allow any unauthorized changes to be done in its internal logic once it is deployed in blockchain.

14.2.2 WORKING OF BLOCKCHAIN

The blockchain can be thought of as a digital copy of a conventional public ledger holding sequence of blocks. Basic building blocks and its structure are illustrated in Figure 14.1. Every block point to its immediate previous neighbor using a reference. This reference is the hash value of the previous block (Parent Block). The sibling block hashes are also stored on the blockchain in case of Ethereum. In the blockchain, the first block is referred as a genesis block.

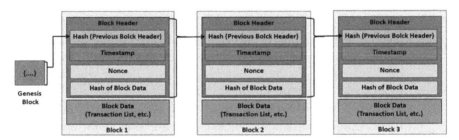

FIGURE 14.1 Blockchain as sequences of blocks.

Each block contains two parts: block header and block body. The block header includes (1) Block version which indicates the validation rules followed by blockchain; (2) Parent block hash denoted by a 256-bit hash value pointing to the previous block; (3) Merkle tree root hash which indicate the hash value of all the transactions in the block; (4) Current timestamp; (5) Compact representation of number of bits used in representation of current hashing target; (6) 4-byte nonce (starting with 0 and increasing for every hash calculation.

The body of the block comprises transaction counter and transaction. Depending on the size of the block and the size of each transaction, the number of transactions can be accommodated in the block. Transactions can be authenticated using asymmetric cryptography along with digital signature in an untrusted environment [3].

14.2.3 BLOCKCHAIN TYPES

Blockchain can be classified based on the permission granted to create and publish the block in a chain of blocks. If the permission to publish a new block is given to anyone, it is referred to as permissionless. However, if only specific user publishes blocks, then it is called a permissioned blockchain. Permissioned blockchain are generally used by an individual, or group of people commonly known as consortium [6, 7]:

1. **Permissionless:** It is a decentralized ledger platform open to all to publish the blocks and does not require permission to be taken from any of the authorities. These are often open-source and can be easily downloaded and used by anyone who wishes to use blockchain. This property gives freedom to users (miners) to read, write, and submit the transaction to the ledger. It is also known as public blockchains. Since it is open to all users, sometimes malicious users may try to publish blocks. To overcome this problem, permissionless blockchain utilizes multiparty agreements (consensus) that need users to pay or maintain required resources while publishing a block. Any participant can join the consensus process to decide whether to add blocks and transactions to the ledger. Consensus models like proof of work (PoW) and proof of stake (PoS) are used in permissionless blockchain. Permissionless blockchains are suitable for open ended and decentralized applications. Bitcoin is a well-known example of a public blockchain.

2. **Permissioned:** In the permissioned blockchain, the users who are publishing blocks need to be authorized by some authority. The authority may be centralized or decentralized. Read and write access are restricted and hence it is also referred to as private blockchain. In permissioned blockchain, any of the users may allow to read the blockchain or read access is restricted to authorized users only. Similarly, anyone can submit transactions, or it may restrict submission only to authorized entities. Permissioned blockchain may be implemented using open source as well as proprietary software. Permissioned blockchain can also use consensus models for publishing blocks like permissionless blockchain, but it does not require the expenses or maintenance of the used resources. Consensus models in permissioned blockchain are faster and computationally less expensive than permissionless blockchain. Private blockchains are centralized systems and mostly suitable for applications which

require high trust and privacy. In this type of blockchain, consensus is decided by selective trusted nodes.

3. **Consortium:** It is semi-private blockchain which makes use of consensus process to be initiated by a selected group of participants that are trusted by the system. Although it does not require verification of transaction by each user reducing time, it makes the systems partially centralized to selected nodes. A group of organizations are assigning the permission to a node to become part of consortium. Table 14.1 shows the comparison of different types of blockchain using various perspectives like user's involvement in consensus process, read permission, possibility of tampering, transaction throughput, latency, and consensus process.

TABLE 14.1   Comparison of Different Types of Blockchain

Property	Public Blockchain	Consortium Blockchain	Private Blockchain
Node participation	All	Selected nodes	Individuals
Read authorization	Public	Public/restricted	Public/restricted
Immutability	Yes	No	No
Efficiency	Low	High	High
Centralized	No	Partial	Yes
Consensus process	Permissionless	Permissioned	Permissioned

14.2.4   CONSENSUS IN BLOCKCHAIN

In blockchain, it is especially important to decide which user will publish the next block in blockchain. This decision is taken by making use of consensus model from a plethora of such models. In a permissionless blockchain, at a time many nodes are competing for publishing a block. They usually do this to win the reward in terms of cryptocurrency and/or transaction fees. These nodes are known to each other only by their public addresses. Every publishing node is influenced by the desire for the reward. Here, each node is motivated by financial gain and in such a situation, why will they help other users who are attempting to publish? Moreover, if multiple such modes are trying to publish at the same time, who, and how the conflict will be resolved? Therefore, to make such decisions in blockchain technology, consensus models are used to allow a group of distrustful users to work together. On joining a blockchain network, every user needs to agree to the initial state of the system recorded in genesis block [8]. Every new block needs to be added after the genesis block based on the consensus model. It is assumed that each block is valid, and it must be validated independently by every user in the blockchain irrespective of the model used. Consensus model works on these assumptions: (1) genesis block; (2) consensus model selection; (3) previous block header hash digest linked with next block; (4) block verification independence. There are many consensus models available in blockchain technology. Some of the commonly used consensus models are discussed in this section:

1. **Proof of Work (PoW) Consensus Model:** In this consensus model, a user publishes the next block by being the first to solve a computationally intensive puzzle. The solution to this puzzle is the "proof" that they have performed work. The puzzle is designed in such a way that solving the puzzle is difficult process but checking whether the solution is valid is easy. All other nodes can easily validate proposed new blocks, and if the block could not satisfy the puzzle, it would be rejected. This puzzle-solving requires significant computation resource consumption. Due to the significant resource consumption of some PoW blockchain networks, there is a mechanism to add publishing nodes to the areas where there is a surplus supply of cheap electricity. The puzzles are independent and do not influence one's chances of solving the current or future puzzles.

   Whenever a publishing node completes the work, they send their block with a valid nonce to full nodes in the blockchain network. The node which is capable to validate and create new blocks is referred to as full node. This node will verify whether the new block is fulfilling the puzzle requirements or not. If yes, then the block is added to their copy of the blockchain and the block is resent to their peer nodes. Verification of the nonce is easy process since only a single hash needs to be checked to see if it solves the puzzle [3, 9].

2. **Proof of Stake (PoS) Consensus Model:** This model is based on the idea that the more stake a user has invested into the system, the more likely they want the system to succeed, and the less likely they want to subvert it. Stake is generally a bunch of cryptocurrencies that the blockchain user has invested into the system may be by locking transactions via special transaction type, sending it to a specific address or keeping it on hold in some wallet. The cryptocurrency cannot be spent once it is staked. Each user's amount of stake is used as a determining factor for publishing new blocks.

Unlike PoW, there is no need to perform resource intensive computations in this consensus process. Since this consensus model utilizes fewer resources, some blockchain networks have decided to relinquish a block creation reward. In this system, instead of generating new cryptocurrency at constant intervals, existing cryptocurrency is distributed among users. In such systems, the reward for block publication is usually the earning of user provided transaction fees [10].

3. **Round Robin Consensus Model:** Round Robin is the conventional consensus model commonly used by some of the permissioned blockchain networks. As the name suggests, every node gets a chance to create a block turn by turn. If a publishing node is not available to publish the block, the system may pass it to the next publishing node if the predefined time limit is over. This model ensures not a single node creates most of the blocks. This consensus algorithm is simple and does not require any cryptographic puzzles. The power requirement is also very less. This model is suitable only for trusted environments and hence cannot be used for permissionless blockchain networks [11].

4. **Proof of Authority/Proof of Identity Consensus Model:** Partial trust of publishing nodes through their known link to real world identities is utilized in this model. The identities of the publishing nodes need to be proven and verified within the blockchain. In this consensus, the identity/reputation of the publishing node is on stake for publishing a new block. Publishing nodes can lose reputation by acting in a way that the blockchain users disagree with, just as they can gain reputation by acting in a manner that the blockchain users agree with. The nodes try to maintain a high reputation to be able to publish the block; the chance of being able to publish a block lower down if the reputation is less. This consensus is only used in trusted environments for permissioned blockchain networks.

5. **Proof of Elapsed Time (PoET) Consensus Model:** In this model, each publishing node requests a wait time from a secure hardware time source within their computer system. A random wait time is generated and passed to the publishing node software and the publishing node becomes idle for that random time duration. On wake up, the publishing node creates and publishes a block over a blockchain and any other publishing node which is still in idle state stops waiting and the entire process is started again. The

correctness of this consensus model is only achieved if the environment is trusted. For untrusted environments, digital certificates can be employed with consensus algorithms for achieving correctness and security [12].

There are plenty of consensus algorithms used in the blockchain network [13]. Table 14.2 shows the comparison of such widely used consensus protocols in a variety of blockchain environments and applications.

14.2.5   BLOCKCHAIN PLATFORMS

Over the decade, blockchain has had a significant impact on various businesses and industries. Many Businesses are keenly interested to integrate blockchain into their existing infrastructure and witnessed a rise in their revenue model. Such blockchain based applications can be easily developed using blockchain platforms. These platforms are either permissioned or permissionless. There are plenty of blockchain platforms available and can be selected for application development based on the underlying requirements of the application. Table 14.3 summarizes most of the commonly used blockchain platforms in Business and industry applications [22, 23].

14.2.6   CHALLENGES IN BLOCKCHAIN

As an emerging technology, blockchain is facing multiple challenges and problems [3]. Some of the important challenges are:

1. **Scalability:** The blockchain is becoming heavy as daily many transactions are getting added into it, and for validation of transactions, all transactions need to be stored. Moreover, due to block size and time interval restriction for new block generation, transaction processing speed cannot be increased. If the size of blocks is small, then many such transactions may possibly be delayed as miners will not prefer them as resulting in less transaction fees. Larger the block size, the lesser the propagation speed, more the chances of breaches.
2. **Privacy Leakage:** Although blockchain claims to achieve user privacy using public addresses instead of real identities, it does not guarantee the transactional privacy as the values of transaction and public key information are visible publicly.

TABLE 14.2 Consensus Algorithms

	Blockchain Type	Transaction Finality	Transaction Rate	Token Needed	Cost of Participation	Scalability of Peer Network	Trust Model
PoW	Permissionless	Probabilistic	Low	Yes	Yes	High	Untrusted
PoS	Both	Probabilistic	High	Yes	Yes	High	Untrusted
PoET	Both	Probabilistic	Medium	No	No	High	Untrusted
BFT and Variants [14]	Permissioned	Immediate	High	No	No	Low	Semi-trusted
Federated BFT	Permissionless	Immediate	High	No	No	High	Semi-trusted
Round robin	Permissioned	Deterministic	Low	Yes	Yes	High	Trusted
longest chain [15]	Permissioned	Probabilistic	Medium	Yes	Yes	Medium	Untrusted
GHOST [16]	Permissioned	Probabilistic	Medium	Yes	Yes	High	Trusted
TANGLE [17]	Permissionless	Probabilistic	Low	No	No	Medium	Untrusted
Tendermint [18]	Permissionless	Deterministic	High	Yes	Yes	Medium	Semi-trusted
SCP [19]	Permissionless	Deterministic	High	Yes	Yes	High	Trusted
Ripple [20]	Permissioned	Deterministic	Low	Yes	Yes	High	Trusted
Algorand [21]	Permissionless	Deterministic	High	Yes	Yes	High	Trusted

TABLE 14.3   Blockchain Platforms

Blockchain Platforms	Features	Consensus Algorithm	Ledger Type	Smart Contact Functionality	Governance
Ethereum	Decentralized platform characterized by EVM	Proof of work	Permissionless	Yes	Ethereum developers
Hyperledger fabric	Open source blockchain platform designed to build modular blockchain applications	Pluggable framework	Permissioned	Yes	Linux foundation
Hyperledger IROHA	Simple and modular distributed architecture used for developing trusted, fast, and secure applications	Chain-based byzantine Fault-tolerant	Permissioned	Yes	Linux foundation
Hyperledger SAWTOOTH	Modular and enterprise-grade platform used for creating, executing, and deploying distributed ledgers	Pluggable framework	Permissionless	Yes	Linux foundation
OpenChain	Open source blockchain platform designed to handle digital assets	Partitioned consensus	Permissioned	Yes	Linux foundation
STELLAR	Distributed ledger network used for cross-platform asset transfer	Stellar consensus protocol	Permissioned as well as permissionless	Yes	Stellar development foundation
NEO	Open source decentralized blockchain used to issue and manage digitized assets.	Delegated Byzantine fault tolerance	Permissioned	Yes	NEO foundation support
EOS	Secure and highly scalable open-source distributed platform	Delegated proof of stake	Permissioned	Yes	EOSIO core arbitration forum
Hedera hashgraph	Trusted and highly secured platform used to build applications for digital currencies and online payments	Asynchronous Byzantine fault tolerance	Permissioned	Yes	Hedera hashgraph council

TABLE 14.3 *(Continued)*

Blockchain Platforms	Features	Consensus Algorithm	Ledger Type	Smart Contact Functionality	Governance
R3 Corda	Innovative and cost-effective platform utilized in applications like healthcare, supply chain, government authorities, and trade finance, etc.	Asynchronous Byzantine fault tolerance	Permissioned	Yes	Hedera hashgraph council
BigchainDB	Open-source distributed storage system which combines NoSQL and blockchain technology used in applications dealing with identity, financial assets, intellectual property	Federation of nodes with voting permissions	Both permissioned and permissionless	Yes	Big chain DB GmbH

3. **Selfish Mining:** In blockchain, nodes over 51% computing power could eventually have the potential to reverse the blockchain. But recent studies showed that even with less than 51% power can still be dangerous. Blockchain networks can be made vulnerable by cheating using a small amount of hashing power. In this mining, selfish miners keep their mined block with them only on private blockchain instead of broadcasting. As this private branch is longer than the current public chain, all miners will add blocks in it. Trustworthy miners are wasting their resources by mining for this branch, whereas selfish miners are mining without competitors and get more rewards. Many of the rational miners get attracted towards selfish miner's pool and it exceeds 51% making the blockchain unsecure.

14.3 INTERNET OF THINGS (IoT)

With the initiation of the industrial revolution from the 18th century in productions by replacing manual productions to mechanical productions, till the 20th century automated productions with the development of IT and electronics increased productivity with less human intervention. In recent years, due to the merging of information and communication technologies (ICT) incorporated with big data analytics (BDA) and IoT and have made intelligent productions. The "internet of things (IoT)" is the inter-connection of things. In 1999, Ashton [24] invented IoT in the supply chain management; but it is covering many applications domains like mobile, healthcare, personal, home, industries, utilities, enterprise, etc., in recent years as presented by Gubbi [25]. The IoT, in short, IoT is devised from two words namely *Internet* and *Things* according to Ref. [26]. A universal system of interconnected computer networks that uses TCP/IP protocol for communicating worldwide among billions of users is known as the Internet. It is a network of networks, connected by various communication technologies and a carrier of enormous information. According to the international telecommunication units (ITU), more than 50% of the world's population is using the Internet. The numbers of users have increased exponentially compared to users in 2005. Things can be any distinguishable object in the physical world. It can be a living or non-living thing. The living things can be person, animal, or plant whereas non-living things can be any home appliance or industry apparatus. With the evolving technology, the definition of things has changed; but the main goal is to sense our surroundings through objects which communicate and act without human intervention remains the same. The key idea behind IoT is to connect anything (person, plant, sensors, machines, etc.), embedded with software through the Internet which can be remotely monitored and controlled without human intervention.

The simplified definition of IoT is an integration of three main components: things (sensors and/or actuators), software (to process data) and the Internet (to connect everything together). In IoT, "Things" should have a unique identifier to distinguish it over the Internet and should be able to sense the environment to collect primitive parameters for evaluation and perform action accordingly. So, the requirements of "Things" in IoT are recognizing, addressing, and actuating capabilities in the same device. The data gathered by "Things" in IoT is analyzed through the software and delivered correct information to the correct entity at the accurate time and place using processes. The Internet is used to connect all the things together and carry information among them. Things with the unique identification has an ability to communicate with others and sense information from the environment allow us to observe and regulate things from any place in the real world. IoT enables to monitor anything from anywhere through the Internet gives a vast service and commercial opportunities to enhance the financial impact for businesses, governments, industries, hospitals, consumers, and many more entities.

IoT enables the machines to talk to each other and thus supports machine to machine (M2M) communication. The devices remain connected and can communicate transparently. This machine-to-machine communication facilitates automation in work and machines can work without any human intervention and with high speed. As IoT devices are interconnected and they can converse with each other, a huge amount of data is collected. This data will be always helpful in the decision-making process which can range from simple decisions related to the amount of grocery in house to any critical business-related decisions. Also, the collected information can be helpful for monitoring purposes. Finally, the collected information and timely monitoring will help to save time required for performing any task. The time and efforts will be minimized because the devices interact with each other and perform much functionality by themselves without any intervention. The devices can be regularly under surveillance and hence any damage or failure can be immediately handled. The utilization of energy and resources will be less and thus help in reducing the cost. With the IoT anything can be linked to anyone at any time from any place through the internet. This property of IoT has tremendous potential in many applications which makes human life easy, smart, and safe. There are many applications of IoT in various domains like agriculture, energy, finance, industrial, transportation, healthcare, and retail.

14.3.1 CHARACTERISTICS OF IoT

Due to the interdisciplinary nature of IoT, it has various characteristics which vary from domain to domain. The characteristics of IoT are based on the features of connected devices and the communication network used to connect them with each other. The devices used in IoT are smart, compact, programed to automatically on/off, consume less power and easy to use [27]. The key characteristics of IoT are as follows:

1. **Interconnectivity:** Anything can relate to anyone to sense the environment, transfer the gathered information to analyze it and make intelligent decisions through ICT. In IoT, things connected through the Internet can be monitored and controlled from anywhere in the world.

2. **Intelligence:** IoT devices are smart with inherent intelligence as they constitute software, algorithm, and computations. This enables things in IoT to respond to the situation in an intelligent way to perform a specific task.

3. **Dynamic Behavior:** The devices sense the environment which changes dynamically. This leads to dynamic behavior of the devices, as they wake up or sleep, connect or disconnect and based on the context of the device. Also, the numbers of devices are changed dynamically with place and time.

4. **Heterogeneous:** The IoT devices are heterogeneous as they are based on various hardware platforms and can communicate with other devices via diverse communication networks. IoT architecture supports heterogeneity by providing direct connection between heterogeneous networks. This leads to stringent design requirements for scalability, interoperability, and modularity.

5. **Enormous Scale:** There will be noticeable increase in the number of devices that are connected to the current Internet in future, this leads to the huge communication among them which results in generation of tremendous amount of data and its interpretation for applications becomes a great challenge.

14.3.2 IoT ARCHITECTURE

IoT is a technology that builds a system which is independently capable of sensing the environmental changes and act accordingly without human intervention. There is no standard IoT architecture, various architectures of IoT are defined by many researchers, but every architecture [28] comprises the following four layers as shown in Figure 14.2.

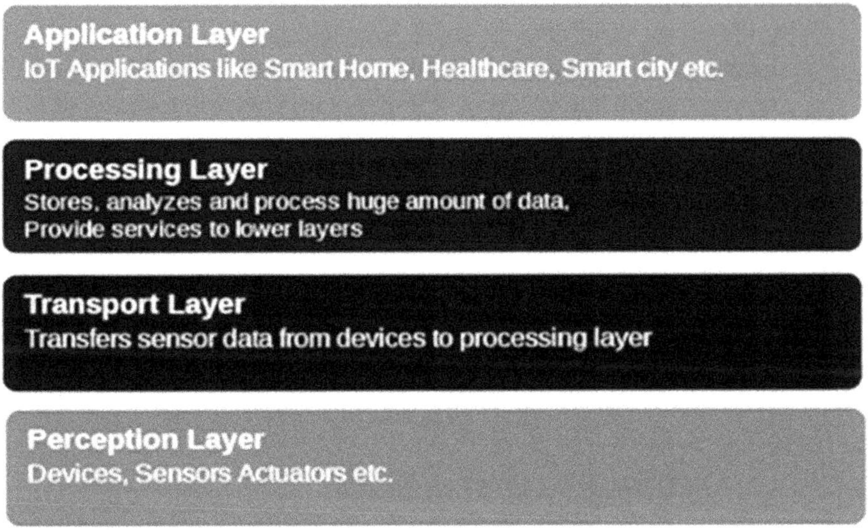

FIGURE 14.2 IoT architecture.

1. **Perception Layer:** The physical layer in IoT is the perception layer which has devices, sensors, and actuators. Sensors sense the environment and gather information about physical parameters in it. A sensor is an electronic device that perceives changes in the surrounding environment like pressure, sound, flow, temperature, motion, etc., and generates corresponding signal/action. Sensors take analog input and produce digital output in the form of electrical signals using an analog-to-digital converter. There are various types of sensors like air pollution, temperature, level, pressure, flow, noise, and speed sensors. An actuator is responsible to perform action based on received data. The data collected and transferred by sensors is useless until it is not converted into intelligence to take corrective action before it makes an impact on the surroundings. For example, generate an alarm if boiler temperature crosses the threshold value or shut the nob down when the tank is filled with fuel. Some of the types of actuators are electrical, mechanical, hydraulic, and manual.

2. **Transport Layer:** The transport layer is responsible for transmission of sensed data from the perception layer to the processing layer and vice versa. The data is transferred using different networks such as Bluetooth, 3G, RFID, wireless, LAN, and NFC.

3. **Processing Layer:** The processing layer plays the role of the middleware. The data received from the transport layer is stored, investigated, and processed at this layer. It also provides a bunch of services to the below layers. It engages various technologies such as cloud computing, databases, and big data modules for analysis.

4. **Application Layer:** The application layer delivers application-oriented services to the user. This layer constitutes various applications where IoT technology can be deployed, for example, smart health where patient's, heartbeat, blood pressure (BP), etc., are monitored remotely by doctor and medicines are suggested accordingly; smart homes where lights switched ON or OFF based on whether someone enters or leaves the room, etc.

14.3.3 IoT PROTOCOLS AND STANDARDS

The IoT is termed as a large grid of associated devices that enables these devices to collect, to process and to transfer data to other devices. To process or send data, IoT devices need to be connected through some communication network, and they must be able to talk to each other. The different IoT protocols and standards help the IoT devices to share data in the proper way. The IoT protocols have specific demand in terms of range, bandwidth, power consumption, etc., hence the existing protocols cannot be utilized for IoT systems. Therefore, some specialized IoT protocols have been evolved, and few existing standards are also used in IoT systems. The data protocols enable communication between low power IoT devices through some wired or cellular network:

1. **Message Queue Telemetry Transport (MQTT):** It is the simple, trivial communication protocol, which operates on the top of the TCP/IP suite. It is used to send data from different sensors to applications. It functions based on publish/subscribe policy [29]. The three major components of this protocol include publisher, subscriber, and broker. The protocol provides acknowledgement for all formats and hence it is more reliable. In the IoT environment, the publishers are the lightweight sensors, the subscribers are the applications and

brokers play the role of mediator. The publishers create the data and pass it to subscribers through the broker. The broker is responsible for ensuring the security by authorizing the publishers and subscribers properly. The protocol is more suitable for small and cheap devices that require low memory, low power. It can operate with low or vulnerable bandwidth as discussed in Ref. [30].

2. **Constrained Application Protocol (CoAP):** It was designed by IETF Constrained RESTful Environment working group in 2013 [31]. The main intention behind the development of COAP is, to use this protocol in restrictive devices and network environments. It is basically designed to translate HTTP models to a lightweight RESTful interface that requires low overhead, low complexity. It operates over the UDP protocol instead of TCP. It supports multicast and broadcast communication with the necessary speed but maintains low bandwidth usage [31].

3. **Advanced Message Queuing Protocol (AMQP):** It is the protocol at the application layer and it is message-oriented, which is approved by International standard OASIS [32]. It is mainly designed for the middleware environment and is used by different financial or banking industries. This protocol operates over the top of TCP. It also follows publish and subscribe policy. Like MQTT protocol, this protocol comprises three architectural constituents, i.e., publisher, subscriber, and broker. But the broker component is different from the MQTT protocol. The broker is a combination of two components: exchange, and queue. It works according to store and forward architecture. The publishers send the messages to exchange component, which in turn stores them into respective queues, according to the topic of the message. The subscriber can access the data from the queue whenever required [33]. The protocol is suitable for heterogeneous environments as it can support many different applications and platforms [34]. The protocol makes use of TLS protocol and SASL for providing security of data and for authentication respectively [35]. The major disadvantage of this protocol is that it needs large memory and high processing power [35].

4. **Extensible Messaging and Presence Protocol (XMPP):** It is a message-oriented communication protocol for IoT environment developed by IETF standard [31]. The protocol is based on XML standard and basically used for interchange of structured and extensible messages in real-time [31]. The protocol is used for a variety

of applications such as multi-party chat, voice calls, instant message exchange, video calls, presence, etc. [36]. This protocol operates over TCP and supports the traditional client-server model. The most important characteristics of this protocol is the ability to recognize any device on the network. Hence it is widely used in the environment where presence-based solutions are needed [37]. The limitations of protocol include no support for end-to-end encryption mechanism, large overhead due to XML data, no guarantee for quality of service (QoS), absence of binary encoding, etc. [35]. Hence XMPP is not completely suitable for a device constrained environment like IoT. But later in literature many improvements are presented to make XMPP suitable for IoT [38–41]. The lightweight specification of XMPP, i.e., XMPP-IoT is developed to apply it in IoT environment. The major aim of XMPP-IoT is to support communication between two machines [41].

5. **Data Distribution Service (DSD):** This protocol is another communication protocol based on publish and subscribe policy. The protocol delivers excellent QoS. The data centric sub-layer handles the delivery of messages to the subscriber. Another sub-layer, i.e., data local is responsible for integrating DDS into the application layer [36]. The data is distributed to the subscribers by the publishers. The subscribers receive data and then deliver to different IoT applications.

14.3.4 IoT SECURITY

Security is an important concern in IoT that introduces a new online privacy concern for consumer's personal data. The IoT devices sense the environment and collect a huge amount of data which includes personal information like name, phone number, etc., along with the user activities. An attacker can acquire knowledge about consumer's life by snooping on the collected data received from IoT home appliances, wearable gadgets, etc. Despite of various benefits of IoT, it has major security and privacy challenges which include multiple technologies and applications, scalability, resource availability, Big Data, mobility, and delay-sensitive service [27]. To address these security challenges in IoT, it is necessary to fulfill the security requirements, which includes confidentiality of data transferred, integrity of data, authentication, authorization, non-repudiation, forward, and backward secrecy. The confidentiality is the among the most critical challenges for IoT environment as the data collected by IoT devices must be securely transmitted to prevent any unauthorized usage. The data collected by IoT devices is used for any certain type of analysis or for making any decision. Hence it is very much essential to maintain integrity of data and assure no data alteration by any malicious entity in the environment. The majority of IoT applications are processing real-time data so availability is also a crucial requirement for proper functioning of the system. The proper access control mechanism should be employed in IoT ecosystem to protect against different malicious attacks. Also, appropriate authentication or authorization mechanisms must be developed to validate the connected device's identity in the network. Table 14.4 represents some solutions present in literature to address some basic security requirements for the IoT environment.

The issues related to confidentiality can be handled by applying different Symmetric or Asymmetric encryption algorithms. The different solutions to ensure privacy in IoT environment are proposed in [42–46]. These solutions apply elliptical curve cryptography, AES-GCM cipher, combination of symmetric and asymmetric ciphers, attribute-based encryption techniques, etc. Along with confidentiality, it is equally significant to preserve the integrity of data in the IoT ecosystem. Different frameworks that apply lightweight cryptographic hash functions, Proof of Trust (PoT), blockchain-based secure firmware update, PUSH based approach to verify integrity, etc., are proposed in literature [44, 47–53]. There exist some solutions in literature to address the authorization issues, authentication concerns and access control [45, 49, 51, 65]. The smart contract-based solution to address the issue related to availability is presented in Ref. [54].

The IoT architecture is divided into four layers: Perception, Transport, Processing, and Application layer. So, it is essential to discourse issues related to security at various layers. The security of perception layer in IoT architecture is relevant with the security concerns at the lower layers of the TCP protocol stack [55, 56]. In IoT, the primary task is a data collection, hence the forging of data collected and destruction of IoT devices is the main security challenge at this layer that are addressed next in this section.

The major attacks at the perception layer are: jamming attack, insecure initialization, malicious code injection attack, low level Sybil and spoofing attack, Insecure physical interface, node capture attack, sleep deprivation attack, etc. The jamming attack can be easily launched on the wireless networks which are built upon shared medium. Jamming attacks affect working of wireless networks by radiating radio frequency signals, which are not pursued by MAC protocol on wireless IoT devices. This mainly influences network functioning and transfer of data between legitimate nodes.

TABLE 14.4 Solutions for IoT Security Issues

Paper and Solution	Confidentiality	Authentication/ Id-Management	Integrity	Availability
Wilkinson et al. [42]	AES-GCM cipher, mixture of Poly 305 and Salsa20	—	—	—
Axon and Michael [65]	Blockchain PKI with privacy awareness	—	—	—
Guan et al. [57]	Bloom filter and pseudonym	—	—	—
Emanuel et al. [43]	Variant of selfish miner: stalker miner	—	—	—
Gong et al. [47]	Lightweight cryptographic algorithms	—	Lightweight hash functions	—
Dorri et al. [44]	Combination of symmetric and asymmetric cryptography	Shared keys within policy header	Lightweight cryptographic hash	—
Roy et al. [49]	—	—	Proof of trust	—
Rahulamathavan et al. [45]	Attribute-based encryption	—	—	—
Hammi et al. [50]	—	—	ECC digital signature	—
Liu et al. [51]	—	—	Trustworthy authentication	—
Kiyomoto et al. [58]	—	Privacy-preserving authorization	—	—
Zhang et al. [54]	—	—	—	Smart contract-based access control
Dorri et al. [44]	Encryption and overlay structure-based blockchain architecture	Hash in transaction	—	—
Lee and Lee [52]	—	—	Secure firmware update based on blockchain	—

TABLE 14.4 *(Continued)*

Paper and Solution	Confidentiality	Authentication/ Id-Management	Integrity	Availability
Kostal et al. [53]	—	Digital signature	—	—
Yohan et al. [59]	—	—	PUSH based approach for integrity of distributed firmware	—
Boudguiga et al. [60]	—	—	—	Blockchain solution for updates availability
Dhakal et al. [61]	—	—	Private blockchain-based integrity verification	—
Jung and Agulto [46]	Blockchain-based integrated network function management	—	—	—
Hernández-Ramos et al. [62]	Elliptic curve cryptography optimizations	Capability based access control mechanism	—	—

Another attack is insecure initialization at the physical layer. The initialization and configuration of IoT using secure mechanisms ensures smooth functioning of the whole system without disrupting network services. The secure mechanism for communication at the physical layer, protect it from access to unauthorized nodes. In low level Sybil and spoofing attack, a malicious Sybil node uses many fake identities to exhaust the system resources and disturbs the IoT functionality. At the physical layer, Sybil nodes may use random fake MAC values for concealing as a different device. This may lead to access denied to real IoT devices. The functioning of IoT devices can also be threatened due to poor physical security, physical interfaces used to access software and testing tools used. Another attack at this layer is sleep deprivation attack, where a fake node militaries real node to drop their energy. IoT devices have low power capacity. To save the battery, the devices are programmed with sleep routine. In IoT, sleep deprivation attack causes sensor nodes to stay awake till their battery gets discharged. In a node capture attack, an attacker may tamper the IoT device, replace it or take control over it. If an attacker captures a node, then the sensitive information may be exposed to the attacker. Along with the node capture attack, an attacker can inject malicious code in the memory of an IoT device which is called a malicious code injection attack. The malicious code that is injected by the attacker performs specific function and gain control over IoT system. The false data detection attack at the perception layer affects the effectiveness of an IoT system, an attacker can replace normal data with dummy/fake data which causes the IoT system to send erroneous responses. In cryptanalysis attacks and side-channel attacks, an attacker can use some techniques to obtain encryption keys from IoT devices by either applying a side-channel attack or timing attack in which encryption keys are obtained based on the time required to execute the encryption algorithm. In eavesdropping and interference attack at the physical layer, IoT devices are majorly communicating over wireless networks. The information transferred over wireless networks can be eavesdropped by an attacker.

The next layer of IoT architecture is a transport layer used to transfer data to processing layers where data is stored, analyzed, and processed [55, 56]. The security at these two layers mainly concerned with availability of network resources, communication, and routing at network and transport layer are discussed next in this section. The network and transport layer attacks in IoT are: replay or duplication attacks due to fragmentation, sinkhole, insecure neighbor discovery, buffer reservation attack, and wormhole attacks, Sybil attacks on intermediate layer and authentication and secure communication, etc. In replay or duplication attacks the IP packets are fragmented due to small frame size during transmission. The reconstruction of fragments in IoT results in buffer overflows, device rebooting, and resources draining. Even frames coming from malicious nodes affect the reassembly of packets which impact on the processing of real packets. In the IoT system, every node is uniquely identified on the network. The data transferred during end-to-end communication must reach securely to the intended receiver to ensure the secure identification process. Before the transmission of data, the neighbor discovery phase performs address resolution and discovers the route. The improper verification of this process results in denial-of-service (DOS). At the receiving node, reassembly of fragments requires buffer space. In Buffer reservation attack, an attacker may exploit buffer space by sending dummy packets resulting in a DOS attack. In sinkhole attack, an attacker processes the routing request and makes a packet route through it where it can perform some malicious activity. In a wormhole attack, an attacker creates a tunnel between two nodes to divert packets to other nodes too, which leads to eavesdropping and DOS. Sybil attacks at intermediate level disgrace the network performance and breach the privacy of data. The Sybil node with false identities in a network may lead to spamming, circulation of malware or initiating phishing attacks. Also, the authentication of IoT devices and users along with the secure transfer of data using cryptography techniques is an important aspect of security. Any security gap at the network or transport layer causes major vulnerabilities. Another concern at transport level end-to-end security is the delivery of data in a reliable manner from source to destination. The authentication mechanism is required with minimum over-head to send data in encrypted form. At the transport layer, session hijacking with false messages leads to DOS. A fake node impersonates as a target node to continue with the session. IoT can be deployed on the cloud. A malicious cloud service provider can access sensitive information transmitted to the destination node.

The application layer is mainly concerned with services requested by users. The security challenges in the application layer are concerned with software attacks [55, 56]. The application layer attacks are discussed next in this section. The first attack is related to constrained application protocol (CoAP), which provides end-to-end security. The messages in CoAP need to be encrypted; also, key management and authentication is required for multicast support in CoAP. The different attacks that lead to data privacy may occur during accessing IoT services through the interfaces like mobile, web or cloud are considered as insecure interfaces. The next security concern exists with respect to insecure software/firmware. The testing code of languages or updating software/firmware may cause vulnerabilities in IoT.

Hence testing of code and updating firmware should be done in a secure manner. Also, to establish communication among heterogeneous entities of IoT a secure middleware needs to be designed for delivering the services. The blockchain characteristics that can be used to address security issues in IoT are presented in Table 14.5.

14.4   BLOCKCHAIN OF THINGS (BCoT)

IoT connects ubiquitous devices using complex network infrastructure and handles heterogeneous data efficiently. However, it faces some challenges including interoperability issues, heterogeneity of devices, single point of failure, privacy, and security of devices and information. Integrating blockchain in IoT reduces the probability of a single point of failure significantly. Blockchain also leverages the reliability and scalability of IoT systems [63]. Moreover, the consensus and security mechanisms help to strengthen IoT security. Various security attacks being launched on perception, network/ transport, and application layers of IoT can be minimized or nullified with the help of integration of significant features of blockchain (Table 14.5). Blockchain is the seamless complement technology to IoT and can be amalgamated to evolve as BCoT. BCoT improves interoperability among various ubiquitous devices, traceability, reliability, and it also provides seamless and autonomous interactions between IoT systems.

14.4.1   PROPOSED ARCHITECTURE OF BCoT

IoT architecture illustrated in Figure 14.2 is further extended by adding components and functionalities of blockchain BCoT. It acts as a blockchain service through some application programming interfaces (APIs) for various applications by hiding heterogeneity of underneath IoT layers. Figure 14.3 shows proposed layered architecture for BCoT.

The lower two layers, i.e., perception layer and transport layer and upper application layer provide the same functionalities as they were providing in IoT. The processing layer of IoT now serves as a middleware layer comprising 4 sublayers namely data and infrastructure sublayer, distributed communication sublayer, platform sublayer and application sublayer [4].

Data and infrastructure sublayer is the lowest sublayer of the processing layer having tight coupling with the transport layer. It consists of all components of blockchain. Data sensed and acquired from IoT devices are wrapped

TABLE 14.5 Mapping of Blockchain Characteristics to Address Security Issues in IoT

IoT Security Issues		Blockchain Characteristics*								
Level	IoT Security Issues	DEC	PER	ANY	SCA	RES	EFF	TRA	SMC	NR
Perception Level	Jamming adversaries	✓	—	✓	—	—	✓	✓	—	—
	Node capture attacks	✓	✓	—	—	✓	—	✓	—	—
	Insecure initialization	✓	—	—	✓	—	—	✓	✓	—
	Malicious code injection attacks	✓	—	✓	—	—	—	✓	✓	✓
	Low level Sybil and spoofing attack	✓	✓	—	—	—	—	—	✓	—
	False data injection attacks	✓	—	✓	—	—	—	—	✓	—
	Insecure physical interface	✓	—	✓	—	—	—	—	✓	—
	Cryptanalysis attacks and side-channel attacks	✓	✓	—	—	—	—	✓	✓	✓
	Sleep deprivation attack	✓	—	✓	—	—	—	—	—	—
	Eavesdropping and interference	✓	—	✓	—	—	—	—	✓	—
Network and Transport Level	Authentication and secure communication	✓	✓	✓	—	—	✓	✓	✓	✓
	Replay or duplication attacks due to fragmentation	✓	✓	✓	—	✓	✓	✓	✓	—
	Session establishment and resumption	✓	✓	✓	—	—	✓	—	✓	—
	Buffer reservation attack	✓	—	✓	—	✓	✓	—	✓	—
	Privacy violation on cloud-based IoT	✓	—	✓	—	—	✓	—	✓	—
	Insecure neighbor discovery	✓	✓	✓	—	✓	—	—	✓	✓
	Sybil attacks on intermediate layers	✓	✓	✓	—	—	—	✓	✓	—
	Sinkhole and wormhole attack	✓	✓	✓	—	—	✓	—	✓	✓
	Transport level end to end security	✓	—	—	—	✓	✓	✓	—	—
Application Level	CoAP security with internet	✓	✓	✓	—	✓	—	—	—	—
	Middleware security	✓	✓	—	✓	—	✓	—	—	—
	Insecure software/firmware	✓	✓	✓	—	—	—	✓	✓	—
	Insecure interfaces	✓	—	✓	—	—	✓	—	—	—

*DEC: Decentralization; PER: Persistency; ANY: Anonymity; SCA: Scalability or more address space, RES: Resilient backend; EFF: High efficiency; TRA: Transparency; SMC: Smart contract; NP: Non-repudiation.

up into data blocks using encryption and hashing security constructs and form basic constructs of blockchain. They are stored on the full nodes in the blockchain network. The ledger of transaction records is stored using a storage component. Some of the nodes in the blockchain network are capable of just sending and receiving the transactions, whereas some can validate the transactions and propagate it to other nodes. This functionality is handled by Propagation and validation components in collaboration with underneath transport layer. Also, there is a special category of nodes referred to as mining nodes which can mine the blocks (generate new blocks).

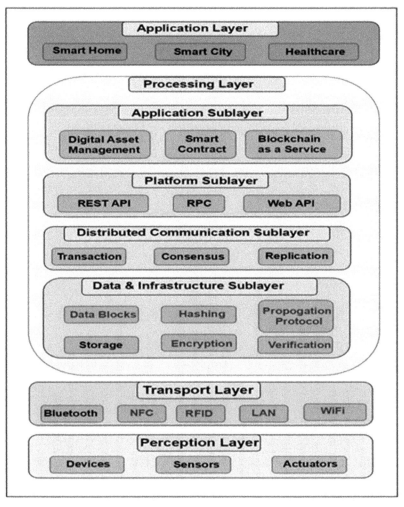

FIGURE 14.3   Architecture of BCoT.

Distributed and Communication sublayer ensures access to data blocks and other properties of blockchain-like fault tolerance, traceability, and immutability. This sublayer is responsible to complete the consensus process for ordering the transactions in the network and updation of the ledger. It uses various basic and specialized consensus algorithms like PoW, PoS, PBFT, GHOST, TANGLE, Ripple, and Algorand.

The platform sublayer ensures the smooth functioning of this middleware layer by facilitating remote procedure calls, web APIs and REST API for the communication between various nodes in the blockchain network.

The application sublayer provides blockchain as a service to the users of various applications running on IoT with the help of smart contracts. The users are permitted to build their own blockchain products for application in hand using smart contracts and other blockchain based solutions. It does not require the creation and management of blockchain based infrastructure. It also provides business logic for managing digital assets and for execution of smart contracts.

BCoT is intended to provide seamless and automated service to IoT. Therefore, the realistic deployment of BCoT is a very crucial and important task. BCoT can be deployed only on a full node which can be a cloud server or edge server. Due to limited storage of IoT devices, they can store partial blockchain data whereas cloud servers can hold entire blockchain. These IoT devices with the collaboration of cloud servers can validate the transactions using available partial data in their memories.

14.4.2 BENEFITS OF BCoT

Amalgamation of blockchain and IoT as BCoT provides benefits in terms of improved and efficient qualities such as interoperability, reliability, scalability, privacy, and security. Blockchain middleware layer facilitates storage of IoT data over blockchain. The data collected from heterogeneous devices are stored and processed using blockchain by establishing peer to peer (P2P) network on the top of segmented heterogeneous network and thus improving the interoperability of IoT. IoT data is stored and processed as transactions which are encrypted and signed by digital signatures on blockchains. Also, the smart contracts updates IoT firmware in a secured way and thus overcome lacunas in firmware security features. This will certainly improve the overall security of the IoT system. One of the striking features of blockchain is traceability which helps in tracing the participating devices and end parties in an efficient way. Immutability property of blockchain helps in achieving reliability by making it impossible to modify or fabricate the transactions in the blockchain. With the help of smart contacts, IoT devices interact with each other in an autonomous fashion which diminishes human intervention and helps in saving the cost [64].

14.4.3 BCoT CHALLENGES

Although the benefits of BCoT are multifold, there are few challenges as well which need to be addressed to fully utilize the strength of BCoT in an ample amount of applications.

Most of the IoT devices have limited computing, storage, and battery capacity. The consensus algorithms used in blockchain need lots of computations and consume huge energy to make it impossible to be executed on low battery IoT devices. Therefore, energy efficiency is essential to allow long-term participation of nodes in contributing seamless services through BCoT. Throughput and latency of the underlying IoT network plays a crucial role in providing a stable network. It may lead to some scalability issues as well. Some time, IoT devices will not be able to provide a stable network due to failure of nodes in the network.

Although BCoT claims to provide significant improvement in security by integrating blockchain into IoT, there are lots of heterogeneous physical, network, and application components and different vulnerabilities of such components. Therefore, security is a major and important challenge for BCoT. Users are identified by hash or public key on the blockchain. Through a series of transactions pertaining to the user, the pseudonymity of the user can be easily cracked.

Over the years, IoT has been widely used in a variety of applications generating massive volume of real time heterogeneous data. As blockchain is combined with it in the BCoT environment, it becomes difficult to use traditional analytics on this data. The computing requirement is extremely high for such analytics schemes making it difficult to be executed on poor computing IoT devices and on anonymous blockchain data [64].

14.5 CONCLUSION

Blockchain technology enables people to share valuable information in a secure and transparent way. It is called distributed ledger technology (DLT) that makes data unaltered and transparent using distributed systems and cryptographic hashing techniques. The characteristics of blockchain include immutability, transparency, decentralization, anonymity, traceability, and non-repudiation. These characteristics ensure the privacy, scalability, and reliability during information sharing over the Internet. This chapter focuses on the integration of blockchain with IoT. The IoT is a network of intelligent things that are uniquely identified, sensed, and react to environmental changes, connected over the Internet. Nowadays with IoT, anything can be connected to anyone through the Internet. This gives enormous potential for IoT in various applications from smart home, smart city, and agriculture to healthcare, etc. Despite the advantages of IoT, there are many challenges like heterogeneity, interoperability, resource constraint, security, and privacy. The brief introduction of blockchain technology along with its characteristics, platform, consensus, challenges, and applications are discussed here. This chapter also introduces IoT along with its characteristics, architecture, protocols, security, challenges, and applications are discussed here. The convergence of IoT and blockchain called BCoT is discussed with the security issues in IoT which can be addressed using blockchain technology. The architecture to integrate blockchain with IoT is proposed along with the challenges and benefits of BCoT.

KEYWORDS

- **artificial neural networks**
- **blockchain**
- **blockchain of things**
- **consensus**
- **convolutional neural network**
- **internet of things**

REFERENCES

1. Panarello, A., Nachiket, T., Giovanni, M., Francesco, L., & Antonio, P., (2018). Blockchain and IoT integration: A systematic survey. *Sensors, 18*(8), 2575.
2. Ramaguru, R., Sindhu, M., & Sethumadhavan, M., (2019). Blockchain for the internet of vehicles. In: Singh, M., Gupta, P., Tyagi, V., Flusser, J., Ören, T., & Kashyap, R.,

(eds.), *Advances in Computing and Data Sciences. ICACDS 2019. Communications in Computer and Information Science* (Vol. 1045). Springer, Singapore.

3. Zheng, Z., Xie, S., & Hong-Ning, D., & Chen, X., & Wang, H., (2018). Blockchain challenges and opportunities: A survey. *International Journal of Web and Grid Services, 14*, 352.

4. Ismail, L., & Huned, M., (2019). A review of blockchain architecture and consensus protocols: Use cases, challenges, and solutions. *Symmetry, 11*(10), 1198.

5. Lauslahti, K., Juri, M., & Timo, S., (2017). *Smart Contracts–How Will Blockchain Technology Affect Contractual Practices?* Etla Reports, 68.

6. Buterin, V., (2015). *On Public and Private Blockchains.* URL: https://blog.Ethereum. org/2015/08/07/on-public-and-private-blockchains (accessed on 10 November 2021).

7. Pilkington, M., (2016). Blockchain technology: Principles and applications. In: *Research Handbook on Digital Transformations.* Edward Elgar Publishing.

8. Palanivel, K., (2019). Blockchain architecture to higher education systems. *International Journal of Latest Technology in Engineering, Management & Applied Science (IJLTEMAS), VIII*(II). ISSN 2278-2540.

9. Monrat, A. A., Olov, S., & Karl, A., (2019). A survey of blockchain from the perspectives of applications, challenges, and opportunities. *IEEE Access, 7*, 117134–117151.

10. Kiayias, A., Alexander, R., Bernardo, D., & Roman, O., (2017). Ouroboros: A provably secure proof-of-stake blockchain protocol. In: *Annual International Cryptology Conference* (pp. 357–388). Springer, Cham.

11. Ahmed, M., & Kari, K., (2018). *Don't Mine, Wait in Line: Fair and Efficient Blockchain Consensus with Robust Round Robin.* arXiv preprint arXiv:1804.07391.

12. Sankar, L. S., Sindhu, M., & Sethumadhavan, M., (2017). Survey of consensus protocols on blockchain applications. In: *2017 4th International Conference on Advanced Computing and Communication Systems (ICACCS)* (pp. 1–5). IEEE.

13. Xiao, Y., Ning, Z., Wenjing, L., & Thomas, H. Y., (2020). A survey of distributed consensus protocols for blockchain networks. *IEEE Communications Surveys & Tutorials, 22*(2), 1432–1465.

14. Vukolić, M., (2015). 'The quest for scalable blockchain fabric: Proof-of-work vs. BFT replication. *International Workshop on Open Problems in Network Security* (pp. 112–125). Zurich, Switzerland.

15. Shi, E., (2019). Analysis of deterministic longest-chain protocols. In: *2019 IEEE 32nd Computer Security Foundations Symposium (CSF)* (pp. 122–135). IEEE.

16. Zamfir, V., (2017). *Casper the Friendly Ghost: A Correct by Construction Blockchain Consensus Protocol.* White paper: https://github.com/ethereum/research/blob/master/ papers/CasperTFG/CasperTFG.pdf (accessed on 10 November 2021).

17. Salimitari, M., & Mainak, C., (2018). *An Overview of Blockchain and Consensus Protocols for IoT Networks.* arXiv preprint arXiv:1809.05613.

18. Kwon, J., (2014). *Tendermint: Consensus Without Mining.* Draft v. 0.6, fall 1, no. 11.

19. Luu, L., Viswesh, N., Kunal, B., Chaodong, Z., Seth, G., & Prateek, S., (2015). *Scp: A Computationally-Scalable Byzantine Consensus Protocol for Blockchains.* https://www. weusecoins. com/assets/pdf/library/SCP 20, no. 20 2016.

20. Schwartz, D., Noah, Y., & Arthur, B., (2014). The ripple protocol consensus algorithm. *Ripple Labs Inc White Paper, 5*, no. 8.

21. Chen, J., & Silvio, M., (2019). Algor and: A secure and efficient distributed ledger. *Theoretical Computer Science, 777*, 155–183.

22. Wang, X., Xuan, Z., Wei, N., Ren, P. L., Jay, G. Y., Xinxin, N., & Kangfeng, Z., (2019). Survey on blockchain for internet of things. *Computer Communications, 136*, 10–29.

23. Macdonald, M., Liu-Thorrold, L., &. Julien, R., (2017). The blockchain: A comparison of platforms and their uses beyond bitcoin. *COMS4507-Adv. Computer and Network Security.*

24. Ashton, K., (2009). That "internet of things" thing. *RFID Journal, RFiD Journal, 22,* 97–114.

25. Gubbi, J., Buyya, R., Marusic, S., & Palaniswami, M., (2013). Internet of things (IoT): A vision, architectural elements, and future directions. *Future Generation Computer Systems, Volume 29*(7), 1645–1660. http://www.sciencedirect.com/science/article/pii/S0167739X13000241 (accessed on 10 November 2021).

26. Madakam, S., Ramaswamy, R., & Tripathi, S., (2015). Internet of things (IoT): A literature review. *Journal of Computer and Communications, 3*(5).

27. Rayes, A., & Salam, S., (2017). Internet of things (IoT) overview. In: *Internet of Things from Hype to Reality.* Springer, Cham, ISBN: 978-3-319-44858-9, () https://doi.org/10.1007/978-3-319-44860-2_1.

28. Sethi, P., & Smruti, R. S., (2017). Internet of things: Architectures, protocols, and applications. *Journal of Electrical and Computer Engineering.*

29. Salman, T., (2017). Networking protocols and standards for internet of things. *Advanced Computing and Communications, 1*(1). http://www.cse.wustl.edu/~jain/cse570-15/ftp/iot_prot/index.html (accessed on 10 November 2021).

30. OASIS, (2012). *Oasis Advanced Message Queuing Protocol (AMQP) Version 1.0.* Retrieved from: https://bit.ly/3HZD1PW (accessed on 10 November 2021).

31. AVSystem, (2020). https://www.avsystem.com/blog/iot-protocols-and-standards/ (accessed on 10 November 2021).

32. Mehedi, H., (2020). https://www.ubuntupit.com/top-15-standard-iot-protocols-that-you-must-know-about/ (accessed on 10 November 2021).

33. Pathaka, A., & Tembhurne, J., (2018). Internet of things: A survey on IoT protocols. In: *3rd International Conference on Internet of Things and Connected Technologies (ICIoTCT).*

34. Rani, D., & Gill, N. S., (2019). Review of various IoT standards and communication protocols. *International Journal of Engineering Research and Technology, 12*(5), 647–657. ISSN 0974-3154.

35. Dizdarevic, J., Carpio, F., Jukan, A., & Masip-Bruin, X., (2018). A survey of communication protocols for internet-of-things and related challenges of fog and cloud computing integration. *ACM Computing Surveys, 1*(1), 1–27.

36. Postscapes, (2020). https://www.postscapes.com/internet-of-things-protocols/ (accessed on 10 November 2021).

37. Mehrotra, N., (2019). https://opensourceforu.com/2019/10/xmpp-a-communication-protocol-for-the-iot/ (accessed on 10 November 2021).

38. Schuster, D., Philipp, G., Dominik, R., István, K., Ronny, K., & Michael, K., (2014). Global-scale federated access to smart objects using XMPP. In: *2014 IEEE International Conference on Internet of Things (iThings), and IEEE Green Computing and Communications (GreenCom) and IEEE Cyber, Physical and Social Computing (CPSCom) (*pp. 185–192). IEEE.

39. Che, X., & Maag, S., (2013). A passive testing approach for protocols in the internet of things. In: *Proceedings of the 2013 IEEE International Conference on Green Computing and Communications and IEEE Internet of Things and IEEE Cyber, Physical and Social Computing* (pp. 678–684). doi: http://dx.doi.org/10.1109/GreenCom-iThings-CPSCom.2013.

40. Hornsby, A., (2009). BaiE.l. µXMPP: Lightweight implementation for low power operating system Contiki. In: *Proceedings of the 2009 International Conference on Ultra-Modern Telecommunications Workshops* (pp. 1–5). doi: http://dx. doi.org/10.1109/ICUMT.2009.5345594.

41. Wang, H., Daijin, X., Ping, W., & Yuqiang, L., (2017). A lightweight XMPP publish/subscribe scheme for resource-constrained IoT devices. *IEEE Access, 5,* 16393–16405.

42. Wilkinson, S., Boshevski, T., Brandoff, J., Prestwich, J., Hall, G., Gerbes, P., Hutchins, P., & Pollard, C., (2018). *Storj a Peer-to-Peer Cloud Storage Network.* Available online: https://storj.io/storj.pdf (accessed on 10 November 2021).

43. Emanuel, F., Vanessa R. L. C., Célio V. N. D. A., & Antônio, A. D. A. R., (2018). A survey of how to use blockchain to secure internet of things and the stalker attack. In: *Journal Security and Communication Networks* (pp. 1–28).

44. Dorri, A., Kanhere, S., Jurdak, R., & Gauravaram, P., (2017). *LSB: A Lightweight Scalable Blockchain for IoT Security and Privacy.* arXiv preprint arXiv:1712.02969,

45. Rahulamathavan, Y., Phan, R. C., Rajarajan, M., Misra, S., & Kondoz, A., (2017). Privacy-preserving blockchain based IoT ecosystem using attribute based encryption. In: *IEEE International Conference on Advanced Networks and Telecommunications Systems (ANTS)* (pp. 1–6). IEEE.

46. Jung, Y., & Agulto, R., (2020). Integrated management of network address translation, mobility and security on the blockchain control plane. *Journal of Sensors, 20*(69), 1–14.

47. Gong, S.,Tcydenova, E., Jo, J., Lee, Y., & Park, J. H., (2019). Blockchain-based secure device management framework for an internet of things network in a smart city. *Sustainability, 11*(3889), 1–17.

48. Dorri, A., Steger, M., Kanhere, S., & Jurdak, R., (2017). Blockchain: A distributed solution to automotive security and privacy. In: *IEEE Communications Magazine, 55*(12), 119–125. doi: 10.1109/MCOM.2017.1700879.

49. Roy, S., Ashaduzzamany, M., Hassan, M., & Chowdhury, A. R., (2018). Blockchain for IoT security and management: Current prospects, challenges, and future directions. In: *2018 5th International Conference on Networking, Systems and Security (NSysS)* (pp. 1–9). IEEE

50. Hammi, M. T., Hammi, B., Bellot, P., & Serhrouchni, A., (2018). Bubbles of trust: A decentralized blockchain-based authentication system for IoT. *Computers and Security, 78,* 126–142.

51. Liu, B., Yu, X. L., Chen, S., Xu, X., & Zhu, L., (2017). Blockchain based data integrity service framework for IoT data. In: *Web Services (ICWS), IEEE International Conference* (pp. 468–475). IEEE.

52. Lee, B., & Lee, J. H., (2017). Blockchain-based secure firmware update for embedded devices in an internet of things environment. *Journal of. Supercomput., 73,* 1152–1167.

53. Kostal, K., Helebrandt, P., Belluš, M., Ries, M., & Kotuliak, I., (2019). Management and monitoring of IoT devices using blockchain. *Journal of Sensors, 19*(856).

54. Zhang, Y., Kasahara, S., Shen, Y., Jiang, X., & Wan, J., (2018). *Smart Contract-Based Access Control for the Internet of Things.* arXiv preprint arXiv:1802.04410.

55. Khan, M., & Salah, K., (2018). IoT security: Review, blockchain solutions, and open challenges. *Future Gener. Comput. Syst., 82,* 395–411.

56. Lin, J., Yu, W., Zhang, N., Yang, X., Zhang, H., & Zhao, W., (2017). A survey on internet of things: Architecture, enabling technologies, security and privacy, and applications. *IEEE Internet of Things Journal, 4*(5), 1125–1142, https://doi.org/10.1109/JIOT.2017.2683200.

57. Guan, Z., Si, G., Zhang, X., Wu, L., Guizani, N., Du, X., & Ma, Y., (2018). Privacy-preserving and efficient aggregation based on blockchain for power grid communications in smart communities. In: *IEEE Communications Magazine* (Vol. 56, No. 7, pp. 82–88). doi: 10.1109/MCOM.2018.1700401.

58. Kiyomoto, S., Basu, A., Rahman, M. S., Ruj, S., Kim, D., Yun, J., Kim, S., et al., (2017). On blockchain-based authorization architecture for beyond-5g mobile services. *The 12nd International Conference for Internet Technology and Secured Transactions.*

59. Yohan, A., Lo, N. W., & Achawapong, S., (2018). Blockchain-based firmware update framework for internet-of-things environment. In: *Proceedings of the International Conference on Information and Knowledge Engineering (IKE)* (pp. 151–155).

60. Boudguiga, A., Nabil, B., Louis, G., Alexis, O., Flavien, Q., Anthony, R., & Renaud, S., (2017). Towards better availability and accountability for IoT updates by means of a blockchain. In: *2017 IEEE European Symposium on Security and Privacy Workshops (EuroS&PW)* (pp. 50–58). IEEE.

61. Dhakal, S., Jaafar, F., & Zavarsky, P., (2019). Private blockchain network for IoT device firmware integrity verification and update. In: *Proceedings of the 2019 IEEE 19th International Symposium on High Assurance Systems Engineering (HASE)* (pp. 164–170).

62. Hernández-Ramos, J., Antonio, J., Leandro, M., Gómez, S., & Antonio, F., (2016). DCapBAC: Embedding authorization logic into smart things through ECC optimizations. *International Journal of Computer Mathematics, 93*(2), 345–366.

63. Sreelakshmi, K. K., Ashutosh, B., & Ankit, A., (2020). *Securing IoT Applications using Blockchain: A Survey.* arXiv (2020): arXiv-2006.

64. Alamri, M., Jhanjhi, N. Z., & Mamoona, H., (2019). Blockchain for internet of things (IoT) research issues challenges & future directions: A review. *Int. J. Comput. Sci. Netw. Secur., 19*, 244–258.

65. Axon, L. M., & Michael, G., (2016). PB-PKI: A privacy-aware blockchain-based PKI. ().

66. Hong-Ning, D., Zibin, Z., & Yan, Z., (2019). Blockchain for internet of things: A survey. *IEEE Internet of Things Journal, 6*(5), 8076–8094.

67. Sultan, A., Muhammad, A. M., & Muhammad, A., (2019). IoT security issues via blockchain: A review paper. In: *Proceedings of the 2019 International Conference on Blockchain Technology* (pp. 60–65).

CHAPTER 15

Blockchain and Its Integration with the Internet of Things: Applications and Challenges

RIDHIMA RANI and MEENU KHURANA

Chitkara University Institute of Engineering and Technology, Chitkara University, Punjab, India, E-mails: rdahiya7@gmail.com (R. Rani), meenu.khurana@chitkara.edu.in (M. Khurana)

ABSTRACT

Internet of Things (IoT) permits different objects to connect with each other and transfer information so that the physical world will get converted into a vast information system. Current solutions in IoT are based upon centralized client-server architecture provided by cloud servers. This centralized client-server architecture requires highly efficient servers and is proved unsuitable in situations in which objects want to exchange services autonomously with data privacy, security, and mutual trust. The exponential growth rate of IoT warrants those new models need to be put forward. This chapter presents the role of blockchain in designing blockchain-based IoT framework having resilience, adaptability, fault-tolerance, security, privacy, trust, and reduced maintenance cost. It also elaborates on blockchain, its applications and challenges. This chapter also classifies prerequisites, applications of blockchain in IoT and challenges in implementing IoT solutions with blockchain.

15.1 INTRODUCTION

Internet of Things (IoT) is a pervasive network of physical entities called people and things. IoT permits different objects to connect with each other and transfer information so that the physical world will get converted into a vast information system. IoT operational technology network known as

IoT fabric is integrated with various technologies like cloud computing and ML nowadays. About 5 billion devices are connected through IoT [1] and it is expected to touch 29 billion by the year 2022. Out of these connected devices 18 billion will be relevant to IoT (NYC). Every connected device will produce and exchange a large amount of data on the internet. In order to effectively manage the extensive growth in IoT as described in (NYC,) there is a need to create a set of protocols and set of layers to provide services to different devices used in IoT. Current solutions in IoT are based upon centralized client-server architecture provided by cloud servers [2], but the growth rate of IoT advises that new models need to be put forward [3]. One of the proposed solutions that came forward in the past was a huge peer-to-peer wireless sensor networks (WSNs) [4, 5] with no piece of information on privacy and security.

Anticipating the security threats this gigantic information system will be put through, researchers should take privacy and security as a major challenge. To a great extent this challenge may be addressed by blockchain deployment. Blockchain deployment in IoT can address the following challenges:

- Distributed architecture, a major challenge in IoT because every node in a distributed network is a point of failure due to its susceptibility to different types of attacks such as distributed denial of service attack [6].
- Central point of failure due to centralized nature of IoT is another challenge.
- Data confidentiality, integrity [2, 7] and security is another challenge as a result of the emergence of new business paradigms and their integration with IoT requiring resource sharing that can be computational power-sharing, unrestricted data access.
- Protection of information from injection attacks that would cause insertion of erroneous data affecting the end result, for IoT deployed in decision support system for data collection from sensors.
- In this era of machine economy where sensors are generating data for trading in an autonomous system, creating trust among communicating parties [8] without the involvement of a central authority thus addressing the non-repudiation problem is another challenge.

Figure 15.1 indicates the evolution of centralized IoT using cloud-central approach after closer of pre-IoT and predicting the distribution of cloud functioning among peers with the help of blockchain in future [3].

This chapter comprises of eight sections. Section 15.2 gives an overview of the evolution of blockchain, Section 15.3 elaborates blockchain architecture focusing on the major revolution in this technology. Section 15.4

describes general application areas of blockchain whereas Section 15.5 focuses on specific application areas of blockchain in IoT and the parameters helping in determining the need of blockchain in IoT applications. Section 15.6 highlights the challenges and opportunities in blockchain-IoT integration, Section 15.7 summarizes these challenges and mentions the future direction of research in integration of the two technologies. Section 15.8 concludes the chapter.

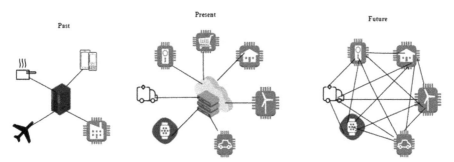

FIGURE 15.1   Architecture of IoT in the past present and future.

15.2   BLOCKCHAIN

Blockchain technology with the underlying technique of putting data in a chain of blocks was put forward for consideration by researchers in 2008 and implemented in the year 2009 [9], in the crypto-currency world of digital currencies with bitcoin as its first and famous application. It is a decentralized platform that allows processing of transactions consequently for sharing of information and computation [10]. It enables multiple reliable domains that do not trust each other, to collaborate, coordinate, and communicate in a coherent decision-making process. It is also known as a public ledger that is used for storing all committed transactions in a chain of blocks. This technology has key attributes like persistency, immutability, anonymity, and decentralization, which are empowered by the amalgamation of different core technologies like digital signatures, cryptographic hash functions and consensus components. Blockchain can be adapted in divergent domains besides crypto-currencies such as digital asset management, online payments, smart contracts [11], public services, reputation systems [12], IoT and security services [13]. It is tamper proof, so it can be adapted by businesses which require high reliability and honesty for captivating their customers.

Blockchain of bitcoin; a crypto-currency, is constantly growing, as every 10 minutes, a new block is added by miners to record the young transactions. Every computer that is connected to the bitcoin network for validating transactions has a full copy of the blockchain, which is automatically downloaded when it joins the network. There is a block called genesis block that keeps record of first-ever executed transaction and blockchain keeps complete record of transactions from genesis block to the recent created block. It is like a spreadsheet for keeping record of all assets and acts like an accounting system for transacting those records on a global level.

The modern world can be understood on the basis of computing models with each new model occurring every 10 years as depicted in Figure 15.2. Mainframe and personal computers appeared as first model and then the internet brought a radical change. The most recent model was mobile and social networking. For the current decade the model that came into existence could be the connected world of computing depending on blockchain cryptography [14].

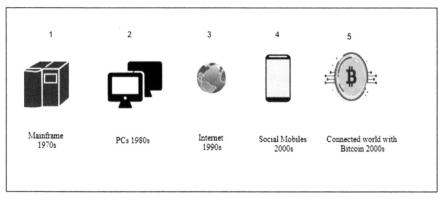

FIGURE 15.2   Confusing computing models: Mainframes, PCs, internet, social-mobiles, blockchains [15].

15.3   BLOCKCHAIN ARCHITECTURE

Blockchain exists as a distributed peer to peer (P2P) linked structure of blocks with each block containing records of transactions committed in a particular timestamp. Each block in the blockchain points to its immediate predecessor called parent block as depicted in Figure 15.3, as well as immediate successor, using their respective hash values as reference.

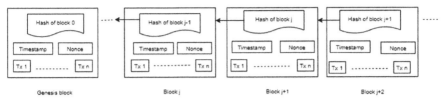

FIGURE 15.3 Example blockchain with continuous sequence of blocks.

15.3.1 BLOCK

A single block in a blockchain comprises of many fields such as the header of the block and body of the block as depicted in Figure 15.4. The header of block further incorporates [10]:

1. **Block Version:** It describes the set of rules to be followed for validation of blocks.

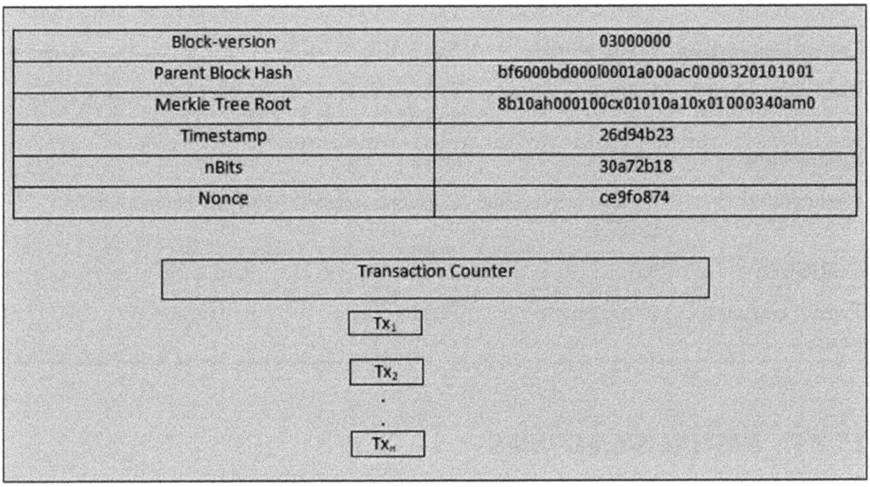

Block-version	03000000
Parent Block Hash	bf6000bd000i0001a000ac0000320101001
Merkle Tree Root	8b10ah000100cx01010a10x01000340am0
Timestamp	26d94b23
nBits	30a72b18
Nonce	ce9fo874

Transaction Counter
Tx₁
Tx₂
.
.
Txₙ

FIGURE 15.4 Structure of block in blockchain.

2. **Previous Block Hash:** It is a hash value of 256-bits for pointing to the parent of the block.
3. **Root Hash of Merkle Tree:** It is the hash value of all transactions within the current block.
4. **Timestamp:** Current timestamp in seconds as per universal time as long as 1 January 1970.

5. **nBits:** It refers to the current hashing target to be achieved (difficulty level) in a compact format.
6. **Nonce:** It is a 4-byte field, conventionally begins with 0 and expands for every hash calculation.

Table 15.1 depicts the comparison among different types of blockchain, based on its characteristics. Body of a block comprises of transactions and transaction counter. The maximum count of transaction a block of blockchain can store depends upon the size of the block and size of the transaction. Blockchain makes use of asymmetric key cryptography (MET) for validating the authenticity of transactions. Bitcoin blockchain uses cryptographic techniques for processing of transactions such as elliptic curve cryptography (ECC). Digital signatures which are based on asymmetric key cryptography are used in blockchain. A brief overview of digital signatures is explained next.

TABLE 15.1   Comparative Analysis of Private, Public, and Consortium Blockchain

Characteristics	Public Blockchain	Private Blockchain	Consortium Blockchain
Consensus approval	By all miners	Single organization	Only selected set of nodes
Read access rights	Public	Either restricted or public	Either restricted or public
Efficiency level	Low	High	High
Immutability	Almost impossible to alter	Could be vandalized	Could be vandalized
Centralized	No	Less	Partial
Type of consensus process	Permissionless	Permissioned	Permissioned

15.3.2   DIGITAL SIGNATURES

Digital signatures follow two phases; Signing phase and verification phase. For example, if a user A wants to send a message to user B. (1) user A will encrypt the message with his private key and send it to user B along with original data in the signing phase. (2) After receiving the message B decrypts it with A's public key in the verification phase. Along these lines B could easily verify whether the data is manipulated or not. Blockchain uses Elliptic Curve Digital Signature algorithms [16].

15.3.3 CHARACTERISTICS OF BLOCKCHAIN

The characteristics which are supported by blockchain are summarized below:

1. **Anonymity:** Any blockchain user with his generated address can connect with blockchain network without revealing his real identity. In addition to that, a user can hide his identity by generating multiple addresses in case of information leakage.

2. **Decentralization:** It is achieved using private and public key pair between any two peers in blockchain network. There is no central authority to validate the integrity of transaction and to keep a record of transactions in blockchain. In this way blockchain reduced the central server cost significantly in contrast to conventional transaction system. Replication of data and consensus algorithms are helpful in maintaining the quality of data in decentralized system. It also helped in alleviating the performance barrier at central servers.

3. **Persistency:** It is nearly impossible to rollback and discard a transaction once it is included in the public ledger. Only committed transactions are accepted by honest miners and invalid transactions get discovered immediately.

4. **Auditability:** Each of the transaction in a blockchain is saved with its timestamp. Therefore, any previous record can be traced by the user by accessing any anonymous node in the blockchain. As in the case of bitcoin blockchain iteratively any transaction can be traced. In this way identifiability and transparency of data stored on blockchain is improved.

5. **Openness [17]:** Any anonymous user can generate a request for data from blockchain due to its open-source nature and can create his personal relevant applications through open interfaces.

15.3.4 REVOLUTION IN BLOCKCHAIN TECHNOLOGY

- For convenience purposes, the divergent kinds of activities in the revolution of blockchain are divided into three categories: Blockchain 1.0, 2.0, and 3.0 [5]. Blockchain 1.0 is related to the deployment of cryptocurrencies such as digital payments, cash transfer. Blockchain 2.0 involves more extensive financial applications such as smart contracts, smart property, stocks, bonds, mortgages. Blockchain 3.0 involves applications in the areas of literacy, health, science, government, culture, and art as depicted in Figure 15.5 that is adapted and modified from [18].

- Beside this blockchain can also be categorized as public, private, and consortium blockchain [19]. In case of public blockchain every node becomes part of consensus mechanism, in consortium only selected or validated nodes can take part in consensus and in private, this mechanism is controlled by the single organization.

- Currently consortium blockchain framework for business perspective is being developed by Hyperledger [20]. Ethereum is also providing tools for creating consortium blockchains [21]. Private blockchains are under implementation by many companies for evaluation and effectiveness. Comparison among different types of blockchains on the basis of their properties is summarized in Table 15.1.

15.3.5 CONSENSUS ALGORITHMS CLASSIFICATION AND ROBUSTNESS

Consensus among unreliable nodes in blockchain is a variation of Byzantine General's Problem [22]; a group of Generals on the battlefield not trusting each other but they have an inclination for some coordinated communication mechanism to reach a consensus on whether to attack or not. This is an untrustworthy situation. Blockchain also suffers from the same problem as there is no central node, assuring that ledgers on all distributed nodes are the same.

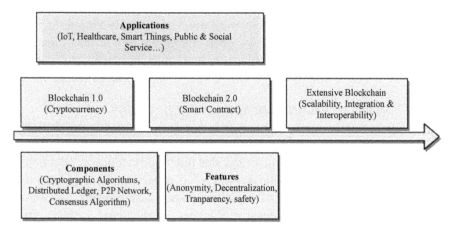

FIGURE 15.5 Development of blockchain.

To ensure the consistency of ledgers on all node's protocols are required. The different consensus algorithms used in blockchain are listed below:

1. **Proof of Work (POW):** It is a Bitcoin network consensus approach [9]. POW approach requires calculation of hash values of constantly changing block header by all nodes in the network. Consensus is reached if the calculated value becomes less than or equal to a pre-decided threshold value. The nodes involved in the calculation of hash are designated as miners and the consensus procedure is called mining. Mining in POW performs complex computer calculation resulting in wastage of resources.

2. **Proof of Stake (POS):** It is an alternative to POW which saves a lot of resources. It requires people to prove the amount of currency under their ownership because people with more currency are less prone to attack the network. In this approach richest person will dominate others in the network. An alternative to this is randomization [23] for choosing the next generator.

3. **Practical Byzantine Fault Tolerance (PBFT):** It is the consensus algorithm used in Hyperledger fabric [20]. It is an algorithm based on replication to handle Byzantine faults [24]. It is able to handle up to $1/3^{rd}$ malicious byzantine replicas. The complete process consists of three phases: pre-prepared, prepared, and commit. A node would move in next phase only after receiving votes from $2/3^{rd}$ of all nodes. PBFT is not based upon any type of hashing like POW. Antshares (ant,) has developed delegated PBFT (dPBFT) on the bases of PBFT. In dPBFT only a set of professional nodes are involved instead of all nodes to keep record of transaction.

4. **Delegated Proof of Stake (DPOS):** It is also implemented like POS on the basis of stake, with the only difference that DPOS delegates are elected for validating a block. This delegation results in significant improvement in block validation time due to less number of block validators, leading to fast transaction confirmation. DPOS is already implemented as a backbone of Bitshares [25].

Table 15.2 is describing the difference among different consensus protocols based on the properties given by Ref. [26].

TABLE 15.2   Comparison of Consensus Algorithms

Properties	PBFT	DPOS	POW	POS
Identity management of node	Permissioned	Permissionless	Permissionless	Permissionless
Energy saving	Yes	Partial	No	Partial
Admitted adversary-power	<33.3% faulty replicas	<51% validators	<25% computing power	<51% stake
Example	Hyper-ledger fabric	Bitshares	Bitcoin	Peercoin

15.3.6   SMART CONTRACTS

Smart contract is a pre-written code that utilizes both the blockchain and electronic data interchange (EDI) protocols. They do not require a middle man and are visible to every user. A smart contract without the involvement of a third party performs automatic execution of contract, keeps ground level contract rules, and verifies and evaluates the outcome. They play a vital role in the supply-chain industry for global distribution. Like in health-care industry, a patient's surgery can be scheduled using smart contracts. These contracts perform mining for related caregiving nodes and also perform initial setup of blockchain. These care-giving nodes become part of the private blockchain in which no single participant is the data owner and all partners are part of a consortium. All of them can read and write from and into the blockchain. If a node writes some data into blockchain then it must be validated by the community of practice or consortium. Only after validation, this data gets shared with other external repositories and nodes. In this way, different services can be advanced with the help of smart contracts, which were facing bottleneck issues due to privacy protocols and complex logistics [27].

15.4   APPLICATION AREAS OF BLOCKCHAIN

Blockchain technology has diverse application areas. In this section applications of blockchain are categorized. Figure 15.6 presents major application areas of blockchain.

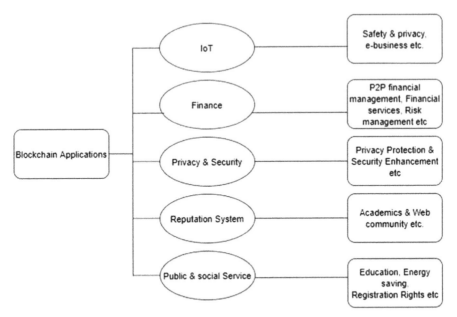

FIGURE 15.6 Application areas of blockchain.

15.4.1 GOVERNANCE SERVICES

The robustness provided by blockchain through its accountability, safety, immutability, and automation features for handling of public records helps in increasing the efficiency of services provided by government and reducing corruption. Blockchain is capable of providing the same governance services that are provided by the state and its authorities in a decentralized way but without any reduction in validity of services. Some examples of such type of services are voting, marriage contracts, attestation, registration, and taxes [14].

15.4.2 BLOCKCHAIN IN IoT

The main objective of IoT is to allow smart objects to interact over the internet with minimal human intervention in exhaustive data collection and providing services. To achieve this target IoT was built on conventional central server system. This approach requires highly efficient servers and is proved unsuitable in situations where objects require exchanging services autonomously. Other issues include data privacy [28], security [29, 30] and mutual trust required while using central servers. The built-in features of blockchain make them fit for developing a fabric for cloud computing in general. The main objective of making blockchain based IoT framework is to achieve resilience, adaptability, fault tolerance, security, and privacy, trust, and reduced maintenance cost [31].

15.4.3 FINANCE SERVICES

Blockchain is playing a vital role in financial fields like financial asset management, economic transaction [32], and prediction markets. Blockchain is helpful in the justifiable growth of the global economy by giving benefits to banks, consumers, and to the whole society [33]. Blockchain-based applications are going to be used for securities, derivative contracts [34], and paper money in the global financial system. This technology is helpful in achieving tremendous performance gains in operations like loan management, auditing, cryptocurrency payments and exchanges through e-wallets, thus reducing cost and time in conducting audits. Blockchain can be applied to different financial application areas for clearing and settling financial assets, and many of the software companies are working to offer now blockchain-as-a-service (IBM).

15.4.4 REPUTATION SYSTEMS WITH BLOCKCHAIN

In public services offered by blockchain, we can see that proof of identity, proof of reputation, proof of existence are the services that can be provided to the public without the intervention of official authorities. Blockchain in the education sector can be used as an alternative to educational reputation currency [12] to measure learning outcomes to further store them in virtual wallets. Learning is earning is a smart contract application for students to get reward for their performance in education. Secure and immutable nature of blockchain makes it suitable for storing performance data of learners that can be trusted and used later in talent acquisition [35]. Because education is more diversified, decentralized, and disintermediated nowadays, so we need to maintain more reputation, proof of learning and trust in certification.

15.4.5 SECURITY AND PRIVACY WITH BLOCKCHAIN

A large amount of personal and private data is handled by centralized, public, and private organizations. Blockchain technology can be deployed for strengthening the security of such a big data [36] generated by IoT applications. The security services that can be provided by blockchain includes: authentication, integrity, confidentiality, and data privacy. The conventional way to provide data privacy is through access control list (ACL) rights to owners of data and encryption techniques to prevent others from accessing the data [37]. Hiding the identity of the user is major concern from a privacy point of view in IoT. Blockchain provide pseudo-anonymous privacy to users. In the case of bitcoin, hash values are used to classify the users of blockchain in place of their real identities to keep them hidden and anonymous within the system unless practiced attacks are executed [38]. Internet censorship is prevented with one of the non-currency implementations of blockchain called Namecoin. It is an altcoin that is used to verify domain name system (DNS) registrations and it is not controlled by any corporation or government. The advantage of Namecoin is that it can be used by anyone to share the information publicly, who is feasibly suppressed for sharing information on the internet. The main benefits of Namecoin are security, efficiency, privacy, and censorship resistance. Alexandra [39] is another open-source project based upon blockchain that provides secure and decentralized freedom of speech. Both these systems can be enhanced with pseudonymous approach of blockchain to hide an individual's identity, enabling security and privacy [14, 40]. To enhance the security of modern power systems against cyber-attacks Liang et al. [41] proposed the use of a distributed blockchain-based protection framework. Use of docker containers (Con,) in IoT and their benefits are described by [42].

15.4.6 BLOCKCHAIN IN INSURANCE SECTOR

Many aspects of the insurance industry can be improved with the potential benefits of blockchain. The insurance sector faces many disruptions due to slow claim processing and manual paper work. Smart contracts in the blockchain system after meeting some specified conditions are able to trigger an action. The blockchain is able to verify and process insurance claims instantly without human intervention, once they are uploaded by a customer. Logistics cost is saved with an increase in device-internet connectivity in IoT. The risk prediction power of insurance industry has enhanced owing to regular flow of information among devices connected through cloud due to blockchain integration. For example, in health insurance, a central database can be created with the help of blockchain to collect information from hospitals, and companies can gather data from this database to speedup sign-ups of customers and processing of claims [43]. Privacy and security features of blockchain helps in secure processing of health-care information which is desirable in health insurance. With the help of blockchain and ML, a healthcare startup EMRChain (EMR) is building a platform to provide immutable audit-trail of data and patient's health forecasting respectively. This platform is acting as an interface between private insurance providers and hospitals. It is providing fast data access and quick decision support due to inter-operable system. Shared Blockchain among all companies helps in inspection and reduction of fraudulent claim risks. Introduction of anti-counterfeit solutions in supply chain management with blockchain are tried by Blockverify (blo, a). Another organization, Dynamis (dyn,) has proposed to implement blockchain in providing unemployment insurance to people by collecting data from professional networks on execution of smart contracts. InsurETH (ins,), offering travel delay insurance works on blockchain-based execution of Ethereum smart contracts, by keeping flight delay information for resolving claims. Blockchain is used here to keep flight delay information based upon which claims are resolved.

15.5   BLOCKCHAIN AND IoT INTEGRATION AND APPLICATIONS

15.5.1   *DETERMINING REQUIREMENT OF BLOCKCHAIN IN IoT*

A blockchain is not considered appropriate for every IoT application. Typically, for certain IoT scenarios directed acyclic graph-based ledgers [44] and conventional distributed databases are good solutions [3]. Figure 15.7 is depicting a flow-graph for deciding the type of blockchain that must be chosen depending upon the need of IoT application. Fernandez-Carames and Fraga-Lamas [3] has described features of IoT application, which gives an idea of blockchain applicability in IoT. If these features are required in an application only then the developers should consider developments of IoT using blockchain. These features are described below:

1.   **Peer-to-Peer Exchange:** IoT communication occurs from IoT nodes to gateways which further route the information to cloud or remote server. Intelligent swarms [45] and mist computing [46] are specific applications which require communication at the node level, otherwise node level communication is not so common in IoT. Communication among nodes at the same hierarchy also happens in fog computing with local gateways [47, 48].

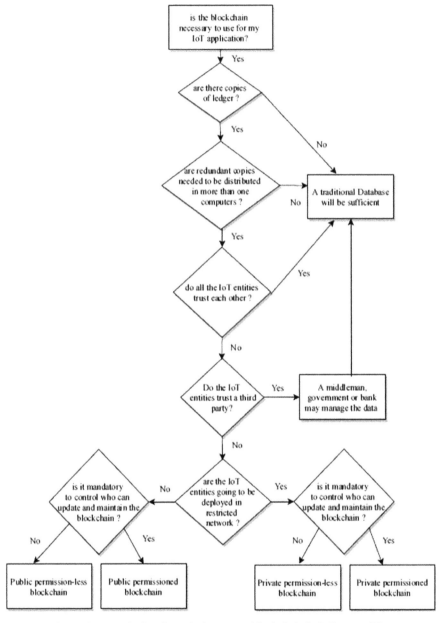

FIGURE 15.7 Flow graph showing whether to use blockchain in IoT or not [3].

2. **Decentralization:** This phenomenon is required in IoT applications if there is no central system to be trusted, but blind trust still exist

on banks and government agencies by many users, so if there is no trust-less environment there is no need of blockchain.

3. **Payment Systems:** There are certain applications in IoT which perform economic transactions with trusted third parties but many applications do not. Moreover, traditional payment systems are sufficient enough to perform economic transaction in a centralized environment.

4. **Transaction Logging with Time-Stamp:** If security is guaranteed and attacks are rare then time stamping and sequential storage of transactions can be easily full filled with traditional databases.

5. **Robust Distributed Systems:** These systems can be easily implemented with clouds and servers and any type of traditional database systems [49]. Need of blockchain occurs if there is a trust-less environment in the entities which are managing distributed computing.

6. **Micro-Transaction Collection:** Not all IoT applications need to keep a record of every transaction, but some of them as in [50, 51], for audit-ability purpose or for applying big data techniques [52, 53]. Use of side chains [54] is an efficient solution in this case. There are some applications where communication is expensive, like, remote agriculture monitoring. For such applications use of IoT nodes is common which will wake up every hour for collecting sensors' data. The collected data is recorded on local systems and transmitted once a day altogether in a single transaction [55].

Figure 15.7 summarizes through a generic flow diagram, the type of blockchain that must be opted depending upon IoT application [3].

15.5.2 APPLICATIONS OF BLOCKCHAIN IN INTERNET OF THINGS (IoT)

The aim of IoT is to allow communication among smart objects in order to provide personalized automation services and collect data from internet with little human interference. To fulfill this objective centralized server architecture is used in IoT for data handling, device authorization and coordination services. High-end servers are required for this approach, and it is proved unsuitable in situations where anonymous data sharing is required. Keeping in view the benefits offered by blockchain technology and their potential impact, developers, and researchers are trying to create decentralized applications for IoT using blockchain. Few of these applications are discussed in this section [56].

15.5.2.1 BLOCKCHAIN FOR IoT PRIVACY

Recently decentralization using blockchain has been seen as a solution to issues of privacy in IoT. Due to the decentralized nature of blockchain, once IoT devices are integrated with this technology, malicious users would not be able to perform different types of malicious activities to impact the integrity of data in the IoT environment, thus leading to enhanced data privacy. All types of interaction over blockchain are publicly available and verifiable. IoT data stored on-chain and off-chain is encrypted and authorized access policies can be enforced on the blockchain. The first step towards this authorized access mechanism is to ensure data ownership for users of IoT data so that users have full control over; how their data will be accessed and when. One of the proposed solutions for private ownership of IoT data is FairAccess [57, 58] where data owners have full control to give access to their IoT data. Smart contract is used by FairAccess to give privileges to users who want access rights to their data in exchange for service or monetary benefits [56]. IBM and Samsung [59] are trying to promote device autonomy under the project titled autonomous decentralized peer-to-peer telemetry (ADEPT) and to do this they are ensuring execution of code at edge device level using blockchain technology. This autonomous project uses some protocols: Ethereum, BitTorrent, Telehash for blockchain, file sharing and messaging, respectively. Authentication, engagement, checklists, and contracts are provided by blockchain technology. Proof of concept based smart contract in blockchain technology, applied in smart washing machines for buying detergent supplies from retail stores.

15.5.2.2 TRUSTLESS IoT ARCHITECTURE WITH BLOCKCHAIN

IoT ecosystem offers its services in a centralized environment using cloud infrastructure for storing and processing of the data from IoT devices. Devices in the IoT ecosystem interact with users, collect sensitive data, and intimate to the users. Though the data in the IoT ecosystem is widely available through cloud services, it is still stored and managed by a central authority which could lead to privacy and security breaches in IoT. This security and privacy breach problem could be solved either by using trustful architecture that is maintained by using secure algorithms to store IoT data. The other approach is a trustless architecture [60] which follows a peer-to-peer approach for transaction validation among participating entities. IoTChain [61] has proposed a trustless architecture using blockchain where different devices in the IoT framework can register themselves for sharing, storing, and organizing data streams without interference of any trusted third party. Trustchain [62] is another trustless architecture which is scalable and Sybil attack resistant and it uses NetFlow as a consensus algorithm in place of POW to guarantee trustworthiness of peers. Trustchain makes use of parallel chains to keep record of transactions of all the participating entities. Trustchain is responsible for identifying faults if transactions stored in one chain do not match with identical transactions of the other involved parties and refuses further services to those peers responsible for the faults [56].

15.5.2.3   BLOCKCHAIN-IoT IN ENERGY SECTOR

Applications of blockchain to internet of energy (IoE) [63–65] or to IoT are benefiting the energy sector also. Authors of Ref. [66] are proposing a blockchain-based approach in which IoE/IoT devices are paying for services to each other without human involvement. In this chapter potential of the system is shown with an implementation: a smart grid is connected with smart cable to pay for the electricity consumption. In addition, a single-fee micro-payment protocol is also presented for aggregating multiple small payments into a single large transaction, for reducing the transaction fees in cryptocurrencies such as Bitcoin [3]. In LO3 Energy (LO3) a blockchain based Microgrid of energy has been illustrated in South Australia, Southern Germany, and Brooklyn (USA). Grouping of energy storage, electricity generation and loading is done in the form of microgrids. A community energy marketplace is built using this project and a peer-to-peer energy network is created to coordinate with the power grid. This blockchain-energy platform is the first of its kind which allows devices to perform energy sales directly and securely among participants of micro-grid.

15.5.2.4   BLOCKCHAIN-IoT IN HEALTHCARE

IoT in healthcare is another application area of blockchain. A trace-ability application is described in Ref. [67] making use of sensors in IoT and blockchain technology for verification of data integrity and accessing temperature records in the supply chain of the pharmaceutical industry. For the transportation of medical products, this verification is very judgmental because it would help in ensuring the medical conditions and quality of medical products like humidity and temperature. In this application, a sensor is attached with every shipped parcel to transfer the data to blockchain. A smart contract is used on the blockchain to determine whether the received value of collected data through sensors is within the prescribed range or not. There is another application of blockchain in IoT described in Ref. [68] where blockchain based architecture is presented for precision medicine and clinical trials [3].

15.5.2.5 SECURITY WITH BLOCKCHAIN IN IoT

While IoT smart devices get connected with each other and with the internet, creating an interconnected complex system, they become vulnerable to different types of web attacks like traffic analysis, Sybil attack, message spoofing, password security, etc., due to centralized architecture of IoT. Access control, data integrity, availability, and confidentiality are the areas of security in IoT provided with blockchain to protect the information system against these attacks [56]. Research lab named Chain of Things (Cha,), provided integrated IoT and blockchain solution Maru, by assigning universal identity to devices for interoperability and security. Devices are provided with universal identity for interoperability, security. Three case studies implementing proof of concept over Ethereum network are: Chain of Shipping, to improve security in logistics and shipping industry; Chain of Solar, for connecting solar panels to blockchain in order to store generated energy for different applications and Chain of Security, for providing security to IoT using blockchain.

A blockchain-based solution called Modum (Mod,) improves supply chain process with an aim to facilitate data integrity for physical products. This solution was created to work with different platforms, and it used devices equipped with sensors to record environmental conditions during shipping. Ethereum blockchain-based solution has been developed to distribute medical products. Each time the ownership of goods gets changed, Ethereum smart contracts verify sensor data and validate that the transaction is meeting customer's standards. A mobile application, sensor tags, and a dashboard are integrated together to achieve this solution. Riddle and Code secured the ownership of their everyday object (Rid,) using a solution called Twin of Things. This solution uses cryptography and blockchain, and generates hardware-based digital-identities for all physical objects that are connected. Each device is allowed to become a blockchain node with the help of a secure crypto-chip. The tamper-proof and unique identity of the chip is registered by executing a blockchain transaction using an android application. This chip exists as near field communication (NFC) tag. The chip can interact with other devices in the network after getting validation. At present the solution can work with BigchainDB blockchains, Ethereum, and Bitcoin. Industrial-IoT integration is provided with blockchain of things (BCoT) (blo, b) which is a secure open communication platform. A web service named Catenis is proposed to provide swift integration of Bitcoin blockchain, with an end-to-end encryption. In this web service every IoT device within Gateways and a Catenis hub is represented as a virtual device.

15.5.2.6   BLOCKCHAIN-IoT IN ECONOMIC SECTOR

Slock.it (Prisco,) introduced a blockchain-based framework to deal with privacy, coordination, identity, and security over billions of IoT devices. In this framework a shared economy is created from where without involving any authority IoT assets get rented quickly and securely. A variety of projects they are working upon, one of them is Block charge that is a marketplace providing a charging infrastructure to charge electric vehicles. It is a mobile application-based solution, that activates the smart-plug, charge it with control, and uses blockchain for payment of services availed. Another project they are working on is based on smart lock for automating renting of apartments. Smart contracts are implemented in autonomous insurance network called Aigang (Aig,) using Ethereum, to conduct risk assessment, issue policies and for automatic processing of claims. This network has also made a custom-virtual currency and is offering opportunities for investment with distinct risk levels in distinct product range. Smart contracts are used to automate insurance payments and to order maintenance by intelligent devices which are connected with insurance policies. Further, inclusion of event reporting helps in automatic handling of claims. MyBit (Myb) is a new investment opportunity and financial model that creates an ecosystem in which only a certain number of people are involved that are the owner of IoT assets and share revenues generated through services of this ecosystem. It uses Ethereum smart contract for automation of the process so that the investors automatically get their share from the revenue generated through IoT devices.

Applications of blockchain in IoT are being represented pictorially in Figure 15.8. It is evident from the figure that blockchain can be integrated in almost all major application areas of IoT.

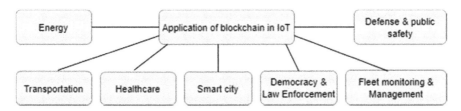

FIGURE 15.8 Applications of blockchain in IoT.

15.6 CHALLENGES AND OPPORTUNITIES IN INTEGRATION OF BLOCKCHAIN AND IoT

This section summarizes the challenges in integrating blockchain with IoT, which is a significant area of research. Blockchain technology was basically designed to operate on powerful computers on the internet which is a long way from physically existing IoT. Blockchain works with transaction which is digitally signed, therefore all the devices capable enough to work on blockchain technology must be furnished with this service. Assimilating blockchain with IoT is challenging [69]. Some of these challenges are described in this section.

15.6.1 SECURITY

Security problems in IoT applications need to be dealt with at different levels because of heterogeneity and lack of performance in devices. In addition, there are other properties of IoT which affect security such as scale, mobility, and wireless communication. Increase in number of attacks on IoT environment and their severe effects inflates the need to create more sophisticated security techniques for IoT. One of the major challenges in integrating blockchain with IoT to enhance security is the reliability of data generated by IoT to store it on blockchain. If the data is already corrupted while it is generated by insecure IoT device, it will get stored on blockchain in that corrupted form only. The reason for generation of corrupt data can be malicious activities like failure of devices, environment or participants affecting IoT architecture. Sometimes the devices do not work properly due to their disconnection, short circuit and so on. Some other factors affecting IoT environment are denial of service (DoS), eavesdropping, and controlling [70]. Due to these reasons, IoT devices must be tested thoroughly and must be placed on the right place before integrating them with blockchain [69].

15.6.2   SCALABILITY AND STORAGE CAPACITY

Blockchain technology is facing scalability and storage capacity as a major challenge these days and if we think about integrating this technology with IoT, then the capacity and storage as inherent limitations make these challenges more eminent. In IoT environment, each device produces data in gigabits; this is a major restriction in integrating blockchain with IoT because at present blockchains are processing only a few transactions per second. In addition, blockchains are not designed to keep large amount of data as produced in IoT. So, an integration of these techniques is a major challenge in terms of storage capacity and scalability [69].

15.6.3   DATA PRIVACY AND ANONYMITY

It is essential to solve the problem of data privacy and anonymity in many applications of IoT. For example, in e-health, personal data is kept confidential when a device is connected with a person. For identity management blockchain is the ideal solution, but there are applications like in bitcoin, where anonymity is important. In IoT problem of data privacy is challenging because securing devices so that their data are not accessed without permission is possible only by integrating security cryptographic software into the devices. The problem of identity management in IoT can be solved with blockchain but privacy and security are still the challenges to be addressed in IoT [69].

15.6.4   RESOURCE CONSTRAINTS

Resources in IoT are limited in terms of communication, storage, and computation while blockchain technology which works in Gigabits (GBs) of memory needs an excessive number of resources. Moreover, the calculations performed by consensus protocols used in blockchain, like POW are also beyond the potential of low-powered IoT devices. As can be seen in Figure 15.9 end-devices and edge-devices used in IoT are not capable enough to be connected directly to blockchain due to high resource demands. Server layer in IoT is ideally suitable for modern blockchain deployment. This server layer would act as an entry point from the centralized architecture of IoT to decentralized architecture of blockchain [71].

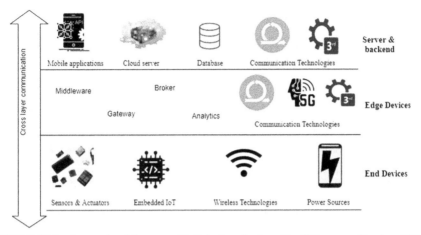

FIGURE 15.9 Layered architecture of IoT devices deployed in different applications [71].

15.6.5 *BLOCKCHAIN INFRASTRUCTURE, LEGAL, AND REGULATORY ASPECTS*

A comprehensive trust infrastructure is required for the efficient functioning of blockchain in IoT. Inter-domain policies and controls are some of the latest approaches which can address the trust-related issues in the deployment of blockchain in IoT. To support use-cases of public interest, blockchain framework must be set up by the government. In addition, development of a proper model for regulatory environment such as national and international regulators of decentralized owner-ships is another issue in amplification of potential use of blockchain in IoT. It may be the case that some blockchain developers show fake results of their blockchain in order to lure more investors propelled by the expected profit [3].

15.6.6 *LATENCY DEMANDS IN IoT*

Different IoT applications typically involve a set of data consumers and data producers. Data consumers are the real actuators who respond to an event. The introduction of blockchain technology will reduce the responsiveness of data consumers because they have to wait for a long for the conclusion of a consensus algorithm before making a decision on an event. Therefore, state-of-the-art blockchain technology is not suitable for IoT environment applications where fully and timely confirmed transactions are the primary requirements [71].

15.7   SUMMARY AND FUTURE RESEARCH DIRECTIONS

In this chapter, we had a review of blockchain as a technology, its latest and greatest applications, and ventures in this area, possibility of integration with IoT in specific application areas. Based on the literature referred for IoT-blockchain applications, Ethereum is the most popular blockchain platform. It provides extensive features as compared to Bitcoin, and expands the applications of blockchain in IoT due to inclusion of smart contracts.

Despite its benefits there are certain challenges faced by the blockchain technology itself, few of them are described here:

- Privacy of transactions is a challenge in blockchain. Several methods have been proposed to improve anonymity property in blockchain [10] such as mixing services [72], zero-knowledge proofs [73] but the solutions for transaction privacy are still required in IoT-blockchain integrated applications.

- Blockchain technology as a distributed P2P network of blocks was basically designed to solve the double-spending problem [9] in bitcoin by maintaining the order of execution of transaction using transaction timestamp as a metric. Thus, blockchain is capable of keeping a robust and auditable record of all transactions. With the advent of blockchain traditional business system is facing serious disruption because the applications and services based on centralized or third-party approval can now work in decentralized environment inevitably. So, there is a need to decide which IoT application should be implemented with decentralized features of blockchain and which of them should be kept centralized.

- The number of cryptocurrencies illustrates blockchain's importance, currently exceeding and growing (Chez,). Such a growth pace could soon create interoperability problems due to the heterogeneity of cryptocurrency applications [74].

- Though the blockchain technology due to its inherent capabilities is able to modify the future of internet systems, it is facing scalability challenge. Block size of bitcoin is restricted to be 1 MB now and mining of new block occurs every 10 minutes. Consequently, the bitcoin network processes 7 transactions per second, showing its ineffectiveness for high transmission trading. On the other hand, keeping a large block size would result in more storage requirements and increased delay in the operation of the network, leading to security threat.

- Another challenge in case of blockchain based cryptocurrencies is selfish mining by miners to increase their revenues. It holds up blockchain development. Hence solutions are required for these problems in order to deploy or integrate this technology with IoT.
- Though blockchain is capable of providing robust security solutions for IoT, but it is still vulnerable [75]. If the hashing power of minor is limited, the consensus algorithm of blockchain can be compromised by an attacker to take control of the blockchain. Similarly, insufficient randomization of private keys can be leveraged for compromising blockchain. To ensure privacy of transactions and to avoid race attacks which results in double-spending problem; there is a need to deploy effective mechanisms.

15.8 CONCLUSION

In this chapter, we explained how major challenges faced by IoT can be leveraged to explore blockchain integration with it. The narrative outline of the chapter started with history of blockchain, its architecture, the role of consensus algorithms in it and applications of smart contracts in implementing blockchain. Decentralization in the cryptocurrency world achieved through blockchain can also be applicable for IoT with no intermediaries. The challenges and research opportunities in potential application areas of blockchain integration with IoT were listed. Those opportunities, if explored, may yield productive outcomes in the near future.

KEYWORDS

- **Blockchain**
- **Blockchain in IoT**
- **Client-server architecture**
- **Information and communication technologies**
- **IoT challenges**
- **Message queue telemetry transport**
- **Security and privacy**

REFERENCES

1. Panarello, A., Tapas, N., Merlino, G., Longo, F., & Puliafito, A., (2018). Blockchain and IoT integration: A systematic survey. *Sensors, 18*(8), 2575.
2. Gubbi, J., Buyya, R., Marusic, S., & Palaniswami, M., (2013). Internet of things (IoT): A vision, architectural elements, and future directions. *Future Generation Computer Systems, 29*(7), 1645–1660.
3. Fernández-Caramés, T. M., & Fraga-Lamas, P., (2018). A review on the use of blockchain for the internet of things. *IEEE Access, 6*, 32979–33001.
4. Triantafillou, P., Ntarmos, N., Nikoletseas, S., & Spirakis, P., (2003). Nano peer networks and p2p worlds. In: *Proceedings Third International Conference on Peer-to-Peer Computing (P2P2003)* (pp. 40–46). IEEE.
5. Ali, M., & Uzmi, Z. A., (2004). CSN: A network protocol for serving dynamic queries in large-scale wireless sensor networks. In: *Proceedings. Second Annual Conference on Communication Networks and Services Research* (pp. 165–174). IEEE.
6. Kolias, C., Kambourakis, G., Stavrou, A., & Voas, J., (2017). DDoS in the IoT: Mirai and other botnets. *Computer, 50*(7), 80–84.
7. Sicari, S., Rizzardi, A., Cappiello, C., Miorandi, D., & Coen-Porisini, A., (2018). Toward data governance in the internet of things. In: *New Advances in the Internet of Things* (pp. 59–74). Springer.
8. Hawlitschek, F., Notheisen, B., & Teubner, T., (2018). The limits of trust-free systems: A literature review on blockchain technology and trust in the sharing economy. *Electronic Commerce Research and Applications, 29*, 50–63.
9. Nakamoto, S., & Bitcoin, A., (2008). *A Peer-to-Peer Electronic Cash System*. Bitcoin.-URL: https://bitcoin.org/bitcoin.pdf (accessed on 10 November 2021).
10. Zheng, Z., Xie, S., Dai, H. N., Chen, X., & Wang, H., (2018). Blockchain challenges and opportunities: A survey. *International Journal of Web and Grid Services, 14*(4), 352–375.
11. Kosba, A., Miller, A., Shi, E., Wen, Z., & Papamanthou, C., (2016). Hawk: The blockchain model of cryptography and privacy-preserving smart contracts. In: *2016 IEEE Symposium on Security and Privacy (SP)* (pp. 839–858). IEEE.
12. Sharples, M., & Domingue, J., (2016). The blockchain and kudos: A distributed system for educational record, reputation and reward. In: *European Conference on Technology Enhanced Learning* (pp. 490–496). Springer.
13. Noyes, C., (2016). *Bitav: Fast Anti-Malware by Distributed Blockchain Consensus and Feedforward Scanning*. arXiv preprint arXiv:1601.01405.
14. Swan, M., (2015). *Blockchain: Blueprint for a New Economy*. O'Reilly Media, Inc.
15. Sigal, M., (2011). *You Say You Want a Revolution? It's Called Post-PC Computing*.
16. Johnson, D., Menezes, A., & Vanstone, S., (2001). The elliptic curve digital signature algorithm (ecdsa). *International Journal of Information Security, 1*(1), 36–63.
17. Lin, I. C., & Liao, T. C., (2017). A survey of blockchain security issues and challenges. *IJ Network Security, 19*(5), 653–659.
18. Lu, Y., (2018). Blockchain and the related issues: a review of current research topics. *Journal of Management Analytics, 5*(4), 231–255.
19. Buterin, V., (2015). *On public and Private Blockchains*. URL: https://blog.Ethereum.org/2015/08/07/on-public-and-private-blockchains (accessed on 10 November 2021).
20. Blummer, B., (2018). *An Introduction to Hyperledger*. https://bit.ly/2W7bCpq (accessed on 10 November 2021).

21. Ray, J., (2018). *Consortium Chain Development.* https://bit.ly/2YAPvJl (accessed on 10 November 2021).

22. Lamport, L., Shostak, R., & Pease, M., (1982). The byzantine generals problem. *ACM Transactions on Programming Languages and Systems, 4*(3), 382–401.

23. Vasin, P., (2014). *Blackcoin's Proof-of-Stake Protocol v2.* URL: https://blackcoin.co/ blackcoin-pos-protocol-v2-whitepaper.pdf (accessed on 10 November 2021).

24. Moore, S., Chang, S., & Bach, S., (2016). Practical byzantine fault tolerance. *American Mathematical Monthly, 27*(4), 1–4.

25. Fabian, S. D. L., (2017). *BitShares 2.0: General Overview.* https://cryptorating.eu/ whitepapers/BitShares/bitshares-general.pdf (accessed on 10 November 2021).

26. Vukolic, M., (2015). The quest for scalable blockchain fabric: Proof-of-work vs. BFT replication. In: *International Workshop on Open Problems in Network Security* (pp. 112–125). Springer.

27. Fiaidhi, J., Mohammed, S., & Mohammed, S., (2018). Edi with blockchain as an enabler for extreme automation. *IT Professional, 20*(4), 66–72.

28. Kumar, J. S., & Patel, D. R., (2014). A survey on internet of things: Security and privacy issues. *International Journal of Computer Applications, 90*(11).

29. Ammar, M., Russello, G., & Crispo, B., (2018). Internet of things: A survey on the security of IoT frameworks. *Journal of Information Security and Applications, 38*, 8–27.

30. Zhao, K., & Ge, L., (2013). A survey on the internet of things security. In: *2013 Ninth International Conference on Computational Intelligence and Security* (pp. 663–667). IEEE.

31. Ali, M. S., Vecchio, M., Pincheira, M., Dolui, K., Antonelli, F., & Rehmani, M. H., (2018a). Applications of blockchains in the internet of things: A comprehensive survey. *IEEE Communications Surveys & Tutorials, 21*(2),1676–1717.

32. Haferkorn, M., & Diaz, J. M. Q., (2014). Seasonality and interconnectivity within cryptocurrencies-an analysis on the basis of bitcoin, Litecoin and name coin. In: *International Workshop on Enterprise Applications and Services in the Finance Industry* (pp. 106–120). Springer.

33. Nguyen, Q. K., (2016). Blockchain-a financial technology for future sustainable development. In: *2016 3rd International Conference on Green Technology and Sustainable Development (GTSD)* (pp. 51–54). IEEE.

34. Peters, G. W., & Panayi, E., (2016). Understanding modern banking ledgers through blockchain technologies: Future of transaction processing and smart contracts on the internet of money. In: *Banking Beyond Banks and Money* (pp. 239–278). Springer.

35. Chen, G., Xu, B., Lu, M., & Chen, N. S., (2018). Exploring blockchain technology and its potential applications for education. *Smart Learning Environments, 5*(1), 1.

36. Puthal, D., Malik, N., Mohanty, S. P., Kougianos, E., & Yang, C., (2018). The blockchain is a decentralized security framework [future directions]. *IEEE Consumer Electronics Magazine, 7*(2),18–21.

37. Salman, T., Zolanvari, M., Erbad, A., Jain, R., & Samaka, M., (2018). Security services using blockchains: A state of the art survey. *IEEE Communications Surveys & Tutorials, 21*(1), 858–880.

38. Pilkington, M., (2015). *Research Handbook on Digital Transformations.* Books.Google. Com (accessed on 10 November 2021).

39. Bingen, J., & Karrarah, A., (1988). The Library of Alexandria: Past and future. *Diogenes, 36*(141), 38–55.

40. Zhang, N., Zhong, S., & Tian, L., (2017). Using blockchain to protect personal privacy in the scenario of online taxi- hailing. *International Journal of Computers Communications & Control, 12*(6), 886–902.

41. Liang, G., Weller, S. R., Luo, F., Zhao, J., & Dong, Z. Y., (2018). Distributed blockchain-based data protection framework for modern power systems against cyber attacks. *IEEE Transactions on Smart Grid, 10*(3), 3162–3173.

42. Xu, Q., Jin, C., Rasid, M. F. B. M., Veeravalli, B., & Aung, K. M. M., (2017). Decentralized content trust for docker images. In: *IoTBDS* (pp. 431–437).

43. Ikeda, K., & Hamid, M. N., (2018). Applications of blockchain in the financial sector and a peer-to-peer global barter web. In: Advances in Computers (Vol. 111, pp. 99–120). Elsevier.

44. Simmons, J., (2019). What is iota? https://www.crypto-news-flash.com/ (accessed on 10 November 2021).

45. Gui, T., Ma, C., Wang, F., & Wilkins, D. E., (2016). Survey on swarm intelligence based routing protocols for wireless sensor networks: An extensive study. In: *2016 IEEE International Conference on Industrial Technology (ICIT)* (pp. 1944–1949). IEEE.

46. Preden, J. S., Tammemäe, K., Jantsch, A., Leier, M., Riid, A., & Calis, E., (2015). The benefits of self-awareness and attention in fog and mist computing. *Computer, 48*(7), 37–45.

47. Lavanya, R., (2019). Fog computing and its role in the internet of things. In*: Advancing Consumer-Centric Fog Computing Architectures* (pp. 63–71). IGI Global.

48. Suárez-Albela, M., Fernández-Caramés, T. M., Fraga-Lamas, P., & Castedo, L., (2017). A practical evaluation of a high- security energy-efficient gateway for IoT fog computing applications. *Sensors, 17*(9), 1978.

49. Datla, D., Chen, X., Tsou, T., Raghunandan, S., Hasan, S. S., Reed, J. H., Dietrich, C. B., et al., (2012). Wireless distributed computing: A survey of research challenges. *IEEE Communications Magazine, 50*(1), 144–152.

50. Wu, Z., Meng, Z., & Gray, J., (2017). IoT-based techniques for online m2m-interactive itemized data registration and offline information traceability in a digital manufacturing system. *IEEE Transactions on Industrial Informatics, 13*(5), 2397–2405.

51. Lomotey, R. K., Pry, J., Sriramoju, S., Kaku, E., & Deters, R., (2017). Wearable IoT data architecture. In: *2017 IEEE World Congress on Services (SERVICES)* (pp. 44–50). IEEE.

52. Cai, H., Xu, B., Jiang, L., & Vasilakos, A. V., (2016). IoT-based big data storage systems in cloud computing: Perspectives and challenges. *IEEE Internet of Things Journal, 4*(1), 75–87.

53. Marjani, M., Nasaruddin, F., Gani, A., Karim, A., Hashem, I. A. T., Siddiqa, A., & Yaqoob, I., (2017). Big IoT data analytics: architecture, opportunities, and open research challenges. *IEEE Access, 5*, 5247–5261.

54. Back, A., Corallo, M., Dashjr, L., Friedenbach, M., Maxwell, G., Miller, A., Poelstra, A., et al., (2014). *Enabling Blockchain Innovations with Pegged Sidechains*. URL: http://www.opensciencereview.com/papers/123/enablingblockchain-innovations-with-pegged-sidechains (accessed on 10 November 2021).

55. Pérez-Expósito, J. P., Fernández-Caramés, T. M., Fraga-Lamas, P., & Castedo, L., (2017). Vinesens: An eco-smart decision-support viticulture system. *Sensors, 17*(3), 465.

56. Ali, M. S., Vecchio, M., Pincheira, M., Dolui, K., Antonelli, F., & Rehmani, M. H., (2018b). Applications of blockchains in the internet of things: A comprehensive survey. *IEEE Communications Surveys & Tutorials, 21*(2),1676–1717.

57. Ouaddah, A., Abou, E. A., & Ait, O. A., (2016). Fair access: A new blockchain-based access control framework for the internet of things. *Security and Communication Networks, 9*(18), 5943–5964.

58. Ouaddah, A., Elkalam, A. A., & Ouahman, A. A., (2017). Towards a novel privacy-preserving access control model based on blockchain technology in IoT. In: *Europe and MENA Cooperation Advances in Information and Communication Technologies* (pp. 523–533). Springer.

59. Veena, P., Panikkar, S., Nair, S., & Brody, P., (2015). *Empowering the Edge-Practical Insights on a Decentralized Internet of Things*. IBM Institute for Business Value, 17.

60. Tai, S., (2016). Continuous, trustless, and fair: Changing priorities in services computing. In: *European Conference on Service-Oriented and Cloud Computing* (pp. 205–210). Springer.

61. Yu, B., Wright, J., Nepal, S., Zhu, L., Liu, J., & Ranjan, R., (2018). Trust chain: Establishing trust in the IoT-based applications ecosystem using blockchain. *IEEE Cloud Computing, 5*(4), 12–23.

62. Otte, P., De Vos, M., & Pouwelse, J., (2017). Trustchain: A Sybil-resistant scalable blockchain. *Future Generation Computer Systems*.

63. Kafle, Y., Mahmud, K., Morsalin, S., & Town, G., (2016). Towards an internet of energy. In: *2016 IEEE International Conference on Power System Technology (POWERCON)* (pp. 1–6). IEEE.

64. Blanco-Novoa, O., Fernández-Caramés, T. M., Fraga-Lamas, P., & Castedo, L., (2017). An electricity price-aware open-source smart socket for the internet of energy. *Sensors, 17*(3), 643.

65. Fernández-Caramés, T. M., (2015). An intelligent power outlet system for the smart home of the internet of things. International *Journal of Distributed Sensor Networks, 11*(11), 214805.

66. Lundqvist, T., De Blanche, A., & Andersson, H. R. H., (2017). Thing-to-thing electricity micropayments using blockchain technology. In: *2017 Global Internet of Things Summit (GIoTS)* (pp. 1–6). IEEE.

67. Bocek, T., Rodrigues, B. B., Strasser, T., & Stiller, B., (2017). Blockchains everywhere-a use-case of blockchains in the pharma supply-chain. In: *2017 IFIP/IEEE Symposium on Integrated Network and Service Management (IM)* (pp. 772–777). IEEE.

68. Shae, Z., & Tsai, J. J., (2017). On the design of a blockchain platform for clinical trial and precision medicine. In: *2017 IEEE 37th International Conference on Distributed Computing Systems (ICDCS)* (pp. 1972–1980). IEEE.

69. Reyna, A., Martín, C., Chen, J., Soler, E., & Díaz, M., (2018). On blockchain and its integration with iot. challenges and opportunities. *Future Generation Computer Systems, 88*, 173–190.

70. Roman, R., Zhou, J., & Lopez, J., (2013). On the features and challenges of security and privacy in distributed internet of things. *Computer Networks, 57*(10), 2266–2279.

71. Ramachandran, G. S., & Krishnamachari, B., (2018). *Blockchain for the IoT: Opportunities and Challenges.* arXiv preprint arXiv:1805.02818.

72. Koshy, P., Koshy, D., & McDaniel, P., (2014). An analysis of anonymity in bitcoin using p2p network traffic. In: *International Conference on Financial Cryptography and Data Security* (pp. 469–485). Springer, Berlin, Heidelberg.

73. Casino, F., Dasaklis, T. K., & Patsakis, C., (2019). A systematic literature review of blockchain-based applications: Current status, classification, and open issues. *Telematics and Informatics, 36*, 55–81.

74. Tschorsch, F., & Scheuermann, B., (2016). Bitcoin and beyond: A technical survey on decentralized digital currencies. *IEEE Communications Surveys & Tutorials, 18*(3), 2084–2123.

75. Li, X., Jiang, P., Chen, T., Luo, X., & Wen, Q., (2017). A survey on the security of blockchain systems. *Future Generation Computer Systems.*

76. Aigang, (2017). https://www.crunchbase.com/organization/aigang (accessed on 10 November 2021).

77. Antshares and the Blockchain, (2016). https://cryptorating.eu/whitepapers/NEO/antshares. pdf (accessed on 10 November 2021).

78. Blockverify Website, (2015). https://www.crunchbase.com/organization/blockverify (accessed on 10 November 2021).

79. Chain of things, (2017). https://www.blockchainofthings.com/ (accessed on 10 November 2021).

80. Chain of things, (2017). https://www.chainofthings.com/ (accessed on 10 November 2021).

81. Chez, M. Cryptocurrency Market Capitalizations, (2020). https://coinmarketcap.com/ (accessed on 10 November 2021).

82. Dynamis Website. http://dynamisapp.com/ (accessed on 10 November 2021).

83. IBM blockchain- enterprise blockchain solutions & services, (n.d.). https://www.ibm. com/in-en/blockchain (accessed on 10 November 2021).

84. Insureth Website, (2016). http://insureth.mkvd.net/ (accessed on 10 November 2021).

85. Internet of things outlook, (2017). https://www.ericsson.com/en/mobility-report/reports (accessed on 10 November 2021).

86. Lo3energy, (2018). https://lo3energy.com/ (accessed on 10 November 2021).

87. Modum, (2017). https://modum.io/ (accessed on 10 November 2021).

88. My bit, (2017). https://mybit.io/ (accessed on 10 November 2021).

89. Prisco, G., (2015). *Slock.it to Introduce Smart Locks Linked to Smart Ethereum Contracts.* https://bitcoinmagazine.com/technical/slock-it-to-introduce-smart-locks-linked-to-smart-ethereum-contracts-decentralize-the-sharing-economy-1446746719 (accessed on 10 November 2021).

90. Riddle and Code, (2017). https://www.riddleandcode.com/ (accessed on 10 November 2021).

91. Simply Vital Health Website, (2019). EMRchain website. http://ww1.emrchain.us (accessed on 10 November 2021).

92. *Survey on Blockchain Technologies and Related Services*, (2015). https://bit.ly/2zZx2vP (accessed on 10 November 2021).

93. What is a Container? (2017). https://www.docker.com/resources/what-container (accessed on 10 November 2021).

94. https://iota-news.com/about-iota/ (accessed on 10 November 2021).

CHAPTER 16

Paradigm Shift of Audience from Television to Video Streaming Apps

GITANJALI KALIA[1] and RAJESH CHAUHAN[2]

[1]*Associate Professor, School of Mass Communication, Chitkara University, Punjab, India*

[2]*Assistant Professor, School of Mass Communication, Chitkara University, Punjab, India*

ABSTRACT

Digital media has penetrated deep into our nerves that we can never think of the day when we are not exposed to digital platforms. There was a time when social media ruled the internet world, but with the increased internet speed and market competition among digital players, OTT platforms are the new leaders. Over the top players like Netflix, Amazon Prime, Voot, Hotstar, Balaji ATL, etc., are ruling the digital world. These video streaming apps have revolutionized the way people consume and react to content. From the change in king of the market from 'Consumer' to 'Content,' a lot has been changed in context to content producer to consumer. They have not only changed the time, date, and venue of our content consumption but have also upsurged new media-watching habits.

In this chapter, the authors have emphasis on the OTT platforms and their current market scenario. The author also focuses on understanding the theoretical perspective from the consumer viewpoint through cognitive dissonance theory where the audience have shifted their viewership from television to video streaming platforms. The chapter also mentions the change in content production and distribution patterns along with changing consumption patterns by consumers. Future aspects of these video streaming aspects have also been discussed at the end of this chapter.

16.1 INTRODUCTION

Media content providers, through video streaming services have revolutionized the way of providing entertainment to its viewers. They have not only changed the time, date, and venue of our content consumption but has also upsurged new media-watching habits. Gone are the days when people had to wait for their preferred television programs and movies to be broadcasted on specific time and day. The upsurge of Smartphone's advanced communication technology has revolutionized the way media content is being consumed. This convergence has led to new media termed as over the top media that has made way for video streaming platforms and services.

An over-the-top (OTT) software can be described as an app or service that offers content over the internet with the support of conventional distribution like cable or broadcast TV. The time period OTT refers to packages and services that are handy over the internet and presents various internet access services, e.g., newbie video aggregation web sites, social networks and so on. Some of the significant examples of OTT can be classified under the head like Messengers (Facebook Messenger, BlackBerry Messenger), Chat apps (Skype, Viber, WhatsApp), video streaming apps, eCommerce websites (Amazon, Flipkart, etc.).

The growth of OTT platforms has the following parameters:

1. **Adaptability of Technology:** The acceptability of any new ICT is entirely reliable on the technological set up of the country and how well they are equipped with it. Countries having excessive pace broadband networks and excessive degrees of phone penetration are maximum suitable to streaming services.

2. **Cost-Effectiveness:** Streaming platforms provide inexpensive access to information, entertainment, and education often. Usually, web players offer loose services to purchasers and use classified ads to recognize revenue.

3. **Social Acceptance of OTT:** The social adaptability to the OTT platforms is based on the education level of the demographics within the country. It is normally seen that social groups of youngsters and teenagers are more acceptable to the OTT platforms as they find programs with their area of interest. OTT platforms are generally interpersonal in nature with single consumer engagement rather than social groups.

4. **Audience is Strength:** The OTT is strengthened by the presence of a huge population over a single OS platform (e.g., Android).

5. **Extend of the Services:** Gamers are at a bonus with regards to scaling up any incremental/new offerings. Gamers on OTT platforms should construct new offerings without investing much in growing the infrastructure.

A video streaming service can be defined as an on-demand online entertainment source that broadcast shows on demand. Video streaming is a sort of media streaming wherein the facts from a video document is continually added via the internet to a faraway person. It allows the video to be considered on line without being downloaded on a pc or device.

India is on the brim of being the fastest-growing market for video streaming platforms. In one of the recent reports, India is set to enter the top 10 OTT video markets by 2022 with a growth rate of 22.6% CAGR. OTT video revenue in India is expected to touch 5,595 crores by 2022.

Another reason for the upsurge of this new media technology is inexpensive data and the increased data consumption. In one of the interviews, Bharti Airtel spokesman said, "The increase in video streaming activities is the result of the dipping data cost that has led to increase in average data consumption by 100% over the past years."

This change has enabled the consumers to consume content as per their preference in the context of information, entertainment, and social activities. Whether it is Netflix, Amazon, ATL Balaji, Hotstar, etc., these video streaming services are expanding in a big way. They are not only changing media gallery but also the way it is consumed technologically. Media has always been used as a medium for gratifying the personal needs of the audience, be that information, entertainment, and mood management needs. They engage with like-minded people and participate through connecting with them and interacting with their content as well as by likes, comments, and following them. They produce their own contents for expressing themselves and accomplishing their needs. These three usages are separate analytically but interdependent in reality. It has been observed that adolescents gratify their need for integration, social interaction, information, and understanding of their social environment primarily through the use of Facebook.

As per the recent BARC report, the common viewership for total TV in 2015 stood at 21.2 billion impressions, which presently stands at 29.2 billion. Youth are considered to be the very best clients of OTT content material and make a contribution 32 according to cent of total TV viewership, the highest among all age businesses. This too, has been developing yr-on-12 months. The impact of OTT players on DTH players has additionally begun displaying. There had been a few disconnections in metros because of the advent of OTT gamers inclusive of Netflix, Hotstar, and Amazon Prime movies. However, it is not always a supply of worry for DTH gamers as our internet additions are pretty excessive. We additionally plan to release our own OTT app in view of the trend,' quoted Anil Dua, CEO of Dish TV.

16.2   VIDEO STREAMING MARKET

To understand the market segmentation of the video streaming platforms, it can be classified and studied under following subheads:

1. **On the Basis of Types:** Video Streaming programs can be segmented on the basis of two major services provided by vendors:

   i. **On-Demand:** The on-demand video streaming provides viewers an exclusive access to a variety of channels and distinguished content along with the option of live screening of events on their preferred platforms. This option provides varied content with pre-scheduled content that provides effortless, preferable, and comfortable viewing.

   ii. **Programmed Video Streaming:** Programmed video streaming option provides the viewers to watch their favorite programs at their convenient timings as all the major channels have their own apps like Voot for Colors, Sony Liv for Sony TV, Hotstar for Star Plus, etc., where people watch their preferred shows at any time.

2. **On the Basis of Revenue Generation Components:** Video streaming market can also be segmented on the basis of revenue generation components:

   i. **Software Platform:** One of the major components while under-standing the video streaming platform are the software's used for handling the demand of online videos and the need of transcoding the data to deliver videos to a large number of end-users. The increasing demand in the software is a huge source of revenue for the OTT service providers.

   ii. **Video Streaming Services:** Advertisers leave no stone unturned when it comes to generating revenue from new business opportunities. Video streaming services are a great source of revenue for the marketers with their increase in demand and subscriptions.

3. **On the Basis of Deployment:** Segmentation on the basis of Video Streaming content being provided to customer:

i.   **On-Premise:** On-premise technique is generally used by the companies to connect third-party services to the application for the integrating the data. Generally, this feature provides the control in the hands of the company with very little control over the additional and external features like security that can be added to the app.

ii. **Cloud:** It is expected to witness an exceptional growth in the next coming years with the bulk storage it provides. With storage spaces like Dropbox, iCloud, Google Drive, SharePoint, and lots of others, it is becoming popular. The exquisite call for increase being witnessed with the aid of video streaming marketplace poses requirements for network efficiency, video processing, and high-carrier best, as a consequence to enhance present infrastructure. Adaptation of cloud-based services will fill the gaps with quicker overall performance, instant increase, and reduction in placement and renovation costs.

16.3   WORLDWIDE GROWTH OF VIDEO STREAMING APPS

The increasing demand of video streaming apps has resulted in millions of subscribers adding to the league every year. The market for video streaming is increasing continuously at a tremendous rate, majorly because of higher internet penetration of the internet in the lives of the people along with proliferating subscribers on social media platforms.

The global video streaming market is projected to increase by 18.3% CAGR during the period from 2019 to 2026.

In another report by prescient and strategic intelligence on 'video streaming market research-global industrial analysis and forecast to 2024 (2019), it can be seen that in the coming years India is expected to be one of the fastest-growing markets in the video streaming industry (Figure 16.1).

Figure 16.2 mentions the present state of video streaming platforms consumed by the consumers [19]. YouTube rules the 15% of the global video traffic while people stay at home followed by Netflix viewers with 11% of global traffic. WhatsApp consumer utilizes 12.78% of Satellite traffic and WordPress being the best blogging platform consumers 4.93% of global traffic.

According to Media Partners Asia, the research firm, as of give up-2017, the hooked-up base of virtual media consoles consisting of dongles and related STBs (set-top containers) stood at 0.7 million. While talking to Mint, Mihir Shah, Vice President Media Partners Asia, disclosed that in the subsequent five years, India may have a gigantic number of clients gaining access to video content material through connected STBs and dongles, equal to the wide variety of active pay-TV HD subscribers nowadays.

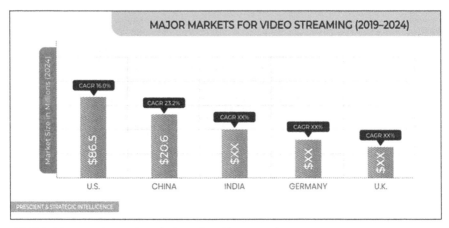

FIGURE 16.1   Major market's holders for video streaming.

Source: Reprinted with permission from: Prescient and Strategic Intelligence Report [1] while studying major markets for video streaming for the period of 2019–2024. www. psmarketresearch.com/market-analysis/video-streaming-market.

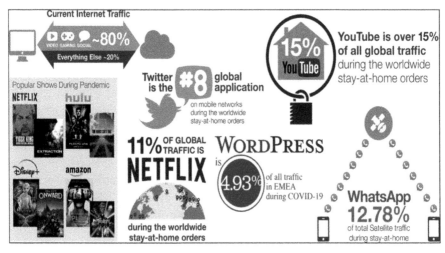

FIGURE 16.2   Platforms used by consumers for consuming video streaming content.

Source: Reprinted from: Global Internet Phenomena Report [19].

16.4 REVIEW OF LITERATURE

Individuals are the usage of smart gadgets such as clever telephones and smart TVs for Video Streaming and browsing the internet. Video streaming can be classified in two headings: On-Call Video Streaming and programed video streaming. In the first option, netizen can access their video content at any factor of time. While in the second option, a viewer can view his content at a scheduled time.

Smartphones are the maximum favored tool for non-public video intake, even as PC/laptops are used greater for video viewing with family and buddies in India. Daily engagement involves hovering for 4-hours and cell screens appeal to greater engagement than another media consisting of television.

Due to digitalization, traditional television has lost their monopoly. OTT services are providing new screens and content to consumers and faster network technology is an additional factor in it. OTT opening has created a road for broadcasters and producers to reach directly to the prospective viewer. Reasonable cost is another factor for the success of the OTT TV. They create content according to the consumers' needs which changes timely. The researcher mainly specified four target groups' users for OTT TV service, i.e., Students, Expats, Content Seeker and Tech Savvy. According to this research chapter, higher data usage is required for using OTT services, hence its generating revenue for telecom operators and creating revenue for service providers due to App purchasing and subscription charges. Various factors like cost, content, availability, high speed internet, smartphones are leading to OTT players. In another research, it was found that viewers chat while watching video streaming apps and often reward the content by sending emoticons [2].

More than-third of the Netflix content of video is in English with Indian language content restricted most effective to Hindi and Bollywood. Amazon Prime centered a much wider institution of audience with less than 65% in their content in English, 25% in Hindi and greater than 10% in different Indian languages. Indians spend 93% of the time online video watching content material in Hindi and regional languages. So, the system of best western content material for the top cease of the market or even western plus Bollywood content material does not maintain the important thing to successful triumphing of the emerging Indian target market for online video streaming [3].

16.5   THEORETICAL FRAMEWORK

Media has not only been used as a source of seeking information but also as a mode of awareness and entertainment. With the changing times and changes in social norms, theorists have tried to explain this phenomenon with the help of theories. The theorist describes this audience media relationship through various communication models and how these mediums are used in influencing and impacting the receiver response.

There are many theories that can be applied to understand the connection between OTT platforms and audiences like uses and gratification theory (UGT) and cognitive dissonance theory. Therefore, let us have a look at the theory of 'cognitive dissonance' by Leon Festinger that lays emphasis on consistency between action, belief, and perception. When applied to media, this theory states that media audience enters the stage of discomfort if the media does not cater as per their needs and requirements. It emphasizes on the psychological discomfort that arises out of inconsistency between the action and belief by watching some particular media channels and programs and rejecting others (Figure 16.3).

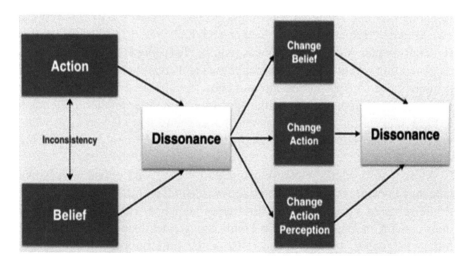

FIGURE 16.3   Theory of cognitive dissonance.
Source: Original Festinger [3]. Reprinted from Elearningindustry.com.

Festinger through his theory spelled out that when content expectation does not match the requirement of the audience, the audience tries to either shift the medium of entertainment or programs that match more to their beliefs. Hence, this theory can be stated to the audience of TV viewers that enter into the stage of discomfort with the emergence of OTT platforms that provide personalized experience. From group viewing to personal viewing, the changing concept can be studied through UGT.

With the changing times and growth of ICTs, the audience had more platforms to explore. UGT hence focus on how media can be used to gratify their needs (Figure 16.4).

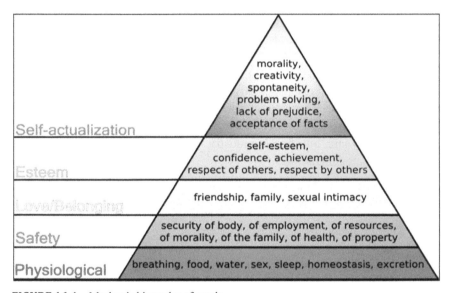

FIGURE 16.4   Maslow's hierarchy of needs.

Source: Created by J. Finkelstein. https://commons.wikimedia.org/wiki/File:Maslow%27s_hierarchy_of_needs.svg https://creativecommons.org/licenses/by-sa/3.0/deed.en.

This theory differs from other media effect theories in that it assumes that individuals have authority over their media usage rather than consuming the media as passive audience. As the UGT states that people use media to satisfy their needs of self-actualization, safety, esteem, physiological, and Love [4].

16.6   CHANGE IN CONTENT PRODUCTION AND DISTRIBUTION

The TV enterprise has been modified from issuer-pushed to client-pushed. Initially, the longevity of the content was determined by the broadcasters and operators, but now the internet with its changed earning model has changed the content consumption [5].

These changes have affected the concept of television altogether. Traditionally it was used to be referred to as a cabinet-like furniture that runs scheduled programming on a small screen with a limited number of broadcast channels. With time, the scenario changed from cable to satellite and net television (IPTV) with masses of channels. In today's time, viewers have access to games, drama, information, and news at their will on the preferred mediums.

16.6.1 EXPERIMENTAL CONTENT

1. Viewers are on top of things, developing personal playlists whilst virtual recorders and selective packages. Commentary moves immediately to social media and hence no longer wait for a week to be broadcasted on a weekly TV or newspaper [6]. This has been going on for years, but the TV industry has recently started to address the associated challenges.

2. **Multiple Channels:** The journey of the TV started with an experiment and with privatization it exploded with multiple numbers of channels being broadcasted on DISTV, Set-Top box, etc. But now, with the upsurge of OTT platforms like smartphones, iPad, laptop, etc. For example, earlier TV shows were produced for restricted networks and movies for theaters, but this difference has been erased with the latest ICTs.

3. **Hi-Tech Devices:** The window viewing has changed with new information technologies coming in the market. From huge television screens to Smartphone screens, media viewing has gone under paradigm shift. OTT service vendors are being impacted the maximum by using new windowing techniques and are becoming valid competition with premium TV for the house video window.

4. **Niche Market:** To avoid competition, many streaming have started to create their own content has thus have attained the status of fullfledged production studios. There has been a paradigm shift in the content creation market. Earlier the content was produced keeping in mind the generalized public and social environment but with the segmentation of the market and diversified audience, the content is produced for the niche market. For example, where Netflix, Disney, etc., are known for the global market and Amazon and Hotstar are known for the regional content.

5. **Global Presence:** From geographical boundaries to global villages, entertainment has spread its wings to every corner of the world, thus the audience has gone from local to global. A few years back, the programs were made keeping the Indian audience in mind like soap operas, documentaries, government programs, etc., but now the programs are made keeping in mind the global audience that contain global concepts.

6. **Reasonable Investment:** There has been a huge shift in the investment made for the earlier television programs with context to outdoor shoots, production techniques, technologies applied, etc. The production and distribution have become more reasonable with the change in production formats.

7. **Independent Content Creators:** Big banners used to have the monopoly in the television and film market earlier, but OTT platforms have given a space to independent directors and creative content producers. OTT platforms are noticing a huge participation from small banners and independent directors who have been earning in lakhs and crores.

16.6.2   *CHANGING HABITS OF VIEWER'S CONTENT CONSUMPTION*

In research by London based firm, it was found that Netflix has majority of content in English with limitation to content for Hindi audience whereas Amazon Prime targeted more of Hindi audience with less than 65% of their content in English, 25% in Hindi and more than 10% in other Indian languages. The research also concludes that Indians spend 93% of the time on online video watching content in Hindi and regional languages [7–9].

In a recent survey carried out by Mint and the Indian arm of market researcher YouGov, suggests that millennial is using social media networks tons extra than older cohorts. The research suggests that the majority of millennialsmillennial-aged among 22 to 37 consumer news via online portals with only a minority of the teenagers looking at TV information or studying newspapers. The research also concluded that 48% of millennials watch on line structures for leisure as compared to 43% who watch Cable TV for the same.

This approach that digital media players have opened new doors for the vernacular content would seize the next set of users:

1. **Original Content:** Earlier the viewers used to watch one type of show but with OTT platform, the experimentation with the program's

formats have commenced. Viewers watch more original content with context to lives shows, web series, documentaries, etc., people from different regions create regional content for regional viewers. It is seen that with Indian consumers having more preference towards vernacular and regional content, spend 93% of their time in watching regional content and only 7% of English content is preferred.

With audience facts at their fingertips, publishers can extract actionable insights into the topics and interests driving the maximum target audience engagement, after which take a records-driven approach to content material introduction, instead of taking pictures in the darkish and publishing content no person reads. The next wake of boom is predicted from tier II and tier III cities, wherein mobile with internet will result in permitting the growth of vernacular and regional content, stated the record.

2. **Live Streaming:** It is the thing that takes the viewer to the place of the event immediately whether it is a laptop, Smartphone, tablet, or iPad. Streaming can be started anywhere; all we need is a Smartphone and high-speed internet and thus OTT players are making the most of it to attract the attention of the viewers.

StreamNow, LiveStream, FacebookLive, Broadcast, and Twitch TV are some of the apps used by the consumer for live streaming.

3. **Personalized Content:** From TV surfing to binge-watching, the channel control has gone in the hands of independent viewers. They watch programs in their own space and time at their preferred platform. For example, four members of the family can watch their preferred programs at the same time. Personalization reflects the precept of push-versus-pull technology, wherein conventional TV is push technology (e.g., factor to multipoint broadcasting), and the internet is a decidedly pull technology. The significance of personalized viewings alternatives has no longer been lost on traditional broadcast and cable programmers. Video carriers indigenous to the internet (maximum substantially, Netflix, YouTube, and Hulu) have turned out to be immensely famous, and the traditional TV networks are actually actively promoting the distribution in their programs online. Traditional television does not now permit family individuals to look at extraordinary suggestions of their private choice at the same time, online television permits this personalization. Digital media is splitting their viewing styles from the common or dwelling room to the person or bedroom [10, 11].

4. **More Options:** Television broadcast programs as per specific time that restricts the quantity of programs broadcasted on television channels. This limitation has been overcome by OTT platforms that provide a variety of options in every category of romance, drama, thriller, action, etc., to be watched by the viewer. With increasing video streaming apps, customers have a variety of options to choose their content.

5. **Flexibility of Watching:** There was a time when TV audiences were called a couch potato due to the non-portability of the television sets, which has been changed by OTT platform that made watching possible anywhere anytime. Also, the platform provides the option to pause and resume watching your selected programs at any time. Now people watch programs on Smartphone's, iPad, laptops, etc., those are portable. Mobility being the signature function of virtual media platforms empowered customers to use media content material everywhere, whenever at their will. Users require flexibility of movement and are not restricted to bodily tied communication networks [12, 13].

6. **Reasonable Charges:** This is one of the features that has made video streaming popular among netizens as they purchase video streaming services at reasonable rates compared to Dish channels. The most successful streaming groups are those that have long passed out of doors the additives of the conventional pay-TV format: broadcast channels, scheduled stay programming, and programming guides. A massive bite of consumers is already paying to get content as consistent with their requirement. Cost of VOD/OTT is also kept minimal which prevents purchasers from thinking twice earlier than making a fee.

For example, to watch your favorite channels through a dish network, you need to purchase a set-top box along with the quarterly or annual subscription, but this hurdle has been surpassed by OTT platforms.

16.6.3 DIFFICULTIES FACED BY CONSUMERS

Though there is a lot of potential for OTT platforms, pain points related to streaming video services are aplenty too. Consumers are still frustrated by technical difficulties. Despite the variety of content offered by the streaming services,' consumers are not satisfied with the amount of available programming. Therefore, there is an urgent need for video streaming services to revise their revenue models [14–16]:

1. **Live vs. Recorded Streaming:** Despite the predictions that live TV streaming will be the hottest functions in 2017, interest in this is diminishing. According to a new Cogent Report StreamOn that focuses on Market Strategies International has observed that mere 11% streamers have been using this service.

2. **Technical Issues:** According to effects from Panthera's Q1 2019 US Mobile Streaming Behavior Survey, Unfortunately, video streaming can result in an expansion of frustrations. From connectivity troubles to rebuffering within the center of a display, consumers are getting much less possible to be ok with the concept of experiencing problems in the course of their viewing revel in, with 57% of respondents within the Penthera survey thinking about frustrations to be unacceptable. Furthermore, 56% of respondents indicated that they absolutely give up and try later if faced with problems that encompass a video taking too lengthy to start playing, buffering, and extended month-to-month information fees. These concerns lead 20% of consumers to end the use of a provider if their streaming enjoyment is less than perfect.

3. **Ad-Oriented Models Along with Revised Strategies:** As extra clients pick out to reduce the twine, broadcasters, and content material owners are confronted with the necessity to devise monetization models that are powerful in the ever-changing video viewing landscape. While the purchaser conduct shift opens up a mess of possibilities, the changing ecosystem additionally affords many demanding situations, as the call for connected TV (CTV) and OTT marketing skyrockets.

16.7 FUTURE ASPECTS OF VIDEO STREAMING PLATFORMS

From the recent reports and research studies, it can be seen that OTT platforms are making an effort to expand every parameter from software's to technology settings. There has been a drastic change in how consumers are consuming online content with respect to his personal preference and convenience of watching. Where companies are trying to provide engaging content to the audience, on the other hand, every effort is being made to increase the data production and storage capacities. With the upsurge of the

5G technology, there is going to be increase in data capabilities and better streaming services will be created. Therefore, televisions will become more customer-driven in the coming future.

Hence, it is expected that the future in video streaming will witness more investments in blockchain technology and artificial intelligence (AI) that will improve the content quality on the OTT platforms.

1. **More Data at Reasonable Rates in Future:** Video streaming generation calls for excessive internet pace which include 4G for streaming real-time video content material. However, 3G and 4G era is available in a few countries, so other countries without advanced telecommunication technologies cannot use it.

   Future will witness more video streaming services offering content at lower rates. With more telecommunications networks expanding their services, people will be able to access content anywhere anytime at reasonable rates.

2. **More Content:** The coming years in the video streaming industry will see more variety and experimentation with respect to its content as compared to the content provided on television channels. Highly personalized and niche content will be produced and distributed to audiences as per their interest like live shows, online games, preferred programs, live movie shows, etc. Music industry is going to emerge in a big way with the help of video streaming platforms. The future will also see the consumption of content through streamed augmented and virtual reality in the coming years.

   It is seen in various reports that Netflix is already experimenting with interactive content that allows viewers to choose their own content. Original content, personalized recommendations, and data-driven algorithms are the only factors that will only grow in coming years.

3. **Competition on Consumer Experience:** With so many changes at the global level in software and technology, the market share of any video streaming app will differ on the basis of content production and consumption and most importantly consumer satisfaction. From free subscriptions to desired viewing, video streaming providers are stretching every wing to reach out to its niche consumer.

   The key players like Netflix, Amazon Prime, Hotstar, etc., have always focused on consumer experience with context to their services. While bringing up Netflix quarterly earnings, Reed Hastings, CEO Netflix quoted, hundreds of video streaming companies in this tremendously diversified market are trying to entertain consumers. Our increase is primarily based on how good our experience is, in comparison to all of the other display time reviews from which consumers can pick out. Our cognizance is not on any competitors; however, we are trying to enhance our level for our members.

Another example of gratifying the consumer experience is video streaming app, YouNow. This app displays programs that are specifically made for the adolescents by the adolescents that provide them the platform to interact and reward the performers through emoticons.

4. **Collaborations:** The future of video streaming services holds a lot of collaborative opportunities in their bag. The recent collaboration of Disney and Hotstar-like Disney Hotstar plus has opened a wide range of programs for its viewers. Another recent example of Jio collaborating with Facebook will open new doors to video streaming apps making extensions with the help of social media platforms.

The set-top field will include a far-off that has a separate Netflix button permitting users to launch the streaming provider. "We have additionally joined fingers with Tata Sky, Vodafone, and Airtel to make it a whole lot simpler for Indian purchasers to look at Netflix, whether on a fixed-top container or on a mobile," says Zameczkowski. In May 2017, Twitter entered into the partnership with 16 new streaming groups which include BuzzFeed, Vox Media, Viacom, the WNBA, and the PGA. This partnership will assist Twitter to grow its customers for video streaming.

KEYWORDS

- **Netizens**
- **OTT platforms**
- **practical byzantine fault tolerance**
- **technologies**
- **television**
- **TV audience**
- **video streaming apps**

REFERENCES

1. Prescient and Strategic Intelligence Report, (2019). *Video Streaming Market Research -Global Industrial analysis and Forecast to 2024(2019) (Graph)*. Retrieved from: https://www.psmarketresearch.com/market-analysis/video-streaming-market/segmentation (accessed on 10 November 2021).

2. Scheibe, K., Fietkiewicz, K. J., & Stock, W. G., (2016). Information behavior on social live streaming services. *Journal of Information Science Theory and Practice, 4*(2), 6–20. Retrieved from https://doi.org/10.1633/JISTaP.2016.4.2.1 (accessed on 10 November 2021).

3. Festinger, L., (1957). *A Theory of Cognitive Dissonance*. Stanford, CA: Stanford University Press.

4. Amor, B. F., (2019). *After Music and TV, what is the Future of Streaming.* World Economic Forum. Retrieved from: https://www.weforum.org/agenda/2019/07/after-music-and-tv-the-next-streaming-revolution-is-already-here/ (accessed on 10 November 2021).

5. App, A., (2017). *State of Video Streaming Apps in Asia*. Retrieved from www.appannie.com/intelligence (accessed on 10 November 2021).

6. Bhawan, M. D., & Marg, J. L. N., (2015). *Regulatory Framework for Over-the-Top (OTT) Services 27* (Vol. 2). Telecom Regulatory Authority of India.

7. Chakravarti, N., (2018). *478 Million Mobile Internet Users by June 2018: IAMAI.* Retrieved from: http://www.asianage.com/technology/in-other-news/020418/478-million-mobile-internet-users-by-june-2018-iamai.html (accessed on 10 November 2021).

8. Denz, A., (2017). *New Study Reveals Consumers Are Not into Live Video Streaming_Business Wire*. Retrieved from https://www.businesswire.com/news/home/20171206006184/en/New-Study-Reveals-Consumers-Live-Video-Streaming (accessed on 10 November 2021).

9. Dhal, R., (2018). *Can Netflix Scale in India*. Retrieved from https://www.linkedin.com/pulse/indian-m-class-premium-ott-rajeev-dhal (accessed on 10 November 2021).

10. Huang, T. Y., Handigol, N., Heller, B., McKeown, N., & Johari, R., (2012). Confused, timid, and unstable. *Proceedings of the 2012 ACM Conference on Internet Measurement Conference - IMC '12*, 225. Retrieved from https://doi.org/10.1145/2398776.2398800 (accessed on 10 November 2021).

11. Liu, Y., Guo, Y., & Liang, C., (2008). A survey on peer-to-peer video streaming systems. *Peer-to-Peer Networking and Applications, 1*(1), 18–28. Retrieved from https://doi.org/10.1007/s12083-007-0006-y (accessed on 10 November 2021).

12. News bureau. (2018). *_We are way behind YouTube and Hotstar in India__ Netflix's Reed Hastings*. Retrieved from https://www.afaqs.com/news/story/53299_We-are-way-behind-YouTube-and-Hotstar-in-India-Netflixs-Reed-Hastings (accessed on 10 November 2021).

13. Rao, A., Legout, A., Lim, Y., Towsley, D., Barakat, C., & Dabbous, W., (2011). Network characteristics of video streaming traffic. In: *Proceedings of the Seventh Conference on emerging Networking Experiments and Technologies on - CoNEXT '11* (pp. 1–12). ACM CoNext. Retrieved from: https://doi.org/10.1145/2079296.2079321 (accessed on 10 November 2021).

14. Sarkar, J., (2018). *India Video Streaming_Indian Video Streaming Grows 23% YoY-Times of India.* Timesofindia.Indiatimes.Com. Retrieved from https://timesofindia.indiatimes.com/business/india-business/indian-video-streaming-grows-23-yoy/articleshow/64488591.cms (accessed on 10 November 2021).

15. Sen, I., (2018). *The Streaming Warriors _ MxMIndia*. Retrieved from https://www.mxmindia.com/2018/03/the-streaming-warriors/ (accessed on 10 November 2021).
16. Shaw, L., (2019). *What the Streaming Wars Mean for the Future of TV.* Bloomberg BusinessWeek. Retrieved from: https://www.bloomberg.com/news/articles/2019-11-30/what-the-streaming-wars-mean-for-the-future-of-tv-quicktake (accessed on 10 November 2021).
17. Van, E. E., & Chow, W., (2018). *Perspectives from the Global Entertainment & Media Outlook 2018–2022 Trending: Trending Now: Convergence, Connections and Trust* (p. 34). www.pwc.com/outlook. Retrieved from: www.pwc.com/outlook (accessed on 10 November 2021).
18. Westenberg, W., (2016). The influence of YouTubers on teenagers. University of Twente. Retrieved from: http://essay.utwente.nl/71094/1/Westenberg_MA_BMS.pdf (accessed on 10 November 2021).
19. COVID-19 Global Internet Phenomena, (2020). *Sandvine*. https://www.sandvine.com/press-releases/sandvine-releases-covid-19-global-internet-phenomena-report (accessed on 10 November 2021).

CHAPTER 17

Implementation of the Quality-of-Service Framework Using IoT-Fog Computing for Smart Healthcare

PRABHDEEP SINGH[1] and RAJBIR KAUR[2]

[1]*Department of Computer Science and Engineering, Punjabi University, Patiala, Punjab, India, E-mail: ssingh.prabhdeep@gmail.com*

[2]*Department of Electronics and Communication Engineering, Punjabi University, Patiala, India, E-mail: rajbir277@yahoo.co.in*

ABSTRACT

Smart cities projects are spreading at a phenomenal rate across the globe. They have an audacious vision to improve local communities 'prosperity through creativity whilst enhancing residents' quality of living by improved public facilities and a healthier climate. Smart cities are constantly seen not only as motivating factors for creativity and economic development but also as a level where wicked challenges can be solved to comfort the lives of their residents. Local authorities then establish appropriate and creative responses to certain diverse problems through technological efforts. Smart healthcare is one of the main services for people of a smart society, as a city with safe citizens integrated across any sphere of operation. IoT in health care offers useful information through the relation to data obtained by smart devices and sensors. Artificial intelligence (AI) plays a leading role in patient observation and helps to identify health conditions early on while Fog computing is in excellent condition for delays-sensitive real-time applications in the health field. In this chapter implementation of the quality-of-service framework using IoT-fog computing for smart healthcare is presented. It uses the idea of Fog computing convergence of AI. The proposed system enables consumer health records to be analyzed in real-time to diagnose the risk for chronic condition at an early level. The functioning of the proposed framework is illustrated by a case analysis of swine flu (H1F1 flu). To model the scenario and test the suggested system, the iFogSim and python language are used. The suggested system is tested in relation to typical quality of service (QoS) parameters such as classification accuracy, overall response time, recall, and f-measure with traditional IoT cloud framework.

17.1   INTRODUCTION

Smart cities are being developed to make society more efficient and sustainable. Every year the government is spending a considerable amount on their traditional city to update into the smart city [1]. Many researchers are working towards implementing smart city applications using the existing computing paradigm. In today's era, everything becomes virtual: each person and thing has a locatable, readable, and addressable counterpart on the internet. The healthcare sector always takes the maximum benefit of these latest technologies to save citizen's life and for health improvement. The application of information technologies in the healthcare system has shown a substantial increase in the level of treatment obtained by patients. Globally there are about 4.6 billion citizens who use mobile broadband subscriptions. This could lead to a world where almost everyone will have a smartphone that is connected to the internet. New trends and phenomena are being distributed more rapidly via doctor prescriptions and recommendations over the internet. Various technologies like cloud computing, IoT, big data, etc., proving their best efforts to the healthcare sector.

17.1.1   INTERNET OF THINGS (IoT)

IoT makes things (physical objects) alive by connecting all the devices, facilities, and services to make a smart society for human beings [2]. The IoT services can be utilized at any time and in any place. The IoT enabled technologies made feasible remote surveillance in the healthcare industry, released the ability to securely and healthily hold patients and encouraged doctors to offer superlative treatment. It has also improved patient involvement and comfort with the smoother and more productive contact with physicians. In comparison, online health surveillance tends to minimize hospital stay time and avoid readmission. IoT also greatly decreases treatment expenses and increases therapeutic outcomes.

The basic structure of an IoT in medical sector system consists of three parts [3]:

- A central server, which stores and processes the patient's sensory data.
- A local gateway that is connected to the internet, such as a smartphone. This can have a 2-way data stream with the sensor and with the server. Usually, some of the data is already pre-processed in this unit before it is sent to the server. When there is an issue in the gateway, then the whole system will be affected and as a result, the real-time data would not be accessible from the cloud server.
- A body sensor that is attached to the patient. This sensor is built as small as possible, but at the same time, it has to have a long lifespan as well. Due to this reason, it cannot have much computing power in it. This can either be wearable or implantable. Depending on the implementation, those sensors can have different communication protocols to transfer data such as Wi-Fi, Bluetooth1, ZigBee2, or 6LoWPAN3.

17.1.2   CLOUD COMPUTING

Cloud computing is a distributed and parallel system of computation which consists of a set of connected computers connected [4]. These are virtualized computers that are provisioned dynamically. A collaboration of one or more resources has been found that is dependent on the service level agreements (SLAs) established through abstraction between the two parties.

In the healthcare sector, this type of computing makes use of remotely placed servers kept in data centers, which have high security, for storage of data and its management, so that hospitals do not have to buy and maintain their IT solutions on site. It provides a more convenient and easier way to access storage, databases, servers, and a wide collection of medical services over the internet. Cloud computing in the healthcare sector allows patients to use the applications without installing and provide access to their data at any system which has access to the internet. This technology increases efficiency by centralizing bandwidth and processing. Further, it helps to access the clinical data anywhere, anytime. It maximizes the efficiency of shared resources with reduced infrastructure costs and makes easier resource reallocation. Cloud computing in healthcare always provides improved manageability with less maintenance.

17.1.3   FOG COMPUTING

In between the cloud and IoT, new computational nodes are finding their natural elbow room, acting both as processing capabilities closer to the ground and as filters over data streams directed towards the cloud. Such geographically distributed nodes can make it possible to respect real-time deadlines and to implement security policies that the cloud alone could not ensure [5]. The new intermediate layer connecting the ground to the sky goes under the name of fog computing. Fog computing uses near-user edge storage, connectivity, control, and many other resources to fulfill low-latency IoT requirements, especially for healthcare and mobile applications, and complement the cloud computation model [6]. To achieve fog capacity, a large scale of sensors and high geo-distributed fog servers, which is also called fog node, are necessary. The data preprocessing at the fog node makes it possible to reduce the response time needed between applications and computing stations. It is capable of improving the performance of latency-sensitive services.

17.1.4   ARTIFICIAL INTELLIGENCE (AI)

AI can be applied to almost all kinds of data but medical data is one of the most critical data. While working with medical data, the utmost accuracy and fast analysis are required [7]. The impact of AI is growing day by day on medical data, due to the number of reasons like remarkable increase in medical data size, nearly impossible to manage it manually, more chances of human errors and their adverse effects, heterogeneity of data, endless hidden patterns in given data, incomplete data, etc. AI could be a great aid to solve these issues to a larger extent [8]. It is evident from existing work that it is always valuable to apply AI techniques on medical data to achieve the best information.

AI in the medical sector can assist in almost every discipline of medicine ranging from fast diagnosis to efficient record keeping, prediction to prognosis. The main objective of applying AI techniques is to effectively perform screening, early, and accurate diagnosis of cancer, heart disease, swine flu, and many others. The applicability of AI in the medical domain is further strengthened by the fact that it could coordinate with different communities associated with medicine domains like patients, physicians, nursing staff, record keeping, and management staff.

17.2   LITERATURE REVIEW

From the last few decades, with the advent of computer technology, many research works have contributed significantly to cloud computing, fog computing, IoT, and AI domain.

Li et al. [9] proposed a logarithm to plan complex workflows on time. Three techniques are suggested and implemented in smooth for the complex modification of accessible virtual machines and active hosts to increase the energy and resource performance of cloud data centers. Finally, the NEAT solution is contrasted to three current algorithms utilizing real-world workflow files, in order to show its superior energy and resource consumption results thus maintaining the timing criteria of workflows.

Javidroozi et al. [1] Identified the intrinsic challenges in the deployment of intelligent cities applications and ecosystems. Presented the smart city operating system that effectively supported the current smart applications, as well as the basis for the future of the internet of cities.

Alrawahi et al. [11] proposed a method for the generation of a QoS-Aware service automatically on the real-time environment. The proposed method produces the basic services Discrete Event System. To compute the QoS-Aware service, an algorithm is proposed, and it applies to the Petri net model. These methods and algorithms are utilized in the system.

Montazerolghaem et al. [12] gave a proposal for an implementation model with QoS compatible with IoT applications with multiple components in the fog infrastructure. The model described the systemic operational qualities, such as latency and bandwidth, the interactions between the components and things in the software, and the company's policies. The state of the art of current IoT QoS techniques was measured. Automated queries were used to map the most important institutional libraries to resolve many study concerns. Several holes in study literature have been established at unique IoT layers.

Motlagh et al. [13] proposed three possible alternatives to effectively incorporate method: UAV Selection, UAV selection holes and fair exchange UAV selection. These approaches use linear integer problem modifications. Although the EAUS solution is targeted at reducing UAV energy consumption, the DAUS solution aims to reduce the length of the UAV. In the meanwhile, FTUS uses a policy framework to align resources and time.

Verma and Sood [14] proposed a fog-assisted, patient-centered IoT eHealth architecture which efficiently ensured a transition from clinically focused treatment to patient-centered medical care. This fog and cloud-based proposed architecture improved the processing of complex data in terms of variety, speed, and latency. For the future health architecture, IoT eHealth's various challenges have been addressed.

Rathore et al. [15] developed, a multi-layer perceptron model, centered on neural networks, for real-time medical device protection. The model achieves 98.1% specificity in the detection of false and real quantities of glucose. The suggested model was tested with a linear vector support system with a marginal precision and recall of just 90.17% accuracy. The plan also measures the framework's durability by utilizing the Bayesian network. The solution suggested improves the durability of the total frame by 18% if just one system is protected and more than 90% if both devices are protected.

Wang et al. [16] has implemented a genetic algorithm that was proposed with two different strategies. The objective was to determine a solution to UCTP by implementing the following types of genetic algorithms (GA): SSGA-Steady-state GA together with LS schemes, GSGA-guided search genetic algorithm, EGSGA-extended GSGA, GALS-GA with both LS schemes and TS method.

Huang and Dong [17] delivered the implementation of the MACE estimation using a wide number of heterogeneous electronic health information. Also, multi-subtype MACE prediction for ACS as a multi-task learning (MTL) issue is analyzed and proposed an MTL-based MACE model to forecast ACS patients' MACE for various subtypes. Adverse learning is introduced into the model to eliminate the conflict between both the general and private latent characteristics of each ACSA subtype.

Xu et al. [18] have proposed a new hybrid algorithm (cAnt-Miner2 with mRMR) outperformed cAnt-Miner2, suggested that it is beneficial to apply feature selection algorithms in terms of better classification rates. The results of experiments concluded that the proposed method is highly effective, and selects the most relevant genes with high accuracy in classification.

Xing [19] concluded that the nature of data plays an important role in selecting the classifiers and also concluded that the combined approach outperformed individual approaches. UCI library is used to fetch the breast cancer datasets. The valid range for all the attributes was set between zero and ten. From this study, it was concluded that the decision tree is less accurate as a classifier and the k-NN classifier achieved.

Huang et al. [20] proposed a classifier based on logical similarity measures. For the comparison measures, the similarity is checked against a clear logical structure, monotonically increasing, or decreasing, and continuous. The similarity comparison measures can be used for classification. The empirical results proved that the logical similarity measure gives better results than other classifiers and the maximum classification accuracy achieved.

Lasaponara et al. [21] proposed that the method be used to automatically map burned and burned areas based on spectral indices and self-organizing mechanism of Sentinel 2. These analyzes were conducted in a fire-ravaged region in Chania, Crete. Three spectral indices of the standardized difference vegetation index, the standardized burn and the sentinel burning field index, which are used to optimize burned areas, are used to quantify differing degrees of fire intensity without using specified thresholds. The findings obtained were checked with an independent data collection, which revealed strong associations with the intensity of satellite fire.

Misbahulmunir et al. [22] proposed a novel approach to handle imbalanced datasets. The results of input and output normalization would be explored to strengthen the clustering of SOMs. The new SOM needs fewer training data relative to previous SOM implementations, increased SOM flexibility in incipient failure detection, and has good diagnostic efficiency.

Ma et al. [23] proposed an improved version of the ant miner algorithm. A data-driven framework for health evaluation is discussed. This modern approach focused on the deep belief discriminative networks and ant-colony optimization which is used to determine the machine's health status. For validation of improved algorithm, two case studies were carried out demonstrating that a positive outcome can be reached.

17.3   PROPOSED FRAMEWORK

In this study, chapter implementation of the quality-of-service framework using IoT-fog computing for smart healthcare is proposed as shown in Figure 17.1, which classifies the user's health status at an early stage and generates alerts to their guardians as well as doctors according to their health condition. The user has two types of information, i.e., static information and dynamic information. User name, contact number, blood group, height, weight, gender, etc., come under static information whereas temperature, pulse rate, blood pressure (BP), etc., come under dynamic information of the user. The system starts with registering the users through the web application along with their static information. The real-time data (dynamic data) is collected through various medical IoT devices. This real-time data is transferred to fog nodes where this data is pre-processed and cleaned through various AI techniques. The architectural view of the proposed system is shown in Figure 17.1 which contains three subsystems: (a) user subsystem; (b) fog subsystem; and (c) cloud subsystem. The user subsystem is responsible to collect the user data which is processed by the fog subsystem and finally, it is stored in cloud repositories placed in the cloud subsystem.

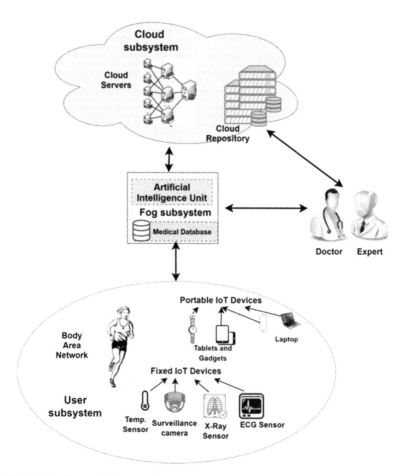

FIGURE 17.1   Proposed framework.

17.3.1   *USER SUBSYSTEM*

The user subsystem monitors the real-time information of the user where desired information related to any disease can be uploaded on the system by IoT based medical devices. These medical devices can be wearable; different types of sensors, various gadgets, etc., to acquire the health data in real-time and provide this data to fog nodes and cloud data centers. IoT based medical devices are categorized into two groups based on the nature of the health data to be collected (1) that are portable attached to the human body directly or indirectly. Body and medical sensors are used to monitor the health condition and keep track of patient health status. These hardware and sensors are used to monitor body temperature, pulse rate, BP, difficulty in breathing status, coughing, tightness of chest, running nose, etc. (2) are not attached to the human body. Fixed smart sensors are used to collect the health status of a patient from the surrounding. The key area of interest of these sensors is to provide remote monitoring, consultation, and diagnosis. These devices need a protocol for communication via fog node. Blue tooth, ZigBee, Wi-Fi, WiMAX, etc., provide their best effort for making a connection of short distance. These wireless technologies can establish both short rage communication as well as long-range communication channels for data transmission.

17.3.2   FOG SUBSYSTEM

Fog subsystem contains the fog nodes which have the processing capability to organize the data generated with the various IoT based medical devices. It is responsible for collecting data from the user subsystem, classifying it, and generates alerts accordingly. This subsystem contains two components device manager and AI unit. The primary role of the device manager is to collect heterogeneous data from the user subsystem and convert to the requisite format whereas the AI unit [24] is to take the data from the device manager and process it through various AI techniques [25]. The data is moved with various phases. Various parameters as accuracy or by using confusion matrix are considered in this phase to check the model. When the model is accepted it feeds to the next phase, classification, as input. The selected algorithm is compared with applying various real-time data.

Every step of the AI unit plays an incredible role in making the process successful. The output of one step becomes the input of the next step. The success of every step depends on the quality of the previous step. The role and working of each step of the AI unit are explained in subsections.

17.3.2.1   DATA PREPROCESSING

The success of the AI unit lies in the hands of preprocessing to a large extent. As the real-time data of the medical sector is always highly susceptible to errors, discrepancies, inconsistencies, missing problems. It is highly required and recommended to first perform the data preprocessing, for emancipating the input data from all the above-mentioned troubles and to shape in the data for further analysis [26].

17.3.2.2   DATA CLEANING

The strength of the AI unit process lies in the fact that before the actual knowledge extraction begins; the incoming data is furnished and polished to make it well equipped for analysis purposes. Data cleaning is an important step and need of an hour as AI works on real-world databases and real data is always highly prone to several problems like noise, missing values, and inconsistencies which makes the data inaccurate and inappropriate for further data analysis [27]. It suggests several solutions to real data problems. Noise is defined as an unexpected value of a measured variable.

It deploys several techniques to solve the noisy data problem like binning, regression, and clustering. The data cleaning process is padded with several routines that attempt to fill in missing values so that data analysis can be successfully performed on complete and meaningful data. Some popular techniques used for filling the missing values are by using global constant, attribute means, most probable value and by calculating mean for a specific class of samples. Data can be inconsistent due to many reasons like a faulty machine, errors in data transmission, technology limitations, different naming conventions, and inconsistent formats for input fields. To remove this incorrectness from the data, knowledge workers can use discrepancy detectors, scrubbing tools, unique rules, consecutive, and null rules.

17.3.2.3   DATA INTEGRATION

Another vital phase of data preprocessing is data integration. Today's materialistic world is expanding at a very fast pace, which makes it obvious to have different heterogeneous sources of data. It is very likely to have data of heterogeneous nature in various shapes. Integrating this diverse data at one commonplace is a big challenge and a pocket full of tissues [28]. Out of which, most common are schema integration and object matching. During data integration, the entity identification problem can be resolved by having metadata along with it.

17.3.2.4 DATA SELECTION

Data mining is applied when voluminous data is to be analyzed, comprising of a large number of attributes and tuples. For a specific purpose, a complete set of data may not be required, so for improvising the analysis process, proper data selection must be performed. If data is correctly fetched, it will reduce the analysis and execution time. It will also amplify the chances of getting the finest results and faster too. Data workers always strive for nuggets from a pool of data [29]. Data selection can be made at two levels: attribute selection and tuple selection. Based upon the nature of the data set for either one of these or both levels of selections are opted. If all the attributes are not required for analysis, then attribute selection can perform using any of the methods like gain ratio, information gain, and Gini index to fetch the best suitable set of attributes from the given pool of attributes.

Despite these effective attribute selection techniques, mining provides with tuple selection measures also. These techniques are dimensionality reduction and numerosity reduction which are applied to fetch the reduced and required number of tuples based upon various conditions. It is always suggested to represent the data in compressed form without data loss, and when the input data can be reconstructed from the compressed data, it is known as lossless representation. Wavelet transform and principal component analysis are two popular lossy selection techniques. Sampling is another important way of selecting the data subset for fast analysis. These samples can be fetched in many ways like picking sample randomly without replacement (SRSWOR), by selecting the data sample randomly but with replacement (SRSWR) and stratified samples can be picked in which whole data is divided into smaller strata, based on specific attribute values, and the sample is drawn from every stratum. This technique gives a fair chance of picking values from every set of values irrespective of their frequency.

17.3.2.5 DATA TRANSFORMATION

Data transformation plays an important role in generating the data in the best suitable shape for data analysis. Data mining has a bag full of transformation techniques like smoothing, aggregation, generalization, normalization, and attribute construction. The basic purpose of all these methods is to transform the given data in the most appropriate form, by either reducing the size of data without distressing its dignity and meaningfulness or by adding new attributes. As in aggregation, summary operations are applied to the data, to consolidate the given set into the precise and more effective form. Generalization is another incredible technique having its root from the concept hierarchy [30]. The numerical attributes, which have a large set of different values, can be transformed to lie between a smaller specified range. In attribute construction, new attributes are constructed to enhance the analysis performance. Thus, data transformation enhances the system's performance by increasing the analysis rate, reducing the data size, and providing the data in the most required format.

17.3.2.6   CLASSIFICATION

Data is always a rich source of hidden information to be used to make smart choices. A classification is a strong tool that can be used for extracting hidden patterns from a given impossible sized set of data, in the form of classes. It is a type of data analysis that is applied to extract different classes from the data based on some selected attribute [31]. The classification works on categorical data that is of unordered and discrete nature. Before the classification process is applied, the given data is pre-processed which may include data cleaning, attribute relevance analysis, and transformation as per requirements. Classification is carried in two phases:

- Learning phase (training); and
- Testing phase.

During the classification process, the classifier model is constructed to take essential and intelligent decisions.

17.3.3   CLOUD SUBSYSTEM

In this subsystem, patient data is processed as well as stored inefficient manner. For patient data storage with their unique ID, various cloud repositories are placed whereas high-end cloud servers are responsible for the processing. Cloud repository is enough capable to store both static and dynamic data of the patient. Static data includes personal information of the patient and the dynamic data consist of as heartbeat/BP/ECG/reports which are continuously updating. The cloud repository is designed with proper authentication and authorization such that no one can access the patient's personal information except the patient himself/herself. The health data can be accessed by doctors, medical officers, government health agencies, and hospitals for analysis purposes.

17.4 CASE STUDY ON H1N1

In recent times, H1N1 is the most rapidly spreading infection virus among vector-borne diseases, which is consequential a new threat to public health globally [32]. The contamination is a form of fluctuation of flu. The cloud contagion was initially distinguished in Mexico in 2009 in America. H1N1 flu is also known as Swine flu, hoard flu, pig flu. H1N1 is a respiratory disease caused by the influenza virus affecting the pigs, which, when infected shows the symptoms like decreased appetite, increased nasal secretions, cough, and listlessness. Influenza viruses are important pathogens of humans, other mammals, and birds. The genetic material of these viruses is separated into eight molecules, called segments, and may change very rapidly. Swine are considered to be crucial for generating genetically novel influenza viruses because they are susceptible to infection with influenza viruses infecting swine, humans, and birds [33]. A major challenge for the health care system is to be providing diagnostic product services at low costs and to diagnosing patients accurately [10].

The proposed framework helps in the implementation of a user-health monitoring system in a clinical environment to cure the swine-flu infection as well as generate alerts to the user, doctor, and government agencies to take the appropriate action at a very early stage of infection. At the user subsystem IoT based health monitoring devices related to swine-flu infec-tions are placed as pain detector is attached with the user body to store the level of pain the patient feels, cough assist mechanical device to collect the current status of cough, the electric thermometer is used to check the body temperature at a prescribed interval, headache detector device is activated if the user feels the headache, eyes monitoring equipment is placed near the user's eye to check the eye irritation level, the smart camera is installed in the patient room to collect the vomiting, nausea, and diarrhea status. At the fog subsystem, various fog devices are installed. All IoT based health devices send their data to the fog subsystem where all attributes are indexed-based on their ranges. The hybrid classifier is applied to this collected data to forecast the user H1N1 infection status and generate alerts to doctors along with health reports of the user. On the other hand, another alert generates to the user to cure the H1N1 infection and provide the diet plan which has to be followed. Further data is transferred to the cloud subsystem to store it in the cloud repository. Where data is analyzed, and again, an alert is generated to the government agencies.

17.5 EXPERIMENTAL SETUP AND PERFORMANCE EVALUATION

Amazon web services are chosen as a testbed for performance evaluation of the proposed framework. To check the accuracy of alert generation at fog subsystem, R language is used which utilized the ML package. The experiment is divided into the following four segments:

1. **H1N1 Data Creation:** To the best of my knowledge, the data set of H1N1 is not available in any government repository as UCI, CDC, NHS, etc., which can be utilized directly for analysis. Even though the internet is not able to find any data set of H1N1, so all possible cases of H1N1 infection are mapped and generated H1N1 data set by applying the following algorithm, which is used systematically under the extreme guidance of physicians, specialist medical officer, medical institutions. No possible cause is left while generating the data set. The symptoms shown in Figure 17.2 are utilized to generate the H1N1 dataset.

    Result: H1N1 data creation

    Input: Patient symptom

    Output: Generate H1N1 dataset

    Step I: N initialize to 1.

    Step II: for N <= number of entries required do

    Step III: Allocate values to significant symptoms of H1N1 based on their probabilities.

    Step IV: Allocate values to the minor symptom of H1N1 based on their probabilities.

    Step V: Create new user data by combining Step III and step IV values generated.

    If (PatientID_Result= = H1N1 positive}

    {
        Same user data is already present then;
        discard this data;
    }

```
{
    Add new user data.
}
    Increment N
}
```

Step VI: End

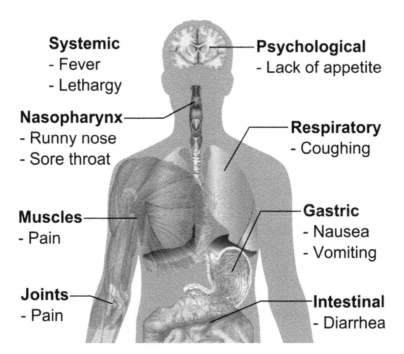

Systemic
- Fever
- Lethargy

Psychological
- Lack of appetite

Nasopharynx
- Runny nose
- Sore throat

Respiratory
- Coughing

Muscles
- Pain

Gastric
- Nausea
- Vomiting

Joints
- Pain

Intestinal
- Diarrhea

FIGURE 17.2 Symptoms of H1N1 [33].

2. **Training and Testing of the Proposed Hybrid Classifier:** The H1N1 dataset generated from the algorithm is further divided. Around 70% of total data is used to train the hybrid classifier, and rest data is responsible for testing the classifier with various performance measures. This hybrid classifier is implemented by an open-source language R. The ML packages are installed in R studio. Window 7 is installed on Intel i7 2.50 GHz with an 8GB RAM machine to take the results of the hybrid classifier. Preprocessing is carried out before entering the classification phase, which includes data cleaning, data integration, data selection, and data transformation. Initially, fourteen

attributes are collected from each patient. For further analysis, the data selection algorithm selects 10 attributes. Smoothing, aggregation, generalization, normalization, and construction of attributes are carried out in the data transformation. In classification phase 10, rotational estimates with 10 reciprocal folds are selected. In terms of classification precision, reminder, and f-measure, the performance of the hybrid classifier is stored.

i.   **Accuracy:** The total number of accurate predictions is separated by the total number of instances to determine the classifier accuracy. The proposed approach offers 81.058% more precision compared with other classifications as seen in Figure 17.3.

ii. **Recall:** The value is measured as the 'No Ratio–True Positive' and 'the cumulative amount of actual positive and false negative' No. Strong recall value demonstrates a more effective methodology of classification. A recall value of 0.93 is obtained in the suggested method, better than other classifiers as seen in Figure 17.4.

iii. **F-Measure:** It is a parameter which finds the precision of the test. The integrated accuracy count and recall value calculated by the formula-

$$(2 \times \text{Precision\_value} \times \text{Recall Value})/$$
$$(\text{Precision\_value} + \text{Recall value}).$$

For efficient classification techniques, the high value of F-measure is needed. An F measure of 0.871 which is higher than other classification strategies is seen in Figure 17.5 is obtained by the proposed data classification.

3.   **Testing the Proposed Framework on iFogSim:** iFogSim is chosen as a testbed for performance evaluation of the proposed framework. It uses the libraries of cloudSim to perform the simulation.

The response time is calculated when the data is accessed at the patients from the fog, with the response time when the data is accessed at the patients from the cloud. Here response time is the time for data transmission from the data generator node to the patient node. When data is accessed from the data center, which is very away from the current location, the response time becomes more as compared to the proposed framework. In the absence of fog nodes, the response time becomes almost 6 times the response time caused by the fog. The comparison of the overall response time is depicted in Figure 17.6 which shows that the proposed framework is better than the traditional cloud-based framework.

4. **Alert Generation:** The process of alert generation is shown in Figure 17.7. The efficiency of alert generation depends upon the total number of true alert cases generated by the proposed algorithm. As shown in Figure 17.8, the proposed hybrid algorithm gives better results compared with other traditional algorithms.

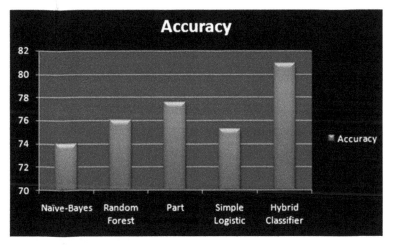

FIGURE 17.3 Classifier accuracy.

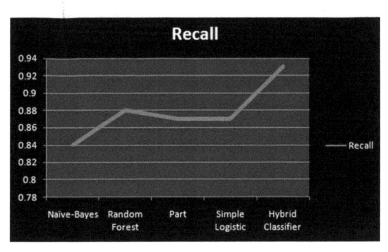

FIGURE 17.4 Recall of classifier.

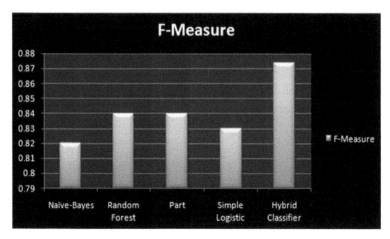

FIGURE 17.5 F-measure of classifier.

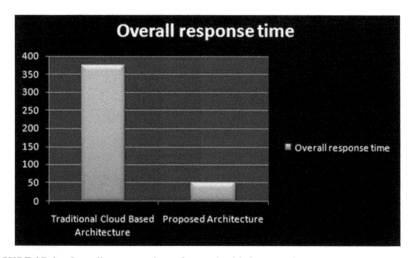

FIGURE 17.6 Overall response time of smart health framework.

The suggestion for diet and some prevention measures are shown below:

1. **Suggestion for Diet:**
   - Avoid cooked food;
   - Take fruits before noon. The number of fruits is as follows;
   - Fruit consumption (In grams) = Body weight (BW) (Grams)/10;
   - Take a diet of fresh vegetables. The quantity of vegetables is;
   - Vegetable consumption (In grams) = BW (KG)/20;

- Take fresh leaves 50–100 grams. Leaves can be mint, radish leaves, Ocimum, etc.

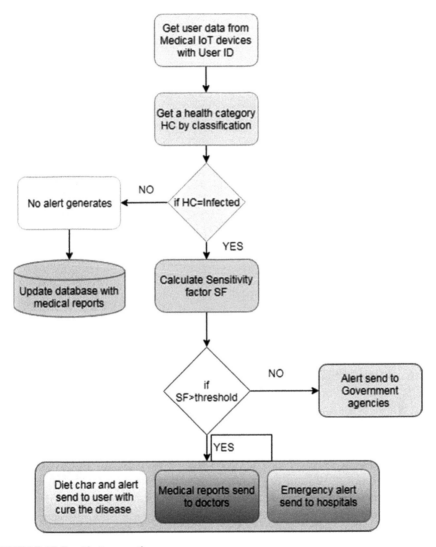

FIGURE 17.7 Alert generation.

2. **Precautions:**
   - Always wear a mouth guard;
   - Wash hands frequently with normal cleaning soaps;
   - Disinfecting contaminated surfaces;

- Avoiding too close contact with the infected person;
- Vitamin D levels should be increased by daily doses;
- Control of the vitamin-D-level is recommended, and at values below 30 ng/ml, vitamin D should be supplied.

However, the role of vitamin D in preventing influenza is not undisputed.

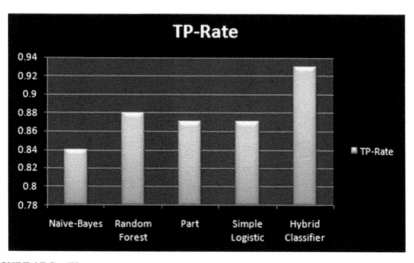

FIGURE 17.8   TP rate.

17.6   CONCLUSION

The H1N1 is an unprecedented global crisis, which leads to an enormous number of deaths, economic losses, and daily disruptions. Restrictive actions taken by most countries have been a quick reaction to establishing the first line of defense and taking time to prepare for the next stages of this pandemic. Cloud/fog computing integrated with AI can help to control this virus outbreak at a little cost. The proposed quality of service (QoS) framework using IoT fog computing to predict and prevent H1N1 is implemented efficiently to control the H1N1 virus outbreak in various regions of the country. The synthetic H1N1 data of the patients can be used to detect patterns and connections between the attributes that are common H1N1 patients. These features can be determined using attribute selection algorithms and classification techniques and used for developing a framework that may help in reducing costs and distinctively improve the quality of care.

KEYWORDS

- **artificial intelligence**
- **connected TV**
- **information and communication technologies**
- **over-the-top**
- **uses and gratification theory**

REFERENCES

1. Javidroozi, V., Shah, H., & Feldman, G., (2019). Urban computing and smart cities: Towards changing city processes by applying enterprise systems integration practices. *IEEE Access, 7*, 108023–108034.
2. Ang, K. L. M., & Seng, J. K. P., (2019). Application-specific internet of things (ASIoTs): Taxonomy, applications, use case and future directions. *IEEE Access, 7*, 56577–56590.
3. Cao, R., Tang, Z., Liu, C., & Veeravalli, B., (2019). A scalable multi-cloud storage architecture for cloud-supported medical internet of things. *IEEE Internet of Things Journal*.
4. Fowley, F., Pahl, C., Jamshidi, P., Fang, D., & Liu, X., (2016). A classification and comparison framework for cloud service brokerage architectures. *IEEE Transactions on Cloud Computing, 6*(2), 358–371.
5. Zhang, R., Xue, R., & Liu, L., (2017). Searchable encryption for healthcare clouds: A survey. *IEEE Transactions on Services Computing, 11*(6), 978–996.
6. Roy, S., Das, A. K., Chatterjee, S., Kumar, N., Chattopadhyay, S., & Rodrigues, J. J., (2018). Provably secure fine-grained data access control over multiple cloud servers in mobile cloud computing based healthcare applications. *IEEE Transactions on Industrial Informatics, 15*(1), 457–468.
7. Ong, Y. S., & Gupta, A., (2019). AIR 5: Five pillars of artificial intelligence research. *IEEE Transactions on Emerging Topics in Computational Intelligence, 3*(5), 411–415.
8. Bozkurt, M. R., Uçar, M. K., Bozkurt, F., & Bilgin, C., (2019). Development of hybrid artificial intelligence based automatic sleep/wake detection. *IET Science, Measurement & Technology, 14*(3), 353–366.
9. Li, C., Huo, L., & Chen, H., (2019). Real-time workflows oriented hybrid scheduling approach with balancing host weighted square frequencies in clouds. *IEEE Access, 8*, 40828–40837.
10. Ahad, A., Tahir, M., & Yau, K. L. A., (2019). 5G-based smart healthcare network: Architecture, taxonomy, challenges and future research directions. *IEEE Access, 7*, 100747–100762.
11. Alrawahi, A. S., Lee, K., & Lotfi, A., (2019). A multi objective QoS model for trading cloud of things resources. *IEEE Internet of Things Journal, 6*(6), 9447–9463.

12. Montazerolghaem, A., & Yaghmaee, M. H., (2020). Load-balanced and QoS-aware software-defined internet of things. *IEEE Internet of Things Journal, 7*(4), 3323–3337.

13. Motlagh, N. H., Bagaa, M., & Taleb, T., (2019). Energy and delay aware task assignment mechanism for UAV-based IoT platform. *IEEE Internet of Things Journal, 6*(4), 6523–6536.

14. Verma, P., & Sood, S. K., (2018). Fog assisted-IoT enabled patient health monitoring in smart homes. *IEEE Internet of Things Journal, 5*(3), 1789–1796.

15. Rathore, H., Wenzel, L., Al-Ali, A. K., Mohamed, A., Du, X., & Guizani, M., (2018). Multi-layer perceptron model on-chip for secure diabetic treatment. *IEEE Access, 6*, 44718–44730.

16. Wang, L., Wan, J., & Gao, X., (2019). Toward the health measure for open-source software ecosystem via projection pursuit and real-coded accelerated genetic. *IEEE Access, 7*, 87396–87409.

17. Huang, Z., & Dong, W., (2018). Adversarial MACE prediction after acute coronary syndrome using electronic health records. *IEEE Journal of Biomedical and Health Informatics, 23*(5), 2117–2126.

18. Xu, C., Gordan, B., Koopialipoor, M., Armaghani, D. J., Tahir, M. M., & Zhang, X., (2019). Improving performance of retaining walls under dynamic conditions developing an optimized ANN based on ant colony optimization technique. *IEEE Access, 7*, 94692–94700.

19. Xing, W., & Bei, Y., (2019). Medical health big data classification based on KNN classification algorithm. *IEEE Access, 8*, 28808–28819.

20. Huang, M., Han, H., Wang, H., Li, L., Zhang, Y., & Bhatti, U. A., (2018). A clinical decision support framework for heterogeneous data sources. *IEEE Journal of Biomedical and Health Informatics, 22*(6), 1824–1833.

21. Lasaponara, R., Proto, A. M., Aromando, A., Cardettini, G., Varela, V., & Danese, M., (2019). On the mapping of burned areas and burn severity using self-organizing map and sentinel-2 data. *IEEE Geoscience and Remote Sensing Letters*.

22. Misbahulmunir, S., Ramachandaramurthy, V. K., & Thayoob, Y. H. M., (2020). Improved self-organizing map clustering of power transformer dissolved gas analysis using inputs pre-processing. *IEEE Access, 8*, 71798–71811.

23. Ma, M., Sun, C., & Chen, X., (2017). Discriminative deep belief networks with ant colony optimization for health status assessment of machine. *IEEE Transactions on Instrumentation and Measurement, 66*(12), 3115–3125.

24. Abadi, H. H. N., & Pecht, M., (2020). Artificial intelligence trends based on the patents granted by the united states patent and trademark office. *IEEE Access, 8*, 81633–81643.

25. Zhang, C., Ueng, Y. L., Studer, C., & Burg, A., (2020). Artificial intelligence for 5g and beyond 5g: Implementations, algorithms, and optimizations. *IEEE Journal on Emerging and Selected Topics in Circuits and Systems, 10*(2), 149–163.

26. Hurtik, P., Molek, V., & Hula, J., (2019). Data preprocessing technique for neural networks based on image represented by a fuzzy function. *IEEE Transactions on Fuzzy Systems*.

27. Rammelaere, J., & Geerts, F., (2019). Cleaning data with forbidden item sets. *IEEE Transactions on Knowledge and Data Engineering*.

28. Dhayne, H., Haque, R., Kilany, R., & Taher, Y., (2019). In: Search of big medical data integration solutions-a comprehensive survey. *IEEE Access, 7*, 91265–91290.

29. Wang, J., Zhao, P., Hoi, S. C., & Jin, R., (2013). Online feature selection and its applications. *IEEE Transactions on Knowledge and Data Engineering, 26*(3), 698–710.

30. Kaplan, E., Gursoy, M. E., Nergiz, M. E., & Saygin, Y., (2017). Known sample attacks on relation preserving data transformations. *IEEE Transactions on Dependable and Secure Computing.*
31. Phan, H., Andreotti, F., Cooray, N., Chén, O. Y., & De Vos, M., (2018). Joint classification and prediction CNN framework for automatic sleep stage classification. *IEEE Transactions on Biomedical Engineering, 66*(5), 1285–1296.
32. Qi, Q., & Tao, F., (2019). *A Smart Manufacturing Service System Based on Edge Computing, Fog Computing, and Cloud Computing*, 86769–86777. IEEE.
33. Park, C., Choi, W., Kim, D., Jin, B., & Lee, J. S., (2019). Highly sensitive detection of influenza A (H1N1) virus with silicon nanonet BioFETs. *IEEE Sensors Journal, 19*(23), 10985–10990.

CHAPTER 18

Machine Learning-Based Electronic Tree Surveillance System for Detection of Illegal Wood Logging Activity

PIYUSH SAMANT,[1] J. SAI PRAVEEN KUMAR,[2] ROHIT GUPTA,[2] ALPANA AGARWAL,[2] and RAVINDER AGARWAL[2]

[1]*Chandigarh University, Punjab–140413, India,*
E-mail: piyushsamantpth@gmail.com

[2]*Thapar Institute of Engineering and Technology, Patiala, Punjab–147001, India*

ABSTRACT

Despite the enforcement of various regulatory and legislative measures to eradicate illegal wood trade and wood logging is still considered as one of the major global socio-economic issues. Till date, limited work has been done specifically to curb illegal wood logging activity and an effective threat recognition system is required. In the present chapter, a novel activity recognition framework has been proposed by the fusion of sensor technology with machine learning (ML) techniques. The proposed framework is able to recognize traditional wood logging activities in a constrained environment. It is a well-known fact that forced vibrations are imparted onto the tree trunks during the wood cutting activity, so vibration data from tree trunks was logged during axe cutting, saw cutting and machine cutting activities by employing a tri-axial accelerometer sensor. Accurate wood logging activity recognition was achieved using ML-based activity recognition method in conjunction with short time windowing technique by extracting various time domain and frequency domain features from the acquired vibration data to form a training feature vector for support vector machine (SVM) classifier. Efforts were made to optimize real time implementation constraints like computation time, memory usage, and accuracy, and a study has been conducted to analyze the effect of training data and number of features forming a training feature vector for SVM classifier on system accuracy. The results were evaluated by K-fold validation technique and the optimum accuracy of the proposed framework is observed to be 97.5%. This framework potentially paves the way for real-time detection of illegal wood logging.

18.1   INTRODUCTION

Forests are considered as 'Green gold,' which play an important role in the ecosystem. More than 30% of the total global land is occupied by the forests [1]. It provides valuable wood species, which have high international demand due to which illegal logging and deforestation has increased. According to the UN Framework Convention on Climate Change (UNFCCC), it is estimated that deforestation accounts for between 1/6 and 1/4 of global carbon emissions [2]. In addition to endangering the environment, illegal logging and deforestation have also emerged as one of the major socio-economic issues. A survey conducted by UNEP and INTERPOL estimated the economic value of global illegal logging to be worth US$ 30 billion, which constitutes 10–30% of global wood trade. This survey also reports that criminals, in recent days, have been employing sophisticated techniques along with older woodcutting techniques at all levels [3]. Various regulatory and legislative measures have been implemented globally to preserve natural resources. However, in many cases, illegal wood smuggling has constantly been reported. Therefore, law enforcement alone is insufficient to eradicate illegal logging and an effective threat recognition system is demanded. This can be achieved by introducing electronic sensor technology and effective signal processing for activity recognition.

The RFID-based tracking system has been developed for detection and identification of illegal tree logging on cedar species in the forests of Ifrane region of the Atlas Mountains and Sandalwood trees in India, respectively [4, 5]. Both these works use RFID tags installed in trees and used handheld readers for tracking the tags in the surveillance zone. RFID tags alone is not an effective option since they are passive threat detection devices and require constant human surveillance. Dhanashree, Chanchal, and Dinesh [6] proposed a tree monitoring system for prevention of illegal woodcutting, which consists of an accelerometer sensor, cameras, GSM, and GPS. Thresholding of vibration signal in the time domain for active detection is performed in this work. Time-domain thresholding is prone to false alerts as a possibility of triggering the set threshold and generation of the false alert is possible by various factors like large sway winds, hurricanes, or animal interference with trees, etc. Chethan et al. [7] implemented a wireless sensor network (WSN) for forest tree monitoring and alert generation based on event detection where false alerts were also considered in addition to thresholding. Oguchi et al. [8] developed an accelerometer-based security system for orchards where a fruit plucking event was detected by considering frequency domain thresholding. The frequency of the vibration signal is considered as the primary feature as certain periodic frequency will be generated on the branches during the fruit plucking activity. It is observed that accelerometer/ vibration sensors are considered effective for sensing the activity accurately, however till date, very few efforts were made to introduce electronic sensor technology to detect illegal wood logging activities. There is a need for an effective mechanism for the cause.

Illegal wood dwellers, these days, use state of the art machinery to cut down the trees and chop the tree in no time [9]. An effective threat classification system has to be developed to detect the event as well as classify the wood cutting device used simultaneously. This is achieved by fusion of sensor technology with effective signal processing and machine learning (ML) techniques. Various algorithms were proposed for activity recognition using machine learning by developing effective feature vector for training the classifier. These activity recognition techniques are applied in a wide area of applications like in medical monitoring applications by Nishkam [10]; Atallah [11]; Piyush [12]. Authors have performed human activity recognition by extracting several time domain and frequency domain features from acquired accelerometer sensor data and perform machine-learning technique for classification of human physiological activity. Tong [13] performed human fall detection by using accelerometer sensor and ML classifier. Mitchell [14] developed an asymmetric human running activity recognition system by extracting time and frequency domain features from the acquired signals from sensors positioned at various body locations and also performed K-fold validation of the obtained results. Similar activity classification was applied in machine condition monitoring application [16] where bearing fault detection and fault diagnostics has been performed by extracting various time-domain features from the acquired accelerometer sensor data and considering SVM classifier, the faults in the bearings were classified. From all the aforementioned works, it is evident that physical events are effectively sensed by accelerometer sensors. Moreover, by performing effective feature extraction along with ML accurate activity recognition can be achieved.

In the current research work, a simple as well as robust mechanism to detect and classify the traditionally followed wood cutting activities is proposed which provides an improved threat recognition and eliminates the false alerts that arise by thresholding techniques. A ML based activity recognition has been implemented where time domain and frequency domain features are extracted by performing short time windowing technique from the acquired vibration signal during various woodcutting activities. A supervised learning based SVM classifier is used for the activity classification, and the results were validated using K-Fold validation technique. Efforts were made to optimize the memory consumption, computation time along with the accuracy of the system where the optimum feature vector and percentage of training data sufficient for the classifier to perform accurate activity recognition.

18.2   METHODOLOGY

18.2.1   SYSTEM SETUP AND DATA ACQUISITION

The vibration data is acquired by positioning a tri-axial accelerometer (ADXL345-analog devices make) on the selected tree samples. The integration schematic of the experimental setup for data acquisition is shown in Figure 18.1. It is simply showing the connection diagram how the actual sensor connection will be there in order to create node wise data collection setup. The selected accelerometer is capable of detecting various acceleration ranges up to ± 16 g with 13-bit ADC. To evaluate the feasibility, the study has been conducted on some of the trees present in the campus. Table 18.1 shows the properties of the selected tree samples. These samples are selected based on their similarities in properties with that of the precious Indian sandalwood trees, where a typical Indian sandalwood tree grows up to 20 meters with girth growing up to 2.4 meters. The prototype accelerometer sensor has been positioned at 3 meters from the point of impact by considering visual security aspects.

Figure 18.2 shows the developed sensor node and acquisition system. Figure 18.2(a) shows a sample of connecting node. Multiple of same nodes are developed and after proper packaging (Figure 18.2(b)) attached with the trees as shown in Figure 18.2(d). Three wood cutting activities are employed in this research as mentioned in Table 18.2. Every wood cutting activity is performed for a period of time on selected sample and the vibration data generated on all axis (ax, ay, and az) of sensor is logged and analyzed using LabVIEW and MATLAB software's respectively. The data collection graphical user interface (GUI) LabVIEW in is shown in Figure 18.2(c).

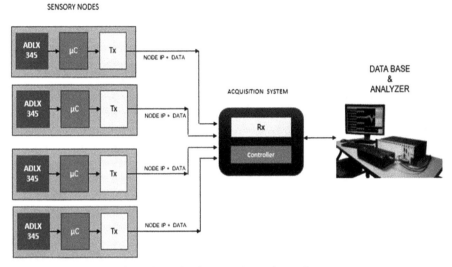

FIGURE 18.1 Integration schematic diagram of experimental setup.

TABLE 18.1 Properties of Tree Samples

Log Sample	Height (in meters)	Overall Girth (in cm)
1	15.25	25.50
2	14.40	22.68
3	14.64	21.98
4	14.25	20.42
5	13.12	19.50

18.2.2 VIBRATION SIGNAL ANALYSIS

18.2.2.1 SENSOR AXIS NORMALIZATION

The tri-axial acceleration data acquired by the sensor is normalized into a single channel by performing root mean square of the signal. This RMS acceleration of the sensor, R (t) is calculated for all the activities by Eqn. (1) and the block representation of the implemented methodology is shown in Figure 18.3.

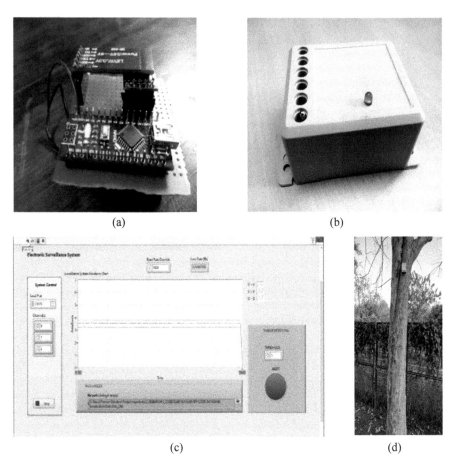

(a)   (b)

(c)   (d)

FIGURE 18.2 (a, b) Accelerometer sensor node; (c) data acquisition GUI in LabVIEW; (d) real time data acquisition.

TABLE 18.2 Type of Woodcutting Activities

Activity	Threat Activity
1	No wood cutting
2	Woodcutting using handsaw
3	Woodcutting using axe
4	Woodcutting using electric machine

$$R(t) = \sqrt{ax(t) + ay(t) + az(t)} \qquad (1)$$

where; $a_x(t)$ is the vibration data acquired on the x-axis of the sensor; $a_y(t)$ is the vibration data acquired on the y-axis of the sensor; $a_z(t)$ is the vibration data acquired on the z-axis of the sensor.

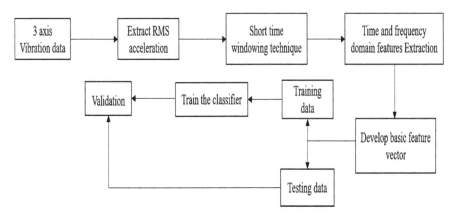

FIGURE 18.3 Block diagram of the proposed framework.

18.2.2.2   *FEATURE VECTOR COMPUTATION*

Time and frequency domain features are extracted from the calculated resultant acceleration data R (t). The list of extracted features is as shown in Table 18.3. Feature extraction is performed by short time windowing technique [14] where the complete vibration signal is divided into windows and all-time domain and frequency domain features were extracted from each window to form a basis feature vector.

18.2.3   *ACTIVITY RECOGNITION METHODOLOGY*

Training data and testing data were generated from the basic feature vector and were used for classification of the employed wood cutting activities by supervised learning SVM classifier. The K-Fold cross-validation of the results was performed and the overall accuracy of the developed system was calculated.

18.2.4   *OPTIMIZATION OF COMPUTATIONAL TIME AND MEMORY USAGE*

Computational time and memory usage are the important constraints during real-time operations, optimization of computation time is computed by observing the effect of varying the classifier training data percentage on the system accuracy and optimization of memory usage is computed by observing the effect of varying the number of features to form basis feature vector on the system accuracy.

TABLE 18.3　　Time and Frequency Domain Features

Feature No.	Features
1.	Mean
2.	Median
3.	Standard deviation
4.	Kurtosis
5.	Skewness
6.	Correlation coefficients
7.	RMS magnitude
8.	Peak to peak
9.	Peak to RMS
10.	Peak frequency
11.	Min frequency
12.	Mean frequency
13.	Median frequency
14.	Power bandwidth
15.	Total band power
16.	Occupied bandwidth
17.	Signal to noise ratio
18.	Equivalent noise bandwidth

18.3　RESULTS AND DISCUSSION

Figure 18.4 shows the x, y, z-axis acceleration data acquired during all the activities. Figure 18.4 shows the x, y, and z-axis acceleration acquired when there is no wood cutting activity performed. Figure 18.5 shows the x, y, and z-axis acceleration acquired when there is a wood cutting activity performed by an axe. Figure 18.6 shows the x, y, and z-axis acceleration acquired when there is a wood cutting activity performed by handsaw. Figure 18.7 shows the x, y, and z-axis acceleration acquired when there is a wood cutting activity performed by an electric machine. Figure 18.5

shows the normalized acceleration data during all the employed woodcutting techniques.

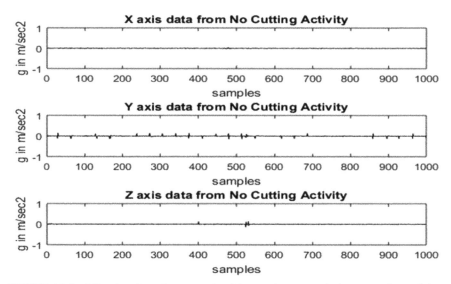

FIGURE 18.4 Vibration data of x, y, z-axis of the accelerometer during no cutting activity.

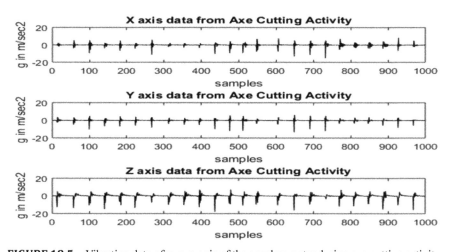

FIGURE 18.5 Vibration data of x, y, z-axis of the accelerometer during axe cutting activity.

Figures 18.4–18.7 indicate that every activity has distinguished signal features and the acquired signal is mostly periodic in nature with slight disturbances. When there is no woodcutting, the signal received is observed to be almost constant, as shown in Figure 18.4. When the woodcutting is performed by axe, the human generally strikes the tree in a periodic way, and the applied impact force of the axe blow on the tree is observed to be comparatively large as shown in Figure 18.5. When a tree is cut using a hand saw, the persons drag the hand saw to and fro on the tree structures, which indeed cause periodic vibrations as shown in Figure 18.6, however, the applied impact force on the tree is observed to be comparatively less than that of axe cutting. Both the axe cutting and handsaw cutting are low-frequency woodcutting techniques, whereas when a tree structure is cut by an electric machine, it produces a vibration of high frequency.

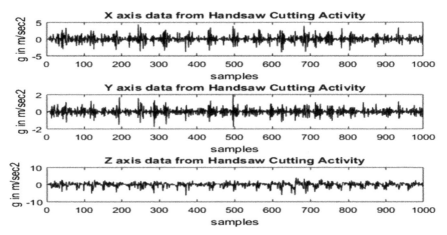

FIGURE 18.6   Vibration data of x, y, z-axis of the accelerometer during handsaw cutting.

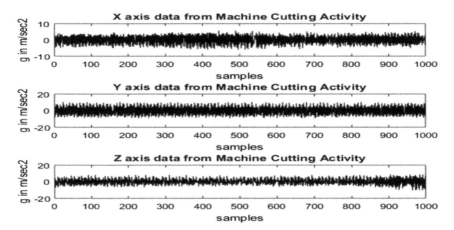

FIGURE 18.7   Vibration data of x, y, z-axis of the accelerometer during machine cutting.

According to the observations, it is evident that all the signals are almost periodic, efforts for extracting the vibration frequencies for every activity was done using the average signals of all types of wood cutting as shown in Figure 18.8. It is observed that the frequency range of the vibrations during no cutting is almost constant and equal to zero, which is shown in Figure 18.9, whereas tree vibration frequencies during axe cutting and hand saw cutting lie between 0 and 5 Hz. However, the amplitudes can differentiate them since axe cutting has high amplitude compared to handsaw cutting. The vibration frequency of machine cutting is observed to lie in between 20–25 Hz. By applying the frequency threshold and amplitude threshold at this stage, basic threat detection was achieved.

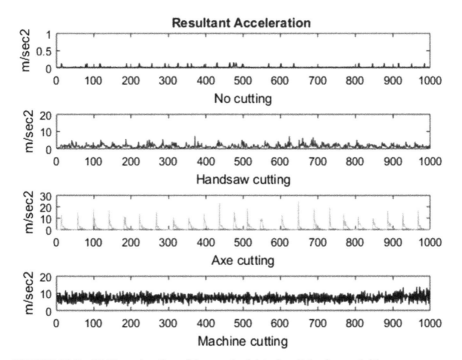

FIGURE 18.8   RMS acceleration of the acquired data for all the four activities.

From the study conducted on selected tree samples, it is observed that tree vibration frequency varies with trunk thickness and as the thickness decreases, vibration frequency on tree trunk increases as shown in Figure 18.10. It clearly shows that the machine cutting activity have highest vibration frequency and n cutting activity have zero vibration frequency.

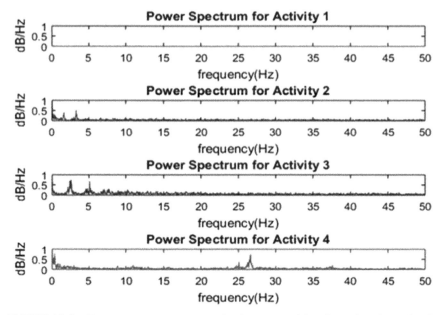

FIGURE 18.9   Frequency power spectrum density extracted for all employed woodcutting activities respectively.

FIGURE 18.10   Vibration frequency during different wood cutting activities on different tree trunks.

To improve threat detection accuracy, other time domain and frequency domain features have been considered for activity recognition. Figure 18.11 shows the accuracy of the individual feature for classification of the activity. It is observed that the accuracy of mean and standard deviation of time-domain signal has a high accuracy of activity recognition compared to the other features.

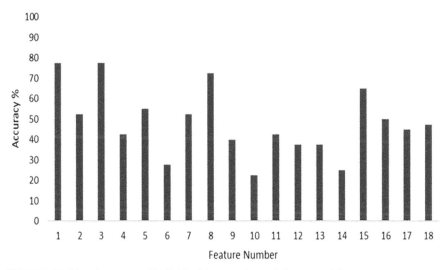

FIGURE 18.11   Accuracy of individual features for activity recognition.

All the 18 extracted features were considered to form a basis feature vector for the classifier and by performing K-fold validation technique along with increasing training data presents the overall accuracy of the system is calculated. In order to optimize the memory usage, computation time and also to verify the effect of a number of features in feature vector on overall system accuracy, the number of features in the basic feature vector are reduced gradually by reducing to top 15, top 10, and top 5 accurate features to form a new basis feature vector for activity classification and overall system accuracy has been extracted with increasing training data present as shown in Figure 18.12. It is observed that the accuracy of wood cutting activity recognition increases with increasing training data and is 100% for maximum training data except for 5 features. It is also observed that the minimum 10 number of top accurate features with complete training data can effectively achieve 100% activity recognition.

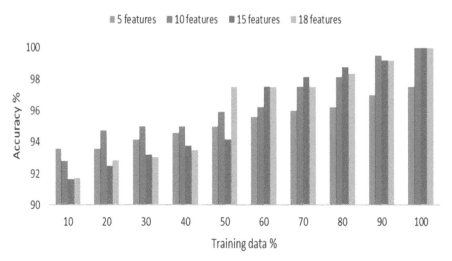

FIGURE 18.12 Analysis of overall system accuracy for different training data and different number of features in feature vector.

From all these experiments, the maximum accuracy of the system with maximum training data during a maximum number of features as feature vector is observed to be 100% and minimum accuracy of the system with least training data during least features as feature vector is observed to be 91.67%. It is also observed that for 50% training data, the basic feature vector containing all 18 features provide high accuracy of 97.50%. It is also observed that 97.50% accuracy has been achieved with only 50% training data by 18 features, whereas it is obtained at 60%, 70% and 90% training data for 15, 10 and 5 featured feature vectors, respectively. Depending on the hardware used and flexibility in choosing the appropriate any of these two optimized values can be used for this particular application. Figure 18.13 depicts the trend of classification accuracy with different training data and number of features. It is observed that with the increase in a number of features, the slope of the output varies and accordingly the accuracy improves.

18.4 CONCLUSION

The proposed framework accurately detects the employed woodcutting activities. It is observed that the tree vibration frequencies on trees are different for different wood cutting activity. The vibration frequencies of tree selected tree trunks during axe woodcutting, handsaw woodcutting ranges between 0–5 Hz and machine woodcutting between 25–30 Hz, respectively. The overall accuracy of the proposed framework ranges from 91% to 100% depending on the percentage of training data considered for activity recognition. Also, the observations show that the mean and standard deviation of the time domain signal can individually provide accuracy up to 77.5%. Top 10 features in feature vector provide 100% accuracy for unconstrained scenarios. For optimum computation time and memory usage, it is considered as 18 and 15 top featured feature vectors for 50% and 60% training data respectively can provide 97.5% activity recognition accuracy. This framework was developed considering real time embedded implementation constraints and can be implemented in real time sensor networks for accurate recognition of malicious wood logging activity.

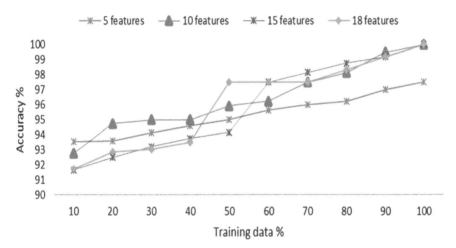

FIGURE 18.13 Trend lines of overall system accuracy.

KEYWORDS

- accelerometers
- activity recognition
- feature vector
- machine learning
- SVM classifier

REFERENCES

1. Food and Agriculture Organization of United Nations, *Global Forest Resource Assessment 2010.* http://www.fao.org/docrep/013/i1757e/i1757e.pdf (accessed on 10 November 2021).
2. Wiley Online Library, Pritchard, D., (2009). *Reducing Emissions from Deforestation and Forest Degradation in Developing Countries (REDD) – the Link with Wet Lands.* Presented for Foundation for International Environmental Law and Development. http://onlinelibrary.wiley.com/doi/10.1111/j.1467-9388.2008.00597.x/full (accessed on 10 November 2021).
3. Nellemann, C., (2012). INTERPOL environmental crime program. *Green Carbon, Black Trade: Illegal Logging, Tax Fraud and Laundering in the Worlds Tropical Forests.* A Rapid Response Assessment. United Nations Environment Program, GRID-Arendal. ISBN: 978-82-7701-102-8.
4. Aboussaid, S., Benbihi, H., & Salih, A. Y., (2013). RFID-based tracking system preventing trees extinction and deforestation. In: *Intelligent Systems Modeling & Simulation (ISMS), 2013 4th International Conference* (pp. 610–614).
5. Srinivasan, S., & Ranganathan, H., (2013). RFID sensor network-based automation system for monitoring and tracking of sandalwood trees. In: *International Journal of Computational Science and Engineering* (Vol. 8, No. 2, pp. 154–161).
6. Dhanashree, P., Chanchal, V. D., & Dinesh, K., (2014). Designing wireless system for disaster prevention. In: *International Journal of Advanced Research in Computer Science and Management Studies* (Vol. 2, No. 6). ISSN: 2321-7782.
7. Chethan, K. P., Aravind, K. G., Jayaraman, S., & Balamuralidhar, P., (2010). FENCE to prevent deforestation using an event-based sensor network. In: *Chemistry and Chemical Engineering (ICCCE), 2010 International Conference* (pp. 322–324).
8. Oguchi, K., Yamashita, S., Terada, S., & Hanawa, D., (2012). Acceleration-sensor-based security system for orchards. In: *Communications and Electronics (ICCE), 2012 Fourth International Conference* (pp. 86–90).
9. Top News, (2012). *Kerala Plans to Insert Chips in Sandalwood Trees.* http://www.topnews.in/law/kerala-plans-insert-chips-sandalwood-trees-2105533 (accessed on 10 November 2021).
10. Nishkam, R., Nikhil, D., Preetham, M., & Michael, L. L., (2005). Activity recognition from accelerometer data. In: *Association for the Advancement of Artificial Intelligence (AAAI)* (Vol. 5, pp. 1541–1546).
11. Atallah, L., Lo, B., King, R., & Guang-Zhong, Y., (2011). Sensor positioning for activity recognition using wearable accelerometers. In: *IEEE Transactions on Biomedical Circuits and Systems* (Vol. 5, No. 4, pp. 320–329).
12. Piyush, G., & Tim, D., (2012). Feature selection and activity recognition system using a single tri-axial accelerometer. In: *IEEE Transactions on Biomedical Engineering* (Vol. 61, No. 6, pp. 1780–1786).
13. Tong, L., Song, Q., Ge, Y., & Liu, M., (2013). HMM-based human fall detection and prediction method using tri-axial accelerometer. In: *IEEE Sensors Journal* (Vol. 13, No. 5, pp. 1849–1856). doi: 10.1109/JSEN.2013.2245231.
14. Mitchell, E., et al., (2015). Automatically detecting asymmetric running using time and frequency domain features. In: *12th International Conference on Wearable and Implantable Body Sensor Networks (BSN)* (pp. 1–6). Cambridge, MA. doi: 10.1109/BSN.2015.7299404.

15. Samanta, B., Al-Balushi, K. R., & Al-Araimi, S. A., (2003). Artificial Neural Networks and Support vector machines with genetic algorithm for bearing fault detection. In: *Engineering Applications of Artificial Intelligence* (Vol. 16, pp. 6576–6665).

16. Samanta, B., & Al - Balushi, K. R., (2003). *Artificial Neural Network Based Fault Diagnostics of Rolling Element Bearings Using Time Domain Features, 17*(2), 317–328.

17. *Analog Devices*. Datasheet for ADXL345, http://www.analog.com/media/en/technical-documentation/data-sheets/ADXL345.pdf (accessed on 10 November 2021).

18. US Forest Service, (1990). Status and cultivation of sandalwood in India. In: *Proceedings of Symposium of Sandalwood in the Pacific*. http://www.fs.fed.us/psw/publications/documents/psw_gtr122/psw_gtr122_rai.pdf (accessed on 10 November 2021).

19. *World Agro-Forestry*. Report on Santalum album, http://www.worldagroforestry.org/treedb/AFTPDFS/Santalum_album.PDF (accessed on 10 November 2021).

CHAPTER 19

Analytics of IoT, SAR, and Social Network Data for Detection of Anomalies in Climate Conditions

VINAYAK ASHOK BHARADI

Department of Information Technology, Finolex Academy of Management and Technology, Ratnagiri, Maharashtra, India,
E-mails: vinayak.bharadi@famt.ac.in; vinayak.bharadi@outlook.com

ABSTRACT

Data analytics has been a widely researched field nowadays as the availability of data as we as the processing infrastructure is growing exponentially. Data analytics for weather prediction is a major researched domain and there has always been a race for precision and accuracy for weather predictions. Three major sources of providing very crucial weather data are IoT sensors, synthetic-aperture radar (SAR) data and social media posts from a particular location. In this chapter, we are proposing a system that takes IoT sensor data, SAR images and Twitter feeds from a geographical location and creates a learning model that will provide a decision-making system for anomaly detection in order to minimize or nullify any casualties. A temperature, pressure, and humidity dataset of BME 280 sensor is processed with K-NN classifiers and the results are presented here, further, the social network data from Twitter is analyzed for the localization of weather anomalies, named entity recognition (NER) and sentiment analysis is used for the same.

19.1 INTRODUCTION

IoT is a network of interconnected physical or virtual 'things' which have defined interfaces to be integrated as an information network in order to communicate with one another, with other such 'things or devices and with services or service providers over the Internet to achieve listed objectives [1]. Big data analytics (BDA) and internet of things (IoT) implementations have become ubiquitous in the past decade. BDA solutions incorporating the machine learning (ML) models are being explored by many researchers. ML has gained wide acceptance in this domain due to its capability to extract the patterns and hidden features in complicated datasets.

IoT sensors are deployed everywhere in a variety of applications [2]. Weather and environment monitorin g and forecasting is a widely used IoT application area that can be further integrated in application areas such as monitoring and management of traffic, precision agriculture, and social engineering. In contrast to previous frameworks that used statistical methods for analysis, the new research techniques use a higher degree of big data solutions and ML methods for forecast using weather and other IoT sensor data [3].

Another prominent data source for real life related events is SAR data. Voluminous data (Hyperspectral, Multispectral) from various types of sensors such as the space borne sensors and the Airborne sensors, with high temporal resolution velocity is available for analysis [4, 5].

People are also sharing the critical information related to natural disasters, extreme conditions or such related events are social media, though the authenticity is questionable semantic data analytics tools can be used on the data collected from various users for understanding the nature of the situation through natural language processing (NLP) [6]. Sentiment analysis comes under a special category of data mining that evaluates the disposition of people's opinions using NLP, text analysis, and last but not the least computational linguistics, which are then used to analyze and extract subjective information from social media and similar sources through the internet. The insight after data analytics quantifies the general public's sentiments or responses toward specific people, ideas, products, or events and reveal the information's contextual polarity. Opinion mining is another name of sentiment analysis [6].

In this study, we propose to gather the large amount of the data generated from the IoT Sensors, and Social Network such as Twitter feeds, process the data and use it for detection of anomalies, extreme weather conditions in real-time [7, 8], use of Synthetic-Aperture Radar (SAR) data is a proposed components and detailed analysis is the scope of the future work. This is a problem coming under BDA as it is processing the large scale of real-time data for near real-time decision-making for the detection and prediction of natural disasters. To extract real-time information from this large-scale data, high-performance computing (HPC) and scalable solutions that reduce the execution time are in extreme demand [9–11]. To address this real-time, a solution using a scalable hybrid parallelism approach using state of the art multi-core GPUs and message passing interface (MPI) is possible [4, 5] for analysis of remote sensing data related to disasters such as cyclones, earthquakes, floods, oil spills, etc. Further, the accuracy of the prediction can be improved if we combine or corroborate the findings with IoT sensors data.

19.2 RELATED WORK

19.2.1 BIG DATA IoT FRAMEWORK

Onal et al. [2] have used Big Data IoT framework considering a weather data case using a publicly available dataset. In detail, a description of all five layers (acquisition, ETL, data processing, ML and decision) in the framework is implemented and Scikit-Learn based k-means clustering is used as a learning model. Analysis of a highly complex dataset with this framework has extracted a meaningful information by taking the maximum cluster value as 4.

Munoz et al. [10] have proposed an integrated architecture for distributing IoT analytics between the core cloud and the edge of the network, considering the inclusion of control of the transport network with distributed edge and cloud resources.

A large amount of recent literature revolves around IoT analytics. Mainly, technique of edge IoT analytics is the popular choice of researchers. Depending on the varying conditions of IoT infrastructure, Refs. [11, 12] presented a facility for automatic transitions between edge and cloud by introducing a flexible architecture for edge IoT analytics. A big IoT sensor data is of no meaning unless it is properly analyzed and processed.

In Ref. [11], an approach to sensor data analytics has been proposed using OpenIoT middleware. Using a mobile crowd sensed data, they have analyzed the flexibility of OpenIoT middleware using real time event processing and clustering algorithms.

Taneja et al. [12] have explained the process of predictive analytics of IoT and have also come up with the challenges faced while implementing the predictive analytics of IoT.

As the number of devices in the edge network is growing fast, and comparatively number of data centers are not scaling as fast, it is desirable to decompose analytics programs in fog-assisted IoT environments, thereby making the edge networks more intelligent [13].

In this work, Kurte et al. have proposed a hybrid approach combining MPI and the emerging graphics processing units (GPUs) for high performance analytics of Remote Sense (RS) data in a disaster situation [4, 5].

In Refs. [14, 15], an improvement on the traditional GPUs based algorithm through the access conflict optimization for simulation of SAR raw data for large locations is proposed, which significantly improves the simulation over the GPUs.

El Rahman et al. [16] have proposed a model for performing sentiment analysis of real data of Twitter feeds. The said approach combines the supervised and unsupervised ML. This approach shows a strong performance on mining texts directly from Twitter.

Hagras et al. [17] have used the Latent Dirchlet Allocation LDA algorithm to identify tweets pertaining to a disaster event of the Tsunami in Japan. They used Twitter data for the training and designed an evaluation algorithm to test the effectiveness of LDA algorithm.

19.2.2   SENTIMENT ANALYSIS AND NAMED ENTITY RECOGNITION (NER)

Sentiment analysis is a quite researched topics, various sources of natural language data has been used by researchers for the same. Quanzhi and Sameena et al. [18] proposed sentiment-specific word embeddings (SSWE) and a weighted text feature model (WTFM). WTFM generates features based on the text negation, tf.idf weighting scheme as well as the Rocchio text classification method. Mohammad et al. [19] have designed the top-performing system, National Research Council Canada's (NRC), as a part of the tweet sentiment analysis track of SemEval 2013 and 2014 [20, 21].

Learning features directly from the extracted tweet text is a popular approach as of now. One way is to produce the sentence representations using word embeddings. Various word embedding formation algorithms are discussed in past research work [22, 23].

Named entity recognition (NER) is the initial step towards information extraction which is aimed at localization and classification of named entities in text into predefined categories (tokens), for example, the names of organizations, events, expressions of times, locations, persons, percentages, monetary values, quantities, etc. [24, 25]. After NER, entity disambiguation (ED) is performed for the mapping of an entity reference from knowledge bases such as Wikipedia or other standard datasets.

For example, 'Yes bank should have a concrete roadmap for addressing the NPA,' for the NER step, we have to identify 'Yes Bank' as a named entity (NE) and further classify it as an organization (ORG), rather than just a grammar word. Then in the ED step of the implementation, several candidates are generated for 'Yes,' such as 'Yes Bank' and the response word 'Yes.' Then after this each candidate is ranked with the context, 'Yes to be chosen as 'Yes bank Ltd.' rather than the response word 'Yes.'

Deep neural networks-based approaches have been explored recently to perform ED. In contrast to the conventional ML methods, the manually designed features are not considered in the deep learning methods. He et al. [26] used Deep NN in ED phase in a pioneering way. Model learnt entity representation via stacked was proposed by them, further they used denoising autoencoders to evaluate the context-entity similarity. Francis et al. [27] used convolutional neural networks (CNNs) to analyze mentions of contexts and the Wikipedia entity. Then the sparse features were added to the networks to capture semantic similarity. The model proposed by Gupta et al. [28] studied the use of Bidirectional long short-term memory (LSTM) LSTMs encoders and context modeling of entity documents with CNNs. In the next step their document information was concatenated with fine-grained types. A neural attention mechanism was proposed by Ganea et al. [29] over the over local context; later they passed the results to global disambiguation.

Akbik et al. have proposed a NER framework FLAIR which is based on deep neural network [24]. In this work FLAIR is used for Sentence Level Analysis of Tweets Polarity and various level of analytics is performed.

In the current research, the automated approach using FLAIR framework [24] is implemented. Automatic methods systems are based on ML techniques rather than on manually crafted rules as in the case of the rule-based systems. The sentiment analysis phase is generally deployed as a classification problem. The text is given as the input to the classifier model and it returns the corresponding polarity as positive, neutral, or negative. The ML classifier has the steps as shown in Figure 19.1.

19.2.2.1 TRAINING AND PREDICTION

The first phase is the training phase, the classifier learns the association between a particular input and the concerned output (tag or token) in the context of the training data set. The feature extraction module generates the feature vector from the text input. Sets of feature vectors and the positive, negative, or neutral tags are given as input to the ML algorithm to generate a classifier model. Next comes the prediction phase, the feature vector as discussed above is generated from the input text data and given as input the model generated above for the prediction of the tags as positive, negative, or neutral.

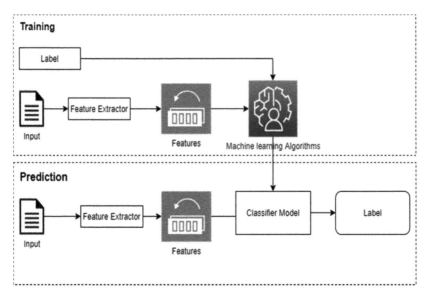

FIGURE 19.1 The training and prediction processes.

19.2.2.2   *FEATURE EXTRACTION*

The computer cannot understand text, it can understand only binary data or the numbers, the text should be converted into the numerical representation, and this is called the feature vector. The components of feature vector consist of frequency of a specific word or expression from a predefined lexicon of polarized words or dictionary. This is also referred as text vectorization. Previously people have worked on the bag-*of-words* or *bag-of-ngrams* with their frequency [21–26].

19.2.2.3   *CLASSIFICATION ALGORITHMS*

Various statistical model such as Logistic Regression, support vector machines (SVMs), Naïve Bayes, as well as Neural Networks are used in the classification process:

1. **Naïve-Bayes:** These classifiers are part of probabilistic algorithms family. These classifiers use the Bayes's Theorem for the prediction of text category;
2. **Linear Regression:** These algorithms use the correlation between the inputs and predict Y based on the input set X;

3. **Support Vector Machines (SVMs):** These algorithms map the input text vectors in a multidimensional space, the different categories are mapped to different of this vector space and the membership of a particular point will decide the category;

4. **Deep Learning:** A diverse set of algorithms using artificial neural networks (ANNs) to process data.

19.3 PROPOSED MODEL OF DISTRIBUTED DECOMPOSED DATA ANALYTICS

Weather forecasting systems rely on data from the satellite or their own networks and data collection labs. Their prediction can be further enhanced and made in real-time by adding the real time data of IoT, remote sensing satellites (SAR) and Social Networks.

As the data is to be acquired from social media, synthetic aperture radar (SAR) Images and IoT sensor data in real-time. It is very difficult to get actual location data of SAR as it needs Remote sensing satellite access, however we are using publicly available SAR datasets [30] and simulating the situation based on SAR data available to us.

Here we propose a framework for the analysis of data from IoT sensors and satellite images at a specific region along with the social network feeds such as Twitter (environment, Geo-spatial, and Social) data to generate the prediction about extreme weather conditions or anomalies in real-time.

The proposed system will be taking input from following resources:

- IoT sensors deployed at a location (air temperature, wind-speed/pressure, humidity, and visibility);
- Social network feeds-live twitter stream;
- SAR images.

The proposed framework is shown in Figure 19.2. The analytics on the gathered large volumes of data will be done in three phases as discussed in subsections.

19.3.1 DATA ACQUISITION PHASE

The data is gathered from the various sources as discussed, this will be passed and sent for stored locally. Sensor's data is captured over IoT network interface. SAR data from the Satellite network and the social network feeds from Twitter API.

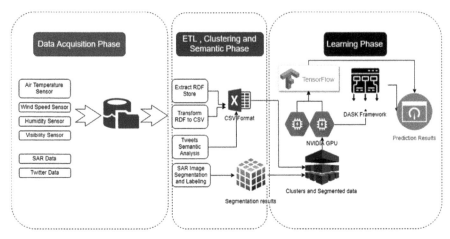

FIGURE 19.2   The proposed architecture of distributed decomposed data analytics of IoT, SAR, and social network data by means of clustering and event processing.

19.3.2   *ETL, CLUSTERING, AND SEMANTIC ANALYSIS*

To address the interoperability issue, semantic web solutions are proposed using:

- Modeling of the input data using resource description framework (RDF);
- Standard data formats such as JSON-LD, Turtle, and N3 [1] are used to develop the Web Ontology Language (OWL) protocols.

Location Specific Twitter feeds will be processed with semantic algorithms along for finding out specific phrases describing extreme events.

Further SAR images are processed with K-means clustering for and the clusters will be labeled to generate a k-means clustering using a library such as ScikitLearn. This clustering will reveal hidden pattern in the input data.

19.3.3   *LEARNING PHASE*

Learning algorithm will be implemented in Python on Scikit-learn, Pandas, NumPy, FLAIR [24] and Dask [31] libraries and frameworks will be used. The Dask library supports the scaling on GPUs; hence the performance improvement in a multi-GPU environment can be tested on Dask framework. The conceptual design is depicted in Figure 19.3. The data from each of the source will be acquired and processed in parallel and real-time in three phases as discussed above.

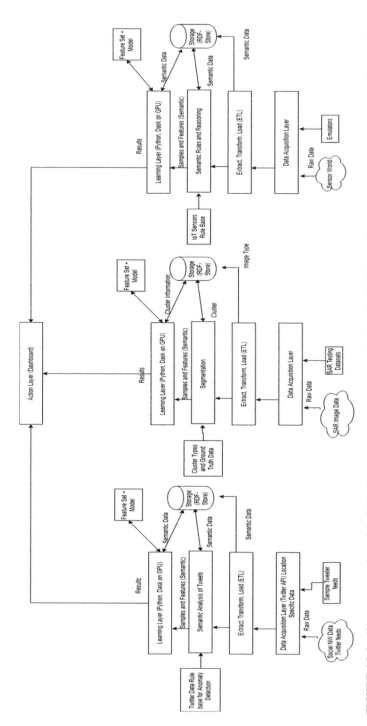

FIGURE 19.3 The conceptual model of distributed decomposed data analytics of IoT, SAR, and social network data by means of clustering and event processing.

19.4   EXPERIMENTAL METHODS AND RESULTS

The data analytics is done at two levels: first at the sensor data analytics and second at the social network data analytics.

19.4.1   SENSOR DATA ANALYTICS

The initial implementation is focused on the IoT sensor data analytics. BME 280 is a commonly used IoT sensor for sensing temperature, humidity, and air pressure [32]. A dataset having 100,700□ samples is used for the analysis of temperature, air pressure and humidity data. The Python panda's library test dataset is used here for the research. The data description is as in Table 19.1.

TABLE 19.1   Data Description for BME280 Data

	Temperature	Humidity	Pressure
Count	100,700	100,700	100,700
Mean	78.65	24.87	971.04
Std. Dev.	1.54	2.72	0.55
Min	76.51	18.56	970.06
25%	77.28	23.37	970.54
50%	78.36	25.43	971.08
75%	79.77	27.05	971.52
Max	108.96	36.77	996.029

The plot of temperature, pressure, and humidity is shown in Figure 19.4. Scikit-learn library was used to implement the K-NN Classifier The K-NN Classifier was used for the classification process, the N was varied from 1 to 8, The final training and testing accuracy was as follows:

- **Training Accuracy:** 0.998409.
- **Testing Accuracy:** 0.997365.

The confusion matrix is as in Table 19.2.

The performance plot relating the number of N and the classification accuracy is shown in Figure 19.5. This classification will further be used for detection of anomalies in temperature, pressure, and humidity. The real time data from BME 280 sensors deployed at various locations will be captured at a cloud-based server, and the anomaly detection will be performed to predict the weather conditions, this is the future scope.

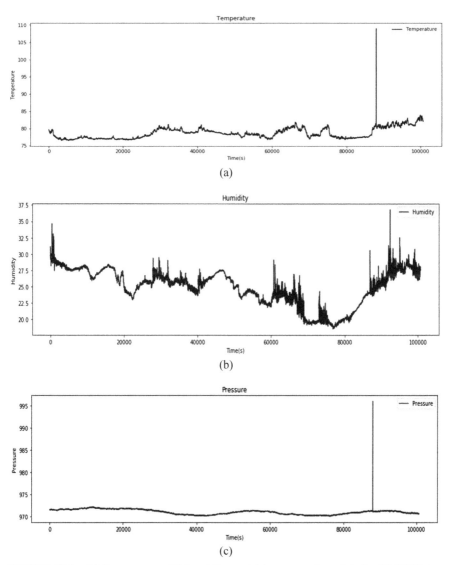

FIGURE 19.4 (a) Temperature; (b) humidity; and (c) pressure data plots for BME280 data used for the prediction analysis.

TABLE 19.2 Confusion Matrix

Predicted True	0	1	All
0	**17,301**	41	17,342
1	46	**22,847**	22,893
All	17,347	22,888	**40,235**

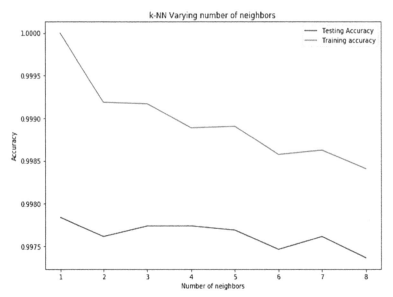

FIGURE 19.5   Performance of K-NN classifier.

19.4.2   *TWITTER DATA ANALYTICS*

Now the methodology for the sentiment analysis of the Twitter data will be discussed. The process follows some stages as given in Figure 19.6.

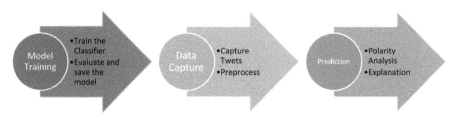

FIGURE 19.6   Sentiment analysis: Training and evaluation pipeline.

Flair framework [24] is used here for sentiment analysis purpose. Flair allows the combination of various kinds of word embeddings together; this results in greater contextual awareness of the classifier model.

Flair framework consist of contextualized representation called string embeddings at its core. Flair generates the character sequences by breaking the bigger sentences into smaller character sequences. This data is then fed to a pre-trained bidirectional language model for learning of the character level embeddings. Using this process, the model learns to identify the case-sensitive characters (for example, proper nouns from similar-sounding common nouns) and other natural language patterns like syntactic patterns accurately. This process makes Flair framework capable for efficient NER.

19.4.2.1 MODEL TRAINING FOR SEQUENCE TAGGER AND TEXT CLASSIFIER IN FLAIR

For the sentiment analysis of the tweets, we first need to set up the NER using FLAIR. The FLAIR framework has two components for this namely Sequence Tagger and Text Classifier. Sequence Tagger separates the tokens and Text Classifier gives the polarity of the tokens (Figure 19.7). The sequence tagger and text classifier are trained first. Both of them are trained with parameter optimization using HyperOpt [34] on WNUT 17 Database [35].

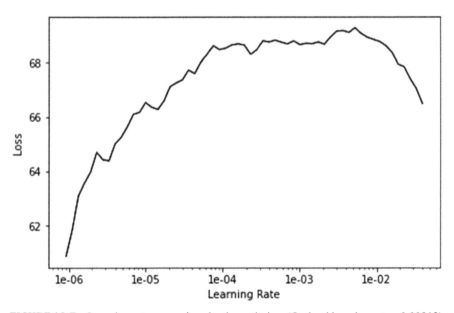

FIGURE 19.7   Learning rate curve given by the optimizer (Optimal learning rate = 0.00912).

Sequence tagger model is trained with FlairEmbeddings, Corpus details are as follows:

Corpus: "Corpus: 4907 train + 545 dev + 500 test sentences"
-Workshop on Noisy User-generated Text (WNUT'17) Database.

The classifier parameters were as follows:

learning_rate (LR)=0.001, batch_size=32, max_epochs=150,
embeddings_storage_mode='gpu'

The precision and recall parameters obtained are as follows for the Sequence Tagger.

MACRO_AVG: Acc 0.9273 – f1-score 0.961

NUM tp: 111 – fp: 3 – fn: 2 – tn: 384 – precision: 0.9737
– recall: 0.9823 – accuracy: 0.9569 – f1-score: 0.9780

The text classifier is trained with TREC-6 dataset [36].

Corpus: 4907 train + 545 dev + 500 test sentences
learning_rate: "0.1," batch_size: "32," annealing_factor: "0.5"
max_epochs: "150," Embeddings storage mode: gpu

The Precision and Recall Parameters obtained are as followed for the text classifier

MACRO_AVG: acc 0.8732 – f1-score 0.9316
Precision: 0.9727 – recall: 0.9469 – accuracy: 0.9224 – f1-score: 0.9596

Now the Sequence tagger and Text Classifier are ready for the Prediction or Classification of the tweets. Next steps are:

- Download the tweets related to the topic of the interest;
- Extracts relevant tags from the tweets (NER);
- Does sentiment analysis on those tweets (polarity evaluation of the tweets).

19.4.2.2   DATA CAPTURE AND PRE-PROCESS

Tweepy [37] is used to capture the Twitter data. Twitter API keys (and of course a Twitter account) are required to make Tweepy work. One can get those by signing up here: www.developer.twitter.com/en/apps.

Once you have your API SECRET KEY as well as API KEY, you can provide the credentials to Tweepy AppAuthHandler to get access to the tweets. Twitter allows maximum 45,000 tweets every 15 minutes. For sentiment analysis purposes various queries are given to the API and a set of tweets is downloaded. The details of query and tweet count is given in Table 19.3.

TABLE 19.3   Summary of Downloaded Tweets with the Topic

Date	Query	Tweet Count
19-Mar-20	Climate change	15,000
28-Mar-20	Raining India	10,000
5-Apr-2020	Raining	45,000
5-Apr-2020	Cyclone	45,000
6-Apr-2020	Cyclone	45,000
	Total	160,000

Following parameters for a tweet are captured:
['tweet_dt,' 'topic,' 'id,' 'username,' 'name,' 'tweet,' 'like_count,' 'reply_count,' 'retweet_count,' 'retweeted']), a snapshot of the sample data is shown in Figure 19.8.

	tweet_dt	topic	id	username	name	tweet	like_count
0	2020-03-28	Raining india	1243845586811141248	RameshK ja	ﻋﻠﻰ-Ramesh K ja	It's raining in Pune, India https://t.co/FbWqhdYVHY	5
1	2020-03-28	Raining india	1243811399150964326	Priyanka ran19	Priyanka Ba wal	Corona is declared non-effective under heat. \nWhen summer was expected in March, it's raining here, in Kuwait. Even... https://t.co/BlmZV6T1Xr	0
2	2020-03-28	Raining india	12437657326277754	NsBumb	NS mb	@BollyNumbers Like the monsoon, the Corona patients are raining heavily on the western part of India !	2
3	2020-03-27	Raining india	1243676077958070274	thomasmatkinsc	Thomas M Atkins	For the first time in my life, I really, really want to be a police man in India. Armed with only rattan canes and... https://t.co/ZpiljodfCG	0
4	2020-03-27	Raining india	1243644898416316416	cahima 1u15	Hi nshu Chh ra	@hopeseekr @ymcamomfmm @narendramodi No the current temperature in India is quite low actually and it is raining ev... https://t.co/6AV3eXLPNG	0

FIGURE 19.8   Sampled tweets data (some part is masked for anonymity).

Once the tweets are captured, they are cleaned to remove any Hashtag symbol (#). The cleaned tweets are given to the Sequence Tagger and the Text Classifier for the sentiment analysis process.

19.4.2.3   *POLARITY ANALYSIS*

The sequence Tagger takes the cleaned tweet as the input and predicts the tags which are the Named Entities of the sentence (tweet). The Named Entities such as Location, Person, Hashtag, Organizations are predicted by the Sequence tagger. Next, the text Classifier predicts the Polarity of the sentence, this polarity indicates the emotion behind the tweet or the sentences, here the polarity value is given as a real number with positive and negative weight of the emotion (Figure 19.9).

	tweet_dt	topic	id	username	name	tweet	tag_type	tag	sentiment	polarity	adj_polarity	like_count
0	2020-03-28	Raining india	12434558658114124¦	╱Kateja	ﺭ⌐Ra ╎ ╽a	sh ╮a	It's raining in Pune, India https://t.co/FbWqhdVHY	LOC	Pune	NEGATIVE	0.999987	-0.999987	5
1	2020-03-28	Raining india	12434558658114124¦	Kateja	ﺭ⌐Ran K	h a	It's raining in Pune, India https://t.co/FbWqhdVHY	LOC	India	NEGATIVE	0.999987	-0.999987	5
2	2020-03-28	Raining india	1243813991509643²¦	Priyan	₃ran19	Pri nka Bar ╷wal	Corona is declared non-effective under heat. \nWhen summer was expected in March, it's raining here, in Kuwait. Even... https://t.co/BlmZV6T1Xr	LOC	Corona	NEGATIVE	0.999863	-0.999863	0
3	2020-03-28	Raining india	1243813991509643²6-	Priyan╽	╷ran19	Priy ka Bara ╷al	Corona is declared non-effective under heat. \nWhen summer was expected in March, it's raining here, in Kuwait. Even... https://t.co/BlmZV6T1Xr	LOC	Kuwait	NEGATIVE	0.999863	-0.999863	0
4	2020-03-28	Raining india	12437657326277775	Nsl ╵mb	NSf ╷mb	@BollyNumbers Like the monsoon, the Corona patients are raining heavily on the western part of India !	LOC	Corona	POSITIVE	0.998277	0.998277	2

FIGURE 19.9   Sampled tweets data with tags and polarity (some part is masked for anonymity).

There was unusual raining in the Pune City of India on 27th March 2020 and this event was trending on the Twitter, this was going on while India was facing the COVID-19 outbreak, this overall sentiment is captured in the analysis (Table 19.4).

TABLE 19.4 Tags, Tag Types and Sentiment Analysis of the "Raining India" Tweets

Tag	Tag Category	Frequency	Polarity (Average)	Likes (Total Count)	Sentiment
India	LOC	57	–0.232423086	672	Negative
Corona	LOC	5	–0.587251496	3	Negative
#India	Hashtag	5	–0.591005993	5	Negative
Pune	LOC	3	0.225422343	8	Positive
#COVID-2019	Hashtag	3	–0.913457374	29	Negative
Delhi	LOC	3	–0.916047017	27	Negative
INDIA	LOC	3	–0.21741273	9	Negative
Maharashtra	LOC	3	–0.304067771	14	Negative
#coronavirus	Hashtag	2	–0.996330559	13	Negative
Indian	MISC	2	–0.981727362	1	Negative
Ahmedabad	LOC	2	–0.999890178	8	Negative
Mumbai	LOC	2	–2.83E-05	1	Negative
Pharmacy	ORG	2	–0.969625771	16	Negative
Coronavirus	MISC	2	–0.987374812	2	Negative
God	PER	2	–0.998883665	2	Negative
#Lockdown21	Hashtag	2	–0.999959826	1	Negative
Indians	MISC	1	–0.999993086	21	Negative

Form the sentiment analysis, it can be substantiated that there was a rain in the Pune City, India, and the Pune City People are positive about this, however at a broader level as it is not usual to be raining at this time and as COVID-19 outbreak is their there is a negative sentiment about this event at the national level. The NASA's Global Imagery Browse Services (GIBS) also support these findings. The images on that day as shown in Figure 19.10; Clear rain clouds can be seen over the Pune city. Figure 19.11 is the summary of the polarity of the sentiments against various location tags.

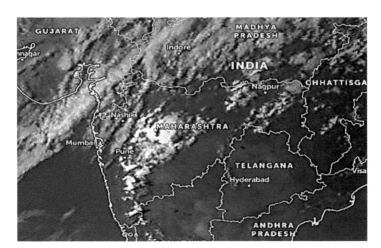

FIGURE 19.10   NASA's global imagery browse services map for Pune city on 27th March 2020 (the city names are overlaid [38]).

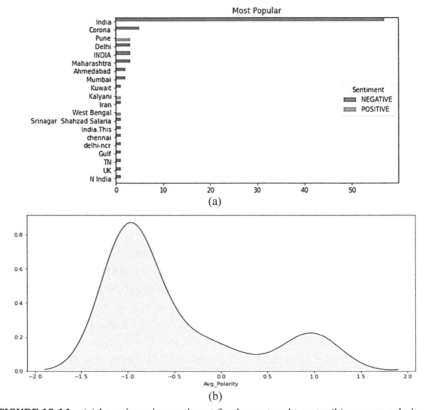

FIGURE 19.11   (a) Location wise sentiment for the captured tweets; (b) average polarity.

19.4.3 CYCLONE DATA ANALYTICS

The above-mentioned process is carried out for all the queries in Table 19.3, the key events and the findings are discussed here. Total 160,000 tweets were analyzed on the FLAIR framework, using LSTM [24] based classifiers. The implementation was done in Python on Google Colaboratory infrastructure. The results for tweet polarity are presented in the following sequence, Organization, Hashtag, Location, and the Polarity map.

On April 5 and April 6, total 90,000 tweets were scraped from tweeter and the Sentiment analysis with NER was performed. The NER clearly indicates a high number of tweets from Solomon Island where Cyclone Harold was present. Actually, two main cyclones are part of this study, Harold, and Irondro [38], cyclone Harold was present over the city Vanuatu, Solomon Islands, towards east of Australia, and Cyclone Irondro was present at the west side of Australia. As the cyclone Harold was affecting a larger population, the effect is reflected in tweet analytics (Figure 19.12).

Table 19.5 shows the progression of the Tropical Cyclone Harold as it moves from Tropical Depression to Category 4 Cyclone.

TABLE 19.5   Cyclone Harold 2020 (Vanuatu, Solomon Islands) Progression, Source-Zoom Earth Readings [38]

Date	Cyclone Category	Wind (mph)	Pressure (bar)
31 March 2020	Tropical depression	23	NA
1 April 2020	Tropical depression	23	NA
2 April 2020	C1 (Category 1) tropical cyclone	46	1000
3 April 2020	C1 tropical cyclone	52	999
3 April 2020	C2 tropical cyclone	63	990
4 April 2020	C3 tropical cyclone	104	966
4 April 2020	C4 tropical cyclone	127	946
5 April 2020	C4 tropical cyclone	132	950
6 April 2020	C4 tropical cyclone	121	950

The NER is performed and Location and Hashtags are separated, the plots are given in Figure 19.13.

The analytics shows that from 31 March to 6th April 2020, the Cyclone word was trending or most popular or maximum tweeted at the location Vanuatu and Solomon Islands, these locations are at the center of the Cyclone Harold. In the Twitter trends, the words Vanuatu and Harold are having higher rank, as the Cyclone Irondro has not impacted much human population as compared to cyclone Harold, the word Irondro is on the 8th Rank.

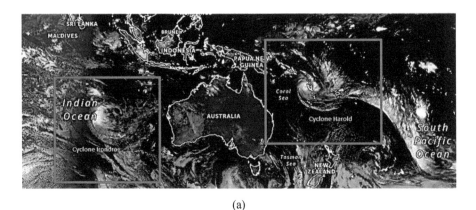

(a)

(b)

FIGURE 19.12   (a) Satellite image of cyclone Harold and cyclone Irondro on 5th March 2020; (b) enlarged image of cyclone Harold (Adapted from: NASA's global imagery browse services (GIBS) [38]).

The overall sentiment is negative as the cyclone is having destructive nature and negative impact on the human civilization.

Thus, the tweet analytics has clearly identified the anomalies and located them. This can be used to have a real time impact analysis of the natural disasters and improve the accuracy of the weather condition predictions.

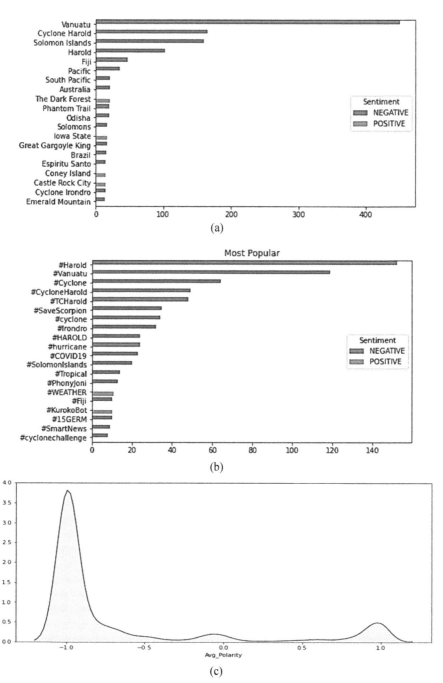

FIGURE 19.13 Satellite image of cyclone Harold and cyclone Irondro (NASA's global imagery browse services (GIBS), and zoom earth [38]).

The accuracy can be further improved by real time analysis and segmentation of the SAR data, this is the future scope of the research.

19.5   CONCLUSION AND FUTURE WORK

In this chapter, a framework for distributed decomposed data analytics of IoT sensors, SAR, and social network data by means of clustering and event processing are proposed. The results for BME 280 Sensor data by the K-NN clustering approach is presented and the accuracy was 0.9973 for prediction was achieved. Further, the sentiment analysis was performed on the Twitter data using the NER. The NER and sentiment analysis was performed using FLAIR on 160,000 tweets. The sequence taggers and classifiers were trained with optimized parameters and later on used for NER analysis and prediction of the polarity. The analytics clearly located the cyclone Harold and its negative impact on human civilization. The location, hashtag, and organization-based analysis can be further used for planning about the counteractions for specific events and further actions. The future work is to combine SAR and social network data along with the IoT sensor data and use other neural network classifiers for the prediction of real time anomalies in weather conditions.

ACKNOWLEDGMENT

We acknowledge the use of imagery provided by services from NASA's Global Imagery Browse Services (GIBS), part of NASA's Earth Observing System Data and Information System (EOSDIS).

KEYWORDS

- **IoT analytics**
- **named entity recognition (NER)**
- **natural language processing**
- **sentiment analysis**
- **synthetic aperture radar (SAR) data**
- **Twitter feeds**

REFERENCES

1. Taneja, M., Jalodia, N., & Davy, A., (2019). Distributed decomposed data analytics in fog enabled IoT deployments, *IEEE Access*, *7*, 40969–40981.
2. Onal, A., Sezer, O. B., Ozbayoglu, M., Dogdu, E., & Can, A., (2017). Weather data analysis and sensor fault detection using an extended IoT framework with semantics, big data, and machine learning. *IEEE International Conference on Big Data (BIGDATA).* doi: 10.1109/BigData.2017.8258150.
3. Chin, J., Callaghan, V., & Lam, I., (2017). Understanding and personalizing smart city services using machine learning, the internet-of-things and big data. In: *Industrial Electronics (ISIE), 2017 IEEE 26ᵗʰ International Symposium* (pp. 2050–2055). *IEEE,*
4. Kurte, K., Bhangale, U., Durbha, S., King, R., & Younan, N., (2016). Accelerating big data processing chain in image information mining using a hybrid HPC approach. *IEEE International Geoscience and Remote Sensing Symposium (IGARSS)* (pp. 7597–7600). Beijing.
5. Kurte, K., Bhangale, U., Durbha, S., King, R., & Younan, N., (2016). Big data processing using HPC for remote sensing disaster data. *IEEE International Geoscience and Remote Sensing Symposium (IGARSS)* (pp. 5894–5897). Beijing. doi: 10.1109/IGARSS.2016.7730540.
6. Chong, P., Karuppiah, E., & Yong, K., (2013). A Multi-GPU framework for in-memory text data analytics. In: *27ᵗʰ International Conference on Advanced Information Networking and Applications Workshops*, 411–1416. Barcelona. doi: 10.1109/WAINA.2013.238.
7. Samiappan, S., (2018). Texture classification of very high resolution UAS imagery using a graphics processing unit. *IGARSS 2018 - 2018 IEEE International Geoscience and Remote Sensing Symposium* (pp. 6476–6479). Valencia.
8. Praveen, P., Babu, C., & Rama, B., (2016). Big data environment for geospatial data analysis. *International Conference on Communication and Electronics Systems (ICCES)* (pp. 1–6). Coimbatore.
9. *European Space Agency-Earth Online Data*. https://earth.esa.int/web/guest/data-access (accessed on 10 November 2021).
10. Munoz, R., Vilalta, R., Yoshikane, N., Casellas, R., Martinez, R., Tsuritani, T., & Morita, I., (2018). Integration of IoT, transport SDN, and edge/cloud computing for dynamic distribution of IoT analytics and efficient use of network resources. *Journal of Lightwave Technology, 36*(7).
11. Patel, P., Ali, M. I., & Sheth, A., (2017). On using the intelligent edge for IoT analytics. *IEEE Intelligent Systems, 32*(5), 64–69.
12. Taneja, T., Jatain, A., & Bajaj, S., (2017). Predictive analytics on IoT. *IEEE International Conference on Computing, Communication and Automation (ICCCA2017).* ISBN:978-1-5090-6471-7/17.
13. Hromic, H., Le Phuoc, D., Serrano, M., Antonić, A., Žarko, I. P., Hayes, C., & Decker, S., (2015). Real time analysis of sensor data for the internet of things by means of clustering and event processing, *IEEE International Conference on Communications (ICC).* doi: 10.1109/ICC.2015.7248401.
14. Joshi, V., Manikandan, S., & Srinivasaiah, H., (2017). Overview of airborne SAR data processing algorithms. *IEEE International Conference on Innovative Mechanisms for Industry Applications (ICIMIA).* doi: 10.1109/ICIMIA.2017.7975661.

15. Zhang, F., Hu, C., Hu, W., & Li, H., (2014). Accelerating time-domain SAR raw data simulation for large areas using multi-GPUs. *IEEE Journal of Selected Topics in Applied Earth Observations and Remote Sensing, 7*(9). doi: 10.1109/JSTARS.2014.2330333.

16. Rahman, S., AlOtaibi, F., & AlShehri, W., (2019). Sentiment analysis of twitter data. *IEEE International Conference on Computer and Information Sciences (ICCIS).* doi: 10.1109/ ICCISci.2019.8716464.

17. Hagras, M., Hassan, G., & Farag, N., (2017). Towards natural disasters detection from twitter using topic modeling. *IEEE European Conference on Electrical Engineering and Computer Science.* doi 10.1109/EECS.2017.57.

18. Li, Q., Shah, S., Fang, R., Nourbakhsh, A., & Liu, X., (2016). Tweet sentiment analysis by incorporating sentiment-specific word embedding and weighted text features. In: 2016 *IEEE/WIC/ACM International Conference on Web Intelligence (WI).* doi: 10.1109/ wi.2016.0097.

19. Mohammad, S. M., Kiritchenko, S., & Zhu, X., (2013). Building the state-of the-art in sentiment analysis of tweets. *International Workshop on Semantic Evaluation 2013.*

20. Nakov, P. S., Rosenthal, Z., Kozareva, V., Stoyanov, A., & Wilson, T., (2013). *Removal-2013 task 2: Sentiment analysis in twitter.*,

21. Martínez-Cámara, E., Martín-Valdivia, M. T., Urena-López, L. A., & Montejo-Ráez, A. R., (2014). Sentiment analysis in Twitter. *Natural Language Engineering, 20*(1), 1–28.

22. Collobert, R., Weston, J., Bottou, L., Karlen, M., Kavukcuoglu, K., & Kuksa, P., (2011). Natural language processing (almost)from scratch. *J. Mach. Learn. Res., 12*, 2493–2537.

23. Mikolov, T., Sutskever, I., Chen, K., Corrado, G., & Dean, J., (2013). Distributed representations of words and phrases and their compositionality. In: *Proceedings of NIPS.*

24. Akbik, A., Bergmann, T., Blythe, D., Rasul, K., Schweter, S., & Vollgraf, R., (2019). FLAIR: An easy-to-use framework for state-of-the-art NLP. *Proceedings of the 2019 Conference of the North American Chapter of the Association for Computational Linguistics (Demonstrations)* (pp. 54–59). doi: 0.18653/v1/N19-4010.

25. Wang, Q., & Iwaihara, M., (2019). Deep neural architectures for joint named entity recognition and disambiguation. In: *2019 IEEE International Conference on Big Data and Smart Computing (BigComp).* doi: 10.1109/bigcomp.2019.8679233.

26. He, Z., et al., (2013). Learning entity representation for entity disambiguation. *In Proc. 51st ACL*, 30–34.

27. Francis-Landau, M., Durrett, G., & Klein, D., (2016). Capturing semantic similarity for entity linking with convolutional neural network. In: *Proc. NAACL-HLT, 2016* (pp. 1256–1261).

28. Gupta, N.,Singh, S., & Roth, D., (2017). Entity linking via joint encoding of types, description, and context. In: *Proc. EMNLP*, (pp. 2681–2690).

29. Ganea, O., & Hofmann, T., (2017). Deep joint entity disambiguation with local neural attention. In: *Proc. EMNLP* (pp. 2619–2629).

30. NASA's Global Imagery Browse Services (GIBS), part of NASA's Earth Observing System Data and Information System (EOSDIS).

31. *Dask-A Flexible Library for Parallel Computing.* https://docs.dask.org/en/latest/ (accessed on 10 November 2021).

32. *BME 280 Sensor, Data.* https://www.bosch-sensortec.com/products/environmental-sensors/humidity-sensors-bme280/ (accessed on 10 November 2021).

33. Kaggle, (2019). *BME 280 Sensor Dataset.* https://www.kaggle.com/faisalawan/bme280 sensordata (accessed on 10 November 2021).

34. Bergstra, J., Yamins, D., & Cox, D. D., (2013). Making a science of model search: Hyperparameter optimization in hundreds of dimensions for vision architectures. In: *Proc. of the 30th International Conference on Machine Learning (ICML 2013).*

35. Diego, R. J., (2020). https://github.com/juand-r/entity-recognition-datasets/tree/master/data/WNUT17 (accessed on 10 November 2021).

36. Voorhees, E., & Harman, D., (2000). Overview of the sixth text retrieval conference (TREC-6). *Information Processing & Management, 36*(1), 3–35. https://doi.org/10.1016/S0306-4573(99)00043-6.

37. Hill, A., & Harmon, R. J., (2020). https://github.com/tweepy/tweepy/blob/master/docs/index.rst (accessed on 10 November 2021).

38. Cyclon Harod and Irondro Data, (2020). NASA EOSDIS Global, Full Resolution Imagery, https://worldview.earthdata.nasa.gov/?v=30.9521484375,-86.302734375,267.0673828125,13.259765625&t=2020-04-02-T04%3A53%3A01Z&l=Reference_Labels,Reference_Features,Coastlines,VIIRS_NOAA20_CorrectedReflectance_TrueColor,VIIRS_SNPP_CorrectedReflectance_TrueColor(hidden),MODIS_Aqua_CorrectedReflectance_TrueColor(hidden),MODIS_Terra_CorrectedReflectance_True-Color (accessed on 10 November 2021).

CHAPTER 20

Proposed Framework for Improving Localization Using Bluetooth Low Energy Beacons

RAKHI AKHARE,[1] MONIKA MANGLA,[2] NARENDRA SHEKOKAR,[2] and SMITA SANJAY AMBARKAR[1]

[1]*Lokmanya Tilak College of Engineering, Navi Mumbai, Maharashtra, India, E-mail: smita.ambarkar27@gmail.com (S. S. Ambarkar)*

[2]*Dwarkadas J. Sanghvi College of Engineering, Mumbai Maharashtra, India*

ABSTRACT

Localization has become an attractive area of research during past decades. Outdoor localization had gained intensive interest of the researchers since its inception but indoor localization had experienced lack of attention of researchers during the past few decades. Resultantly there are various recognized technologies for outdoor localization like GPS, GLONASS, Galileo, etc., but technologies for indoor localization is still in its infancy. Authors in this chapter aim to present state-of-the-art for various developments in the indoor localization. This chapter aims to propose use of Bluetooth Low Energy (BLE) devices beacons for indoor localization. The reason for selection of BLE devices is its competence and capability to support mobile smart devices that leads to an exponential rise in its application.

Using this technology, the authors also present a framework for detecting COVID-19 patients. Recently, the whole world is witnessing the pandemic outbreak of coronavirus. The chapter also discusses a similar case study of an application launched by GovTech (Government Technology Agency of Singapore), the IT agency of the Singapore in association with the Ministry of Health (MOH). This application is based on the

BLE, which supports and supplements efforts of the nation to reduce the spread of COVID-19.

20.1   INTRODUCTION

The process of localization process estimates the co-ordinates and position of a wireless sensor node in an open space or closed space. These wireless sensor nodes attempt to determine their position with reference to anchor nodes (nodes that are conscious of their position) in the network. During the past few decades, localization has grabbed an overwhelming attention and interest of researchers owing to its real-life application in various domains. It has deployed its application in tracking the location of animals in a zoo, location of a mobile device, etc. Earlier, this application was limited to outdoor localization only. However, in the past decade, researchers are getting attracted towards devising efficient approaches for indoor localization also. This scope for research in indoor localization has attracted numerous industry and academic researchers resultantly this research area has been intensified.

Several technologies are there in existence for localization. The most prominently technology for communication is global positioning system (GPS), an approved most adept technology for outdoor localization. However, it bears several disadvantages [1] despite its widespread application. The most concerning issue is that it needs a direct line-of-sight (LoS) among communicating nodes. Also, it necessitates specialized hardware. Moreover, the power consumption in GPS is very high. Also, its accuracy and efficiency are strongly affected by the noise in the environment and other interference. However, GPS has observed widespread deployment in outdoor localization; it has limited application in indoor localization. Hence, it demands different technologies for indoor localization. Some of the widely accepted technologies for indoor localization are Bluetooth, IEEE 802.11, Zigbee, and RFID, etc., each having their own strength and limitations [2]:

1. **IEEE 802.11 (also known as Wi-Fi):** It is generally used to provide connectivity to various devices in a public, private, and commercial organization. Over time, the coverage distance of Wi-Fi has expanded up to 1 km owing to technological advancements. Most of the smart devices in the current scenario are Wi-Fi enables and thus advocates its establishment as an ideal choice for localization. Sufficient

numbers of Wi-Fi access points are deployed for communication. These access points can be utilized for localization by using them as anchor points, thus eliminating the requirement for specialized infra-structure. Though, as the Wi-Fi networks are primarily deployed for communication purpose, it needs to implement efficient algorithm to improve localization accuracy.

2. **Radio Frequency Identification (RFID):** Another promising technology for localization is using RFID. It can basically communicate using electromagnetic transmission among transmitter and RF enabled circuit. Here, readers are used which are competent in communicating to RFID tags. Data emitted by RFID tags can be read by RFID readers using predefined protocols. RFID systems have been broadly classified into active RFID and Passive RFID. The reader may refer to Ref. [2] for detailed understanding of active and passive RFID.

3. **Zigbee (IEEE 802.15.4):** It is an energy-efficient, low cost and low data rate communication standard. It is primarily used in wireless sensor networks (WSNs). Although Zigbee provides optimal perfor-mance for localizing sensors in a WSN, but most of end devices are not ZigBee enabled. Resultantly, it observes limited application in localization purpose.

4. **Ultra-Wideband (UWB):** This technology can also be employed for very short-range communication such as peripherals of PC. It can be widely deployed for indoor localization as it is resistant to external interferences. However, UWB has experienced very slow progress in its standards leading to its limited usage in user devices.

5. **Visible Light Communication (VLC):** It is another developing technology for speedy data transfer using visible light in the range of 400 to 800 THz. Basically, it uses light sensors to estimate the location and emitters direction. Here, LEDs emit a signal which is sensed by the sensor and uses it for localization. The prime advan-tage of VLC is its wide scale proliferation. However, it also has a constraint that it requires a LoS between LED and sensor to perform localization.

6. **Bluetooth (or IEEE 802.15.1):** It is also an exciting communication and localization technology to connect fixed and/or movable wire-less devices within a particular range. This Bluetooth technology has evolved into BLE, which provides improved data communication at a rate of 24 Mbps within a range of 100 meters. BLE primarily

works on the concept of received signal strength (RSS). Although BLE is competent for localization purpose in its original form yet two leading companies Google Inc. and Apple Inc. have recently proposed two BLE based protocols namely iBeacons and Eddystone respectively for context aware localization. BLE has observed its widespread employment for indoor localization. The comparative analyzes of all these technologies have been presented in Table 20.1.

During comparative analysis of various communication technologies as presented in Table 20.1, it is observed that BLE and RFID both are potential candidates for indoor localization. However, BLE has few additional features over RFID that establishes its competence for indoor localization. The most significant and exciting feature of BLE is that it can communicate with other technologies. Hence, it can communicate with smart devices in the vicinity, and the aggregated data is transferred to the cloud.

During a survey of literature, it was noticed that several technologies were implemented for indoor localization, but they failed to give acceptable results due to additional cost and limited performance in comparison to BLE. Thus, it is agreed that BLE is primarily implemented for indoor localization considering its capability and infrastructure requirement. Here, authors would like to mention that indoor positioning experiences a deprivation of its extensive application in real life. The prime causes of this deprivation are excessive power consumption, expensive cost, and inadequate accuracy.

The chapter is organized in various sections. The various communication technologies have been introduced in Section 20.1. This section also presents a comparative analysis of various technologies and thus maintains the completeness of the chapter. Section 20.2 focuses on the related work in the domain of localization. Section 20.3 discusses the working principle and challenges for BLE to maintain completeness of the chapter. Few prevailing use cases are presented in Section 20.4 and authors present the proposed model in Section 20.5. Lastly, Conclusion, and future scope for research is discussed in Section 20.6.

20.2   LOCALIZATION AND RELATED WORK

This section clarifies the concept of localization and also present related work. As already discussed, localization is the process of estimating the position of an object (wireless node) within an environment. The localization

TABLE 20.1 Properties of Various Communication Technologies

Technology	Localization Purpose	Power Consumption	Features
GPS	Outdoor	Very high	• Needs specialized hardware • Need line of sight for communication • Strongly influenced by interference
Wi-Fi	Couple of meters	Moderate	• Widely available, high accuracy • No complex hardware needed • Effected by noise • Needs complex algorithms
Bluetooth	100 m	Low	• Localization accuracy is low • Effected by noise
RFID	200 m	Low	• Wide Range • Requires low power • Low localization accuracy
UWB	10–20 m	Moderate	• Immune to interference • Requires extra hardware and high cost
Visible light	1.4 km	Relatively higher	• Wide-scale availability and high accuracy • Range is affected by obstacles • primarily requires LoS

has been broadly classified into outdoor localization and indoor localization, each having its own principal localization technologies.

20.2.1   OUTDOOR LOCALIZATION

GPS remains the most prominent technology for outdoor localization till date. As mentioned previously, GPS works on the LoS and employs various methodologies for localization. The most prominent wireless protocol for GPS is IEEE 802.11. Additionally, there have been few other localization approaches in existence for the past few years, such as time of arrival (ToA), time of flight (ToF), angle of arrival (AoA), and time difference of arrival (TDOA). All these approaches require extra equipment that further escalates the setup cost, thus limiting their widespread usage. For a detailed understanding of these technologies, readers may refer to Ref. [3].

20.2.2   INDOOR LOCALIZATION

The technologies used for outdoor localization cannot perform effectively for indoor due to obstacle in line of sight inside the building. Moreover, it is also influenced by parameters like building structure, capacity of radio transmitters and receivers, etc. Therefore, indoor localization needs to employ some technology like radio networks which can function even in the interior of building.

As outdoor localization employs techniques like AoA, ToA, TDOA, and ToF, indoor localization uses received signal strength indicator (RSSI). This specialized technique is necessitated for indoor localization as LoS is not feasible within a building. RSSI is based on WLAN and provides a complex data set. The rationale behind usage of RSSI indoor localization is that it does not need any specific hardware in addition to existing WLAN infrastructure. Similarly, it can also employ the approach of Fingerprinting (a building dependent approach) for indoor localization. In fingerprinting approach, fingerprint database is created during the training phase. Later during the positioning phase, fingerprint database is utilized in association with the signal strength to determine object location.

The efficiency of a localization methodology may be evaluated in terms of some performance metrics. Among several metrics, some widely accepted metrics are cost, accuracy, complexity, precision, scalability, and robustness, etc. In the literature, various researchers have proposed different localization approaches as discussed in a subsequent section.

20.2.3 *CURRENT STATE-OF-THE-ART IN OUTDOOR LOCALIZATION*

The technology of GPS has been deployed for PC-class nodes in outdoor localization [4]. However, this is prevented from deploying on all the nodes owing to size, cost, and power constraints of all nodes. The authors in Ref. [4] address the localization for such constrained devices by leveraging radio frequencies for localization. Furthermore, the proposed model does not require extensive infrastructure and preplanning. Here, the authors use two different approaches for RF-based localization system based on RSS and connectivity.

The similar work of localization is undertaken by authors in Ref. [1]. In this, the authors present a hybrid approach for outdoor localization that combines built-in sensors and Wi-Fi signal data in smart phones. This hybrid approach helps in achieving low power requirement and enhanced accuracy. The proposed approach works in two phases. The first phase collects a database of offline Wi-Fi fingerprint using crowdsourcing which includes GPS statistics also. This information is matched with real-time Wi-Fi and GPS during the second phase to perform localization. It is observed in Ref. [1] that fingerprinting is a promising solution over comparative localization methods.

The work of outdoor localization is also undertaken by authors in Ref. [5]. For the same, authors present an integral invariant for outdoor environments, a faster localization method. Here, the image is partitioned in to sub-images and integral invariant of each grid is calculated individually. These invariants are combined to form a feature vector. Authors in Ref. [5] suggest combining this method with a particle filter method to further enhance the localization accuracy.

Authors in Ref. [6] also work for outdoor localization by using an appearance-based approach. For the same, two types of image feature algorithms namely SIFT and SURF have been employed to compare images. It is demonstrated in Ref. [6] that SURF outperform the conventional algorithms for image comparison in terms of time and accuracy. This approach can be used as a basic method for localization of mobile robots. It is noticed in Ref. [6] that SIFT also gives good performance in indoor localization and acceptable performance in outdoor environment. This difference in performance is owing to the fact that outdoor images are affected by lighting, shadows, and seasonal changes, thus obscuring the process of image matching. Research is evolving to match outdoor images in different environmental conditions.

Another method of differential GPS and odometry using Kalman filter has been proposed by authors in Ref. [7] to navigate mobile robot in outdoor environment. Here, curbs are identified using laser range finding, which is later used for localization of robot. In this, laser range finders are used to estimate obstacles which help in building a map. Thereafter, authors in Ref. [8] propose a hybrid navigation approach to robot localization that aims to provide more sophisticated and robust results. Few technologies that have been integrated are Wi-Fi/UWB, GNSS/GSM, and GNSS/GSM/Wi-Fi. Here in Ref. [8], the authors develop a new hybrid model for localization named as localization information fusion system (LIFS) that involves two steps. The first step uses two different technologies to perform its theoretical study.

Thus, it is observed that outdoor localization has been rigorously researched upon by various researchers and efficient approaches have been proposed for the same.

20.2.4   CURRENT STATE-OF-THE-ART IN INDOOR LOCALIZATION

Several researchers have been working in the field of indoor localization in order to devise efficient and effective approaches for the same. Here, the authors discuss some prominent work in this regard. The majority of the methods for indoor localization use BLE beacon-based positioning methods. Also, during the past few decades, BLE proved its competence in indoor localization. Resultantly, authors present detailed information about the working principle of BLE to enhance readers' understanding.

BLE is low energy (1 mW typical transmitter output), low-cost technology for indoor localization that also operates in the 2.4 GHz ISM band [9]. BLE devices are used with Wi-Fi access points. It is driven by consumer devices like smart phones and hence connect with low power sensors as it does not require a long handshake period of classic Blue-tooth 2.2. Modern smartphones are generally equipped with BLE transceivers, resulting in an emerging user base.

Additionally, BLE are cost-effective in comparison to Wi-Fi that further motivates installation of BTLE transmitters in constrained locations where it becomes difficult or even impossible to replace battery. Here, the radio signals emitted by BLE beacons are received by mobile devices. The distance of beacon from mobile device is indicated as signal strength as transmission time depends upon the involved distance. Thus, with an increase in distance between mobile device and transmitter, the strength of signal starts weakening and transmission time increases.

Here, it is worth noting that beacons should be installed in the infrastructure (ex. building) in a manner so as no portion of the infrastructure remains uncovered by its range. For instance, if a beacon is installed at point P, its visibility range can be considered as a circle of radius α and center at P. Here, the maximum distance within which beacon receives a signal is indicated by α as shown in Figure 20.1.

The visibility range is represented by a circle of four beacons is illustrated in Figure 20.1. Now, the region excluding circular disks is not present in the coverage range of beacons and cannot be localized. Hence, placement of beacons should be decided with utmost care so as to cover the maximum area so as to ensure effective and efficient localization.

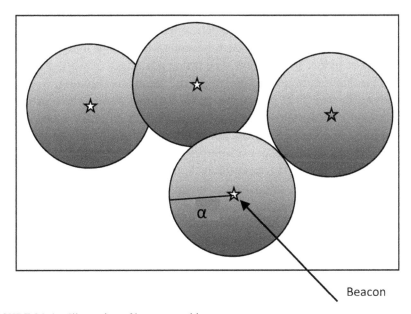

Beacon

FIGURE 20.1   Illustration of beacons and its range.

Fingerprinting and triangulation are the most commonly used techniques for BLE localization in order to estimate location. In *triangulation*, it takes help of numerous transmitters to estimate location. For the same, a few popular techniques are TDOA, ToA, AoA, etc. However, it has some limitations. It necessitates perfect synchronization of all the devices failing which it may give incorrect results. Another limitation of time to travel approach is inference of various environmental factors. Fingerprint is another popular approach that works by creating a fingerprint database and uses two phases. In the first phase, i.e., training phase, RSSI, and location vector are collected which are later used in the second phase to estimate the location in the building.

For the same, neural networks and k-nearest neighborhood algorithm are some commonly used algorithms. However, a reference fingerprinting map (RFM) is created during initial setup in fingerprinting-based methods.

Authors in Ref. [10] proposed a graph optimization-based method to estimate the beacons using fingerprinting-based method and range-based method. Here, a BLE-enabled mobile device is used to collect initial inertial and RSSI readings. These inertial readings are further processed to approximate constraints in the environment. These constraints are further used to form cost functions with least square structure which enables the user to estimate the position of beacons at different times. The most exciting feature of this framework is its enhanced accuracy. A similar work is performed by authors in Ref. [11] by proposing a triangulation technique that uses direction-of-departure (DOD) from multiple BLE beacons which helps to calculate RSSI, thus aiding in indoor localization. The prime advantage of work proposed in Ref. [11] is that it does not require any major setup and planning.

Authors in Ref. [12] propose a novel Kalman filtering fusion method that integrates trilateration and dead reckoning. It employs a device with BLE module that saves a significant amount of energy and thus improves RSS. It also suggests using environmental context information to further enhance the positioning accuracy. It is demonstrated using an experimental setup in Ref. [12] that this Kalman based fusion method has positioning accuracy of less than one meter. Similarly, authors in Ref. [13] also use a fingerprinting technology where localization is done using 3 different phases viz. BLE deployment, BLE identification and node position identification. Here, authors also consider the room environment where BLE beacons are deployed on ceiling. When any smart device enters in the range of BLE, the beacons with the highest RSSI value are selected. Thereafter, information about BLE tag and user is transferred to the webserver. Suggested methodology performs localization through comparison of RSSI values. Hence, it is easy to implement but compromises in accuracy due to interference.

It is noticed during the literature survey that accuracy and time delay have always been huge challenge in BLE fingerprinting method [14]. The authors in Ref. [14] analyze how window size influences the positioning accuracy and Cramér-Rao lower bound (CRLB) using RSS. The authors also propose an enhanced CRLB model. This enhanced CRLB model analyzes the association between delay and accuracy. It also provides a reference for deciding the window size. The authors also propose a WFC (weighted fingerprint construction) method to reduce the fluctuation in the RSS value, thus improving the localization accuracy. As a result, enhanced CRLB model gives enhanced accuracy in optimized time.

Authors in Ref. [15] also propose a BLE beacon's RSSI and geometric distance from current beacon in fuzzy framework to estimate Euclidean distance which eventually leads to localization. It is observed in Ref. [15] that the fingerprinting algorithm combined with fuzzy logic type-2 gives optimal performance for indoor localization. This algorithm is quite helpful to visually impaired persons in unknown environment and thus may be used to guide their movement.

It is worth noticing that BLE generally uses RSSI to locate the target object in the indoor space. However, RSSI has a limitation that its accuracy as the atmospheric factors disturbs the accuracy of reading and may generate false results [16] affecting the widespread deployment of BLE. For handling this issue, existing approaches use threshold value range for RSSI to determine if each RSSI value is within the stated range [17–20]. Also, the authors in Ref. [21] strongly support BLE for indoor localization as it uses mobile devices like smart phones and tablets. In the later phase, a database created using fingerprints is created to the object.

It is evident from the literature survey that BLE is the most significant and promising technology for indoor localization. Hence, authors plan to discuss a few associated challenges in order to enhance readers' knowledge.

20.3 CHALLENGES FOR INDOOR LOCALIZATION

This section discusses the existing challenges in indoor positioning systems as follows:

1. **Accuracy:** The positioning system accuracy is determined by the nearest calculated position to a target object. Various systems give different levels of accuracy. For instance, RADAR has an accuracy of 2–3 meters [22]. However, ultrasonic signals of cricket system have an accuracy of 2 cm approx. [23]. Hence, accuracy of a localization problem is highly related to its application domain and is still a challenging area of research.

2. **Range of Coverage:** The area which can be sensed by a sensor is called the range of coverage for the device. Each positioning system has its own range ranging from 5 meters to 50 meters. Ability to obtain a coverage of more than 60 meters is still a challenging task.

3. **Security:** Although the security aspect of indoor positioning has taken a backseat, it is an important aspect specifically in personal network (PN) used to position objects and people within their personal space.

iBeacon protocol that associates a definite location with a particular Bluetooth signal. This is done by continuous broadcasting of an advertising packet containing a UUID (universally unique identifier) that aids in the identification of a particular beacon. Additionally, it also contains a value which helps to calculate relative distance from beacon. Hence, it is used to help in region-monitoring which is based on users' location and regions created by network of beacons. Here, it is worth mentioning that these features of iBeacons have some additional challenges viz. handling messy signals, tracking, triangulation, frequency variance, and protecting identity theft.

4. **Spoofing:** Public broadcasting of UUID by a beacon may cause sniffing by any third-party. This may lead to impersonation of that beacon anywhere in the environment. It also enables third parties to take advantage of existing beacon network.

5. **Denial of Service (DoS):** It aims to render the device non-operational. Broadly DoS in context of iBeacons, attacks in two ways. Attacks either drains battery life through constant activity or to attack the stack layer to crash beacon. Among these, battery drain attacks are of significantly applicable to lightweight beacons as it has small battery capacities. The major hurdle in the adoption of iBeacon is identification of dead beacons and their replacement.

6. **Hijacking:** In hijacking, any unauthorized person with the help of tools gains access iBeacon's configuration layer and controls its operational settings, thus leading to ransomware attack also. The adverse impact of this kind of attacks in the context of various applications is presented in Table 20.2.

TABLE 20.2 Applications Adversely Affected by the Attacks

	Location-Based Rewards [24]	**Indoor Navigation [25]**	**Proximity-Based Advertising [26]**
Spoofing	Abuse of rewards	• Misdirect users	• Spam
			• Piggy-backing
Denial of service	• Congestion, unavailability of service	• Unavailability of service	• Loss of potential advertising
		• Loses customers	
Hijacking	• Deception of data	• Swapping of location	• Falsification
	• Data lock, need to pay ransom	• Data lock	• Data lock

7. **Complexity:** It is another challenging issue as it involves hardware, software, and operation factor. Different indoor localization systems have varying levels of complexity.

8. **Precision:** Accuracy, also called precision can be measured as the mean errors in calculated location and actual location of the target object. However, localization systems consider the consistency of the system as an important factor of the performance.

9. **Robustness:** Ability to withstand missing signals or the absence of some RSS signals determines the robustness of the localization system. Ability to achieve acceptable level of robustness is a challenging issue for indoor localization.

10. **Scalability:** The scalability of localization system ensures the efficiency to handle large positioning scope. Generally, increase in positioning scope results in performance degradation and such a system is said to be poorly scalable. A location scope normally scales along two axes viz. geography and density. Here, geographical scaling refers to increase in covered area whereas density scaling refers to increase in units located per unit geographic area. Hence, scaling along density leads to congestion of wireless signal further leading to requirement of complex calculation.

20.4 USE CASES OF BLE

In this section, we discuss some use cases of BLE in terms of localization. According to authors in Ref. [27], BLE can be employed for the realization of smart cities, automotive industry, agriculture, airport, and museum, etc. Authors suggest that BLE can be used to control the brightness of the lights at road junctions in response to the approaching vehicles. According to Ref. [27], California has adopted LED streetlights which operates in response to real time data. Similarly, it aids managers and ground staff of smart sports venues to take decisions regarding up keeping of the pitch or ground. BLEs can also be integrated in agriculture to gain other useful information like temperature and chlorophyll levels in plants. Thus, it brings a sustainable and efficient revolutionary transformation in food production. Usage of BLE is also recommended to improve passengers' experience at airport by helping them to find their baggage, restaurants, and other services. Moreover, it can also improve operational efficiency at airport using predictive analytics.

As per authors in Ref. [28], BLE can also successfully implement to monitor blood pressure (BP), thus resulting in a homemade BP monitoring device. BP measurement data is processed and transmitted using a single BLE, user get this information on their smart phone. Similarly, authors in Ref. [29] suggest usage of BLE for a wireless electrocardiogram (ECG) monitoring system. Such automated ECG monitoring system consists of a single-chip ECG acquisition module and a Bluetooth module. Here also, the ECG is monitored, and the captured reading is sent through a Bluetooth link that can display the same on smart-phone.

BLE is also suggested to be used for marketing system by authors in Ref. [30]. In this chapter, BLE, and smartphones can be used for a highly scalable marketing system by sending push notifications to users. These notifications are pushed based on the real-time locations of customers within the mall. This approach aims to increase the sales in the mall by detecting the locations of customers and pushing them personalized promotional offers through smart-phone. Usage of BLE in such system drastically reduces the power consumption so as to maintain long-term monitoring. Moreover, BLEs can also be exploited to provide safety to workers working in adverse conditions like workers working in mines, chambers, etc. For the same, each worker wears a BLE beacon tag while entering the zone. With the help of this BLE tag, the position of worker can be traced in case of emergency. This can help to perform rescue operation if required so as to avoid any unavoidable circumstances.

20.5 PROPOSED FRAMEWORK FOR INDOOR LOCALIZATION

A framework for indoor localization using BLE is proposed in this section. The proposed framework can be implemented in any organization for indoor localization. The motive behind selecting hospital is that it is a challenging environment with diverse source of interference (in terms of noise) that may impede indoor localization. Hence, if the proposed framework performs well in such an environment, it can be effectively deployed in any organization.

It is evident that hospital systems may also employ RFID technology for localization. However, RFID technology has several limitations that limit its application. Hence, the authors of this chapter attempt to proposed localization architecture using Bluetooth technology. In the proposed framework, small low energy transmitter device of *beacons* (also known as *iBeacons*) play a very crucial role in localization as it emits radio signal towards proximate devices. These radio signals are invariably used as identifier signals as it contains beacon ID number and its RSSI value. Here, beacons broadcast its id around 10 times within a second. Figure 20.2 demonstrates the component and architecture of positioning system. The beacons are deployed in the hospital so as entire a hospital is covered through Bluetooth technology. It may vary depending upon the application requirement.

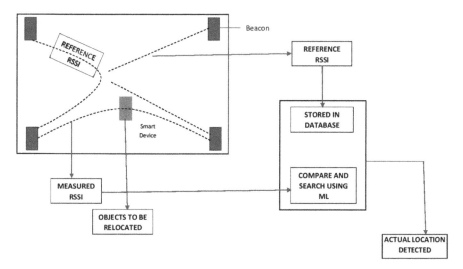

FIGURE 20.2   Architecture of proposed framework.

The suggested architecture assumes BLE tags placed over object which is to be localized. It is also attached with 3V battery power which goes up to 2.5 years span due to low power consumption by BLE. As mentioned previously, a BLE tag interacts easily with Smartphone and thus does not require any specific configuration. Also, BLE tags transmit the signals regularly which are received by the smartphone.

As shown in Figure 20.2, the database is connected to a smartphone. This database maintains the information about BLE tags IDs. Moreover, the calibrated readings of the BLE tags are also stored in the database with reference to different positions of the smartphones. Here, the smartphone acts as a receiver for iBeacons as well as BLE tags. Both these values with respect to predefined reference points are also maintained in the database. Thus, each recorded entry from beacon contains i) the beacon ID (the unique identifier of the beacon), (ii) the signal strength (RSSI) captured by smartphone application from the specific beacon. RSSI is used to determine the location of mobile from the iBeacon transmitter. Similarly, each recorded entry from tag consists of i) BLE tag ID and ii)RSSI to determine the distance of tag from mobile device. These entries play a crucial role in the localization. A single entry in the database stores the reading from iBeacons and tag. The key component of the proposed localization method is concrete calibrations of BLE tags and beacons.

Finally, the purpose of localization is to analyze object movement. It compares the distance with calibrated to calculate the gap. This database consists of a huge number of entries, which eventually results into bigdata. When the tagged object moves, it transmits the ID which is used to estimate the distance. The efficiency of searching can be further enhanced by employing ML algorithms. The most commonly used ML algorithms for localization are KNN, NN, and Random forest, etc.

For localization, the distance is calculated using the following equation:

$$Distance1 = \sum_{i=1}^{m} (\sqrt{(RSSI(B)ref - RSSI(B)measured)^2}$$

$$Distance2 = \sqrt{(RSSI(T)ref - RSSI(T)measured)^2}$$

Where Distance1 gives the distance of *iBeacon* and smartphone and Distance2 indicates the same among smartphone and BLE tag. These two distances are compared by the application and locate the object. The flowchart depicted in Figure 20.3 shows the working of the proposed architecture in detail. The performance enhancement of the proposed approach over existing approaches is presented in the subsequent subsection.

20.5.1 PERFORMANCE EVALUATION OF PROPOSED APPROACH

This section performs the comparative analysis of the proposed approach with prevalent approaches for localization. As evident, the proposed approach suggests usage of fingerprinting method for localization that has several advantages over AoA localization method [31]. As per the findings by authors in Ref. [32], AoA method performs accurately in a constrained region. Moreover, the localization within few centimeters remains difficult for AoA. Fingerprinting method of localization performs efficiently over AoA; hence the proposed architecture is an effective choice for improved efficiency and security as AoA is also vulnerable to security attacks.

Here, authors would like to mention that fingering also bears some limitations when applied to a dynamic environment as it necessitates regular maintenance of reference-fingerprinting map, an energy intensive task. This limitation is addressed in the proposed approach as it recommends maintenance of reference-fingerprinting map during initial setup only. Thereafter, as per the suggested approach, reference-fingerprinting map is updated only when there is a change in position of reference points. Usage of Gaussian filter in the proposed approach further enhances the efficiency of the suggested approach as it aids in enhanced positioning accuracy by removing noise.

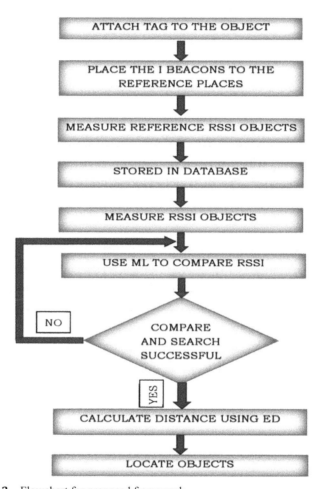

FIGURE 20.3 Flowchart for proposed framework.

From the above features, it is evident that the proposed approach outperforms the traditional localization approaches owing to implementation of fingerprinting localization technique and Gaussian filter. The limitation of fingerprinting is addressed by updating the populating reference-fingerprinting map during initial setup and location change only. Hence, the proposed approach is an efficient, simple, and cost-effective solution for indoor localization in any unrestricted environment.

20.6   CONCLUSION

In this chapter, the authors have presented a comprehensive analysis of the usage of BLE for indoor location, and its comparison to the currently dominant Wi-Fi. It is concluded that BLE outperforms Wi-Fi even when AP placement is identical. Additionally, lower variation in signal strength leads to gain in yield in comparison to Wi-Fi in terms of positioning methods that employ fingerprinting. BLE is having high scan rate and low power consumption. While comparing RFID and BLE, it is observed that RFID is an expensive choice in comparison to BLE. Moreover, RFID can perform localization at a few checkpoints only while BLE is capable of recognizing the complete itinerary of the object under study. In addition, BLE transceivers are cost-effective, which further strengthens its widespread employment. Thus, it is concluded that BLE outperforms the RFID and Wi-Fi during the study. In summary, we expect that BLE has promising future scope for indoor localization.

The proposed approach uses fingerprinting mechanism of localization. Using fingerprinting, the proposed approach outperforms conventional localization techniques by giving enhanced accuracy and efficiency. Proposed approach also suggests using a Gaussian filter to eradicate the effect of noise. Hence, the proposed approach is accurate, economical, user friendly, secure, and efficient. The proposed approach can further be enhanced by incorporating some hybrid approach. The work can also be extended further to populate the reference-fingerprinting map in response to dynamic access points. It should target on devising energy-efficient solution for the same.

KEYWORDS

- **Bluetooth low energy**
- **electrocardiogram**
- **localization**
- **machine learning**
- **RSSI**
- **signal strength**

REFERENCES

1. Du, H., Zhang, C., Ye, Q., Xu, W., Kibenge, P. L., & Yao, K., (2018). A hybrid outdoor localization scheme with high-position accuracy and low-power consumption. *Eurasip J. Wirel. Commun. Netw.*, *2018*(1). doi: 10.1186/s13638-017-1010-4.

2. Zafari, F., Gkelias, A., & Leung, K. K., (2019). A survey of indoor localization systems and technologies. *IEEE Commun. Surv. Tutorials*, *21*(3), 2568–2599.

3. Kul, G., Tavli, B., & Özyer, T., (2014). *IEEE 802.11 WLAN Based Real-Time Indoor Positioning: Literature Survey and Experimental Investigations, 34*, 157–164.

4. Bulusu, N., Heidemann, J., & Estrin, D., (2000). GPS-less low-cost outdoor localization for very small devices. *IEEE Pers. Commun.*, *7*(5), 28–34. doi: 10.1109/98.878533.

5. Weiss, C., & Masselli, A., (2007). Fast outdoor robot localization using integral invariants. *Int. Conf. Comput. Vis.*, no. Icvs, pp. 1–10.

6. Valgren, C., & Lilienthal, A., (2007). SIFT, SURF and seasons: Long-term outdoor localization using local features. *Proc. Eur. Conf. Mob. Robot., 128,* 1–6. [Online]. Available: http://citeseerx.ist.psu.edu/viewdoc/download?doi=10.1.1.84.2497&rep=rep1&type=pdf (accessed on 10 November 2021).

7. Kim, S. H., Roh, C. W., Kang, S. C., & Park, M. Y., (2007). Outdoor navigation of a mobile robot using differential GPS and curb detection. *Proc. - IEEE Int. Conf. Robot. Autom.*, pp. 3414–3419. doi: 10.1109/ROBOT.2007.364000.

8. Belakbir, A., Amghar, M., & Sbiti, N., (2014). Sensor data fusion for an indoor and outdoor localization. *Radio Electron. Commun. Syst., 57*(4), 149–158. doi: 10.3103/S0735272714040013.

9. Zhao, X., Xiao, Z., Markham, A., Trigoni, N., & Ren, Y., (2014). Does BTLE measure up against WiFi? A comparison of indoor location performance. In: *European Wireless 2014; 20th European Wireless Conference* (pp. 1–6).

10. Zuo, Z., Liu, L., Zhang, L., & Fang, Y., (2018). Indoor positioning based on Bluetooth low-energy beacons adopting graph optimization. *Sensors (Switzerland), 18*(11), 1–20. doi: 10.3390/s18113736.

11. Kikuchi, K., (2017). *DOD-Based Indoor Localization Using BLE Beacons*, 4, 5.

12. Röbesaat, J., Zhang, P., Abdelaal, M., & Theel, O., (2017). An improved BLE indoor localization with Kalman-based fusion: An experimental study. *Sensors (Switzerland), 17*(5), 1–26. doi: 10.3390/s17050951.

13. Memon, S., Memon, M. M., Shaikh, F. K., & Laghari, S., (2018). Smart indoor positioning using BLE technology. In: *4th IEEE Int. Conf. Eng. Technol. Appl. Sci. ICETAS 2017* (Vol. 2018, pp. 1–5). doi: 10.1109/ICETAS.2017.8277872.

14. Ai, H., Zhang, S., Tang, K., Li, N., Huang, W., & Wang, Y., (2019). Robust low-latency indoor localization using Bluetooth low energy. *Proc. ION 2019 Pacific PNT Meet.*, pp. 58–72. doi: 10.33012/2019.16793.

15. Al-Madani, B., Orujov, F., Maskeliūnas, R., Damaševičius, R., & Venčkauskas, A., (2019). Fuzzy logic type-2 based wireless indoor localization system for navigation of visually impaired people in buildings. *Sensors (Switzerland), 19*(9), doi: 10.3390/s19092114.

16. Kim, D. Y., Kim, S. H., Choi, D., & Jin, S. H., (2015). Accurate indoor proximity zone detection based on time window and frequency with Bluetooth low energy. In *FNC/MobiSPC*, (pp. 88–95).

17. Andersson, T., (2014). *Bluetooth Low Energy and Smart Phones for Proximity-Based Automatic Door Locks*.

18. Klokmose, C. N., Korn, M., & Blunck, H., (2014). WiFi proximity detection in mobile web applications. In: *Proceedings of the 2014 ACM SIGCHI Symposium on Engineering Interactive Computing Systems* (pp. 123–128).

19. Liu, L., Qi, D., Zhou, N., & Wu, Y., (2018). A task scheduling algorithm based on classification mining in fog computing environment. *Wirel. Commun. Mob. Comput.*

20. Liu, S., Jiang, Y., & Striegel, A., (2013). Face-to-face proximity estimation using Bluetooth on smart phones. *IEEE Trans. Mob. Comput., 13*(4), 811–823.

21. Kriz, P., Maly, F., & Kozel, T., (2016). Improving indoor localization using Bluetooth low energy beacons. *Mob. Inf. Syst., 2016.*

22. Disha, A., (2013). A comparative analysis on indoor positioning techniques and systems. *Int. J. Eng. Res. Appl., 3*(2), 1790.

23. Liu, J., (2014). *Survey of Wireless Based Indoor Localization Technologies.* Dep. Sci. Eng. Washington. Univ.

24. Velazco, C., (2013). *MLB's iBeacon Experiment May Signal A Whole New Ball Game for Location Tracking.* Setembro.

25. http://www.nextome.net/en/indoor-positioning-technology.php   (accessed   on   10 November 2021).

26. http://www.timesunion.com/tuplus-local/article/ (accessed on 10 November 2021).

27. Andersson, M., (2014). *Use Case Possibilities with Bluetooth Low Energy in IoT Applications* (Vol. 2). White Pap.

28. Lin, Z. M., Chang, C. H., Chou, N. K., & Lin, Y. H., (2014). Bluetooth low energy (BLE) based blood pressure monitoring system. *Proc. 2014 Int. Conf. Intell. Green Build. Smart Grid, IGBSG 2014* (pp. 3–6). doi: 10.1109/IGBSG.2014.6835225.

29. Yu, B., Xu, L., & Li, Y., (2012). Bluetooth low energy (BLE) based mobile electrocardiogram monitoring system. *2012 IEEE Int. Conf. Inf. Autom. ICIA 2012* (pp. 763–767). doi: 10.1109/ICInfA.2012.6246921.

30. Zaim, D., & Bellafkih, M., (2016). Bluetooth low energy (BLE) based geomarketing system. *SITA 2016 - 11*th *Int. Conf. Intell. Syst. Theor. Appl.* doi: 10.1109/SITA.2016.7772263.

31. Monfared, S., Nguyen, T. H., Petrillo, L., De Doncker, P., & Horlin, F., (2018). Experimental demonstration of BLE transmitter positioning based on AOA Estimation. *IEEE Int. Symp. Pers. Indoor Mob. Radio Commun. PIMRC* (Vol. 2018, pp. 856–859). doi: 10.1109/PIMRC.2018.8580796.

32. Cominelli, M., Patras, P., & Gringoli, F., (2019). Dead on arrival: An empirical study of the Bluetooth 5.1 positioning system. *Proc. Annu. Int. Conf. Mob. Comput. Networking, MOBICOM*, 13–20. doi: 10.1145/3349623.3355475.

Index